The Deregulation of the Banking and Securities Industries

The Deregulation of the Banking and Securities Industries

Edited by
Lawrence G. Goldberg
Lawrence J. White
New York University

Lexington Books
D.C. Heath and Company
Lexington, Massachusetts
Toronto

Library of Congress Cataloging in Publication Data

Main entry under title:
  The Deregulation of the banking and securities industries.

  Papers presented at a conference sponsored by the Salomon Brothers
Center for the Study of Financial Institutions, Graduate School of Busi-
ness Administration, New York University, held at the Center, May 18-19,
1978.
    1. Banking law—United States—Congresses. 2. Securities—United States—
Congresses. I. Goldberg, Lawrence G. II. White, Lawrence J. III. Salomon
Brothers Center for the Study of Financial Institutions.
KF974.A2D4   346'.73'082   78-19705
ISBN 0-669-02720-0

Second printing, September 1980

Published simultaneously in Canada

Printed in the United States of America

International Standard Book Number: 0-669-02720-0

Library of Congress Catalog Card Number: 78-19705

Contents

Preface

On 18-19 May 1978, the Salomon Brothers Center for the Study of Financial Institutions, Graduate School of Business Administration, New York University, sponsored a two-day conference, "The Deregulation of the Banking and Securities Industries." The conference brought together people from the regulated firms and institutions, government regulators (past and present), and academics to exchange ideas and viewpoints. The two editors of this volume were the organizers of the conference. Our intent was not to have another conference of academics talking to themselves; rather, we wished to encourage an interchange among the regulated, the regulators, and interested outside parties. We believe we succeeded. This volume is the outcome of that conference.

Special thanks are due to many people associated with organizing and running the conference. Edward I. Altman, Ernest Bloch, and Arnold W. Sametz served as able chairmen for three of the sessions. Mary Jaffier, Ligija Roze, and Penny Stone provided the organizational back-up and day-to-day supervision, keeping track of people, places, and papers; without them the conference would have unraveled long before it began. Finally, Arnold W. Sametz provided constant advice, encouragement, and assistance; without him, there would have been no conference.

November 1978

Lawrence G. Goldberg
Lawrence J. White
Graduate School of Business
  Administration
New York University

1 Introduction

Lawrence G. Goldberg and
Lawrence J. White

Financial markets are among the most heavily regulated areas in the American economy. Price regulation, entry regulation, and safety regulation have been pervasive in both the banking and securities industries, and most of these regulations are with us today. The origins of many of these regulations can be found in the 1930s, following the debacle of 1929 and the early 1930s for both the securities and banking industries.

There have been, though, some recent efforts at deregulation and the easing of constraints. In the securities area, the Securities and Exchange Commission (prodded by the Department of Justice) in the early 1970s was no longer willing to tolerate the collusive fixing of brokerage rates, and by 1 May 1975 all commission rates had become unfixed. The SEC has been pressuring the exchanges to ease their restrictions on transactions taking place away from an exchange floor. And the SEC has permitted the expansion of options trading to five exchanges. In banking, some states have eased branching restrictions. Negotiated Order of Withdrawal (NOW) accounts allow depositors in New England commercial banks, savings and loan associations, and mutual savings banks to earn interest on checking accounts. Share drafts allow the depositors in credit unions to do the same. In early May 1978, less than two weeks before the conference was held, the Federal Reserve and the Federal Deposit Insurance Corporation proposed that commercial banks be allowed to transfer funds automatically from a depositor's savings account to his or her checking account; on 1 November 1978 this proposal was put into effect. The prohibition on the payment of interest on checking accounts has been seriously weakened, if not eliminated.

But the trend has not been all in one direction. The SEC has increased its reporting and disclosure requirements for publicly owned companies generally. Its determined push for a "National Securities Market" may foreclose other trading arrangements. In October 1977, in the wake of alleged trading irregularities, the SEC suspended further expansion of options trading to new markets until a complete investigation had been completed. In banking, the nonbanking activities of one-bank holding companies are far more tightly constrained than they were a decade ago. In the wake of a few large bank failures of the mid-1970s, bank reporting and inspection appears to be more stringent. And the "redlining" controversy has led to greater public pressure on depository institutions to channel their investments in certain directions.

Finally, banks and securities firms seem to be edging closer to each other in

1

some areas. Some banks would like to broker stocks and bonds to the public; to underwrite a broader range of securities issues; to take a more active role in private placements; and to offer a wide range of financial advisory and management services to their clients. At least one brokerage firm is offering its margin customers a facility that looks suspiciously like a checking account. The Glass-Steagall Act has for the past 45 years provided an uneasy—and to some, an unnatural—dividing line between the banking and securities industries. The advances of technology may make that dividing line increasingly difficult to defend.

The Salomon Brothers Center for the Study of Financial Institutions, Graduate School of Business Administration, New York University, decided to hold a two-day conference to explore these questions in depth. The conference, held on 18-19 May 1978, included a wide range of participants from the regulated firms and institutions, from the regulatory agencies, and from academia. A fertile exchange of ideas and views took place. The papers presented at the conference and the comments of discussants provide the contents of this book.

Before offering a brief introductory summary of these papers, we believe it is worthwhile to state some of the broad themes that emerged from the papers and discussion.

First, though deregulation is in the air and is hotly discussed (particularly among economists), it is far from a ubiquitous trend. Instead, there seem to be three separate trends that more or less can be linked to the three types of regulation. In the area of price regulation, there is a trend toward deregulation. The unfixing of brokerage commissions is the clearest example. The NOW accounts, credit-union share drafts, and automatic savings transfer provide others. One senses that, but for the special problem of the thrift institutions (savings and loan institutions and mutual savings banks), Regulation Q and allied ceilings on deposit interest rates would have disappeared by now.

The freeing of prices will not be a quick and easy proposition; those who benefit from regulated prices are quite prepared to fight strenuous political delaying actions. But, as Deputy Comptroller of the Currency C.F. Muckenfuss indicated in his oral presentation to the conference, the intellectual arguments that have been advanced in favor of price competition are being absorbed by both the legislative and executive branches of government. Parenthetically, one month before the conference took place, the Civil Aeronautics Board proposed that domestic airlines be allowed to cut their fares by 50% without advance notice. And the week following the conference, a joint House-Senate conference committee broke a long stalemate and voted to approve a bill that would decontrol natural gas prices by 1985.

In the area of entry regulation the trend is more mixed. Some states have eased branching restrictions, but de novo entry is still tightly controlled at the state and national levels. The SEC permitted wider trading of options but then refused to sanction yet further expansion of trading. The present New York Stock Exchange (NYSE) Rule 390 pertaining to transactions away from the exchange is less restrictive than the former Rule 394. But the shape of the future national market and its possible restrictions on alternative trading arrangements is still highly uncertain. And only minor changes in the Glass-Steagall Act (primarily to allow banks to underwrite municipal revenue bonds) are currently before Congress. The legal prohibitions on the banks and securities firms invading each other's turf are likely to remain in place. Perhaps the intellectual arguments in favor of entry have not been as compelling as those in favor of more price competition. Perhaps those whose interests would be harmed by entry are more able to band together politically to repel the invaders than they can to stop price competition.

Finally, in the area of safety regulation, the trend is clearly toward more regulation. Bank failures and the bankruptcy of large firms generally are considered to be politically embarrassing events. There is little recognition, as Michael Redisch pointed out in his comments, that this is one of the consequences of competitive capitalism; if the more successful firms are going to win the race, others are going to have to lose and possibly lose big. Instead, regulators and legislators wish to protect virtually all parties concerned under virtually all circumstances. Depositors, stockholders, and investors are to be protected from fraud, "manipulation," and failure. Inspection and reporting requirements for banks are becoming more stringent. Reporting and disclosure requirements for publicly held companies generally are becoming more extensive. Everything is to be made safer; everyone is to be protected.

A second theme emerging from the conference is a concern among industry members that regulators be even-handed and that regulations be evenly imposed. To the extent that the securities and banking industries do edge closer to each other and compete more, each side is concerned about the differential regulation imposed on the other. As thrift institutions acquire more of the characteristics of commercial banks (like the ability to issue checks), the latter become increasingly restive about the ¼% interest-rate differential in the deposit rate ceilings favoring the thrifts. The prospect of uneven regulation leading to unfair competition is a real one for many industry members.

A third theme is the force of technological change. Electronic tellers and electronic funds transfer may well change the nature of competition among depository institutions. The consolidated tape has brought the trading floors of the various exchanges closer together. Further electronic linking of the exchanges is inevitable, even in the absence of an official National Market System. In the end, it may be the force of technology and the expanded competitive opportunities that it makes possible, rather than the intellectual arguments, that will undermine some of the rigid barriers created by regulation.

We now turn to a brief description of the major papers in this volume. The conference was organized into four sessions. The first session explored a number of the regulation and deregulation problems and issues facing the banking and securities industries. The second session focused exclusively on the securities area. The third session focused on banking. And the final session examined the intersection of the two industries and the tensions created by Glass-Steagall.

In the first session, Roy Schotland provides an overview of regulation and deregulation of both banking and securities. He argues that there is still a need for more and improved regulation: more required information disclosure and more prevention of doubtful business practices in both areas. Morris Mendelson and Simon Lorne focus on the problems of structuring a National Market System. They fear that, if improperly structured, the new system could lead to the demise of the smaller securities firms and create greater hardships in raising new capital for smaller industrial firms generally. They are critical of the SEC's current efforts at mandating a central trading market and argue that any new market structure must be designed to maintain the confidence of the small investor. Lee A. Pickard's paper provides a stinging critique of current SEC policies. He argues that the SEC has not done any cost-benefit analysis to support many of its recent actions such as the suspension of the expansion of options trading. Part of the problem is that Congress, in the Securities Acts Amendments of 1975, provided the SEC with only vague goals and objectives that provide far too little direction on how to proceed. Finally, Patric H. Hendershott examines one of the major cornerstones of banking regulation, deposit rate ceilings. Through a multiequation monetary model, he is able to simulate the effects of the removal of these ceilings. He finds that the removal of ceilings would have been beneficial. During periods of high interest rates, mortgage interest rates would have been lower, mortgage volume would have been higher, and housing starts would have been greater. He further demonstrates that variable-rate mortgages would have solved the earnings-squeeze problems for the thrifts that removing the ceilings might have caused. In sum, Hendershott finds that the ceilings have been counterproductive.

In the second session, Michael Keenan reviews the recent experience of the securities industry. The unfixing of prices, the expansion of options trading, and the formation of incorporated publicly held brokerage firms have brought substantial changes in the ways the industry conducts itself. The course of deregulation has not been smooth, however, and erratic regulatory actions by the SEC have generated substantial costs for the industry. Edward I. O'Brien describes the five categories into which much of the regulation of the securities industry falls. He argues for a middle road on regulation: Regulation that prevents abuse and builds investor confidence should be retained, though carefully structured. Robert C. Hall argues that the approach to a National Market System should be through an orderly process of evolution that builds on the strengths of the existing system to create a better one. Future moves should encourage competition among participants in the marketplace, but there must be regulatory oversight to ensure that this competition is fair. Hence there is likely to be a need for greater regulation and self-regulation which is as streamlined as possible. Dan Roberts, Susan M. Phillips, and J. Richard Zecher examine the unfixing of minimum commission rates on the NYSE. They point out that collusive price fixing not only generates high profits for the colluders but also discourages cost-cutting innovations since the innovators cannot reap the full benefits of the innovation by cutting prices and attracting new customers. They contend that until the mid-1960s, the primary effect of the fixed brokerage commissions was probably to reduce innovation; only by the mid-1960s did the excess profits from the fixed commissions become substantial.

The third session focuses on banking. P. Michael Laub analyzes the political economy underlying three major banking issues: deposit ceilings, redlining, and credit allocation. The first has involved efforts at deregulation; the latter two involve efforts at further regulation. He concludes that piecemeal regulatory changes, rather than large-scale regulatory reform, are likely to continue as the pattern in banking. Lawrence G. Goldberg examines the evidence on the competitive impact of bank holding-company acquisitions of both banks and nonbanking firms. He specifically analyzes the changes in market shares of banks acquired by bank holding companies. He finds virtually no changes in market shares in the years following acquisition and concludes that the competitive impact of such acquisitions is minimal where no direct competition is eliminated. The case of limiting them by regulation is therefore reduced. Benjamin Wolkowitz discusses the question of bank capital adequacy. There are two major alternatives to regulatory requirements: the discipline of the financial markets (perceived riskier portfolios will require higher rates of return) and variable-rate deposit insurance. Wolkowitz argues that greater reliance on a mix of these two alternatives would reduce the need for direct regulation.

The final session examines the intersection of the banking and securities industries. Franklin R. Edwards argues that the mixing of commercial banking and securities activities, which Glass-Steagall currently forbids, presents problems (in terms of risks of bank failure and conflicts of interest) that are no more serious than those currently posed by the presence of trust departments and the activities of nonbank affiliates under holding-company umbrellas. If trust departments and these other activities are considered appropriate for banks, the securities business should be considered appropriate also. Edwards further points out that the affiliate system, whereby nonbanking activities are organized separately from the parent bank, may generate greater conflicts of interest than if the activities are merged under one unified ownership. James W. Stevens argues that banks should be permitted to expand their role in providing financial services to their customers and to underwrite municipal revenue bonds. But he feels that with these modifications, banks can live with Glass-Steagall. Harvey A. Rowen details the areas in which banks and securities firms currently compete; the breadth of the securities services now being offered by banks "would certainly surprise Senator Glass and Congressman Steagall." Rowen argues that further incursions by the banks into the securities area would both be unfair, since banks are regulated in a far different manner, and socially unwise, since it would lead to a greater concentration of financial power. Finally, David Ratner outlines the areas of intersection, both competitive and cooperative, of the two industries. He too fears the increased economic power consequences of letting the banks expand their financial activities. He points out that competition among regulatory institutions is also present and that justifications for this kind of competition often imply that we do not really believe in the type of regulation that is supposed to be imposed in the first place. He argues that if there are to be several regulatory agencies involved, the division should be by function rather than by constituency.

These papers encompass a wide diversity of views and opinions. As a number of participants characterized the views (of others) on regulatory matters, "where you stand depends on where you sit." Though we (the editors) may not agree with some of the arguments presented here, we did not try to use our heavy editorial hands to mold a monolithic presentation of the issues. Rather, we believe that an understanding of the viewpoints held by the various parties is vital to an understanding of the complexities of regulation and the difficulties of effecting deregulation; hence the papers that follow.

Part I
Overview and Some
Issues

2 An Overview: New Myths and Old Realities

Roy A. Schotland

I have a little dream. I dream of markets that are competitive, with few if any situations characterized by monopoly, oligopoly, or price dominance; where the competition occurs in price or quality of service; where items sold are honestly presented, and purchasers can secure information efficiently; where participation is open to all on nondiscriminatory terms; where most transactions are governed by market terms instead of by conflicts of interest; where new technology or other innovations are seldom if ever delayed by existing relationships or positions; where prices make timely moves reflecting new events; and where stability prevails, with speculative excess as rare as a solid citizen's lost weekend. I have a little dream, then, of an invisible hand that never shakes, has no calluses, and never points in the wrong direction.

Other times I have a different little dream. I dream of regulators who are Platonic guardians: wise and informed yet detached; flexible and responsive yet predictable . . . in short, your typical regulatory commission.

You can see already that I am not a true believer. By no means am I one of the iconoclasts who have concluded that nothing works except their own powers of analysis. But I do not share the ideological temper that pervades so much discussion of regulation in recent years. It is as if many of our leading lawyers and economists, having once come across "Religion and the Rise of Capitalism," decided they must crusade against Irreligion and the Rise of Regulation. For example, one of our most able lawyers, Lloyd Cutler, opened a major article in the *Yale Law Journal* writing of "Our nation's ideological commitment to the free market system. . . ." (Cutler 1975) Surely our nation's ideological commitment is toward free men, and we have made only a pragmatic judgment that free markets are a good means toward assuring free men and an open society. Further, since the nation's beginning we have decided in countless instances not to adhere to the free-market means, choosing instead from a huge range of forms of government intervention, from tariffs limiting free entry of goods, to limits on free entry into so many industries and careers, and even to long-standing price setting in numerous sectors. Yet even informed people talk about free markets as if the line in "The Battle Hymn of the Republic" were "let us die to make markets free."

Though I am from Washington, which has been called an island surrounded by reality, I wish to offer observations about realities that seem to me to be the necessary starting points for discussing deregulation in the banking and securities industries. First I suggest that discussion of regulatory reform suffers from commonplace errors of analysis, communication problems, and considerable bias. Too often false issues are raised, incomplete analyses offered as proofs, and "solutions" proposed with serious but unexamined problems. Second I note a little about deregulation generally, and about some current specifics in regulation of banking and securities. Third I consider one of the many problems that show how Canute-like it is to act as if we were likely to stop adding still more regulation. Last I offer four little suggestions for keeping regulatory reform rolling.

Toward Clarifying Language and Acknowledging Biases

Discussion of deregulation too often is impeded by several problems of communication. The very word *deregulation* is troublesome. Virtually complete dismantling of regulation may be a real issue in natural gas or trucking, but I submit that anyone who thinks it more than academic in banking or securities is having a little fantasy. The real questions before us are of regulatory reform: here a possible elimination of some restrictions; there only a relaxation (like allowing depositories to branch across state lines at least into major metropolitan areas); elsewhere a change from requiring or banning certain conduct to less intrusive safeguards such as mandated public disclosure; everywhere an increased use of experiments (like NOW accounts in several states); and in some places a quiet drift forward, luminously labeled "deregulation without telling" (MacAvoy 1978).

Discussion and analysis of these matters seems plagued with what I call "lump thinking," which more formally, at least in economics, would be called "overaggregating." An attack on Regulation Q, or on *ICC* v. *Camp,* is too often couched as if it were against all bank regulation, or all Glass-Steagall.[1] (Or against all regulation. The heat of advocacy too often makes people sound like anarchists when all they want to do is bomb the ban on paying interest on demand deposits.) It is of utmost importance to recognize that economic regulation involves a panoply of techniques. Dissatisfaction with some of them does not dictate opposition to all of them.

Consider the contrasts in attitude toward the variety of techniques regulating depositories and the securities industry. For example, substantial entry barriers protect existing depositories (but are almost inconsequential for securities firms). Many of us outside commentators would prefer freer entry of new depositories, though with 14,700 banks plus 5,300 thrifts plus credit unions, the barriers have hardly been severe; but would many of us also prefer to reduce regulation over depositories' mergers? Another example: price setting by force of law is particularly condemned, understandably. Price setting occurred in broker-dealer commission rates, and even before its end three years ago, it was hard to find anyone—outside broker-dealer firms—to defend fixed commission rates. Price setting occurs in banking via Regulation Q, authorizing federal agencies to limit interest rates paid to depositors and drawing widespread opposition from many in banking and almost all outside observers (though the opposition would be less excited if it were more realistic about how many ways there are now to get around Regulation Q). But few observers object to such significant non-price interferences with business judgment as loan limits, or as limits on the structure of bank holding companies or of investment companies, or as the intense record keeping, reporting, and examination processes that permeate regulation of depositories and the securities industry.

Or for regulation that draws support as widespread as is the opposition to price fixing, consider deposit insurance and its newer counterpart for customers of broker-dealer firms. There, argument is limited to just what further regulation may be needed to protect the insurance fund or to just what should be the basis used for charging premiums. Consider also governmentally mandated public disclosure, merely another technique of regulatory intervention. There is debate over how to make disclosure more efficient, and some observers believe disclosure in some settings has not been effective. But a wide consensus maintains that this regulatory technique makes markets both more efficient and more fair, and the clear trend is to spread disclosure requirements, not to dismantle them.

A last technique, which probably should be the most controverted form of regulation in finance, is the device first used by Pope Alexander VI in 1493, when he issued a "bull of demarcation" dividing new lands between Spain and Portugal: the turf divider. Talk of "our nation's ideological commitment to the free market system" is fanciful in light of our passion for Balkanizing American finance. We have Balkanized quite literally in our geographic barriers surrounding depository institutions, as well as Balkanizing functionally between banks and thrifts, and between banking and investment banking.

In a second kind of lump thinking, regulation is equated with all forms of government intervention. For example, a noted academic, leading off a significant new book on regulating business, adds the price-controlled sector (allegedly about 10% of the GNP) to the sector subject to health and safety regulation so as to conjure up "the control sector" and then points out with horror that that monster has grown recently from about 7% to nearly 30% of the GNP—worse yet, a development with "apparently no commensurate benefits" (MacAvoy 1978).

Regulation itself is merely one of several forms of government intervention. Political power is used to regulate private conduct whenever any law is made establishing civil or criminal liability or taxes are levied with inevitable side effects even when revenue raising is the sole goal. But we don't think of such interventions as "regulation." When we talk of "unregulated markets," we do not mean jungles; we know that such markets are still subject to the rule of law intervening against violence, fraud, etc. Indeed, those who have discovered that regulation is no free lunch and leap to blame it for inflation (Houthakker 1977) and much of our other ills should look into such nonregulatory interventions as our judges' extraordinary development of liability for defective products or malpractice. The ways in which that development has occurred make regulators of financial institutions look almost like Platonic guardians.

Regulation, even broadly conceived, is characterized by continuous administration by some specialized body of people who, in another era, would have been called experts. Regulation is specialized along one of three lines (cf. Jones): (1) generally applicable like state corporate law or federal antitrust or securities law; (2) specific like regulation of drug safety or auto safety or coal mine safety; or (3) specific economic regulation, the kind of regulation before us. And economic regulation not only has a range of methods as already noted but also a range of goals from avoidance of conflict-of-interest abuses, to financial stability, to protecting consumers.

Since the industries we are considering are intensely regulated in such a variety of ways and for such a variety of reasons, it is worth noting whether a plea for change is anarchist, abolitionist, revisionist or perhaps only tinkering.

Lump thinking about regulation is particularly misleading when we get to the "costs" of regulation. *Lump 1:* Costs are usually discussed as if they were total losses, though mostly they are redistributions of wealth. Every cost is someone's gain, and many of these redistributions bring overall gain. For example, required financial disclosure is often discussed as if it were only a cost burden on corporate issuers, which might be reasonable if the only redistribution were to accountants, lawyers, and printers since such redistribution lowers overall output of goods and may indeed be an overall cost. But we cannot stop there. Mandated disclosure of financial data redistributes funds by helping issuers that look better in the light of full disclosure to out-compete (in the financial markets) other issuers that look worse. Or corporate insiders surrounded by disclosure requirements are impeded from taking unjustifiable rewards, which helps their stockholders for whom such impediments are protections. To the extent that savers lack confidence in public investment media, they are likely to reduce their total savings or put savings into such unproductive forms as gold jewelry. Regulation via deposit insurance, by pulling money out of mattresses or gold jewelry, has importantly increased overall productivity. Regulation of securities markets cannot with similar directness bring funds forward because regulation cannot eliminate securities' inherent elements of riskiness. But regulation can reduce some risks by making more information efficiently available and by increasing confidence in the integrity of the markets and of issuers, thus lowering the cost of corporate capital, leading to greater productivity.

Further, the lumpy treatment of costs so often ignores what costs would be borne if there were no requirements. For example, without required disclosure, with its fairly specific mandates as to what shall be told and how, prices are likely to experience two upward pressures. For one, consumers or investors come forward less readily if information is not efficiently available. For another, without information efficiently available, competition tends to occur not so much where we want it, on quality and price, as on "efficiency" of manipulating or avoiding disclosure. Voluntary disclosure is selective at best, depending not on what makes the market more efficient, but on what helps the individual firm. Even where market pressures do arise for substantial disclosure, comparability will be nil or unnecessarily expensive.

Such costs of the *absence* of regulation are inevitable even in markets where buyers are sophisticated and stakes are large. For example, I recently surveyed the market for institutional investment management (Schotland 1978). Every year billions of dollars in pension funds and other institutional accounts flow to new managers; there are many money management firms, so competition for new accounts is intense; the service rendered is unusually susceptible to quantification and comparison; and the buyers—the pension fund and other institutional trustees and staffs—are relatively highly sophisticated. Yet, since the buyers are not as knowledgeable as the sellers and since there are no guidelines about what data should be disclosed, there are considerable difficulties in getting data about as basic a matter as investment performance, let alone in evaluating such data. These difficulties are acute enough to generate a new industry of consultants and a "growing uproar" (Rohrer 1977). The problem is almost wholly one of inefficient information flow since the presentation of data without uniform guidelines leads to variations that defy comparative evaluation. For example: Firms freely choose—and freely change—the periods on which they disclose their performance; whether they give results for all accounts or only "representative" ones; and what indexes are used for comparison. Good investment management seems less a matter of actually managing money than of merchandising the managers. (Before the securities markets became so institutionalized, The Great Truth of Wall Street was "stocks are sold, not bought." Institutionalization of the markets has brought many changes, but The Great Truth has simply gone from the retail level of selling stocks to individuals to the wholesale level of selling investment managers to institutional trustees.)

Surely here is an instance where the costs of regulatory intervention to require and channel disclosure would be low and even productive. After initial costs to develop the requirements, there would be only miniscule costs of administration and compliance. Contrast the gains. The minor gain would be lowering the costs of selecting money managers. The major gain would come from increasing the flow of funds to firms that are more able investors: More funds in more rational hands will increase the efficiency of our investment markets. Here then is a case for low-cost regulation with even economic benefits outweighing the costs (and there may be less direct benefits as well such as heightened confidence in securities markets), hardly to be obscured by lumpy focus only on costs.

Lump 2: Sometimes it is recognized that there is redistribution rather than total loss, but the gainers are simplistically lumped as one group, losers another. For example, Regulation Q has been beaten on as subsidizing inefficient depositories and borrowers at the expense of savers. Virtually no attention has been given to analysis suggesting that lower-income people would gain less through higher rates on savings than they would lose through higher costs of borrowing. That analysis (done under their highly regarded economist, the late Nathaniel Goldfinger) may be wrong, but it is responsible for the AFL-CIO's support for Regulation Q. Considering all the ink thrown at Regulation Q, such analysis has been unwarrantedly ignored.

Lump 3: Costs of regulation often include costs that would be borne in any event or are the costs of living under law or under democracy. Financial firms, dealing with cash, inevitably have substantial record-keeping and reporting burdens because there is such need to protect both the firms and customers against Robin Hood and his less noble imitators. Many of these requirements would be complied with even if left to firms' own choice. Or there are costs of participating in the process of shaping laws and regulations. After a study of its own costs of regulation, Dow Chemical alleged that it spent $5 million in 1975 on salaries and expenses for testifying on federal regulatory matters (*Business Week* 1977). Would any of us prefer systems in which we need not worry about any burden of our own participation in lawmaking? Dow alleged that $750,000 of the $5 million was "excessive." Since Dow has refused to release the study even to an American Bar Association study of regulation headed by John McCloy, no evaluation can be made of their figures or characterizations. By Dow's lights, total regulatory costs for their domestic operations in 1975 came to $147 million, of which the "excessive" category came to $50 million and the "questionable" to $10 million, curiously round numbers when contrasted with the $147 million figure. To use one other example outside finance, AT&T has had huge costs of participation in the FCC's unprecedented, years-long formal rate proceeding; but a huge proportion of those costs went into the company's unprecedented self-study, leading to many new, wholly voluntary, presumably productive changes. Last, it seems always assumed that regulated firms are highly efficient in meeting regulatory requirements. Did Dow need to spend as much as $5 million on one year's federal testimony?

Lump 4: Costs of regulation are treated as if there were no costs of transition to a less regulated scene. Broker-dealers know how horrendous the costs of deregulation can be. Such costs are not merely the loss of profits that had been generated by protection from competition but also fewer securities analysts, fewer sources of research, fewer underwriters, all having serious impacts outside the industry. Nor is it just the more efficient firms that can bear the costs of transition; firms with more diverse products survive better than firms concentrated just where the deregulation has an impact. Also the new, less regulated scene tends to be much more concentrated[2]—as has happened in the securities industry, as is now happening in domestic aviation, and as is predicted for trucking.

The costs of transition just noted are well known. They point up the need for careful analysis to minimize the costs of transition and to make sure that escaping the costs of regulation is worth the costs of transition. But further, even if transition is easy, what of the costs of living with the new regime? It is worth examining what has happened to commission rates since "deregulation" in May 1975, for developments here are a reminder that escaping the problems of regulation brings us back to the problems of free markets.

I was part of the great majority who thought fixed commission rates one of the leading horrors of our financial markets. I still think that, but now I believe reasonable people could differ. I am not even sure that fixed commission rates are gone. Am I wrong to be troubled about the following three things?

Concern 1: One firm, Merrill Lynch, now essentially sets rates for almost all retail business, without any SEC oversight. True, other firms can and do deviate microscopically from Merrill Lynch's retail rates. True also, there is a happy emergence of discount broker-dealers, but they do a tiny proportion of individuals' total volume, and only relatively sophisticated investors—indeed, only readers of financial publications—are even aware of them. Are retail customers likely to benefit as one firm becomes more dominant?

Concern 2: Today's retail rates are based far less on costs or rational profit targets than on the old fixed rates, although huge changes have occurred— especially in options markets—since those old rates were set. Consider the differences in current commission charges on four different kinds of invest- ments, each at $5,000, each unquestionably usually involving different costs for the broker-dealer—but none involving such cost differences as warrant the differences in the prices charged:

$5,000 in options—20 contracts, $250 @	$183.70
$5,000 in 100 shares of common or preferred stock, $50 @	$80.00
$5,000 in 5 corporate bonds $1,000 @ 5-year or shorter	$25.00
5-year or longer;	$50.00
$5,000 in Treasury bonds	$10.00

Whatever might have been true before the days of a central depository and other recent advances from the quill pen era and without suggesting that the SEC should try to assure a rational rate structure, ought not the SEC look into whether these differences are justified?

In fact, there is little or no cost justification because there is very little retail-price competition. Broker-dealers compete for retail customers mainly by competing for registered representatives who, like magnets, bring with them clusters of accounts. And first-time investors tend to pay little if any attention to transaction cost differences between firms. Such costs are so small a proportion of the sum being invested that differences in the rates charged apparently are ignored. At least, these seem to be the only sound inferences from the fact that major firms' efforts to draw customers by advertising rate differences have been so unsuccessful that most of the rate inducements have been discontinued, whereas there has been virtual war among major firms in 1977-1978 over getting and holding retail account executives.

Even at the level of institutional rates, one can question the rationality of the present across-the-board X-cents-per-share treatment. A little pension fund, of which I am a trustee, in February bought $100,000 worth of Phelps Dodge, or 5,000 shares, at a commission of $500; and $100,000 worth of Monsanto, or 2,000 shares, for a commission of $300. There is not even remotely a 66% difference in the cost of handling such transactions. The basis of such charges is simply out of date. Another troublesome aspect of institutional rates today: Large bank trust departments, which do most of their business in orders of fewer than 1,000 shares, are getting rates as low as 4.5 cents per share for such smaller orders, but paying around 15 cents per share for larger orders. Instead of a volume discount by size of order, there is a volume discount for total business transacted. Smaller institutional investors cannot command equally low rates. How does this affect competition among institutional money managers for accounts to manage? Perhaps there is no feasible alternative to this situation. But how far it is from the pre-May-Day vision.

Concern 3: Options produce about twice as much gross commissions for firms and registered representatives as do equities, with some but nowhere near proportional differences in costs; and further, options tend to turn over more. Don't those facts create a set of incentives totally at war with an important (but already too feeble) doctrine, suitability?[3] Many firms try to reduce the registered representatives' incentive to mislead customers into options, by actively discouraging small orders in options. However, at least one major firm, Paine Webber, exacerbates the "wrong" incentive by *increasing* the registered representatives' proportion of gross commissions on small options orders (*Wall Street Letter* 1978). The extreme current difference between rates for equities and for options exists because the CBOE simply copied the old NYSE fixed rates for stocks, which were much higher for low-priced shares and so were conveniently much higher for low-priced option units. The option rate was further inflated artificially: Stocks can be bought in odd lots, down to a "unit" of even a single share so that basing stock commission rates on per-share price is reasonably realistic. But in options, the smallest purchasable "unit" is a contract of 100 shares. If the CBOE had been realistic, they would have used, for the hypothetical $250 contract, the NYSE rate for one $250 share. Instead, option commission rates were inflated about 20% by using the NYSE rate for 100 shares at $2.50 each.

Even if only three years have elapsed since May Day, isn't that more than long enough to inquire whether rates are structured reasonably rationally, are not structured to injure investors or unnecessarily discourage direct public participation in the markets, are not causing unfair discrimination among institutional customers, and are not forcing such concentration in the industry that rate regulation will have to be brought back?

By setting forth the results of deregulating commission rates to show the costs of transition and the problems in living with an unregulated regime, I do not mean to suggest that there are no wasteful costs of regulation or that removing such waste is not worthwhile. I mean rather that lumpy thinking is itself costly: It misleads by obscuring real problems, real lines of possible solution. There is also danger in the simplistic belief that cost-benefit analyses of these matters will be more beneficial than simply costly. All of us are for careful consideration of trade-offs, but that is as far as cost-benefit analyses are likely to take us on a huge array of regulatory matters—*if* such analyses do not misleadingly give measurable factors undue weight over less measurable ones (*Stanford Law Review* 1972).

Aren't costs of regulation so often lumped—instead of being recognized as a dispersion of gains, losses, inevitabilities, and inefficiencies—because reality makes it far harder to secure agreement that the regulation under attack is just a wasteful sacred cow ready for slaughter?

Lumpy thinking is merely a form of sloppiness. But the ideological fervor that infuses deregulation discussions seems to promote sloppiness so that paradoxically, lump thinking is often accompanied by its first cousin, failure to consider related problems together. For example, the NYSE's Rule 390 (setting requirements that orders in listed stocks be "brought to the floor" and thus participate in the public markets) cannot be attacked responsibly unless the abolitionist attack includes concrete proposals for safeguards against all the nonmarket factors that would likely infest the proposed more "competitive" new system of free choice as to where to execute orders.

Sloppiness is not limited to lumping what shouldn't be lumped and separating what should not be separated. Sloppiness in studies of regulation causes such odd treatment of facts that it is hard to imagine any explanation other than ideological fervor, as when so prominent an economist as Stigler is guilty of "a large number of data errors, virtually all of which biased the results in favor of his hypothesis" (Mendelson 1978). An early example, the study that has become almost legend in the literature about regulation's "costs," Huntington's "Marasmus of the ICC," was at once shown to have unnecessary, major gaps in its data as well as other flaws, yet that study has been repeatedly relied on by "scholars" who fail to note the replies to it (Jaffe 1954). Similarly troublesome gaps appear in studies figuring significantly in the current controversy over trucking deregulation.[4]

Sloppy problem analysis that selectively ignores aspects of reality is one side of the deregulatory ideologues' coin. The other side is proposing "solutions" that seem clearly superior to current methods, ignoring the fact that a proposal may already be in use. For example, a noted academic beats on what surely is one of the most beatable agencies, OSHA, arguing understandably and voguishly that an incentives approach via taxes or fines would be superior to the current approach of setting procrustean standards:

> In the OSHA case, that would come essentially to a requirement that workers' compensation provide payments to injured workers through an insurance scheme based on higher premiums on those plants and those corporations where the accident rates are higher. We are many decades from such an improvement in workers' compensation, however, because the arguments have been denied by the safety professionals on grounds that it is still too early to tell, in the history of OSHA operations, whether there are significant malfunctions from the process (MacAvoy 1978).

"Many decades away from such an improvement" may be ambiguous, but it certainly seems to suggest that it will be a long time before beknighted regulators see the wisdom of the sound commentator's solution. In fact, about 85% of all workmen's compensation premium dollars are based on experience ratings (although only about 15% of all employers because it has been deemed impractical to differentially rate small employers). Rates are set by an industry organization, the National Council of Compensation Insurers (Williams 1969). Rather than blithely beating on an obviously poor regulatory program, surely it would be more useful to get the facts and put forward concrete proposals—like telling OSHA to study the long-standing workmen's compensation experience and to consider how, if at all, OSHA may differ with respect to using more of the incentives approach. Surely it is unrealistic to expect the very regulators one is faulting to find their own way to better programs.

The sloppy or "selective" treatment of reality is so pronounced in the studies of regulation that Ronald Coase has warned against the "thoroughly bad" method of comparing actual performance under regulation with " 'an ideal norm derived from the familiar optimum conditions of economic theory' " (Coase 1970).

Not only are real regulation and theoretical markets discussed as if they belonged to the same world but also in language which, I submit, is itself biased.

"Market failures" or "market imperfections," versus "why regulation fails" (Schuck 1975): It would be no less biased—though in the other direction—to talk of "regulatory imperfections," or to ask "why markets fail." I am reminded of Thurman Arnold's distinction between courts and agencies:

> A court is a body of judges whose decisions are either (1) right, (2) caused by the fault of someone else (usually—the legislature), or (3) unfortunate but unavoidable accidents due to the circumstances that no human system can be perfect.

> An agency is a body which if it happens to make a wrong decision, has no one to blame but itself, and if it happens to make a right decision offers us no assurance that it will do so again (Arnold 1961).

I realize I am tilting against accepted usage, but wouldn't neutral analysis and communication be promoted if we acknowledge that both markets and regulation have strengths and weaknesses, not "imperfections"? Markets are weak, to put it kindly, at taking care of "spillovers," at assuring adequate equity, even at staying competitive excesses, etc. Regulation is weak at finding the right ground between rigidity and ad hoc ruler-under-the-fig-tree discretion; regulation even has many problems of determining and adhering to the relevant public interest.

The inability of markets to limit such "spillovers" as pollution, to avoid such sheep shearings as selling new issues to anyone who will buy, or to avoid speculative excesses that recur almost as frequently as tulip bulbs blossom are not "failures" but are inherent weaknesses. Market failures, rather, ought to refer to such events as industry-wide collapses like the "back-office mess," which drowned broker-dealers in 1967-1970, or like the catastrophic 1971-1973 overexpansion, which by 1975 drowned real estate investment trusts and our whole real estate sector.

Lest there be doubt, I do not equate markets with the private sector or regulation with the public sector, although generally the equation fits. It is not private overreaching but inherent limits on markets' working to further the public weal, which requires the bulk of our regulatory interventions. For example, isn't there more similarity than difference between the problems of private pension plans that led to ERISA, and the situation of state and local pension plans, 25% of which have not had an actuarial review in 10 years or more, half of which are not subject to outside audit, and 70% of which do not know or do not disclose the market value of their assets? (U.S. House of Representatives 1978) Regulatory elaboration of pension, tax, environmental, equal employment standards, etc., is necessary not only as long as we have capitalism but as long as we have people. (Might one of the best routes to deregulation be depopulation?)

A final impediment in communication about deregulation is that the principal participants speak different languages. Deregulation discussions are fortunately not the exclusive province of lawyers and economists, but our presence does dominate. The very strengths of our professional training and work create some of the communication problems and even biases in so much of the writing in this area.[5] Lawyers trained and experienced in analyzing A's rights against B are prone to forget to consider how their proposed answer might have an impact on third parties and on the future. I fear we lawyers lack the systematic orientation at which economists are so good. Lawyers' substantial concern for justice tends to make us attend too little to what may be the costs of correcting perceived injustice. On the other hand, economists' great ability in measurement may tend to cause them to attend too little to the immeasurable.

Lawyers may have too little skepticism about the efficacy of the law, economists too little about the efficiency of markets. Lawyers may think too idealistically about political process; economists may think too infrequently about political process.

Perhaps that is why we so often fail to see that the political process from which every regulatory program emerged is itself a strong kind of free market, albeit with "buying" power distributed differently from economic markets. (However, the political and economic "markets" are importantly related through such linkages as campaign financing and lobbying.) Too often it is forgotten that every regulatory program itself emerged in response to a perceived market weakness like conflict-of-interest abuses or a perceived market failure like auto manufacturers' neglect of auto safety. The perceptions may err, but they must be widely shared and important, since political processes move only on problems that matter to many people. In a democracy the process of deciding which problems require action and what action they require is more open and competitive than a great deal of our economic process. And not even politicians come up with only misguided, inefficient solutions. Indeed, E.B. White defined democracy as "the recurrent suspicion that more than half of the people are right more than half of the time" (White 1943).

By no means should I be read as denying that we have a severe problem of too much regulation, too slow, too inflexible, etc., ad nauseam. My own regulatory reform agenda would be long. It would include some abolition (for example, Regulation Q); some relaxation leading perhaps toward abolition in the future (for example, easing geographic barriers on depositories); much lifting of burdens on small firms where regulatory goals end up largely as entry barriers; and much reduction of substantive requirements in favor of more flexible, less intensive ones such as full disclosure (for example, for banks' capital adequacy). And high on my agenda would be an effort to have regulators give more emphasis to activating and educating private-sector forces. For example, if regulators would inform banks' boards of what internal safeguards a bank should have against conflicts of interest, there would be less need to rely on regulatory alertness, and less improper conduct in the first place (Twentieth Century Fund 1975). If regulators recognized how much aid market discipline could bring to regulatory efforts to assure a safe and sound banking system, then the ridiculously obsolete 1864 requirement that each bank must publish its latest balance sheet would be replaced by a requirement that each bank publish instead key data and ratios about itself, side by side with comparative figures on similar size banks in the same region. Better-informed stockholders and large depositors can better protect their interests, which in many ways are part of the public interest that regulation exists to promote.

Since regulation emerges in response to perceived market weaknesses, isn't one avenue of regulatory reform the reform or strengthening of the market?[6]

Toward Full Disclosure about Reforming Regulation

Roderick Hills, speaking as SEC chairman exactly two years ago to the Investment Company Institute about "rationalizing the regulatory process" and claiming that he believed "that regulatory agency is best which regulates least" announced that the first step the SEC had taken to carry out his view was to change the division of investment management regulation by dropping the word *regulation* from the title. One week earlier he testified at the House Commerce Committee in support of an SEC-initiated bill to give the Commission power to set minimum qualification standards limiting entry into investment advising and also to require minimum net capital or bonding (even for advisers who never handle other people's money but only publish advice) (Hills 1976).

That kind of rhetorical flourish covering up an indefensible effort to add unsound regulation[7]—an effort that would have succeeded even in that brief heyday of deregulation but for the strong opposition from one member to the Senate Banking Committee, Jesse Helms—typifies the four hurdles that face people interested in improving financial regulation.

First, we face a general sense of "the unlikelihood of change" (Wilson 1971) because of the complexity of the scene and the difficulty in changing even simple established relationships. Second, despite the fascination with these matters, they lack the public clamor that draws political energies. Third, improvement requires general, wide-ranging efforts to build into the regulatory system mechanisms devoted to improving the system; but not enough people can be interested in such efforts. Fourth improvement requires also deep digging into countless particulars, but not enough people can be interested in such plodding. The persons most responsible for the quality of regulations, the regulators themselves, are understandably more interested in what they perceive to be new problems than in improving the treatment of old problems. Isn't that part of why regulation proliferates? Isn't there more excitement and "news" in requiring, for example, disclosure of previously private information than in plodding through existing disclosure requirements to decide which are unnecessarily complicated and which have become simply unnecessary?

A little sense of history may help us see how hard it is to reform regulation, utterly apart from political disinterest and private vested interest. One of the core goals of regulatory reform is simplification; but that goal often conflicts with others, like the goal of assuring fair regulation. A nice example of how sisyphian is the task of improving regulation, how hard it is to simplify, arose in New York as early as 1806: In 1803 the state incorporated a turnpike company and authorized the governor to appoint three commissioners to examine the road from time to time, each commissioner to be paid $3 a day by the company, but the inspection to be limited to two days a month. In 1804 the scheme was improved by providing for inspection on complaint, but this required structuring a process for hearings, appeals, and penalties. That reform went too far, so in 1806 it was necessary to provide sanctions for unfounded complaints and to authorize appointment of appraisers and inspectors. Codification, albeit without the aid of the American Law Institute, came in 1807 (Hunter 1917).

Today no part of the Carter Administration is working at general across-the-government regulatory reform, except perhaps for whoever recently produced the Executive Order calling for such leaps forward as writing regulations "in plain English" (shades of the well-intentioned, ineffective post-Civil War state constitutional provisions imposing similar "restrictions" on state legislatures).[8]

To turn from general to specific efforts, I have been unable to find anyone in the banking regulatory agencies or SEC who keeps a straight face if asked about deregulation. We do almost nothing to reduce or improve existing regulation, but we add and add. Consider the contrast between first, significant new regulation; second, reduced or "improved" regulation; and third, changes wholly outside regulation or perhaps in that wonderful realm of "deregulation by not telling."

First, ERISA alone is a near-revolutionary recent rise in finance-related regulation. Other major increases have occurred recently in:

corporate issuers' accounting and other disclosure requirements;

markets for state and local securities;

markets for commodities and options;

"antiredlining" requirements;

real estate settlement procedures;

banks' reporting requirements and intensity of examinations;

supervision of U.S. banking abroad;

unprecedented limits on insiders' transactions at thrifts, banks, and investment companies and also on trust department conflicts of interest, training, and competence.

Second, significant items of "improved" or reduced regulation, or "deregulation by not telling":

NOW accounts and their permutations, from the thrifts' debit cards to new uses of old machinery like telephone transfer as well as much new machinery, and most recently to the banks' impending automatic transfer accounts;

in the early 1970s but quiet since then, the Bank Holding Company Act's erosion of geographic and functional barriers;

the steady drift toward easier state branching laws;

variable-rate mortgages;

SEC's April 1978 hearings on easing registration and reporting requirements for "small business"; and

SEC's 1975 "FOCUS" streamlining of broker-dealer reporting.

To this second list may be added a third, of changes essentially outside regulation:

money market funds—what a grand tooth pulling for Regulation Q;

municipal bond funds and trusts;

Mortgage-backed bonds;

"crosses" almost wholly within a trust department or investment advisory firm—Citibank now does 2% of its huge volume through broker-dealers by crosses at only 1 cent per share; and

"market inventory funds," that is, "crosses" wholly between a single pension plan's several investment managers.

Admitting these little lists' nonexhaustiveness, isn't it clear that regulatory proliferation continues? If we consider also the ever-rising intricacies that are added to existing requirements, can doubt remain?

Far more disturbing than the comparatively little actual results or pending work—despite the volume of talk about improving regulation—is the failure of even important lawmakers to get the message that regulation has its limits and its costs. For example, in SEC Chairman Hills' talk noted earlier, he singled out as among the "requirements I'm not sure we need" the SEC rules on investment company sales literature. He was pointing to a leading example of overcomplex, ineffective regulation:

the existing system of mutual fund advertising rules and the folklore which has grown up regarding the distinctions and over-laps between regular generic ads, underwriter generic ads, limited tombstone advertisements, expanded tombstones, combined tombstones, summary prospectuses, abbreviated prospectuses, supplemental sales literature and dealer-only material (Investment Company Institute 1978).

For almost a decade the SEC has been "working" at simplifying investment company advertising. The progress has been as great as you would expect around tombstones, but the need for improvement is substantial. On the one hand, the existing system keeps investment companies under unfair competitive disadvantages. On the other hand, the crazy quilt of requirements fails to protect investors from seriously incomplete, even misleading information; for example, no data on relative riskiness and misleading "mountain charts." As if progress on these rules is against the rule, the commission recently proposed limiting print ads to 600 words, banning radio or TV ads and prohibiting direct mailings. Now there's the spirit of deregulation.

Perhaps the outstanding example of recent faith in regulation's omnipotence and low cost comes from the New York City Council. In April 1978 the Consumer Affairs Committee head proposed a set of "Truth-in-Menu" regulations, including: giving prices per pound if, as in steaks or lobsters, prices differ for larger servings; using specified sizes of type for cover or service charges; and for all beverages, showing both the ounces and metric measure.

I fear regulation has its true-believer proponents as well as similar opponents.

A Typical Current Need for Added Regulation

Far too often we say "there ought to be a law," far too frequently do legislators care more to "get a bill" than they care about the bill's contents, far too common is the temptation to "straighten out" an area rather than trying to tailor the intervention to the perceived problem provoking attention. These tendencies have understandable causes, but we need to develop more restraint.

Perhaps it is inconsistent with a call for more restraint to put forward instances where increased regulation is better than the alternatives (which is all we claim for democracy). But my earlier plea for regulating disclosures about institutional investors' performance illustrates how difficult it is to develop the restraint just called for. To point up further how Canute-like is any call for "no new starts"[9] in regulation, consider how strong is the case for regulating real estate investment trusts (Schotland, forthcoming).

REITs involved at their peak over $21 billion in assets (a tenfold growth in five years). Their decline was not merely a disaster for stockholders, taking the industry's market value at end-1974 to 15% of what it had been in January 1973; the decline also inflicted immeasurable injury on construction firms and workers and on the real estate markets in many regions. Ordinary failure in the marketplace is no reason for regulatory intervention, but the REITs' failure stemmed in part from causes that cry for regulation.

Few people realize that the REIT structure, wholly a creature of the Internal Revenue Code and its limited focus, is uniquely ridden with conflicts of interest:

Like investment companies but no other segment of corporate America, REITs are "externally" managed, with management's interest lying wholly in the "advisory" and related fees. Management almost never holds any ownership interest in the REIT itself, unlike almost all corporate management in the nation.

Unlike investment companies, REITs have been almost completely unlimited in leveraging, and the more leveraging of the portfolio, the higher the management fee.

Unlike investment companies, REITs have been almost completely unlimited in transactions between the REIT and its management or their affiliates. Moreover, almost all such transactions involve hard-to-price real estate investments, so unlike publicly traded securities.

Unlike investment companies, REITs could use (and stock in most of the major ones were sold by using) the name of the sponsor-adviser, for example, the Chase Manhattan or the First Wisconsin REIT, names that were misleading invitations.

Unlike investment companies, REIT managements have derived massive income from almost always undisclosed fees in addition to the management fee.

Unlike investment companies, which at least since 1970 have had moderating limits on managerial or advisory compensation, REIT advisers' total fee income has been estimated by the leading REIT investment analysis firm to have been too high by $100-110 million per year during the halcyon days of 1971-1973, with a number of firms netting as profit over 50% of their gross fees. Such excessive fees were arrived at with no arms-length bargaining and with almost wholly inadequate disclosure.

Unlike investment companies, which have had a weak but not wholly hollow requirement of "independent" directors, REITs had a superficially similar requirement, but a director qualified as "independent" even if he were, for example, counsel for the REIT management or a borrower from the REIT.

In 1940 Congress passed legislation intensely regulating a tiny financial industry—investment companies—which had been all but annihilated by the 1929-1933 crash and a slateful of scandals. By regulating obvious conflict-of-interest problems and thus augmenting investor confidence, the 1940 act has proved to be the Magna Carta of a $50-billion industry.

Isn't there a strong case for enacting a version of the Investment Company Act, appropriately adapted to REITs? If the REIT concept is economically viable at all—and it appears to be, going by market experience since the speculative excess was exorcised by the 1973-1974 disaster—aren't steps to make REITs more sound and more fair, worthwhile even at the price of adding to our plethora of regulation?

Four Steps Toward Improving Regulation

Without reiterating familiar wisdom, familiar because it does cover the fundamentals, I offer four little suggestions:

1. Before President Carter was elected, a massive study of appointments to the FTC and FCC from 1952 to 1972 was published by the Senate Commerce Committee, with strong recommendations to improve regulatory commission-level appointments by raising the visibility and openness of the White House selection process and ending the Senate's charade-level treatment of advice and consent to such appointments (U.S. Senate 1976a). In January 1977, the Senate Government Affairs Committee adopted similar recommendations (U.S. Senate 1977). While my orientation is such that I applaud many of Carter's regulatory appointments, this administration's process—for all its pronouncements about a new wave—has been not a whit better than prior administrations'. If there were a single key to better regulation, it would be the simple one of getting more good people, and improved selection process can do much toward that goal.

2. To speak truth, even if unrealistic: It is nonsensical to have the Congressional Governmental Affairs Committees' majorities in the hands of the same party as the White House. I like checks and balances better than blank checks. Some committees are more than normally representative of the majority party. Is it unrealistic even to try to make the Governmental Affairs Committees *less* than normally representative of the majority party?

3. To continue in the vein of increasing countervailing voices, but in this instance to be wholly realistic: We should have representative, expertly constituted advisory committees for each agency (or even each major program) to write annual "counterreports" on where the agency committed errors of omission or commission. The reports would be somewhat like the Brookings' annual analyses of the U.S. budget, or like the statements of the "Shadow Open Market Committee." We do not need consensus in such counterreports and would never get consensus if such committees are as representative as they ought to be. But we would have informed, timely aid in making congressional oversight agendas more fruitful. We would, in essense, institutionalize a sober second thought for each agency. I have proposed this in detail in congressional testimony (U.S. Senate 1976b). I'm told that the proposal's only flaw is the threat it contains to congressional staffs' wish that the members shall rely on them to understand regulatory programs.

4. Further in the vein of increasing the variety of informed forces at work on regulatory improvement: I submit that the major companies and trade associations do far too little—almost nothing—to *initiate* concrete alternatives to existing regulatory requirements or processes rather than merely to react, to nay-say, and to bewail "regulatory interference."

Without a larger investment of the private sector's singular talent to meet these regulatory challenges that are more complex than the rhetoricians would have us believe, it is up to us academics to cultivate these gardens. That means remembering our role as analysts and as advocates who acknowledge biases. And even if we do contribute as best we can, it is easier to point the way than to get the roads built. But we may be able to keep the growing concern for regulatory reform from going in the wrong direction or from just spinning wheels, making noise but going nowhere.

Notes

1. One professor noted the difficulty of a three-hour discussion of deregulation with a truckers' association, in which the professor meant only economic regulation; the truckers thought from his language that he meant all regulation, including safety, and it was not until the discussion's end that the confusion ended (McAdams in Martin and Schwartz 1977, p. 104).

2. The occurrence of concentration does not necessarily mean that "destructive competition" prevails, but predictions were more optimistic than seems borne out (see, for example, Mann 1975). Such predictions may have gone awry in part because as automatic data processing has replaced clerks, the ratio of fixed costs to total costs has risen; thus even if aggregate supply of services has lost little elasticity (or even become more elastic), ease of entry of new firms or flexibility of market shares has declined sharply.

3. According to decisions under this doctrine, part of the congressional policy of the Exchange Act is to ensure that a customer will not be misled into buying a security that is unsuitable, for example, more risky than is consistent with his investment objectives.

4. Several studies rely on other countries' experience with deregulation of trucking without even considering geographic and other differences between those countries and the United States (Moore 1976 and Nelson 1976; see Spychalski 1975).

5. "Conferences dealing with public policy issues and heavily attended by both economists and lawyers have not always been known for the quality and clarity of discourse nor for the high level of agreement on important questions" (Martin and Schwartz 1977, p. xv).

6. "What is advocated here is the reverse of the policy actions of the 1930s. Then the aim was to mitigate competitive forces in order to preserve the structure of financial markets; here the aim is to increase competitive forces by [improved disclosure], letting the structure adapt as efficiency requires" (Phillips 1975).

7. The American Law Institute's recently approved *Official Draft of a Federal Securities Code* (forthcoming) regrettably proposes authorizing the SEC to promulgate standards with respect to investment advisers' "operational

capability" and "training, experience, competence, and other qualifications" [Section 703(e)]. This is done with no note of the differences between investment advisers who handle customers' money and those who do not.

8. There is an impressive *Regulation Research Program* of empirical studies funded by the National Science Foundation since 1975, including several promising studies of costs and benefits of regulation of consumer financial services. There is also an impressive study on the reform of economic regulation generally by the American Bar Association's Commission on Law and the Economy.

I should note explicitly that many of the problems I describe in analyses of regulation are particularly pronounced in the work of legal academics who have embraced economics with more enthusiasm than expertise and use it as part of their attack on the simpler faith of the New Deal and Nader types who have tried to solve problems by regulating them.

9. This was the label for the Eisenhower Administration policy toward public hydropower projects. Its tone of moderation fades when one notes that existing dams and plants are even less susceptible to dismantling than regulatory agencies; and dynamiting the dams would have been quiet compared to the noise that would have arisen over efforts to sell the dams to private power companies.

References

Arnold, Thurman. In Gellhorn, Walter, "Summary of Colloquy on Administrative Law." *Journal of Society of Public Teachers of Law* 6 (London 1961):70.

Business Week. "Dow Chemical's Catalog of Regulatory Horrors," 4 April 1977, p. 50.

Coase, Ronald H. "Comment" on "Measuring the Success of Regulation in Terms of Its Economic Effects." In *The Crisis of the Regulatory Commissions*, edited by Paul W. MacAvoy, pp. 53-54. New York: Norton, 1970.

Cutler, Lloyd N., and Johnson, David R. "Regulation and the Political Process." *Yale Law Journal* 84 (June 1975):1395.

Hills, Roderick M. Address before Investment Company Institute. (Washington: SEC, 26 May 1976); Hearings on Investment Advisers Act Amendments before U.S. Subcommittee on Consumer Protection and Finance, 94th Cong. 2d sess. (20 May 1976):17-27.

Houthakker, Hendrick. "Economic Aspects of Deregulation." In *Deregulating American Industry,* edited by Donald L. Martin and Warren F. Schwartz. Lexington, Mass.: Lexington Books, D.C. Heath, 1977, pp. 1, 4-5.

Hunter, M.H. "The Early Regulation of Public Service Corporations." *American Economic Review* 7 (September 1917):569, 570.

Investment Company Institute. *White Paper* (prepared statement to SEC) *on*

Regulation of Mutual Fund Advertising (4 February 1978). Washington, D.C., p. 2.

Jaffe, Louis L. "The Effective Limits of the Administrative Process: A Reevaluation." *Harvard Law Review* 67 (May 1954):1105, at 1108.

Jones, William K. "Legal Regulation and Economic Analysis." In *American Assembly: Law in a Changing America.* Englewood Cliffs, N.J.: Prentice-Hall, 1968, pp. 75, 76-77.

MacAvoy, Paul W. "The Existing Condition of Regulation and Regulatory Reform." In *Regulating Business: The Search for an Optimum.* San Francisco: Institute for Contemporary Studies, 1978.

Mann, H. Michael. "The New York Stock Exchange: A Cartel at the End of Its Reign." In *Promoting Competition in Regulated Markets,* edited by Almarin Phillips. Washington, D.C.: Brookings Institution, 1975, pp. 301, 312.

Martin, Donald L., and Schwartz, Warren F., eds. *Deregulating American Industry.* Lexington, Mass.: Lexington Books, D.C. Heath, 1977.

Mendelson, Morris. "Economics and the Assessment of Disclosure Requirements." *Journal of Comparative Corporate Law & Sections Regulation I* 49 (1978), p. 57.

Moore, Thomas Gale. "Trucking Regulation: Lessons from Europe." Washington, D.C.: American Enterprise Institute, 1976.

Nelson, James C. "The Economic Effects of Transport Deregulation in Australia." *Transportation Journal* 15 (Winter 1976):48.

Phillips, Almarin, ed. *Promoting Competition in Regulated Markets.* Washington, D.C.: Brookings Institution, 1975; *Competitive Policy for Depository Financial Institutions.* Washington, D.C.: Brookings Institution, 1975, pp. 329, 366.

Rein, Martin, and White, Sheldon H. "Can Policy Research Help Policy?" *The Public Interest* 49 (Fall 1977):119.

Rohrer, Julie. "Pension Fund Consultants—The Tail That Wags the Dog." *New York Times,* 18 June 1977, § 3, p. 1.

Schotland, Roy A. "Picking Investment Managers." *Pensions & Investments,* 24 April 1978, p. 61 (and see p. 8).

_____. "Conflicts of Interest in Real Estate Investment Trusts." New York: Twentieth Century Fund, forthcoming.

Schuck, Peter H. "Why Regulation Fails." *Harper's,* September 1975, p. 16.

Securities and Exchange Commission. Staff Report on *The Securities Industry in 1977,* 22 May 1978.

Spychalski, John C. "Criticisms of Regulated Freight Transport: Do Economists' Perceptions Conform with Institutional Realities?" *Transportation Journal* 14 (Spring 1975):5.

Stanford Law Review. "Cost-Benefit Analysis and the National Environmental Policy Act of 1969" 24 (June 1972):1092.

Twentieth Century Fund. *Conflicts of Interest in Securities Markets,* forthcoming. See, for example, Herman, Edw. S., "Conflicts of Interest in Commercial Bank Trust Departments," and Brooks, John, "Conflicts of Interest in Corporate Pension Fund Asset Management." New York: Twentieth Century Fund, 1975.

U.S. Congress, House, Committee on Education and Labor, Subcommittee on Labor Standards, *Report on Public Employee Retirement Systems.* Washington, D.C.: 1978.

U.S. Congress, Senate, Committee on Commerce, Committee Print. *Appointments to the Regulatory Agencies.* 94th Cong., 2d sess., April 1976a. Committee on Government Operations, Committee Print. *Study on Federal Regulation: The Regulatory Appointments Process* 95th Cong., 1st sess., January 1977.

U.S. Congress, Senate, Committee on Banking, Housing and Urban Affairs, *Hearings on Federal Bank Commission Act–1976,* 94th Cong. 2d sess., February-March 1976b, pp. 163, 174-177.

Wall Street Letter, 9 January 1978, p. 4.

White, E.B. "The Meaning of Democracy." *The New Yorker,* 3 July 1943.

Williams, C. Arthur, Jr., "Insurance Arrangements under Workmen's Compensation," U.S. Department of Labor, Bulletin No. 317, 1969, pp. 74-75.

Wilson, James Q. "The Dead Hand of Regulation." *The Public Interest*, Fall 1971, p. 57.

3 Regulation in a National Market Environment

Simon M. Lorne and
Morris Mendelson

Prefatory Note

In a review of a book by the current chairman of the Civil Aeronautics Board, our colleague Louis B. Schwartz wrote:

> Skeptical as he is about regulation, Kahn nevertheless defends it against extreme attacks from right and left. The Chicago School of economists, who argue that regulation is a useless and expensive exercise that saves the consumer nothing in the long run, get a respectful hearing, but eventually run into some devastating questions about cases where regulatory agencies demonstrably cut hundreds of millions of dollars from the bills that consumers had to pay.[1]

The authors share Kahn's attitude towards regulation. We do not have an unwaivering faith in either regulation or competition. Some regulations are clearly useful. Others are counterproductive. Clearly the former should be retained and the latter eliminated. In between there are some question marks.

It is inevitable, however, that in any written product representing a collaboration between two authors, disagreement between those authors is possible and, in some instances, not fully reconcilable. A possible resolution of such differences is often compromise, but in some circumstances that is not an appropriate approach. In the present paper, such a situation exists. Divergence is apparent primarily with respect to the national market system: Professor Mendelson, one of the first persons to advocate a computer-assisted national trading system for securities, with a capacity both to store all limit orders and to execute them [A "hard" composite limit order book (clob) or file], is committed to the development of such a system. Professor Lorne is neither committed to that view nor wholly convinced by it.

Rather than seek to align these disparate views, we have instead chosen to have Professor Mendelson "sign" the national market sections. Professor Lorne should not be considered to have endorsed the views expressed by Professor Mendelson in these sections.

The authors wish to acknowledge the helpful comments of Leigh E. Tripoli, supervisor of regulatory research, AT&T, and Junius W. Peake, senior vice president, R. Shriver Associates.

31

Introduction

There are two reasons why this paper examines the regulation of the securities industry and couples that examination with the national market system developments. First, and perhaps more important, it is clear from the Securities Acts Amendments of 1975[2] and subsequent developments[3] that we are moving toward some kind of national market system with greater oversight by the SEC of whatever self-regulatory organizations may arise or survive. Regardless of the form that system may ultimately take, it clearly will be a new world, and it is important to question whether the regulations of the old should be imported to the new.

Second there is some current disaffection with governmental interference with competitive forces. Deregulation is now in vogue in Washington as well as on Lake Michigan since the ascendency of the University of Chicago brand of liberalism with the capture of Washington by the Republicans in 1968. These challenges, however, appear to be essentially rhetoric. The failure to deregulate cable TV, maritime trade, and the trucking industries, despite the brightness of initial prospects, is noteworthy. Even in the case of the successful deregulation of airlines, to date the deregulation has been essentially de facto rather than de jure[4] and is largely attributable to Alfred E. Kahn, Chairman of the CAB. The most obvious regulatory change in the securities industry has been the elimination of fixed commission rates, but this has been a reduction in self-regulation rather than in governmental regulation.[5] Whether the securities industry may be more susceptible than other industries to effective reductions in regulation is yet to be seen.

When we speak of the securities industry in this analysis, we refer to securities exchanges and firms that are registered broker-dealers. We do not therefore consider the regulation of the issuance of securities or regulations primarily affecting corporate issuers and people affiliated with them as within the scope of this analysis.[6] Nor do we consider the market for government and municipal securities, which has not yet been subject to substantial regulation.[7] We propose rather to confine our inquiry to four questions. First, why have we, as a society, chosen to regulate the securities industry, and particularly those aspects of it dealing with trading of equity securities, to the extent that we have? Second, given the general rationale for the existence of a regulatory scheme, what specific rationales support the varying types of regulation that are presently found affecting the securities industry? Third, what will be the characteristics of the marketplace of the future? Finally, what are sensible goals for and approaches to securities industry regulation in the future?

Under "Why Regulate the Industry," Mendelson examines the justification of the attempt of the Securities and Exchange Commission (SEC) to restructure the securities industry. He points out that the arguments used to justify the retention of anticompetitive rules constitute, insofar as they are valid, justification for the SEC's venture into designing market structure. However, he notes that most of those arguments are not themselves sufficient reason either to retain anticompetitive rules or to accelerate the change in market structure. He argues that the major justification for Commission action lies in the possibility that the U.S. industrial structure will be modified in a highly undesirable way if such action is not taken. The early implementation of price and time priorities in trading is necessary if this is to be avoided. In the second major section, "The Forms of and Reasons for the Specific Regulatory Structure," we note that the different regulations seek to accomplish a number of different goals. These goals are categorized and examined. It is reasonably clear that a shift to a hard consolidated limit order book (clob) or file[8] or even a less radical structural reorganization will have implications for future regulation. In the third major section, "The Market Form of the Future," Mendelson argues that the direction in which the SEC is permitting the market structure to drift will make the regulatory problems more complicated than necessary and that the end result will not be the achievement of the stated goals. Mendelson also argues that in spite of SEC opposition, the only way to realize those goals is via a hard clob. He argues that a hard clob will enormously simplify regulation and surveillance. In the final section, "Regulation of the Future Securities Industry," we examine the propriety of the regulatory goals we identified in the second section. We argue that procedural rules will have to be modified and adapted to the evolving system but that those changes are not likely to be radical. We reaffirm the necessity of investor confidence and the need for its reinforcement. Rules relating to customer safety do not require much comment. However, what we term "fiduciary rules" are found to be less satisfactory. The account executive is a living conflict of interest, acting as both investment adviser and salesperson. Clarification and reform in this area are needed. Suitability rules do not seem to have caught up with modern portfolio theory and should be reconsidered. In general, protective regulation should be eliminated, but there is always the possibility that the elimination itself will create serious dislocations. In all such cases, however, care must be taken that elimination will not result in unduly disadvantageous consequences.

It may be useful at this juncture to make an introductory comment concerning general philosophic differences between self-regulation and governmental regulation. It seems clear that most organized groups—doctors, lawyers, and accountants are but a few—prefer self-regulation to a free market. "To some extent, that is the result of aims to assure professionalism and to establish standards." In part, it is no doubt due to fears of overly restrictive governmental controls in the absence of effective self-regulation. In part, perhaps a large part, it may be due to a desire to exclude others from participating in the activity. If, as a society, we could conclude that all self-regulation was the result of the first, or even the first two, motivations, we might prefer self-regulation, for it is often more efficient and knowledgeable than governmental regulation. But determining the reason for, or even the effect of, self-imposed regulation is often a most difficult endeavor. The critically difficult task of deregulation is tied to determining the permissible limits of self-regulation.

Why Regulate the Industry?
Morris Mendelson

An important initial inquiry in any analysis such as this is, "Why do we regulate the securities industry in general and its activities with respect to trading equity securities in particular?" I focus on the case of the push for a national market system, the aspect of securities industry regulation that has received a great deal of recent consideration.[9] I am skeptical of the typical defense of this type of regulation in terms of the liquidity of the market for "listed" securities. Instead, I look for justification in terms of the implications for the structure of American industry and the political and economic consequences of that.[10]

The development of a national market system had its impetus in the development of institutions as a countervailing power to the exchanges and in technological change. These developments set in motion forces beyond the complete control of the securities industry, the investors, or the regulatory agencies. They made possible new ways of doing business that are more efficient than the old ways. Barriers to access are crumbling. We can call for the SEC to go slow[11] in the development of a national market system, but we cannot stop the present structure from unraveling and developing into something other than what it is today.

The push for a national market system is often attributed to the *Institutional Investor Study,*[12] but in fact the concept was discussed much earlier, certainly as early as 1969.[13] The 1975 Amendments specifically directed the SEC

> to use its authority . . . to facilitate the establishment of a national market system for securities . . . in accordance with the findings and to carry out the objectives set forth in paragraph [above] . . . The Commission is authorized in furtherance of the directive [above] . . . by rule or order, to authorize or require self-regulatory organizations to act jointly . . . in planning, developing, operating, or regulating a national market system. . . .[14]

Nowhere does the act specify the nature of a national market system or the justification for forcing its development other than to note that "the securities markets are an important asset which must be preserved and strengthened."[15]

An important theme pervading the current disenchantment with regulation is that competition can be as, if not more, effective than regulation.[16] A partiality toward regulation by competition and some reservations about surrendering all paternalism are enshrined in the 1975 amendments.[17] That act calls for a national market system that is envisaged as a competitive market but with a shift in regulatory powers from the self-regulatory organizations (SROs) to the SEC.[18]

A question that arises frequently but is seldom discussed is why the stock market should be singled out as the area into which the SEC should venture to attempt to restructure, to act positively and design or encourage a particular form of market organization rather than simply play the role of policeman.

Why is it important that the stock market be the one market in a market economy where all bids and offers be allowed to meet? No similar concern has been expressed about the bond market or even the options market, and certainly no such theory has been advanced with respect to markets for other goods and services. The rationale advanced by Chairman Williams when he addressed himself to the cause for SEC concern with restructuring the market was couched in terms of securities markets but was clearly more applicable to the stock market than to the securities market in general. He noted:

> The securities markets serve as the vehicle through which capital is channeled from private hands into what are, ultimately, national priorities—the creation of jobs, the provision of equipment and facilities necessary to produce the goods and services which define our standard of living, and the assurance of economic security for our citizens.... The securities markets are at the heart of our society; those markets are the stimulus and the source of life blood for the most successful economic system in the history of the world. We cannot afford to let the public lose confidence in the fairness and integrity of our capital markets or of the corporations and businesses which those markets have financed and which they sustain.[19]

Equity is indeed the keystone to corporate capital structure. The growth rate of corporate equity determines the growth rate of the corporate sector. To be sure, the bulk of corporate equity is generated internally, but that growth cannot be perfectly synchronized with the growth of equity requirements. The external markets must be relied on. No doubt, individual investors' perceptions of the fairness of the securities markets will be affected by the market structure, but it is not clear that the total supply of equity will be significantly affected by that perception. It is easy to attribute the decline in the number of holders of listed stock to the trauma of the securities industry.[20] Certainly the treatment of small investors by many of the brokerage houses was hardly likely to encourage such investors to stay in the market. Nevertheless, with high probability, the real deterrent to participation in the market has little or nothing to do with the structure of the market. Instead, it is the result of the abysmal performance of the market in recent years. The withdrawal of individuals from the market may itself have affected the level of the market somewhat, but hardly as much as the failure of profits to keep pace with inflation and the failure of the return on equity to match the performance of fixed-income securities. Since the diminished availability of equity capital is unrelated to market structure, concern with the aggregate flow of equity can hardly justify the SEC's intervention in the evolutionary consequences of letting the breath of competitive air brush the stock market.

In recent years the most traumatic deregulatory events for the securities industry have been the abolition of fixed commission rates[21] and the prospective removal of restrictions on upstairs market making, the Rule 390 issue.[22] Major segments of the securities industry have vigorously resisted these changes. The resistance has been premised on the importance of a viable and liquid stock market and has implicitly or explicitly considered the government (and its agent the SEC) responsible for preserving that viability and liquidity. It follows that if the government does have that kind of responsibility, it extends to more than simply maintaining the status quo. It includes seeking out superior alternatives if such alternatives exist, and it includes staying alert to developments that may ultimately erode the features of the market that make it attractive.

If the proponents of no change or even go slow simply maintained that the commissioners should abstain from regulating a particular area of the market, their case would be much stronger. But they ask the commissioners to provide an umbrella against the discomforts of the antitrust laws even if only temporarily. The minimum-commission rate system was a price-fixing scheme and could operate only under such an umbrella.[23] In unregulated industries, price fixing and restraint of trade are illegal per se.[24] The exchanges have lost the battle on commission rates, but they are still fighting to prevent or postpone the abolition of rules that force principal trades by members to take place on the floor of an exchange. Rule 390 is obviously a device designed to restrain trade and as such can also exist only under such an umbrella. These umbrellas can be defended only on grounds that the SEC is justified in seeking to accelerate a national market system and that the market is uniquely important. Given those grounds, the SEC has an obligation to try to maximize the allocational and operational efficiency.

Indeed, we do have cause to be concerned about the liquidity of the stock market. The equity investor has a different problem from the bondholder. Variations in the issuer's fortunes cause only minor variations in the quality of its debt. Deterioration of credit is usually a prolonged affair. With rare exceptions minor variations in an issuer's fortunes have a significant impact on the value of its equity. While the market seems to reflect new information with amazing rapidity, recipients of information often do not know whether that information is yet reflected in the price of the stock.[25] Given the speed with which information is reputed to be reflected, they may wish to divest themselves of the stock rapidly. The prerequisite for such rapid divestment is a highly liquid market. If the market is not liquid or is not perceived to be liquid, the investors run the risk of watching helplessly as the value of their investments melts while they wait for someone to buy their stock. Under such circumstances they are likely to seek other outlets for their funds and hence to curtail the supply of equity to American corporations.

The need for liquidity is pervasive. It is not confined to investing individuals. It is equally sought by institutional investors. Indeed, institutional investors have been known to incur relatively high costs to dispose of particular holdings quickly.[26] If one accepts the premise that American industry must have a significant source of external equity, one must concede the need for liquidity. That might indeed be considered justification for the regulation of the stock market in particular, the capital markets in general, and the very existence of the SEC. Unless it can be shown, however, that liquidity might be significantly different in the alternative forms of the national market system that we can visualize, we still cannot justify SEC intervention in the restructuring of the market on liquidity grounds.

There remains, however, a solid reason why the SEC should intervene. One can argue that the SEC should let industry develop its own devices, provided that industry does not introduce anticompetitive rules. That, however, is no guarantee that the resulting market will be competitive. The commissioners currently face a conundrum that has caused them to step warily. If they force Rule 390 to be struck, liquidity and continuity of the markets are going to depend on the actions of market makers. The SEC seems not so concerned with the absence of market makers as that market makers will confine themselves to what might be considered first-tier stocks to the detriment of capital flow to the smaller and less glamorous firms.[27]

Indeed, the argument goes further. The larger, well-capitalized firms will no longer direct their orders to the exchanges. There will be an attrition of the order flow on the exchanges, and two undesirable consequences will follow from that. Smaller, less capitalized brokerage houses will find the auction market on which they depend for their livelihood withering. They will be forced to direct their orders to the large market makers. But since the large wire houses will be market makers, investors will have no need for the smaller regional firms. The securities industry will become increasingly concentrated. Public orders will no longer meet public orders without the intervention of a dealer, and individual investors will be at the mercy of the market makers as, presumably, they are on the over-the-counter market. The investor may become increasingly vulnerable to price gouging.

There are, however, limits to the extent to which we can look to the OTC market for guidance on what would happen if a dealer market developed. At first glance, it would appear that instead of simply becoming the sole operators in the field, the major firms would develop correspondent relationships with the many small firms scattered throughout the country. After all, this is how the OTC market is organized. The wire houses, however, are unlikely to service any particular correspondent for long. If they want to tap a particular market area, they would be better off having their own offices there. They may engage in correspondent relationships initially to determine the depth of the market, but once that becomes apparent, they have much more control with their own offices. The fact that the small firms have many good producers does not guarantee their survival. Most of these producers can be lured away by the major firms. Moreover, it is probable that the correspondent apparatus exists in the OTC market because the firms exist. The firms exist because they can earn an attractive return in the listed stock business. Their ability to survive an intensely competitive environment in listed securities where order flow is critical is far from clear.

The more important consequence is that with the demise of the smaller firms, it may become increasingly difficult for small industrial firms to tap the public market for equity. The only way they will be able to finance expansion is through merger into larger firms that do have access to the public market. Whether one considers this the most likely outcome, one must consider it a serious possibility. Thus the form of the national market system may determine not only the shape of the securities industry but also the structure of each and every industry that may need to tap the public market. If that is the case, it is difficult to see how the commissioners can stand idly by and let industry develop the market system it finds most convenient. There is no reason to believe that natural forces will bring about a market system that is hospitable to easy access by firms of all sizes. Indeed, competitive forces are likely to develop a system that is quite the opposite.

With the existing market structure, order flow is important to market making. Economies accrue to the market makers with larger order flow, and this reinforces their capacity for attracting order flow.[28] The ability of small- and medium-sized firms to survive in such an environment is questionable. A market designed so that market makers depend on order flow is inherently inhospitable to small firms and is highly likely to curtail significantly access of small issuers to the public equity markets.

Most economists, when considering the merits of regulating the securities industry, point out that the regulations can be judged on the basis of their contribution to equity and/or their contribution to efficiency.[29] The contributions to efficiency in turn can be categorized into contributions to operational or allocational efficiency. Having noted that, they typically proceed to minimize their comments on equity.[30]

In keeping with this tradition, I have paid some attention to ethical considerations, but my concern with efficiency is somewhat different from the traditional concern. There is an extensive body of economic literature assessing the effectiveness of a variety of regulations.[31] My principal concern with regulation in this part of the paper is with the merits of SEC intervention in the restructuring of the securities industry. It is hardly likely that the restructuring in one form rather than in another is going to have much impact on the so-called informational efficiency of the market. Informational efficiency is a necessary but not sufficient condition for allocational efficiency.[32] It is hardly likely that the securities traded on the system that ultimately evolves will trade at prices that fail to reflect available information. If there is a dealer market instead of a continuous-auction market, the operational efficiency may decline, and to the extent that allocational efficiency depends on operational efficiency, the former type of efficiency will be impaired. A researcher, however, would be hard pressed to prove that the benefits of eliminating the operational inefficiency would merit the costs.

It is, however, quite possible that an unguided national market system will lead to a securities industry structure that will have grave consequences for the industrial organization of the United States. The increasing concentration of industry will hardly improve the allocation of resources, and the social consequences can hardly be appealing. The only alternative may be to modify the Glass-Steagall Act of 1933 and let the banks back into the investment banking business to reintroduce competition.[33] Unfortunately, that cure may turn out to be worse than the disease. This is not a case for detailed regulation nor the preparation of a blueprint of a national market system. It is instead an argument for the early implementation of the price and time priority rules the SEC has recommended. The implementation of these rules cannot be postponed until a national market system is in place. On the contrary, such rules should provide the incentive for industry to develop a system with which it feels comfortable. The alternative is to allow the securities industry to drift into a degree of concentration that will create antitrust problems. The task of the SEC is to develop trading rules that more or less force the sharing of order flow and thus negate a major force for concentration.

The Forms of and Reasons for The
Specific Regulatory Structure

Having considered the broad scope of the purposes served by intervention in the market structure itself, it is useful to turn to the specific sorts of regulations that are applied to the industry as a whole. For while the essential importance of capital markets may justify a government presence, it seems clear that other purposes are also being covered by existing regulation. An examination would seem to support the proposition that once we have decided to permit regulation of the securities industry, we have lowered our social expectation of freedom from regulation. Once government involvement is accepted, it seems to become easier to accept involvement in aspects of the industry that might otherwise have justified a principle of nonintervention.

The securities industry is subject to many different regulations, from many different sources, with many different purposes. At the federal level, regulations affecting the industry are imposed by the Securities and Exchange Commission, the Municipal Securities Rulemaking Board, the Commodity Futures Trading Commission, the Board of Governors of the Federal Reserve System, and others, and the industry is directly and substantially affected by regulations adopted under the Employee Retirement Income Security Act and the Internal Revenue Code. Beyond that, virtually all fifty states, the District of Columbia, and Puerto Rico have pervasive regulatory schemes affecting the members of the industry and securities transactions touching their borders. And finally, the stock exchanges and the National Association of Securities Dealers have substantial regulatory authority over member firms, which include by far the majority (in terms of importance, however measured) of securities industry members.

A comprehensive review of the regulatory activities of each of the above agencies is beyond the scope of this overview. However, the major impetus for most regulations affecting the securities industry was the stock market collapse of 1929. In response to that catastrophe and its aftermath, two fundamental needs were perceived: the need to eliminate inappropriate dealings in securities and the need to restore public confidence in securities markets in order to make investors willing to risk their capital. The Glass-Steagall Act, the margin rules of the Federal Reserve Board, and certain other provisions of the Securities Exchange Act of 1934 are examples of the congressional response to the former concern. The Securities Act of 1933, the Investment Company Act of 1940, and other provisions in the Securities Exchange Act of 1934 can be seen as responsive to the latter. While many of such provisions may continue to serve a valid purpose, particularly in an environment that has developed in such a manner as to accommodate them, the possibility of overreaction should not be ignored. Furthermore, it is reasonable to question whether the needs of forty years ago remain current, especially in the face of experience in other countries that appear to have developed reasonably sound capital markets with substantially different regulatory structures. While we would not advocate ignoring the past, we would caution against an unyielding commitment to its dictates.

A number of useful generalizations can be made about the types of regulations that have been established, their apparent purposes, and their effects. While it is not always easy to divine the specific purpose that any given regulation was designed to serve, the basic aims of the Securities Acts, culminating in the Securities Acts Amendments of 1975, are those suggested previously: the protection of investors and the encouragement of the broader public interest as affected by trading in securities. A review of the various regulations and of the literature suggests that most regulations have been adopted to satisfy one or more of five identifiable needs, which are discussed below. While these are not the only categories that could be selected, they are useful ones for the present analysis.

Finally, there are many regulations that are not directed at the securities industry but that have a substantial effect on it. For example, the "prudent man" standards established under the Employee Retirement Income Security

Act seem to have had a dramatic effect on certain securities that might once have been an appropriate part of an investment portfolio but under the newer standards may be thought no longer to be a permissible investment, even as a relatively small part of a portfolio.[34] Similarly, congressional tax policies in the capital-gains, dividend, estate tax, tax-shelter, and other areas have a substantial effect on the securities industry; they can critically affect the future of the industry and should not be ignored. If the capital markets are sufficiently important to be subjected to substantial regulation, the impact of measures that affect the market but are designed for other purposes is surely deserving of considerable attention. Such matters, however, are beyond the scope of this examination.

Procedural Regulation

This category probably encompasses the bulk of the Self Regulatory Organization (SRO) rules and is dealt with most easily. Quite simply, it will always be necessary for some authoritative body to establish the ground rules for transactions in securities.[35] Generally acknowledged procedures for making bids and offers, for accepting them, for making payments and deliveries, and the like are necessary if costly misunderstandings are to be minimized. Some procedural rules will have substantive effects, however, and it would be an error to accept all rules designated as "procedural" without examining the consequences of their adoption. For example, the efficient operation of a widespread market with widely separated participants demands one or more rules to determine which of two or more offers at the same price is to be accepted when an offsetting order is encountered at that price. While a price priority would seem a clear requirement of fairness, the choice between a price-time priority and a price-size priority should be the result of a careful consideration of such values as transactional efficiency and public market confidence.

Investor Confidence

Other regulations are designed to create an atmosphere of confidence in the fairness of the securities markets: the primary reason for regulation of the industry. Concern with that issue, of course, was significantly affected by the 1929 crash, but there are important social reasons for wanting investor confidence. Both self-regulatory and governmental restrictions have sought this goal. From a professional viewpoint, this concern can be seen as an internal need of the industry; unless the public can trust industry members and the markets, there will be relatively little securities business. From a broader perspective, as recognized at least since 1934, it is also a social need in a quasi-capitalist economy.

The ability of enterprises to obtain capital is obviously critical to the economy. In the United States that ability has depended on the existence of secondary trading markets that have sufficient depth to assure liquidity and that are generally regarded as fair and efficient. This has led us, for example, to proscribe trading on the basis of inside information even though there may be no affirmative obligation to disclose that information.[36] To a substantial degree, regulations that may owe their existence primarily to other concerns may also be justified as serving this purpose. For example, regulations resulting from the view of the securities broker as a fiduciary, discussed below, such as mark-up restrictions[37] or the NASD's Interpretation with Respect to Corporate Financing,[38] tend to increase confidence in the fairness of the marketplace itself. Similarly, rules designed to process small orders through the same channels as larger orders such as even the current version of off-board trading proscriptions[39] may improve investor confidence in the market's fairness. There is no evidence that competition has always been an adequate substitute for many of these regulations.

Customer Safety

The frequency with which customer funds and securities are left in the control of brokers also generates rules designed to protect those assets. The establishment of the Securities Investor Protection Corporation, the net capital rules of the various authorities,[40] and bonding requirements[41] are examples of such regulations. Again, competitive forces did not protect the victims of the paper crisis.

Fiduciary Regulation

A number of regulations imposed by the exchanges, the NASD, and the SEC are grounded in the notion that the broker-dealer has a fiduciary sort of relationship to its customers. For example, exchange suitability rules, requiring a knowledge of customers and a reasonable matching between customers' needs and desires and the securities recommended to them, restrictions on mark-ups in principal transactions imposed by the NASD, responsibilities to avoid churning, and the like, are all in large part the result of viewing the broker as having a fiduciary relationship to the customer (although it may sometimes be hard to distinguish between rules responding to the fiduciary concept and rules designed to increase market confidence, discussed previously, since any such rules may be seen to have both results).[42] It is likely that the basis for this fiduciary duty is twofold. First many members of the securities industry not only purchase and sell securities (as agents or for themselves) but also serve as investment advisers, accept the management of discretionary accounts, and in other ways seek to have customers repose confidence in them. That is, they seek to have customers treat them as fiduciaries.[43] Second it is common practice for many customers to leave securities or funds in the control of their brokers. The custodial aspect of the relationship suggests a fiduciary responsibility by itself, and further it increases the likelihood that the broker's recommendations will be accepted, even in nondiscretionary accounts, thereby reinforcing the perception of brokers as fiduciaries. But whatever the cause, it is clear that at the legal level we do view a securities salesperson as fundamentally different from a car salesperson or a suit salesperson and impose substantial regulations to dictate behavior of the securities salesperson with respect to clients.

Protective Regulation

Finally, we are left with the sorts of regulations, primarily adopted by SROs, that have given rise to recent suspicions and increased control over SROs[44] — regulations that appear designed to serve the interests of member firms or SROs themselves rather than the broader public interest. A general test of the validity of any given regulation may be the extent to which it serves appropriate public needs rather than the protection of the regulated. Reasonable people may differ as to the propriety of any given protective regulation, but inevitably its justification will be framed in terms of the alleged beneficial purpose it serves. Minimum commissions, for example, certainly served primarily the purpose of protecting securities firms rather than customers. Its defenders, however, still argue that the public was better served then than now.[45] Off-board trading proscriptions, though primarily designed as protective measures, are defended in terms of their alleged public benefits.[46] It may be that whether such protective regulation is socially desirable depends on a number of conditions and on the assumptions made as to social goals. More often than not, however, implicit in the defense is the support of a cross-subsidy that would clearly not be politically feasible if it were suggested as a direct subsidy. Minimum commissions were defended as a desirable subsidy paid by institutional investors to small investors. Certainly the results of the negotiated-commission environment suggest strongly that such a subsidy was being paid. Yet it is not likely that anyone would suggest, much less accept, a direct tax levied solely on large investors tied directly to periodic payments made solely to small investors.

If an argument that a protective regulation has significant public benefits can be made successfully (which is essentially a political question), it might be justified. However, regulations that are identifiably protective—or even primarily protective in nature—must certainly be subjected to substantial scrutiny.

Almost all regulations designed to control the securities industry fit into one or more of the five categories identified. However, this is a time of change in the industry, a time of scrutiny, a time of restructuring. Consequently, many existing rules will of necessity be changed; many others should be. Following Professor Mendelson's discussion of the market of the future, each of the preceding categories of rules will be reconsidered with a view to establishing a more sensible approach to regulation.

The Market Form of the Future
Morris Mendelson

As far as the trading process is concerned, the critical regulatory question of the future is whether the regulatory authorities are going to be faced with regulating the use of a small centralized market core with broad competing forces in the industry as a whole with special privileges for none, or with regulating an allegedly integrated host of market centers, each with its own privileged cast, competing with each other for order flow. The regulatory problems of a network of market centers are far more complex than those of a single market center. Special privileges must be circumscribed by regulatory safeguards against their abuse.[47] While market centers are not natural monopolies, concentrated order flow does provide competitive advantages. In the absence of regulatory protection, one center tends to dominate. Competing market centers generate the need for a whole host of regulations that simply disappear when the focus of competition is shifted from market centers to market makers. For example, among the problems that have plagued the Intermarket Trading System (ITS) are the rules on opening trading. They must be designed so that they do not give one center an advantage or embarrass other centers.

Just as market centers are not natural monopolies, neither are market makers, but concentration is likely to be the result when market making depends critically on order flow. That is why competing specialist systems have never worked. In spite of the open outcry, competing specialists do not have equal access to order flow. Away from the market, orders flow to the favored specialist. At some point the difference in order flow becomes decisive, and the favored specialist can serve the brokers better than its competitors. From that point the advantage becomes cumulative. The only method for preventing that is a system of sharing the book. The only way to do that is to make the book electronic, but once the book is electronic, the future of exchanges as market centers becomes dubious.

Trading requires much less regulation when the much maligned black box is used. There ceases to be a problem of equal or equivalent regulation of market makers since many of the regulations that currently circumscribe the specialists' activities such as NYSE Rule 113 would no longer be needed. Once the orders are entered in the national book, their times are effectively inscribed in stone. Market makers can give precedence to their own orders or to those of favored customers only by leaving a highly visible trail of what they have done. They would first have to withdraw the customer's order and substitute the favored order. Even that would be meaningless since their favored order would not have priority over any other order in the system at that price. There need be no rules about "firm" quotes since bids and offers may be hit as long as they are in the system. There is no problem of defining the best market or the best execution. There need not be any differentiation in the treatment of round and odd lots. In the process of settlement there need be no rules relating to the resolution of differences. While this is only a partial list, regulation also becomes vastly simplified because the audit trail becomes much clearer. Many steps that are needed for effective audit trails simply slow the trading process too much to be required today.

Unfortunately, in spite of the operational, regulatory, and cost advantages of computer-assisted trading, even the limited version of a national market system envisioned by the SEC is hardly likely to come to pass in the near future. Part of the difficulty lies in the manner in which the SEC has chosen to operate. It has repeatedly given the industry deadlines, it has occasionally suggested "Shape up or else," and it has repeatedly retreated. In their testimony on Rule 390, Mendelson, Peake, and Williams, the coauthors of *The National Book System*,[48] told the SEC that if the Commission retreated, its credibility would be impaired.[49] Nothing it has done since suggests that the testimony was in error. Certainly the industry is not behaving as though the 30 September 1978 deadline is any more serious than the earlier ones. September 30 is likely to come and go without significant progress toward a national market system having been made.

The route chosen by the SEC clearly involves increasing regulation at what looks like a compound rate rather than deregulation. By building the national market system with component parts, the SEC has encouraged the proliferation of authorities, each of which has to be regulated. There is already the CTA, the Consolidated Tape Association. We shall next have the Consolidated Quotation Association. Can we expect the Common Message Switch Authority, the Intermarket Linkage Authority, and the Consolidated Limit Order File Authority? And will these have to be linked to the option market authorities like the Option Price Reporting Authority? Each step requires cooperation among market centers committed to destroying each other. Delay is endless, and the SEC is reduced to refereeing family quarrels and determining whether ampersands should appear on the tape.

The members of the industry, many of whom have much to gain and some of whom may lose advantages, are not much help. For a variety of reasons the firms have allied themselves with the exchanges. They have assumed that there is an identity of interests, though on occasion one sees traces of doubt on that score. Industry leaders are preoccupied with their own problems of adjusting to a rapidly changing scene: They are certain only that ahead of them lies change, and they are highly uncertain of both the character of that change and the most appropriate steps to take to deal with whatever environment evolves. They are extremely unsure of what their competitors are going to do. They are too preoccupied with anticipating their competitors and seeking to maintain their place in the sun to devote the energies required to cope with building a system in which they may thrive. The fact that some system designs may destroy most of the firms need not deflect them from their course so long as they feel reasonably sure that they will be among the survivors. Some firms, because of their stature, operating advantages over competitors, and long-established ability and willingness to be helpful to the specialist, may enjoy preferential treatment on the exchanges and may be reluctant to give that up for an impersonal national market system. Many, influenced by fear of the unknown and their comfort with the old system, resent all this "tinkering" and deplore the changes that have adversely affected their profitability. Many are rightfully resentful of the endless hours spent in futile wrangling over the shape of things to come. There has consequently been a tendency to abandon to the exchanges the responsibility for developing the national market system.

Unfortunately, the exchanges are ill-designed to assume the leadership role. The strength and *raison d'etre* of the NYSE have been its order flow. Orders are directed to that exchange because that is where the orders are—hence the most likely place to realize a rapid and satisfactory execution. Because of the large flow of orders to the exchange, the specialists can take significant positions in many stocks relatively safely, knowing full well that their positions can be laid off rapidly against this never-ceasing flow of orders. They are hardly likely to design a system that they believe will reduce or even share that order flow. Similarly, the competing exchanges are hardly likely to subscribe to a system that they do not believe will assure them of at least as large an order flow as they have had. They are therefore unlikely to encourage the development of a system that will facilitate the development of upstairs market making. In any system designed to preserve the order flow to market centers, upstairs market making can develop only if member firms carve their own order flow out of the flow to existing market centers.

This has had an impact on the direction of structural developments. Market making requires capital. Essentially, a market maker is simply a buffer providing timely executions for customers and preventing the stochastic imbalances in the flow or orders from creating undue fluctuations in the prices of stocks.[50] Smoothing the fluctuations in prices is not, however, the objective of market makers. It is the consequence of servicing customers. In the process the market maker must position securities periodically and finance those securities while it positions them. In today's market this means deflecting capital from other uses. While a number of older hands in the industry find the new environment uncongenial and hence seek to retire themselves and their capital, the stock market is not hospitable to the flotations of brokerage house issues. As a consequence, most firms are not particularly anxious to engage in or expand upstairs market making. On the other hand, every major firm recognizes that it cannot refrain from market making if competitors do not. All other things being equal, institutions prefer to avoid the cost of using intermediaries. Hence every major firm with a significant institutional business recognizes that if it is to retain that business, it will have to be a market maker of sorts. Inevitably then member firms will become market makers. It follows that competition will drive the firms to try to capture major market shares. Under the existing system the sine qua non of being an effective market maker is order flow—hence the drive to attract order flow. This drive takes two forms: the acquisition of firms with a large existing order flow and the sacrifice of commission income to attract order flow. These account for the low rates at which many institutional orders are executed. Insofar as they are loss leaders, the burden of bearing the costs of the executions is shifted to the investing individuals.[51] It is a simple matter of cutting prices sharply where the demand is highly elastic and raising them where the demand appears to be relatively inelastic. Quite perversely, cross-subsidization has been reversed.

Given the initial conditions of this market, competitive forces are unlikely to nurture a market system hospitable to a competitive environment. The whole concept of competitive market centers is alien to such an environment. If market centers are competitive, they are competitive for order flow. If small firms are to survive, an order they receive must have the same probability of being matched with another public order as an order received by a major firm. The only system under which this can be so is one with a central limit order file with execution capability.

However, instead of encouraging the development of a hard clob, the SEC seems to be following a policy that can be described only as perverse. Chairman Williams has noted that

[the] permanent components of a mature system—must be tested for consistency with the following criteria:
Do they provide for interaction of all orders?
Do they contemplate the linkage of all markets and market makers in the same security? And
Do they provide for and create or tend to lead to the creation of a truly national auction based on price and time priorities?[52]

The NYSE ITS satisfies at most one of the above criteria and is not designed even eventually to satisfy the others. And yet the SEC delays removing its umbrella to let a hard clob show its worth. Ostensibly attempting to encourage the participation of individuals to nourish a competitive securities industry and to provide the greatest possible access to the stock market, the SEC appears to be following the policy least likely to achieve the preceding objectives. It has treated the one type of market that is most likely to further those ends as though it had a bad smell, which, if acquired, might offend those it has been charged to regulate.

The Commission's own program consists of six elements: (1) a composite-quotation system; (2) an intermarket order-routing system with a message switch linking orders to all markets, enabling brokers to route orders from their offices to any market; (3) a central file for public agency limit orders; (4) a refined consolidated transaction reporting system; (5) the designation of the types of securities qualified for trading in a national market system; and finally, (6) the abrogation of Rule 390.[53]

This is a beautiful illustration of the creativity of the SEC in devising ways of wasting the industry's money. Consider the first item, the composite-quotation system. For purposes of developing a national market system, it is redundant and will be expensive to build. It will display the bids and offers of the various market makers. No broker, however, will be obligated to execute against the best bid or offer.[54] It is not clear why most market makers would want to insert their bids and offers. They will do so only because the SEC regulations require this.[55] They have three possible defenses against customer suits for failing to fulfill their fiduciary obligations: The size of the system was not adequate; they were afraid that if they tried to hit the best bid-offer, they might miss, and by the time they turned around to hit the one they did in fact hit, that might not be there either; or the best bid-offer on the system is not necessarily the best in the market. Public bid-offers may be superior, and the broker would have failed in his fiduciary duty if he did not investigate the possibility of their existence. Unfortunately, that involves taking a calculated risk. Once an order is sent to the floor of an exchange, it may be too late to retrieve it and try again. Of course, if the order can be relayed from the floor, the latter excuse no longer holds. That type of modification, however, is the death knell of the regional exchanges. Why send an order directly to a regional when the pattern of the order flow makes it more probable that the best execution will take place on the NYSE and better bids and offers of the regionals can always be reached from that floor? Most brokerage-house managers would direct orders to the NYSE in such a system. That would mean that regionals would get orders only when their bids and offers were superior to those on the NYSE floor. Simply matching the NYSE's bids and offers would be of no avail, and if NYSE specialists guarantee members against better prices on the regionals, the specialists on those exchanges will find themselves engaged in a very futile endeavor. The only executions they will find themselves engaged in will be at prices the NYSE specialists judged to be out of line. It must be recalled that in spite of the alleged firmness of the bids and offers, no market maker need stand by his quote if a trade took place in a short time interval preceding the receipt of the commitment to trade. Eventually improvements in the routing system may weaken these defenses. In the meantime the brokerage community will be very uncomfortable because of its vulnerability. The task a wire house faces in this type of environment is impossible. With its large flow of orders there is currently no way it can possibly route the orders to the best market of the moment. If it gets uncomfortable enough, it may take matters into its own hands by developing the necessary system without the help of the exchanges, either jointly or each firm for itself, and so may threaten the viability of the houses that encounter difficulty developing routing systems.

The redundancy of a consolidated quotation system comes from the fact that once a clob is in place, the quotations system will contain very little information not obtainable from the clob.

The second component is ambiguous. An intermarket routing system would presumably enable a floor broker to deliver orders to the best bid or offer he sees on the CRT on the floor. It is my belief that the message switch linking orders to all markets the SEC has in mind differs in important respects from the Securities Industry Automation Commission's common message switch. The latter switch is designed to receive orders from any computer system the broker may choose to use and automatically direct orders to the post at which the stock is traded. The system works well as long as there is limited market-making competition. Given the existence of more than one market maker, that system is designed to channel the order to a system-designated destination unless the broker countermands the system's instructions. As I noted, large volume brokers cannot manually determine to which market orders should be directed. The new switch is supposed to have the capability of determining which market is the best for each order and automatically directing it there. This type of switch can obviously never become operative until the industry agrees on an algorithm by which the switch can determine the best market. A charitable estimate of the length of time it will take the industry to reach such an agreement is five years. If the present direction of development is not altered, one should not be surprised if the debate on the algorithm is not resolved in the next decade.

If the switch is successfully developed, there is no point to the intermarket routing system. The switch itself is an intermarket routing system. The switch must also have the capacity of rerouting if it is found that the bid/asked the broker tried to execute against is no longer there. I cannot resist noting that the advocates of the hard clob would not dream of attributing as much discretion to a computer as the SEC is considering with this switch.

It is incredible that the SEC even considers ITS as a step in the direction of the national market system. It clearly provides no limit order protection. It is a minor improvement on a teletype linkage of the various markets and at best cannot be effective until some device for determining the prices in other market centers is in place.

The SEC has failed to articulate how the character of the exchanges will change with the implementation of an electronic order-routing facility. Once a clob is introduced, executable orders will be directed by the switch. When it arrives at the best market, surely it takes no more than a cleark to deliver the order to the party responsible for the bid or offer. It is not clear that a firm would be wise to entrust limit orders away from the market to floor brokers. If the market moves toward the limit prices, the locality for the best execution may be another market center to which it would be easier to send the order from upstairs than from a floor. One must therefore wonder what function that floor brokers will be expected to perform. If, in addition, brokerage firms can enter orders in the central limit order file directly from their offices, who is to be responsible for their execution, especially when public order meets public order? It is not clear why the specialist from one market center rather than the specialist from another should get paid for matching the order.

The urgency with which commissioners assure the securities industry that the clob will not lead to an electronic market is puzzling.[56] If such a development is inevitable, why should the commissioners be anxious that it not happen?[57] The grounds on which the commissioners base their assurances are not at all clear.[58] The SEC may not wish to see a hard clob develop from a soft clob, but that may not make the development any less likely.

The object of the clob is the protection of public agency limit orders and the provision of time and price priorities. In effect, this must be a book priority rule. To be executed, therefore, all orders will have to pass through the book. Why then should the orders be scattered to the winds only to come to rest in a single place? Why, if a computer contains matched orders, do the orders have to be removed from the system to be executed? If public limit orders are all to end up in the same electronic book, the specialist, as guardian of the agency orders, is redundant. Paying him for execution of such orders will surely involve very contrived arrangements. Any real movement toward a national market system must at the same time be a movement toward a hard clob, the commissioners' protests notwithstanding. The NYSE knows this and has behaved accordingly. Quite rationally it has placed as many stumbling blocks as it could on the road to the national market system. The SEC seems to have mistaken these boulders for pavement.

As already noted, a number of regulatory problems that would beset the system envisaged by the SEC simply would not exist with a hard clob. There would be no need for the multiplicity of SROs we have today. There would be no need for a CTA and a CQA and presumably a CFA. Time and price priorities could easily be established. The definition of a best execution would cease to be a problem. The requirement that bids and offers be firm would simply cease to exist. A market maker's bid or offer in a clob with execution capability is executed when it is matched. It is as simple as that. It would be too late to say, "I did not mean it." There would be no such thing as retreating from a price because the firm had just engaged in a trade at that price. In a hard clob such a trade would have wiped out the bid or offer. A hard clob—and only a hard clob—makes possible a truly locked-in trade and vastly simplifies the clearing process.

Unfortunately, the longer a hard clob is delayed, the more concentrated will the industry become as the major firms maneuver for order flows. In a real sense the exchanges are sowing the seeds of their own destruction. As the industry grows increasingly concentrated, so does the order flow. The large firms will have less and less need for the floors. Market making may not be profitable per se, but increasingly it is the key to institutional business and to investment banking. The pressure to make markets is considerable. The ultimate threat to Rule 390 is not the SEC's regulatory authority but the developing ability of the major firms to withdraw from the exchanges. If the SEC's devotion to the auction market system is not pure rhetoric, it should be encouraging experimentation with hard clobs, not assuring the exchanges that their antipathy to black boxes is shared. When a hard clob was tried in the form of the Regional Market System, the SEC stood idly by and let the exchanges abort it. When this is all we can expect from the best regulatory agency, the vogue for deregulation is hardly surprising.

Regulation of the Future Securities Industry

While the precise form of the future market may be in doubt, that it will be different from the present market is beyond question, and to some extent changes in existing regulations will be essential. It is therefore an appropriate time to step back, to view the entire spectrum of regulations affecting the industry, and to reconsider their sensibility in the emerging environment.

Of the five categories of regulations identified in the second major section of this paper, relatively little comment need be addressed to procedural rules and customer safety rules. The large bulk of existing regulations designed to establish procedures for trading in securities appears reasonably suited to those purposes. Some changes will certainly be necessary to accommodate the developing national market, advances in the clearing process, further movement toward the immobilization of certificates, and the like. While there must always be concern that procedures are not adopted that interfere with significant policies such as preferences to be given among competing orders, most procedural regulations do not by themselves raise significant issues of policy.

Existing rules pertaining to the safety of customer funds and securities—net capital requirements, audit requirements, customer-reporting requirements, and the like—serve beneficial purposes, apparently without creating inappropriate burdens. To the extent that any such regulations can be relaxed or simplified without jeopardizing the safety of customers, they should be, but in general, major policy issues do not appear to be raised in this area.

With respect to the three other categories of regulations identified earlier, greater comment is appropriate. Furthermore, the multiplicity of regulatory authorities deserves particular critical attention.

Sources of Regulation

There can be no question that any regulation, if it is beneficial, should itself be dispensed efficiently. As a first measure, we would therefore propose federal preemption of state regulation of brokerage activities except where a firm's activities would otherwise be exempt from all such regulation. The securities industry is particularly characterized by interstate transactions. The requirement that a securities firm be subject to the licensing and regulatory provisions of each state in which it has an office or even has customers (the latter subject to some exceptions) is duplicative, expensive, and inefficient where those regulations are not designed to serve any purpose distinct from those of national authorities. The situation is not comparable with the regulation of securities offerings in which state authorities have a protective, "fair, just, and equitable" regulatory approach as contrasted with the disclosure orientation of the federal statutes. Instead, it is a situation in which a number of regulatory provisions exist and require substantial attention but nonetheless serve no purpose different from that served by other regulatory authorities that have a national jurisdiction. While state regulation may be appropriate for those few securities firms whose activities are so limited as to be exempt from other regulatory provisions, they create a substantial cost with no discernible public benefit for most securities firms.

Whether even further consolidation of regulatory authorities will be appropriate may depend to a substantial degree on the form taken by the future market. If the form is a network of exchanges, the current regulatory structure—primary regulation by the exchanges subject to substantial SEC oversight—may be appropriate. However, if a more centralized national market system is established (as Professor Mendelson would urge), that marketplace should be operated by a body with appropriate representation both from the securities industry and the investing public. Whoever operates such a single monopoly market, if one develops, should have the primary burden of regulating access and those phases of trading that are integrally related to the market and that warrant regulation. The locus of that regulatory authority should be on the trading system itself.

Investor Confidence

Maintaining investor confidence in the securities markets is among the most important reasons for continued regulation of the securities industry. It is particularly important that the securities markets be, and be perceived as being, fair. The efficiency of the market in allocating capital depends on its ability to maintain appropriate relationships among securities prices. Furthermore, the ability of the economy as a whole to allocate capital efficiently requires that people view competing markets as being equally fair. If securities markets generally, for example, were thought to be subject to manipulation or other sources of unfairness, with the result that the individual investor believed savings and loan institutions were inherently more fair than securities markets, individuals would naturally prefer a savings and loan to a security investment if the attributes of expected return were otherwise comparable. Since the institutions that compete with securities for capital tend to be regulated heavily by bodies whose primary charge is perceived as the maintenance of public confidence, there is obvious reason to strive for comparable confidence in the securities markets.

Accordingly, we think it important that whatever the form of the future market, care should be taken to ensure that small orders are executed in a fashion that does not, in fact or in appearance, tend to operate to their disadvantage relative to large orders. Confidence could be jeopardized by the existence of parallel nonintegrated markets for the trading of any given security. Therefore, when the national market develops, it should be in the form of a single market or a linked network with shared information, and to the extent feasible, it should be the exclusive means of executing trades. In a hard clob system where orders are given a price-time priority, the appearance and reality of fairness would seemingly be automatic. Whether similar characteristics can be provided in a network-type system remains to be seen. A specific "best-execution" rule would be desirable to maximize confidence if the burden of any such rule on industry members is not too great. It would not be rational to impose a great hardship on industry members in an attempt to obtain relatively negligible benefits for "small investors." Indeed, if the hardships were great, they would presumably result in costs, which, when passed on, would negate those benefits.

One interesting question that may not have received sufficient attention to date is the extent to which the average investor has confidence in the regulatory activities of existing securities exchanges over listed companies. In many areas of corporate law it is demonstrable that the changes in corporate regulation viewed as desirable have been imposed by the stock exchanges rather than the legislatures. At a time when "shareholder rights" have become a significant issue, some of the most important such rights have been given to shareholders by the authority of the stock exchanges.

As a consequence, it is possible that the securities exchanges or their successor market authority may generate such confidence by their very existence so that investors as a general rule tend to think that transactions executed on an auction market may be more fair than transactions executed in the over-the-counter market. It would therefore be important to maintain such confidence-building appearances.[59] Such considerations may be irrelevant to efficient trading, but we should not ignore the psychological reaction of investors to different market structures, particularly if our purpose in restructuring includes increasing confidence.

Finally, it seems clear that existing substantive regulations such as anti-manipulative rules that have as a substantial part of their basis the maintenance of investor confidence should not be relaxed as long as a more competitive environment does not render them redundant.

Fiduciary Rules

There is substantial doubt as to whether the rules we have characterized as fiduciary in nature are beneficial. It was noted earlier in this paper that such rules tend to be the result of either activities by brokers seeking to have customers who repose fiduciary-like confidence in them or the retention by firms of customer assets, giving rise to traditional bases for fiduciary duties. However, with respect to the pure salesperson, this concept is in some significant respects at odds with reality. The normal account executive does not consider himself or herself a fiduciary but rather a salesperson. Indeed, the firm is hardly likely to let him or her think otherwise. But normal perceptions of sales-persons—including perceptions held by investors—are directly contrary to those we have of a fiduciary. Moreover, when the account executive's only activity is trading securities for a customer, one might wonder why we impose suitability rules and the like that are intended (with dubious success) to make that sales-person's activities fundamentally different from those of one who sells cars, suits, or other items. Investor confidence requirements might justify some more strict view of the obligations of a securities salesperson; it is doubtful that they should be as extensive as they presently are. Furthermore, suitability rules have been established on the faulty premise that suitability is determined by the nature of the investor rather than by the portfolio to which the security might be added, a premise that is rebutted by modern portfolio theory. Equally important, to the extent that such regulations may cloud the distinction between the securities salesperson and the investment adviser or custodian, it may be that a regulatory compromise has been developed providing rules that are inappropriately strict for the salesperson and inappropriately lenient for the adviser or custodian.

Accordingly, a reexamination of the roles of the securities salesperson, the investment adviser, and the custodian should be undertaken. To identify different responsibilities for people in each of these three categories, it is appropriate to recognize that one person might simultaneously perform two or all three roles with respect to a given customer. In such cases that person should not be exempted from the fiduciary obligations of any of the roles.[60]

Protective Regulations

A substantial part of the recent movement toward a national market system, which began with the abolition of the minimum-fixed-commission schedule, has effectively been a movement away from regulations that are solely protective in nature. By and large, such regulations are undesirable, and the progress being made toward their elimination is appropriate. It should be recognized, however, that the securities industry in its current form has grown up around the regulations that exist. Accordingly, the elimination of any given protective regulation could disrupt the trading markets and should be revoked with due caution and only when there is a reasonable basis for believing that the revocation will not have substantial long-term disadvantageous consequences.

Conclusion

The foregoing has been a brief review of the regulatory scene in the securities industry. It includes a rationale for the current mode of regulation, a critique of the direction being given to the development of the national market system, a contrast of the regulatory problems associated with a hard-clob-type market and alternative forms of a national market, suggestions for decreasing duplication of regulation and for modification of regulations in the light of developments since their regulation, and the direction of market reform. While it is not usually a productive exercise to reinvent the wheel, it is appropriate to focus attention on the extent to which regulation of the securities industry continues to serve a legitimate national interest as we move toward a central market.

Notes

1. Louis B. Schwartz, "Review of A.E. Kahn's *Economics of Regulation: Principles and Institutions,* Vols. 1 and 2." *Antitrust Bulletin* 17 (Winter 1972):1151-69, 1158 (footnote omitted). Note that the FTC recently claimed that its antitrust settlement with Levi Strauss will save consumers $50 million per year in reduced prices (*Wall Street Journal,* 21 April 1978, p. 1).

2. Public Law No. 94-29 (4 June 1975). Henceforth this act will be referred to as the "1975 amendments."

3. For example, the adaption of certain rules to apply to markets other than the New York Stock Exchange (NYSE); net capital rules [SEC Release No. 34-11497 (26 June 1975), 40 FR 29795] and antimanipulative rules [SEC Release No. 34-11942 (19 December 1975) 48, n. 155, 41 FR 4507, 4519, No. 160]. A consolidated reporting system is in place [SEC Release No. 34-12138 (25 February 1976)]. The Commission adopted rules governing the dissemination of quotations from exchanges and third market makers [SEC Release No. 34-14415 (26 January 1978)]. Off-board trading rules have been modified [SEC Release No. 34-11942 (19 December 1975), 41 FR 4507, and 34-14325 (30 December 1977), 43 FR 1327], and still further changes have been proposed [SEC Release No. 34-13662 (23 June 1977), 42 FR 33510]. The SEC has

proposed the development of a consolidated quotation system [SEC Release No. 34-14415 (26 January 1978)]. See also SEC Release No. 34-12159 and National Market Advisory Board hearings and report on a composite limit order book. Finally, note that the NYSE has been developing the Intermarket Trading System.

4. Air fares have been dropping, and further drops can be expected as a result of CAB plans to permit airlines reduce fares by up to 50% without approval. Rules limiting discounts are now being ignored (*Wall Street Journal*, 21 April 1978, p. 1.

5. While the views have often been expressed (and we do not here purport to accept or to challenge such views) that the ICC is captured by the trucking industry, the FCC by the broadcasters, and the like, the SEC has usually been viewed as an exception to the rule. See G.W. Schwert, "Public Regulation of National Securities Exchanges: A Test of the Capture Hypothesis," *Bell Journal of Economics* 8 (Spring 1977):128-50.

6. Although the propriety of the scheme by which regulatory securities issuances and issuers and their affiliates is not examined in this paper, it has been subject to recent inquiry elsewhere. See *Report of the Advisory Committee on Corporate Disclosure to the Securities and Exchange Commission, House Committee on Interstate and Foreign Commerce,* 95th Cong., 1st sess., Committee Print 95-29 (3 November 1977); see also M. Mendelson, "Economics and the Assessment of Disclosure Regulation," *Journal of Comparative Corporate Law and Securities Regulation* 1 (January 1978):49.

7. However, in recent years there has been movement toward greater regulation of the municipal securities industry. See Securities Exchange Act of 1934, §§ 3(a)(17), 3(a)(29)-(33), 15B, 17(a)(1), 17(b),(c), all as amended by the 1975 amendments, to establish the municipal Securities Rulemaking Board and to provide for the regulation of dealers in municipal securities, and Senate Bill 2339 (95th Cong., 1st sess.) introduced 1 December 1977, which would provide substantial disclosure regulation for municipal securities issuances.

8. A *hard* clob is one with an execution capability.

9. See *Statement of the Securities and Exchange Commission on the Future Structure of the Securities Markets* (1972), 37 FR 5286; *Policy Statement of the Securities and Exchange Commission on the Structure of a Central Market System* 11 (1973); reports of the Advisory Commission on a Central Market System (11 October 1972); SEC Release No. 34-12159 (2 March 1976); views of the National Market Advisory Board (see letter to the chairman and the commissioners of the SEC, dated 28 January 1977); SEC Release No. 34-14416 (26 January 1978).

10. The nature of this inquiry should be clear. The basic question is: Why should Congress direct the SEC to push the development of a national market system? The SEC itself needs no further justification than the fact that the 1975 amendments specifically direct the SEC to do so. Indeed, it follows from my

argument that the question to be addressed to the SEC is why it has been so slow. See *Oversight of the Functioning and Administration of the Securities Acts Amendments of 1975,* a report by the Subcommittee on Oversight and Investigations and the Subcommittee on Consumer Protection and Finance of the House Committee on Interstate and Foreign Commerce, 95th Cong., 1st sess., Committee Print No. 95-27 (15 November 1977). That report baldly states, "The Securities and Exchange Commission . . . has not vigorously used its authority to facilitate the establishment of a national market system" (p. 1). Unfortunately, there is little about the composition of the current Commission to encourage the belief that it has changed its ways.

11. Lee A. Pickard, "New Perspective at the SEC," *New York Times,* 27 November 1977, Section 3, p. 6F.

12. *Institutional Investor Study Report,* H.R. Doc. No. 92-64, 92d Cong., 1st sess., pt. 1 (10 March 1971). For such an attribution, see SEC Release No. 34-14416 (26 January 1978) 17 CFR, Part 240:5.

13. See C.E. Youngblood, "The Argument for a Publicly Owned Stock Exchange," *Financial Analysts Journal* 25 (November-December 1969):104-107; letter submitted to the SEC by Donald E. Weeden dated 19 December 1969. It might be noted that Weeden refers to an NYSE version of the central marketplace, which presumably predates Weeden's letter. Also compare comments of Weeden and Co. in connection with SEC Release 34-8791 (31 December 1969). In response to an earlier SEC Release No. 34-8328 (5 June 1968), the then chairman of the NYSE, Gustave Levy, maintained that NYSE Rule 394 was "essential to the *maintenance* of a central market" (emphasis added). Clearly there were some differences in the concept referred to and the concept of a national market system currently being considered.

14. 1975 Amendments, § 11A.(a)(2). See also U.S. Congress, House, Securities Acts Amendments of 1975—*Conference Report* (hereinafter, *Conference Report*), 94th Cong., 2d sess., H. Rept. 94-229 (May 1975):92.

15. 1975 Amendments, § 11A.(a)(1). *Conference Report*, pp. 92-5, 99.

16. See, for example, *Securities Industry Study,* Report of the Subcommittee on Securities, Committee on Banking, Housing, and Urban Affairs, U.S., Congress, Senate, 1st sess., 1973, p. 2.

17. Compare 1975 Amendments, § 11A.(c) (3)(A) and (4)(A).

18. See § 19.

19. Harold Williams, "The Future of the Securities Industry," Gustave L. Levy Memorial Lecture, Twelfth Annual Conference on Wall Street and the Economy (28 January 1978):5-6.

20. The number of shareholders of NYSE listed stock declined from 30.9 million in 1970 to 25.3 million in 1975. The New York Stock Exchange, *1977 Fact Book:*50.

21. SEC Release No. 34-11203 (23 January 1975), 40 FR 7394.

22. SEC Releases No. 34-11942, 35-13662, and 34-14325. It is interesting

to note that in his speech cited above in note 19, Chairman Williams got his priorities backward. In listing the factors that would induce the Commission not to remove off-board trading restrictions, he lists the possibility of diminishing "existing opportunities for investor orders to be executed without the participation of a dealer" first. Yet the Act clearly makes that subordinate to the other factors he mentions. See § 11A(a)(1) (C)(v).

23. The Sherman Act, 15 U.S.C. § 1. These actions appear to be minimally permissible for regulated industries as long as they are necessary to make the regulatory scheme work. See *Silver* v. *New York Stock Exchange,* 373 U.S. 341, 357 (1963), where the court held that the Securities Exchange Act of 1934 "contained no express exemption from the antitrust laws or, for that matter, from any other statute . . . ," and that "[r]epeal [of the antitrust laws] is to be regarded as implied only if necessary to make the Securities Exchange Act work, and even then only to the minimum extent necessary." The Supreme Court upheld the NYSE rate structure against antitrust attack in *Gordon* v. *New York Stock Exchange,* 422 U.S. 659 (1975).

24. *Silver* v. *NYSE* [373 U.S. 341 (1963)]; *Gordon* v. *NYSE et al.* [422 U.S. 659 (1975)].

25. Irwin Friend, "The Stock Market and the Economy: The Economic Consequences of the Stock Market," *American Economic Review* 62 (May 1972):212-215; James H. Lorie and Mary T. Hamilton, *The Stock Market: Theories and Evidence* (Homewood, Ill.: Irwin, 1972), pp. 96-97, 100.

26. *Institutional Investor Study,* H.R. Doc. No. 92-64, Vol. 4, pp. 1721 ff. Also see Alan Kraus and Hans R. Stoll, "Price Impacts of Block Trading on the NYSE," *Journal of Finance* 27 (June 1972):587.

27. SEC Release 34-13662, Sec. IIIA (23 June 1977).

28. Robert W. Doede, "The Monopoly Power of the New York Stock Exchange," Ph.D. dissertation, University of Chicago (1967). The economies of scale discussed here are distinctly different from the economies claimed by the industry during the commission rate controversy. Those allegedly arose from large fixed costs. The statistical evidence simply did not support the contention that such economies existed. The economies I refer to are simply a reflection of information begetting information. Such economies are a sufficient condition for destructive competition. Freedom of entry is of no avail because the new entrant has no effective way of generating demand for his services.

29. See, for example, I. Friend, "Economic Foundations of Stock Market Regulation," *Journal of Contemporary Business* 5 (Summer 1976):1.

30. Of the several authors cited in Friend, "Economic Foundations of Stock Market Regulation," most say absolutely nothing about equity.

31. For a summary, see Friend, ibid., pp. 7-25.

32. Ibid., p. 4.

33. Banks are effectively prohibited from underwriting corporate securities by § 21 of the Glass-Steagall Act as amended, 12 U.S.C.A. § 378. However,

Comptroller of the Currency John Heimann has called for a fundamental reexamination of that Act. Bureau of National Affairs (BNA) *Securities Regulation and Law Report,* No. 450, A-18 (26 April 1978).

34. Under the prudence standards of ERISA, it remains unclear whether each investment in a portfolio must be "prudent" or whether that standard applies to the portfolio in its entirety, although there is some appropriate movement toward acceptance of the portfolio approach. See Shirley Scheibla, "Revamping ERISA," *Barrons,* 1 May 1978, p. 4; Benjamin C. Korschot, "Prudent Investing—Before and After ERISA," *Financial Analysts Journal,* July-August 1977, p. 18. Obviously that difference is of substantial importance to the market for securities since the quantity of total investment funds subject to ERISA is very large, and removing those funds from the market for more risky securities therefore involves significant and far-reaching consequences.

35. Cf. the rules of the Association of International Bond Dealers.

36. See, for example, *SEC* v. *Texas Gulf Sulphur Co.,* 401 F.2d 833 (2d Cir. 1968), *cert. denied,* 394 U.S. 976 (1969); *SEC* v. *Shattuck Denn Mining Corp.,* 297 F.Supp. 470 (S.D.N.Y. 1968).

37. NASD, Rules of Fair Practice, Art. III, § 4.

38. Interpretation of the NASD Board of Governors, "Review of Corporate Financing," pursuant to NASD Rules of Fair Practice, Art. III, § 1.

39. NYSE, Rule 390.

40. For example, SEC Rule 15c3-1, 17 Code of Fed. Reg. § 240.15c3-1.

41. For example, NYSE Rule 319.

42. For a recent consideration of the extent of the broker's fiduciary duty, see *Rolf* v. *Blyth, Eastman Dillon & Co., Inc.,* CCH, Federal Securities Law Reports ¶ 93,275, 2d Cir. (3 January 1978).

43. Indeed, recent advertisements by investment firms, featuring account executives stressing that "the customer always comes first" and that their duties are to the customer, tend to support this view. They are not, however, different in any significant degree from comparable statements in automobile dealers' advertisements.

44. See Securities Exchange Act of 1934 §19(b), (c), as amended by the Securities Acts Amendments of 1975, providing substantially greater authority of the SEC over SRO rules.

45. That view is implicit in, for example, studies showing institutional brokerage must in the current environment be supported by retail brokerage. See "SIA Sees Retail Trade Becoming More Important as Profits from Institutional Business Decline," BNA, *Securities Regulation and Law Report,* No. 436 (18 January 1978): A-3.

46. See SEC Release 34-13662 (23 June 1977).

47. For example, NYSE Rule 113.

48. J.W. Peake, M. Mendelson, and R.T. Williams, *The National Book System: An Electronically Assisted Auction Market* (Parsippany, N.J.: R. Shriver Associates, April 1976).

49. Testimony of Mendelson, Peake, and Williams, SEC Hearings File No. 4-180 (23 August 1977).

50. Harold Demsetz, "The Cost of Transacting," *Quarterly Journal of Economics* 82 (February 1968):37-38.

51. While commissions may have covered the cost of execution, they apparently did not cover the full costs of the services rendered. For example, in February 1978 Donaldson, Lufkin, and Jenrette set maximum institutional discounts. The letter announcing the policy decision explains that at the then low rate levels, brokers would not be able to continue to provide research [*Wall Street Letter* 9 (6 February 1978):2]. The following week the head of one firm accounced, "It just doesn't make business sense to continue operating such a high cost (research) department with seemingly no way of getting paid for the service" [*Wall Street Letter* 9 (13 February 1978):10]. Finally, Goldman Sachs announced, "We feel that it is both necessary and timely to encourage an overall increase of the commission revenue in order to assure the continuation of vital investment services" [*Wall Street Letter* 9 (20 February 1978):10].

52. Williams, "The Future of the Securities Industry":11.

53. SEC Release No. 34-14416 (26 January 1978): text accompanying n. 44-64.

54. SEC Release No. 34-14415, § III B.

55. SEC Release No. 34-14415, § III A.

56. Ibid.: 33-35.

57. "The Commission . . . does not intend its determination to proceed with development of a Central File for public limit orders to be interpreted as a decision to force all auction trading into an electronic [*sic*] system with automatic execution capabilities" (SEC Release No. 34-14416:37).

"There seems to be widespread doubt over the Commission's sincerity in making that statement. However, I sincerely believe that current specialist systems are compatible with, and can survive, the Central File" (Roberta S. Karmel, "The Resolution of Broker Dealer Conflict of Interest in Market Executions," speech to the Compliance and Legal Seminar sponsored by the Securities Industry Association, Sarasota, Florida, 20 March 1978, p. 21).

"The Commission is, of course, aware of the concern expressed by some that a central file will inevitably lead to an electronic market—the so-called black box. That is neither the intent nor the likely consequence of the Commission's proposal" (Williams, "The Future of the Securities Industry":15-16.

58. The reason given by Commissioner Karmel is irrelevant. She noted that the electronic national book was rejected because of a "serious concern about the broker-dealer conflicts of interest which could surface in such a system" ("The Resolution of Broker Dealer Conflict of Interest" p. 18). She overlooks the fact that while one of the virtues of the national book system is that it facilitates the development of competing market makers, the elimination of the

specialist is not a technical necessity. There is no technical reason why the specialist cannot be given a franchise and a brokerage commission on every order entered in the book and ultimately executed, even though brokerage firms entered those orders directly. The absurdity of this is patent, but aside from the specialists' fees, all the economies we have claimed for the national book system could still be realized. See also Peake, Mendelson, and Williams' letter to the National Market Advisory Board (10 June 1976), in which they discuss another scheme for retaining specialists.

59. To date, the notion of "qualified securities"—those qualified for trading in a national market system—that is emerging in the national market discussions does not seem to consider this objective. See, for example, SEC Release No. 34-14416, text accompanying n.24-n.25. If the national market system evolves as a single market, which is the only market for trading in most securities, such considerations probably should not be pertinent. However, the only way in which market regulation in such an environment could generate the sort of investor confidence currently resulting from exchange regulation of listed companies would be by a form of corporate regulation that would approximate federal or national quasi-governmental corporate standards—a topic that has generated considerable controversy in recent years. Furthermore, if the element of discretion is removed from acceptance for listing (or its equivalent), the fact of listing may well lose all significance as a source of investor confidence. On the other hand, the emerging national market system may make available additional information or provide other bases for increased confidence.

60. Similarly, a firm that elects to perform more than one role with its associated fiduciary obligations should not be exempted from them simply because conflict is impossible to avoid.

4

A Need for a Change in Direction in Regulation of the Securities Markets

Lee A. Pickard

One of the problems of expanding regulation in the manner occurring in the financial sector today is the inability to identify with any degree of precision the costs of such regulation and the substantive changes that result from it. Practically everyone professes the desirability of minimizing or avoiding burdensome and unnecessary regulation, but unfortunately those most responsible for many of the important decisions in the regulatory area find their heart is elsewhere when confronted with a perceived inequity that they believe can be remedied through regulatory action. In the deliberative stage little attention is given to the cost of new regulation, and of greater importance its anticompetitive impact. A sense of outrage causes them to act as, for instance, the Securities and Exchange Commission (SEC) recently did when it discovered abuses in the options area. There the commission chose to prevent these markets from further expanding existing programs for option trading while it undertook an investigation.[1]

The release announcing the moratorium on further expansion of the options markets cited a number of concerns such as fictitious trading by options specialists and overtrading to attract order flow (none of which appeared to relate to investor harm or loss in any substantive way) and alleged deficiencies in the surveillance mechanisms of exchanges. Whether the Commission's action, depriving the securities markets of a continued economic expansion of the option vehicle as a medium of investment, was warranted by this questionable conduct is impossible to determine. The sense of concern was clearly manifested in the release. The legal case for the action was carefully documented. Yet there was a total absence of cost-benefit analysis respecting the action. The Commission's duty to consider the competitive impact of the moratorium[2] was disposed of as follows:

> Proposed Temporary Rule 9b-1(T) simultaneously restricts the expansion of all existing options pilot programs, and temporarily defers the institution of new programs. It presently appears to the Commission that to the extent any burdens on competition are engendered by proposed Temporary Rule 9b-1(T), they are necessary and appropriate to insure investor protection and to protect the public interest, in furtherance of the purposes of the Act. (Release No. 14056)

Some existing options markets and other private interests may benefit from the moratorium as new or expanding markets will not be able to compete with them. For the indefinite future, investors will not have exposure to new products in the options area. It may have been a correct decision to impose a moratorium, but a complete analysis is lacking.

Professor Paul McCracken, former chairman of the Council of Economic Advisors, has said,

> The single most important source of economic waste comes from failure to identify and evaluate what is being given up when we go for something that itself is "good."

In the regulatory process it is nearly always impossible to identify the full consequence of the action or "what is being given up." It is almost universally the case, however, that something is being given up. Practically every form of regulation is anticompetitive and carries with it a cost burden. Congress, in the Securities Acts Amendments of 1975, attempted to address this critical aspect of regulation by amending the Securities Exchange Act of 1934 to require the Commission in making rules to "consider among other matters, the impact any such rule . . . would have on competition."[3] In practice, this requirement of the new law has been easily dealt with by Commission lawyers who need only assert, without quantitative analysis, a finding of egregious conduct or that a proposed action exists for the purpose of carrying out the broad objectives of the securities acts.

In spite of the fact that the Securities Act Amendments of 1975 and the accompanying legislative history purport to embrace competition as a major objective and to have as a goal the removal of unnecessary regulatory restrictions wherever possible, the new law in both respects is deficient in accomplishing such results. Besides embodying a number of new restrictions on economic activity, which will prove troublesome for the foreseeable future, the 1975 amendments launch major regulatory intrusions into areas of the securities and banking industry heretofore unregulated. The 1975 amendments have provided the foundation for comprehensive regulation of municipal brokers and dealers, transfer agents, and clearing and depository facilities and have given the Commission new authority to regulate the markets and all professional participants.[4]

One of the most anticompetitive measures in the 1975 amendments is newly revised Section 11(a). Section 11(a) as finally enacted reflects a compromise on the part of the financial industry to divide up the functions of money management and brokerage. Hammered out in an era of fixed rates, its ostensible purpose was to guard against the abuses of institutional money managers performing brokerage for their managed accounts. Its real purpose was to ensure through legislative fiat that institutions would not be permitted to gain access to exchanges through memberships for the purpose of doing portfolio brokerage. It was to be a shield to protect the brokerage revenues received by exchange members from the threat of direct executions on exchanges by money managers and the resulting loss of brokerage to the members. Of course, competitive rates prove the 11(a) shield to be illusory. The brokerage industry began to realize it had made a bad bargain. But when the provisions of Section 11(a) were reexamined by Congress in hearings in 1977 and 1978, institutional fund advisers, insurance companies, and banks extolled its virtues. These groups did not desire the competition likely to ensue from broker-dealers if 11(a) were amended to permit broker-dealers to both manage money and execute portfolio brokerage for the same accounts.

The wisdom of compelling the separation of the money management and brokerage function was never really explored by Congress. No economic analysis was done respecting the advantages to accounts or efficiencies inherent in the same organization performing both money management and brokerage. "What was given up" was not considered relevant. Rather, a potential conflict was perceived by the legislators (an impression that was reinforced by private groups who would benefit from such a separation), and in the absence of proven abuses, the prohibition was enacted into the 1975 amendments.

Similarly, the Employee Retirement Income Security Act of 1974 (ERISA) is a law designed to impose stringent standards and responsibilities on fiduciaries with respect to the investment activities of employee benefit plans, containing prohibitions on conduct that have not received the necessary scrutiny in terms of cost-benefit analysis. Basically, ERISA prohibits a category of parties including fiduciaries from offering multiple services to pension accounts.[5] Absent an exemption (a number of which have been granted by the Department of Labor and the Treasury), a manager of a pension account may no longer effect brokerage transactions for that account.

In the pension fund area there was little, if any, evidence produced of abuses relating to the fact that fiduciaries engaged in both money management and brokerage for the same account.[6] Even assuming that there had been evidence of abuses arising from potential conflicts, the ERISA legislation failed to examine adequately the degree of economic loss or inefficiency attributable to a mandatory separation of these functions or to explore alternative remedial steps short of an outright prohibition on such multiple activity.

Turning to recent regulatory experience of the Commission, a significant aspect of the 1975 amendments was the directive to the Commission to facilitate the establishment of a national market system. Those amendments significantly enhance the Commission's authority over the market structure and spell out in confusing and contradictory terms the characteristics of a national market system.[7] It would be difficult in this paper to provide a full explanation of the motivation and forces that culminated in the notion that there is a need to restructure our securities markets affirmatively through government intervention. Years and years of public deliberations and studies demonstrating market distortions and other effects of fixed commission rates undoubtedly contributed to the thought that the government should do something. The resistence of a large segment of the securities industry to the removal of fixed rates brought with it a clamor for restructuring. The adverse consequences of one set of regulations (that is, those pertaining to fixed rates) were to be dealt with by other affirmative regulatory measures. However, while the primary causes of market fragmentation identified in these earlier studies such as fixed rates and the absence of a consolidated tape displaying trade information in all markets have in large measure evaporated, the thrust for government involvement in the restructuring of the market has not subsided. The momentum for regulatory reform in the market-structure area continues unabated, in a sense being carried by its own inertia, adopting new premises that seem to be conjectured and unproven in terms of need or from the standpoint of cost-benefit analysis.[8]

The law calling for a national market system is now a permanent fixture. Predictably the Commission, acting under its new mandate, has already instituted several regulatory programs focusing on the need for market restructuring. In January 1978 the Commission adopted a rule requiring all exchanges and over-the-counter markets trading listed securities to collect quotations and quotation sizes from their specialists and market makers and make them available to vendors for display purposes.[9] Further, the quotations given out by broker-dealers (with certain exceptions) are to be firm obligations to buy or sell in the sizes displayed. The rule was adopted, "to facilitate the prompt development of a composite quotation system, an integral component of a national market system."

Whether Rule 11Ac1-1, scheduled to go into effect in August 1978, will accomplish its objective remains to be seen. It is a complex rule, and it will be costly to comply with, especially for regional exchanges and over-the-counter market makers in listed securities. Previously dealers had not disseminated firm quotations because from their experience the quotations were largely disregarded by the investment community. The pricing mechanism for listed securities is primarily the NYSE market. Others making markets in listed securities look to the NYSE market for current and accurate pricing.

Several market makers objected to the cost burdens attendant to compliance with the quotation rule. The Commission attempted to meet their objections by promising exemptions where the cost of compliance proved prohibitive. Nevertheless, no attempt was made to do a cost-benefit analysis of the rule. Premised on broad statutory objectives of dubious origins, the Commission needed to do little more than assert that the rule was consistent with those objectives.

The quotation rule was challenged by the Council on Wage and Price Stability. The Council urged the Commission not to adopt such a rule in the absence of an analysis demonstrating that the benefits of the proposal would outweigh the costs associated with its implementation. In response to the Council, the Commission stated:

> the benefits provided by the Rule, particularly its role in facilitating the establishment of a national market system, outweigh the costs associated with implementation of the Rule. As an integral step in accomplishing the statutory goal of the "linking of all markets . . . [to] foster efficiency, enhance competition, . . . and contribute to best execution" . . . of customers' orders, the Rule is justified even in the absence of inherently speculative efforts to quantify the cost and value of certain improvements in the quality of information which will result. (Release No. 34-14415, p. 48)

The problem with the Commission's response to the Council is that the "benefits provided by the Rule" are no more quantifiable than the "speculative efforts to quantify the cost." In fact, no attempt was made to quantify values on either end.

Given the unfocused objectives of a national market system laid out by Congress in the 1934 Act and the lack of standards upon which to measure the impact of administrative action in this area, the Commission was able to proceed without substantive regard to cost-benefit analysis or competitive impact.

At the same time the Commission adopted the quotation rule, it proposed further initiatives to facilitate the establishment of a national market system.[10] It called on securities exchanges and the NASD to provide order-routing systems, permitting orders for the purchase and sale of listed securities to be sent directly from one market to another, and a "single system" allowing broker-dealers to route orders from their offices to various markets. Additionally, the Commission called for the development by exchanges and the NASD of a central limit order file for public agency orders in listed securities. The stated objectives of this file would be:

> to make available a mechanism in which public limit orders . . . can be entered and queued for execution in accordance with the auction trading principles of price and time priority and by means of which such orders can be assured of receiving an execution prior to the execution of any other order by a broker or dealer in any market at the same or an inferior price. . . . Execution priority for orders entered in the Central File over all other orders would be required by rule. (Release No. 34-14416, pp. 34-36)

The Commission disclaims that such a limit order file will force all trading into an electronic system with automatic execution features. However, few knowledgeable people have been able to envision how such a limit order file (with its price and time priorities) will operate effectively except as an electronic system with automatic execution capabilities.

The Commission's initiatives in the January release reflect the government's strong involvement in market restructuring. In contrast, the securities markets have historically been the product of the private sector. Individual market centers developed or implemented new methods of trading securities and communication systems for order transmission and executions, vastly improved procedures for clearing and settling trades, and more comprehensive and effective surveillance reports and techniques. To the extent that there has been a need for improvements in our markets, normal economic processes have produced them in most instances. The course elected by the Commission under its new authority threatens to change all this.

Whether a mandatory "single system" for routing orders to a market or a central limit order file is either legally justified under the 1975 amendments or, more importantly, in the best interest of the public investor, is highly debatable.[11]

As previously noted, an important facet of the Commission's limit order file is the proposal that limit orders from the public be executed prior to the execution of professional orders at the same price. The proposition that in a competitive setting, "public" orders should come ahead of professional orders at the same price regardless of time of entry has never been substantiated as desirable for an efficient market. Under such an arrangement, the disincentives to market making could well leave public investors without sufficient market-maker capacity when needed. The January release merely asserts the desirability of such a priority, without economic analysis or explanation of its competitive impact.[12]

In support of these major structural reforms in the securities markets, the Commission relies on general assertions of enhancing "best-execution" possibilities and ensuring competition and refers to objectives found in the 1975 amendments. Whereas the legal basis for such actions is carefully documented by the Commission, the cost of implementing or operating these new systems is not discussed. There is no reference to possible savings to the securities industry or investors by virtue of implementing systems of this type. The January release is devoid of supportive economic analysis or cost justifications. In responding to the Commission's January release for one of the systems called for—a message-routing switch—the NYSE agreed to cooperate but questioned the need for such a system. They pointed out that several systems similar to what the Commission wants are already operating.

Conclusion

The Commission has become deeply involved in economic regulation at a time when its overall resources are strained and its capacities to undertake cost-benefit analysis or to assess competitive impact are weak. In some measure,

Congress is responsible for the Commission's involvement in market structure and securities processing matters. The legislative history leading up to the 1975 amendments is woefully lacking in analysis or fact finding to support the necessity of the government's becoming involved in such undertakings as the creation of a national market system or a "national system for clearance and settlement of securities transactions."

The 1975 amendments are replete with vague goals and objectives that offer far too little direction to the Commission and the public on how to proceed. Under the circumstances Congress should revisit this law with a view to relieving the Commission of such dubious tasks as imposing a new trading system on the securities industry and allow it to focus its full attention on preventing fraud, strengthening standards of conduct, and enhancing disclosure where it has performed well in the past.

Notes

1. SEC Release No. 14056, 17 October 1977.

2. See discussion of Section 23(a)(2) of the Securities Exchange Act of 1934, *infra.*

3. Section 23(a)(2); also, see Sections 6 and 15A of the 1934 Act which require as a condition of registration of exchanges and securities associations that their rules not impose any burden on competition not necessary or appropriate in furtherance of the Securities Exchange Act of 1934.

4. While the procedures for exercising authority by the Commission have been formalized beyond what they were previously and are more open to public scrutiny (see in particular Sections 19, 23, and 25 of the 1934 Act), the new law has not imposed more responsibility on the Commission to justify the economic impact of its decisions as the agency, by virtue of congressional direction, expands beyond its traditional role of preventing fraud, overseeing self-regulatory action and compelling disclosure.

5. See Section 406 of ERISA.

6. In general, those responsible for pension accounts seem capable of determining whether a fiduciary is properly serving the account in a multiple capacity and whether the overall service is adequate. Moreover, it would not appear that a fiduciary is necessarily conducting himself improperly under traditional trust law merely because he performs a brokerage function in addition to his advisory service for an account. Disclosure and monitoring are techniques utilized to ensure proper performance by fiduciaries in areas of perceived conflicts.

7. See Sections 11A, 15, 15A, 17A, and 19 of the 1934 Act, which provide the Commission with elaborate authority over all phases of market activity to accomplish the goals of a national market system.

8. One of the new premises allegedly justifying reform is the need for greater limit order protection. The Commission in its January 1978 release (34-14416) proposes the implementation of a central limit order file for public agency orders pursuant to its authority conferred by the 1975 amendments. In the Commission hearings on the proposed removal of off-board agency and principal restrictions (Rules 394 and 390 of the NYSE), industry opponents of removal of these rules argued strongly that they were necessary to protect limit orders. Unfortunately, the assumption that limit orders need any special consideration or treatment for an efficient market or that the present market structure (or one that might evolve in the future) is not capable of ensuring adequate executions for limit orders has not been demonstrated or explored in any significant manner.

9. Securities Exchange Act Release No. 34-14415 adopting Rule 11Ac1-1.

10. Securities Exchange Act Release No. 34-14416, 26 January 1978.

11. The Commission's request for a "single" system for routing orders to markets and for a central file for limit orders may be incompatible with a principle objective of the 1975 amendments [Section 11A(a)(1)(C)(ii)] calling for "fair competition among brokers and dealers, among exchange markets, and between exchange markets and markets other than exchange markets." In the final analysis, mandatory systems of this type leave little room for diversity in market functions and may lead to the demise of individual market centers.

12. The Commission recently approved an electronic trading facility of the Cincinnati Stock Exchange (Release No. 14674, 18 April 1978). One of the characteristics of the electronic facility is a rule providing for priority of public orders over professional orders at the same price. The rule was initiated by the sponsors of the facility on the premise that the Commission would require such a rule as a condition of approval. Thus without any clear idea of benefit or cost, such a priority is now a procedure of an operative market.

5

Deregulation and the Capital Markets: The Impact of Deposit Rate Ceilings and Restrictions Against Variable Rate Mortgages

Patric H. Hendershott

Numerous regulations of financial institutions and markets are candidates for dismantling. Some examples are restrictions against investments of some institutions in particular assets (federally chartered savings and loan purchases of consumer credit and mortgages with variable rates and payments); restrictions against thrifts (savings and loans and mutual savings banks) in many areas of the country issuing third party payment accounts; and restrictions against the payment of interest above some level on certain assets (prohibition of interest on checking accounts and on bank reserves held at the Federal Reserve, limitations on yields on savings deposits, and usury ceilings). While removal of each of these restrictions probably has merit insofar as consumers would be provided a greater return on their savings or better services at equal or lower cost, only a few are likely to have a significant impact on capital markets. These few are the subject of this paper.

By "impact on the capital markets," I mean a change in the yields on and issues of various types of long-term debt. Now some contend that virtually nothing can significantly influence the relationships among these yields and thus the relative user costs of capital of relevant nonfinancial capital outlays. As a result financial restrictions and selective credit policies have no real impact.[1] Others believe that market segmentation and credit rationing exist most everywhere, allowing an enormous potential impact for financial arrangements and selective credit policies.[2] I find myself somewhere in between, having provided evidence that relative security supplies have no influence on the spread between yields on corporate and Treasury bonds (Cook and Hendershott 1978), but that federal support of the home mortgage market has altered the spread between yields on home mortgages and corporate bonds (Hendershott 1977*a*, chapter 16). In general, selective credit policies will have some impact on the relationship between the yields on two classes of securities only when there is an absence of a large quantity of funds that are indifferent at the margin between

The author gratefully acknowledges research support from the Department of Housing and Urban Development under grant H-2650.

the classes.[3] There are two cases where an absence seems to exist. First, at any time only households in a particular tax bracket, usually around the 30% bracket, are indifferent between long-term-taxable and tax-exempt securities. Second, only mutual savings banks or financial institutions still participating in the home mortgage market seem to be sensitive to the relative yields on home mortgages and taxable bonds. Portfolio restrictions have rendered savings and loans insensitive, and there is little evidence of sensitivity in the behavior of commercial banks.

Removal of deposit rate ceilings and restrictions against variable-rate mortgages (VRMs) are likely to have significant capital market effects. In addition, their removal would probably cause large income transfers between different types of financial institutions and/or households with different characteristics. These transfers are in many instances as interesting as the capital market effects. The first section of this paper reviews both the motivations underlying the imposition of the restrictions on deposit rates and the issuance of VRMs and the apparent impact of restrictions. The remainder of the paper contains some simulation results measuring the likely impact of higher deposit rates and the existence of VRMs on capital market rates, the composition of nonfinancial investment, and the profits of depository institutions during the 1973-1975 period.

The Rationales for Deposit Rate Ceilings and Restrictions Against Variable Rate Mortgages

The relationship between ceilings on deposit rates and restrictions against variable-rate mortgages is straightforward; the latter give rise to a need for the former during periods of rising interest rates.[4] Because savings and loan associations (SLAs) are effectively restricted to investing in residential mortgages, the further restriction against VRMs results in the SLAs' infamous maturity-imbalance problem—short-term liabilities and long-term assets.[5] When market interest rates rise unexpectedly, SLAs earning low past rates on all but their current mortgage investments would experience sharp reductions in earnings, possibly to negative levels if they were to pay deposit rates that are competitive with either the open market or with rates that commercial banks, whose investments have a much shorter effective term-to-maturity, could afford to pay. Deposit rate ceilings prevent SLAs from suffering declines in earnings.

Table 5-1 illustrates the differential impact of rising interest rates on the retained earning of commercial banks (CBs) and SLAs. In the periods 1965-1970 and 1972-1975 when interest rates rose substantially, retained earnings of SLAs fell slightly while those of CBs rose significantly. In both periods the annual growth rate in bank earnings exceeded that of SLAs by about 15% if the impact of extraordinary increases in loan-loss provisions in 1974 and 1975 on bank

Table 5-1

Retained Earnings of Insured Commercial Banks (CBs) and Savings and Loan Associations (SLAs) and Yield on 3-5 Year Treasuries
(millions of $ and percentage points)

	CBs	SLAs	Treasury Yield
1965	1312	805	4.22
1970	2804	781	7.37
1972	3462	1648	5.85
1975	4225 (4761)[a]	1337	7.55

Source: *FDIC Annual Reports, Savings and Loan Fact Book*, 1977, Table 74, p. 92; *Federal Reserve Bulletin*, various issues.

[a]Adjusted to abstract from the extraordinary rise in loan-loss provisions. The rise was approximately $2 billion. Assuming an effective tax rate of 0.33 and a dividend pay-out rate of 0.6, retained earnings would have been $536 million higher [(0.67)(0.4)($2,000)].

earnings is removed. In contrast, when a period of stable or declining interest rates follows one of rising rates, thrifts fare better than CBs because of the lagged impact of the earlier increase in rates on thrift interest income. The data in table 5-1 are also consistent with this hypothesis; between 1970 and 1972 SLAs' retained earnings doubled, while those of banks rose by less than 25%.

The aggregate data also shed some light on the rationale for deposit rate ceilings and the behavior of regulators of the ceilings. Ceilings have apparently been set so that thrifts will not suffer declines in income if they keep their deposit rates in line with those of banks. This may explain the lowering of bank ceilings in 1966. On the other hand, when thrift income begins to rise due to the lagged impact of rising rates on interest income, as it did in the late 1960s and early 1970s, rate ceilings are raised (early 1970 and mid-1973). But at no time is the increase enough to lower thrift income substantially.

This analysis, combined with the sharp rise in thrift earnings in 1976 and 1977, suggests that rate ceilings would be raised in early 1978 when deposit flows fell off significantly. Instead, two new depository instruments were introduced: a six-month certificate with ceiling rates on bank-issued accounts equal to that on six-month Treasury bills and on thrift issues one-quarter point higher, and an eight-year account with ceiling rates one-quarter point higher than those existing on six-year accounts. Both new accounts carry $10,000 minimums. The purpose of these accounts seems to be to minimize disintermediation with a minimum increase in the interest expense of depository institutions. The $10,000 minimum balance emphasizes in the bluntest way that depositors with limited financial resources are those who bear the burden of deposit rate ceilings.

The potential loss of either SLA deposits to banks or earnings and the detrimental impact this loss might have on housing construction is, of course, the reason usually advanced for the reduction in ceilings on savings accounts at

CBs in 1966 and the extension of ceilings to thrift deposits. An alternative, somewhat less idealistic explanation that is consistent with the new savings account instruments created in the spring of 1978 runs along the lines of Stigler's general theory of regulation (1971). In this theory regulation follows from the lobbying efforts of the institutions themselves rather than the desire of policy makers to achieve some lofty goal. This is surely consistent with Andrew Brimmer's interpretation of the rollback in ceilings on bank deposit rates in 1966 as a response to the appeals of smaller CBs. Stigler's theory is also consistent with the SLA legislative efforts to retain rate ceilings and Jaffee's analysis of the benefits accruing to thrifts from this regulation (1976, especially pp. 71-73).[6]

The profitability for CBs of deposit rate ceilings (accompanied by restrictions to limit disintermediation to open-market securities—the $10,000 minimum on purchase of Treasury bills established in 1969 and restrictions against floating-rate note issues by private firms imposed in 1974) is consistent with the data in table 5-1. The rise in bank-retained earnings was particularly rapid between 1965 and 1970, when the ratio of retained earnings to total assets rose from 0.38% to 0.54%. While SLAs did not fare well during the 1966-1975 period, their retained earnings about doubled between 1975 and 1977, returning the ratio of retained earnings to total financial assets to near the 1965 level. Moreover, earnings will rise further as old low-yielding mortgages continue to be rolled over at the new higher rates.

The FHLBB began pushing VRMs as a solution to the SLA maturity-imbalance problem in the late 1960s. In 1969 the FHLBB informed the congressional committees concerned with financial institutions and housing that they planned to issue regulations allowing VRMs. Owing to negative congressional sentiment, the regulations were not issued. Again in 1974 the FHLBB proposed the issuance of such regulations, and the congressional committees agreed to hold hearings in 1975. The result of the hearings, however, was proposed legislation to prohibit the issuance of VRMs.[7]

The two principal arguments against VRMs seem to be that rising interest payments, when they are called for, are "unaffordable" and "inequitable." Regarding the ability of homeowners to make payments that rise with increases in deposit rates, increases of more than one percentage point in the thrift cost of funds are unlikely to occur in the absence of a significant rise in inflation and thus money incomes. Having a VRM outstanding would simply mean that the housing component of a homeowner's budget would rise along with the other components. Moreover, the inflation would be generating housing capital gains for the household that would more than offset greater household interest outlays. If any inequities exist, they would seem to be in the current system. Existing homeowners reap substantial capital gains without even paying the going cost of funds, depositors do not earn even a positive real after-tax rate of interest, and potential first-home buyers and households wishing to change

residences pay especially high yields or find mortgage funds unavailable altogether due to deposit rate ceilings necessitated by restrictions against VRMs.

The principal results of employing deposit rate ceilings instead of allowing
rates on existing mortgages to rise during the 1966-1975 period were three:

1. Depositors, particularly those with less financial sophistication and lower
   incomes-wealth, lost untold interest income. Existing homeowners gained
   by not paying the going cost of funds.
2. Commercial bank profits rose sharply. Because banks shield their profits by
   investing in tax-exempt securities, bank demand for these securities also
   increased greatly, lowering borrowing costs of state and local governments
   relative to what they otherwise would have been.
3. Housing production was very unstable, rising when mortgage credit was
   ample and falling in response to the credit crunches of 1966, 1969-1970,
   and 1973-1974. As a result home building is a risky, labor-intensive
   industry, and housing prices are higher than they otherwise would be.

The simulation results reported in the following sections provide some evidence
regarding housing cycles, the profitability of different financial institutions, and
the relationship among sectoral borrowing costs in a deregulated housing-finance
system.

The Impact of Increases in Deposit Rates

Substantial differences in opinion exist regarding the likely impact of increases
in deposit rate ceilings on thrift earnings and housing activity. Some argue that
thrifts would lose substantial funds owing to the competitive advantages of CBs
during periods of rising interest rates and that housing activity would be
curtailed. Others contend that housing activity would be greater in the absence
of deposit rate ceilings because thrifts could then offer higher yields during
periods of rising interest rates and thus channel more funds into mortgages.

Determining the likely impact of the removal of rate ceilings is a complicated matter. The first step is to decide how CBs and thrifts (SLAs and mutual
savings banks) would set deposit rates in the absence of rate ceilings. Next is
deducing how fund flows, including the Federal Reserve's supply of reserves, and
open-market interest rates would differ because of changing deposit rates. The
movements in market rates and fund flows would influence and be influenced by
the deposit rates offered by the institutions, thrift earnings, and housing outlays.
Determination of the impacts on earnings and housing is the third step.

In considering how deposit rates would have differed in the absence of
ceilings, it is useful to begin with the observed relationship between yields on
U.S. government securities and certificates having the same maturity. Because

the certificate rates of the different institutions generally move quite closely, we shall consider only those on SLA certificates. The Treasury yields are those for the first day of the quarter as computed by Salomon Brothers; the certificate yields on SLA new issues as supplied by the model builders at the Federal Reserve. The interest payments on certificates are assumed to be compounded daily, and the yields have been adjusted to a bond-equivalent basis.[8]

How much ceilings were depressing yields seems to depend heavily on the maturities that one considers (see table 5-2). For one- and two-year maturities, treasuries paid more than certificates for a three-year period from the second quarter of 1973 (732) to the first quarter of 1975 (751), and the difference was large much of the time. For example, the one-year Treasury rate exceeded the one-year certificate rate by a minimum of 55 basis points, and the average spread was 143 basis points. This average spread was almost as great as the 162 basis-point average spread during the 691-704 period. There was a major difference between the 1969-1970 and 1973-1975 periods, however. In the earlier period one-year maturities were the only certificate game in town,[9] while during much of the latter period four- and six-year certificates were widely available.

The spread between yields on longer-term U.S. and certificate securities differs greatly from the spread on shorter terms. During the same eight-quarter period in which the spread on short terms never fell below 55 basis points and averaged 143 basis points, the spread on four-year accounts exceeded 55 basis points only twice, and the average was slightly negative. Looking closely at the

Table 5-2
Spreads Between Yields on U.S. Treasury Securities and SLA Certificates with Different Maturities
(basis points)

	One Year	Two Years	Four Years	Six Years
731	−15	−26	−5	−
732	114	73	65	−
733	158	60	−58	−
734	138	48	−71	−
741	78	32	−77	−70
742	187	138	20	21
743	255	180	70	70
744	160	155	44	45
751	55	75	−32	−60
752	−37	14	−36	−54
753	35	67	−3	−18
754	138	153	80	47
761	−22	16	−32	−40
762	−46	13	−37	−45

Source: Data on treasury yields computed by Salomon Brothers. Data on SLA new issues supplied by Federal Reserve System.

four-year column in table 5-2, we see that certificates were at an absolute disadvantage only in 732, the quarter before higher ceiling rates were established on four-year accounts, 742-744, and 754, when Treasury yields temporarily blipped upward. That is, certificates were at a competitive disadvantage for more than brief periods only during the 742-744 interval.

The next issue is what rates would institutions have in fact offered in the absence of rate ceilings, relative to available Treasury yields? Because the interest lost when certificate funds are withdrawn early or borrowed against far exceeds the cost of selling a Treasury note, certificates would have to command higher yields than treasuries to attract investors.[10] And the evidence from the July-October 1973 period when ceilings were removed altogether on four-year certificates suggests that institutions might in fact be willing to offer ½ to ¾ percentage points more on certificates during periods of intense demands for funds. The spread data in table 5-2 are −58 and −71 basis points for 733 and 734.[11]

With this evidence we have selected the fourth quarter of 1972 (724) to the fourth quarter of 1975, the most recent period of rising interest rates, as the period for simulation. The basic assumption is that CBs would have kept the spread between their new issue certificate rate and a weighted average of the current and lagged one and two quarters one-year Treasury bill rate at its 723 value of 70 basis points throughout the 1973-1975 period. This means that banks would have offered on average 82 basis points more in 1973, 104 basis points more in 1974, and 92 basis points more in 1975, assuming that the one-year Treasury rate were unchanged. (An increase in the Treasury rate results in even higher certificate rates, and decreases imply lower deposit rates.) As we shall note, higher CB retained earnings during this period (see table 5-1) provided banks with ample resources to pay these higher yields. Competition from banks is likely to have led thrifts to offer similar rates (data from July 1973 to October 1973 support this conjecture), so thrifts are assumed to match the increases in the bank deposit rate. While the thrifts would experience declines in income, they would retain their share of the deposit market, a market that would be larger relative to the case where deposit rates are constrained by rate ceilings.

How thrifts and thus the mortgage market and housing would be affected by increases in deposit rate ceiling seems to depend on two factors: First, how interest sensitive are thrift depositors to changes in alternative interest rates? Second, how are market interest rates likely to be affected by increases in deposit rates? Regrettably, we are not or at least should not be very confident in our answers to these questions. While earlier estimates of short- and intermediate-term interest rate elasticities are generally low,[12] the studies are plagued with problems of insufficient observations when a reasonable array of special-deposit accounts exist (four- and six-year accounts were not introduced until 1973 and 1974) and of erroneous data even for this period.[13]

Simulations are run with two different estimates of depositor responses to interest rates. In the first, interest rate coefficients obtained in equations estimated on quarterly data over the 1968-1975 period are employed. The interest rate elasticities implied by these estimates are listed in table 5-3. As can be seen in the far right column, the own rate elasticities range from 0.21 for certificate accounts to 0.77 for passbook accounts, with those for open-market securities and money lying in between. Given the difficulties in estimating these elasticities accurately, we do not have a great deal of confidence in the estimates in table 5-3. In particular, the −0.1 elasticities of certificate accounts with respect to alternative certificate rates and to open-market (Treasury) rates seem much too low. Thus a simulation employing a second, higher set of interest-rate elasticities, those in parentheses in table 5-3, is also run. This set was obtained by arbitrarily raising the elasticities of certificate accounts with respect to alternative certificate yields and to Treasury rates to −1.0 and letting the other rate coefficients adjust. All responses to interest rates are completed within six quarters (65-100% within three quarters), except the substitution between money and passbook accounts, which takes three years for completion.

Estimates of the impact of increases in deposit rates on open-market rates, on the other hand, are almost unanimous in the conclusion that rates will rise, an increase that would be particularly harmful to housing. But these estimates are based on an unrealistic assumption of no response (change in bank reserves) by the Federal Reserve; the reason rates rise is that an increase in bank deposits raises required reserves and thus lowers total security purchases. It seems unreasonable to assume that Federal Reserve policy would be unaffected by an "exogenous" increase in interest rates (real) that lowers ex ante nonfinancial investment. If one assumes that the Federal Reserve would offset any macroeconomic impact of a rise in deposit rates—that is, would keep total ex ante nonfinancial investment at the level that would have existed in the absence of the increase in deposit rates by supplying reserves—then housing could benefit during periods of rising interest rates by the removal of deposit rate ceilings.

The Simulation Model

This brings us to the model to be simulated and the major differences between it and those of earlier investigators.[14] The vehicle employed is a 70 equation quarterly econometric model estimated over data from the 1960-1975 period. Of the equations, 47 are a flow-of-funds financial model that includes markets for home mortgages, other taxable primary securities, tax-exempt securities, demand deposits, and savings accounts at different depository institutions. The financial behavior of households, nonfinancial businesses, state and local governments, each of the depository institutions, and other finance is explained. The three key long-term interest rates to which nonfinancial investment outlays are negatively related—those on home mortgages, taxable bonds, and tax-exempt

Deregulation and the Capital Markets

Table 5-3
Approximate Interest Rate Elasticities Employed in Simulations

Instruments	Passbook Versus Passbook	Certificate Versus Certificate	Passbook Versus Certificate	Passbook Versus Open Market	Certificate Versus Open Market	Money Versus Passbook	Money Versus Open Market	Own Rate Elasticity
				Type of Substitution				
Passbook accounts	0.10 (0.18) 0.10 (1.0)[a]		0.01	0.18		-0.48 (-1.6)		0.77 (1.97)
Certificate accounts		-0.01		0.10 (1.0)[a]			0.21 (2.01)	
Money						0.48 (1.6)	.18	0.66 (1.78)
Securities (taxable debt)				-0.18	-0.10 (-1.0)[a]		-.18	0.45 |(1.36)

[a]Numbers in parentheses were constrained in a second estimation of the asset-demand equations. These constraints caused some changes in other elasticity estimates; the elasticities that changed are in parentheses without [a].

bonds—are, in general, determined by equality between total security issues and purchases in the respective markets.[15] Thus these three yields do not automatically move in lock step with one another, although portfolio substitution creates a tendency for them to move together. This is the first fundamental difference between our model and that employed in most earlier work.

Another nine equations of the model explain nonfinancial gross investment outlays on 1-4 family housing, multifamily housing, fixed investment of nonfinancial businesses, state and local structures, and consumer durables and intermediate variables that are needed to determine the various outlays. Table 5-4 lists the responses of these outlays to increases in the home mortgage rate, the yield on 20-year, Aa new issue utility bonds, and the yield on 20-year choice-rated tax-exempt issues.[16] A second major difference between our simulations and those of earlier researchers is the assumption that total nonfinancial investment outlays will be invariant with respect to changes in deposit rates. More specifically, the Federal Reserve is assumed to offset any macroeconomic impact of the rise in deposit rates, that is, open-market operations will be undertaken such that no changes in total ex ante investment will occur. (The composition of nonfinancial investment can of course change in response to a change in the structure of long-term interest rates.) Given that the Federal Reserve already is pursuing policies to achieve the optimal future timepath of inflation and unemployment in the absence of this disturbance, it is unreasonable to assume that the Federal Reserve would let higher deposit rates alter the selected timepath.[17] This offsetting behavior of the Federal Reserve is achieved in the simulations by having the taxable primary security rate take on the value that keeps aggregate nonfinancial investment equal to an unchanged level of saving. The issues-equal-purchases market-clearing equation for the taxable securities market then determines the required Federal Reserve net security purchases or sales.

Most of the remaining 14 equations explain the interest income, expense, and saving (retained earnings) of the depository institutions.[18] Interest income is related to current and lagged values of yields on and purchases of a variety of securities, and interest expense depends on current passbook-account yields and quantities and current and lagged certificate yields and purchases. To illustrate, an expression for the saving of a depository institution is:

$$SAV = r(1 - t)[R\text{frm}FRM + R\text{vrm}VRM + \text{Other Interest Income} - R\text{pass}PASS$$
$$- R\text{cert}CERT - \delta TFA] \tag{5.1}$$

where r is the retention rate, t is the tax rate, FRM and VRM represent book values of fixed- and variable-rate mortgages, PASS and CERT denote passbook and certificate accounts, average interest rates on assets and liabilities are represented by Rx where x is the lowercase of the variable on which the yield is

Table 5-4
Nonfinancial Investment Responses to a Percentage Point Increase in Various Interest Rates

Lag	Home Mortgage Rate		Corporate Bond Rate		Tax-exempt Bond Rate
	1-4 Family Housing	*Multifamily Housing*	*Consumer Durables*	*Nonresidential Plant and Equipment*	*State and Local Gov't. Structures*
0	−315	−64	−66	—	−102
1	−369	−87	−88	−37	−73
2	−116	−105	−66	−55	−54
3	—	−93	−15	−55	−44
4	—	−67	−10	−37	−42
5	—	−34	−12	—	—
6	—	—	−13	—	—
⋮	⋮	⋮	⋮	⋮	⋮
20	—	—	−5	—	—
Σ	−800	−460	−440	−184	−315

Note: Outlays are in millions of dollars at quarterly rates; interest rates are in percentage points. The interest rate elasticities of the *outlays* are, from left to right, roughly −0.75, −1.0, −0.9, −0.05, and −0.25.

earned (paid), and TFA is total financial assets. The coefficient δ reflects the relationship between operating expenses of the institution and its size. The average portfolio yields on fixed-rate mortgages in turn are expressed as

$$R\text{frm} = R\text{frm}_{-1} \frac{\text{FRM}_{-1}}{\text{FRM}} + R\text{mor} \frac{\Delta\text{FRM}}{\text{FRM}} + (R\text{mor} - R\text{rep}^f)\lambda \frac{\text{FRM}_{-1}}{\text{FRM}} \quad (5.2)$$

where Rmor is the current mortgage rate, $R\text{rep}^f$ is the average yield on the mortgages that are repaid, and λ is the percent of the stock of outstanding mortgages repaid ($R\text{rep}^f$ and λ are both functions of recent changes in Rmor). Multiplying equation 5.2 by FRM, the left side equals the total interest earned on FRMs. This is, moving to the right side, the interest earned last period plus the interest earned on *net* purchases of FRMs during the current period plus any additional interest generated by rolling over old mortgage funds at higher current rates (or dissipated if the current rate is less than the repayment rate).

Other average portfolio yields and costs are explained similarly. A particularly relevant one for the deposit rate simulations is the average cost of certificates. It is assumed that all certificates have a maturity of two years. Assuming no early redemptions, the average cost of certificates is:

$$R\text{cert} = R\text{cert}_{-1} \frac{\text{CERT}_{-1}}{\text{CERT}} + R\text{new} \frac{\Delta\text{CERT}}{\text{CERT}} + (R\text{new} - R\text{new}_{-8}) \frac{\Delta\text{CERT}_{-8}}{\text{CERT}}$$

$$+ (R\text{new} - R\text{new}_{-16}) \frac{\Delta\text{CERT}_{-16}}{\text{CERT}} + \ldots \quad (5.3)$$

That is, gross new issues equal current net issues plus net issues 8, 16, 24, etc., quarters earlier. The assumption of a shorter term to maturity would result in a faster rise in the average cost of certificates, while a longer term to maturity would result in a less rapid rise in the average cost.

The last two equations relate savings of households and the Treasury to the altered savings of the depository institutions. To illustrate, assume that the increase in deposit rates raises household net interest income and institutional net interest expense by X. If we aggregate all institutions for ease of exposition, their decline in savings is given by $r(1 - t_i)X$, where t_i is their marginal tax rate. Households, on the other hand, receive an extra X in interest but lose $(1 - r)(1 - t_i)X$ in dividends. Their after-tax change in income, all of which is assumed to be saved, is $(1 - t_h)[1 - (1 - r)(1 - t_i)]X$. Treasury tax receipts change by $t_h[1 - (1 - r)(1 - t_i)]X - t_i X$, leading to a smaller (larger) deficit and thus fewer (greater) issues of securities. Thus aggregate saving as well as aggregate nonfinancial investment is unchanged, but the sectoral distribution can shift greatly. The detailed measurement of the earnings gains and/or losses of the aggregate depository institutions is the third, and last, important difference between our model-simulations and those of previous investigators.

Low Deposit Rate Elasticities

New-issue certificate rates rise by 75, 60, and 103 basis points, respectively, for the first three years of the simulation (the data given in table 5-5 for the years 1973, 1974, and 1975 actually refer to the periods 724-733, 734-743, and 744-753). The fall in 1974 and rise in 1975 follows from the movement in the

Table 5-5
The Impact of an Increase in Certificate Yields, Low Deposit Interest Rate Elasticities

	1973	1974	1975	Sum
Interest Rates (yearly average in basis points)				
New Issue certificate yield	75	60	103	
Average yield on SLA certificates	24	44	69	
One-year treasuries	11	−33	12	
Home mortgage	−4	−3	−9	
Tax-exempt bonds	8	25	51	
Corporate bonds	5	−13	−	
Deposits and Other Items (end of third quarter, billions of $)				
Deposits at CBs[a]	1.3	3.4	2.0	
Deposits at SLAs	1.4	3.2	2.7	
Deposits at mutual savings banks	0.5	1.1	0.8	
CB reserves	0.1	0.3	0.4	
CB tax-exempts	−1.3	−7.2	−12.6	
Retained Earnings (billions of $)				
CBs	−0.05	−0.33	−0.38	−0.76
SLAs	−0.20	−0.40	−0.70	−1.30
Mutual savings banks	−0.08	−0.16	−0.32	−0.55
Other	0.33	0.89	1.40	2.61
	0	0	0	0
Nonfinancial Investment (billions of $)				
1-4 family housing	0.12	0.14	0.33	0.59
Multifamily housing	−0.03	−	0.10	0.07
State and local structures	−0.06	−0.19	−0.49	−0.74
Other	−0.03	0.05	0.06	0.08
	0	0	0	0
Single-family starts (thousands)	6	4	11	21

[a]Excludes demand deposits and large negotiable CDs at weekly reporting banks.

one-year Treasury rate to which the new-issue certificate rates are tied. The average cost of the entire SLA outstanding stock of certificates rises steadily as outstandings are rolled over at the higher yields. The increased certificate yield generates a relatively small inflow of funds into depository institutions, $2 to $4 billion at thrifts and somewhat less at CBs. Given the investment of these institutions, especially SLAs, in home mortgages, the supply of these funds increases, and the mortgage yield declines by a modest amount (3 to 9 basis points). Housing starts and construction outlays rise in response to this decline.

The decrease in CB earnings due to the rise in certificate rates has an important impact on relative long-term interest rates. The income from tax-exempt securities is attractive to CBs only if banks have profits and thus taxes to avoid.[19] If banks have expenses to deduct from interest income, then the tax treatment of the income is irrelevant; banks will simply choose the investments earning the highest risk-adjusted rates of return. Thus the increase in interest expense relative to interest income causes CBs to shift sharply out of tax exempts (12½ billion by the end of three years), a shift that raises the tax-exempt yield by 50 basis points by the third year. State and local government construction outlays decline as a result.

As noted earlier, the short-term taxable rates and the other long-term rate in the model, that on corporate bonds, are assumed to be moved by the Federal Reserve in a manner necessary to maintain total nonfinancial investment at its predisturbance level. In this case the corporate rate first rises to offset the excess of the increase in 1-4 family-housing outlays over the decline in STL structures and then falls when the decline in STL structures is greater than the rise in 1-4 housing. As can be seen in table 5-5, the changes in the composition of nonfinancial investment induced by the increase in certificate rates is quite minor due to the relatively small shifts in deposits that occur. Outlays on 1-4 family housing rise by a cumulative total of $600 million over the three years, and construction expenditures of STLs decline by $750 million. Other outlays are affected even less.

The final response of interest is the decline in income of thrifts. SLAs experience a cumulative decline in retained earnings of $1.3 billion, and mutual savings banks (MSBs) suffer a $.55 billion loss. The declines are particularly severe in the third year; according to our estimates, aggregate retained earnings of the two industries would have been less than half of the observed amount for 1975 in the absence of ceilings on certificate rates during the 1973-1975 period. Given the dispersion in experiences of different institutions, a number of them would undoubtedly have had negative earnings.

High Deposit Rate Elasticities

We next consider the case in which high deposit rate elasticities exist (the underlying data are listed in table 5-6). Given both the sensitivity of depositors

Table 5-6
The Impact of an Increase in Certificate Yields, High Deposit Rate Elasticities

	1973	1974	1975	Sum
Interest Rates (yearly average in basis points)				
New Issue certificate yield	140	77	20	
Portfolio yield on SLA certificates	58	98	71	
One-year treasuries	84	−28	−118	
Home mortgage	−21	−37	−28	
Tax-exempt bonds	5	20	104	
Corporate bond	40	16	−41	
Deposit and Other Items (end of third quarter, billions of $)				
Deposits at CBs[a]	11.9	26.3	34.8	
Deposits at SLAs	11.3	24.3	31.8	
Deposits at MSBs	3.8	9.3	13.0	
CB reserves	−0.1	0.8	1.3	
CB tax-exempts	4.5	−5.0	−27.3	
Retained Earnings (billions of $)				
Commercial banks	0.25	−0.30	−1.27	−1.32
Savings and loan associations	−0.51	−0.94	−0.72	−2.17
Mutual savings banks	−0.20	−0.40	−0.41	−1.01
Other	0.46	1.64	2.40	4.50
	0	0	0	0
Nonfinancial Investment (billions of $)				
1-4 family housing	0.55	1.45	1.30	3.30
Multifamily housing	−0.26	−0.85	−0.61	−1.72
State and local structures	−0.04	−0.17	−0.90	−1.11
Other	−0.25	−0.43	0.21	−0.47
	0	0	0	0
Single-family starts (thousands)	28	48	36	112

[a]Excludes demand deposits and large negotiable certificates of deposit (CDs).

to interest rates and the sharp rise in certificate yields relative to open-market rates, deposit flows into SLAs and CBs are increased by over $30 billion each by late 1975. Not surprisingly, the resultant mortgage purchases tend to lower the home mortgage rate sharply relative to other yields, and starts and outlays on 1-4 family housing rise much more than in the case where deposit rate elasticities are lower. As a result of this expanded rise in single-family outlays, the yields on other taxable securities must be increased by the Federal Reserve to generate offsetting declines in other investment categories. The sharp rise in short-term rates—the one-year Treasury rate is up by 84 basis points, on average, during the first year—leads to a major difference in the short-run impact of the increased deposit rates on CB income and thus yields on tax-exempt securities. Because the asset portfolio of banks is relatively short term, bank interest income increases more than interest expense for the first year and a half. This raises bank demand for tax exempts and offsets much of upward pull on the exempt yield caused by the rising corporate bond rate that induces households to shift out of exempts and into taxables. Eventually, though, the lagged negative impact of higher bond rates and investment outlays builds up, inducing expansionary Federal Reserve action to reverse the rise in short-term rates. With interest income falling and expense growing owing to the increased certificate accounts and rolling over of existing accounts at higher yields, bank income and thus demand for tax exempts fall sharply. By late 1975 bank holdings of tax exempts are down by $27 billion ($13 billion below the end of 1972 level), and the tax-exempt rate is up by a full percentage point (the ratio of exempt to taxable 20-year rates is up by 0.15).

Because the short-term interest rates with which certificate rates are assumed to rise more rapidly early in the simulation, the average cost of certificates of the thrifts rises more rapidly, and thrift earnings are depressed more in 1973 and 1974. SLAs, for example, lose a $½ billion in 1973 and $1 billion in 1974. Over the three years, they suffer a cumulative loss of $2¼ billion and MSBs lose $1 billion.

The more exaggerated impact of increased deposit rates when deposit interest rate elasticities are greater also generates greater shifts in the composition of nonfinancial investment. More specifically, single-family starts are up by a cumulative total of 112,000, and outlays on 1-4 family housing are increased by $3.3 billion. Half of this increase is at the expense of multifamily housing, and a third comes from STL structures.[20]

Conclusions

The world in which investors are quite sensitive to changes in yields on deposit accounts is probably the world envisioned by both advocates and opponents of removal of deposit rate ceilings. Advocates cite the enlarged deposit market and thus greater funds that thrifts (and CBs) have to invest in home mortgages. As a result, housing fares better during periods of rising interest rates than it would in the presence of ceilings; with higher deposit elasticities, cumulative starts in the 1973-1975 period are 112,000 greater. Opponents of removal, on the other hand, refer to the impact of this scenario on earnings of depository institutions. CBs would have had over a billion less in retained earnings in 1975. Nonetheless, in normal circumstances they could, at least in the aggregate, manage. The data in table 5-1 indicate that CB-retained earnings would have been nearly $5 billion in 1975 in the absence of the extraordinary increase in provisions for loan losses ($4¼ billion without the loan-loss adjustment), and this was up nearly $1½ billion since 1972. SLAs, on the other hand, were in a tighter box. Their retained earnings equaled only $1½ billion in 1972 and fell slightly between then and 1975. The estimated decline in retained earnings would have cut aggregate earnings in half (by two thirds in 1974) and would have caused some institutions to have significantly negative earnings.

Depositors, on the other hand, would have received about $7 billion extra in interest income (about $5 billion in after-tax income) and lost nearly $½ billion in dividends. Households also would have paid 1/4 to 1/3 percentage points less on home mortgages issued during this period and found mortgage funds more available. One-to-four family mortgage debt is up by $28 billion by the end of 1975, only about a tenth of which finances new construction. Finally, households would have earned more on holdings of tax-exempt securities, but they also would have had to pay higher state and local taxes to finance the higher interest payments.

How thrifts would fare in the longer run as a result of paying higher deposit rates during a period like 1973-1975 depends greatly on the subsequent behavior of interest rates. According to our estimates, SLAs would have purchased an additional $25 billion in home mortgages paying an average yield of just over 8½%. If mortgage rates were to fall slightly (not enough for these mortgages to be financed) and short- and intermediate-term (up to six years) open-market rates were to fall significantly, then thrifts would do very well. The average effective cost of financing the mortgages over their life might be only 6½%, giving an average effective spread to SLAs of over 2 percentage points. On the other hand, if interest rates were to rise further (the 1973-1978 period following the 1969-1970 period comes to mind), then the average cost of financing the mortgages could exceed the income from the mortgages, and the incremental $25 billion in mortgages could be an increasing drain on SLA income over time.

Another pertinent factor is the likely impact of higher deposit rates on non-interest-rate competition for funds. Allowing greater interest rate competition for deposits would result in fewer branches, reduced advertising, and elimination of the offering of gifts to those opening new accounts. The decline in these expenses could offset a significant fraction of increases in average interest expense.[21]

Increases in Deposit Rates When Variable-Rate Mortgages Exist

If depositors are interest sensitive, simple removal of deposit rate ceilings would stimulate housing construction, but thrift earnings would be halved or worse in the aggregate. Given the latter, some doubt regarding the viability of the thrift industry could (and should, if interest rates continue to rise) develop. And this could undermine the expansion in housing as most of the housing lobby obviously fear (Hester 1977, pp. 656-657). Fortunately, a device that would both maintain thrift income and stimulate housing activity during periods of rising deposit rates could be easily introduced. Variable-rate mortgages (VRMs) where the rate is tied to the cost of funds would largely "finance" the payment of higher thrift deposit rates, thereby removing this threat to thrift viability as an impediment to the expansion of mortgage lending and thus housing demand. This section attempts to illustrate how VRMs would play this role.

Implementing the Assumptions Underlying the Simulations

The basic assumption is that half of CB, SLA, and MSB home mortgages were in VRMs during the 1972-1975 period. The difficulty in implementing this assumption in a useful manner stems from the sharp jump in interest rates, including the cost of funds of depository institutions, in the 1960s and early 1970s. The cost of funds for SLAs, for example, rose by 170 basis points between 1955 and 1968 and another 70 basis points between 1968 and 1972. Assuming that half of mortgage holdings in 1972 were VRMs would give the institutions substantial additional income even if yields did not rise in the future. And our purpose is to deduce the likely impact of the existence of VRMs during the rising portion of an interest rate cycle, not to calculate the impact in the early 1970s following from the postwar rise in interest rates.

Our method of introducing VRMs is best illustrated by writing a hypothetical expression to explain the average portfolio yield on VRMs that is comparable to equation 5.2 for fixed-rate mortgages:

$$R\text{vrm} = R\text{vrm}_{-1} \frac{\text{VRM}_{-1}}{\text{VRM}} + R\text{mor} \frac{\Delta\text{VRM}}{\text{VRM}}$$

$$+ (R\text{mor} - R\text{rep}^v)\lambda \frac{\text{VRM}_{-1}}{\text{VRM}} + \Delta R\text{cf}_{-1}(1-\lambda)\frac{\text{VRM}_{-1}}{\text{VRM}} \qquad (5.4)$$

where VRM is the quantity of variable-rate mortgages, $R\text{vrm}$ is the average yield on the VRM portfolio, $R\text{mor}$ is the current or new-issue mortgage rate, λ is the percent of the stock of outstanding mortgages repaid each quarter, $R\text{rep}^v$ is the average yield on the mortgages that are repaid, and $R\text{cf}$ is the cost of funds of the institution. The repayment rate should be last period's portfolio yield, $R\text{vrm}_{-1}$. In order that the introduction of VRMs does not arbitrarily jump the interest-income stream flowing to depository institutions, the VRM portfolio yield in the period prior to the start of the simulation is arbitrarily set equal to the FRM portfolio yield, that is, $R\text{vrm}_{-1} = R\text{frm}_{-1}$. To keep the yields on VRMs and FRMs equal in subsequent periods, *except for the impact of increases in the cost of funds raising the portfolio yield on VRMs,* the repayment yield on VRMs is set equal to that on FRMs.

The simulations are run over the same 724-754 period as before with the CB certificate rate again set equal to 70 basis points plus an average of current and recent one-year Treasury rates and thrift certificate rates tied to the bank rate. In preliminary simulations, the cost of funds jumped rapidly because certificate rates rose quickly. In order to approximate California-type dampers on VRMs, the change in the cost of funds was simply set equal to 12½ basis points in all quarters from 732 to 754, that is, beginning in the third quarter of the simulation. Because these simulations closely approximate the ones without VRMs in all respects but one, only that in which the higher deposit interest rate elasticities are assumed is reported.

Results

The simulation results are summarized in table 5-7, which has the same form as tables 5-5 and 5-6. Comparison of tables 5-6 and 5-7 reveal close similarity in all but the retained-earnings variables. The responses of the interest rates, deposits, and the nonfinancial investment variables are so close in fact that these parts of table 5-7 will not be discussed.

Comparing the total impact on retained earnings (savings) during the three years, we see that all depository institutions suffer smaller declines in income when VRMs exist, and households experience smaller gains. Moreover, the percentage reduction in the decline in income for a sector is smaller the smaller a portion of its portfolio the sector has invested in home mortgages. The CB loss is cut by 17%, the MSB loss is cut by 27%, and the SLA loss is cut by 58%. All of this is as expected.

What might be somewhat surprising and disappointing is the fact that SLAs still lose nearly a billion dollars. However, this can easily be explained by looking at the impact in individual years. Note that all the negative impact on SLA income occurs in the first two years. Because dampers have been placed on the rise in the rate on VRMs—the rise does not start until the third quarter of the simulation and is then limited to 12½ basis points per quarter—interest expense for SLAs initially rises much more rapidly than interest income generated by VRMs. By the third year, however, interest income has caught up. (And having more than half their home mortgages in VRMs would mean that SLA interest income would catch up faster.) Further, even if interest rates and the average cost of certificates continued to rise in the future, income from VRMs would cover the increased interest cost until the maximum 2½-percentage-point restriction on the increase in the rate on VRMs became binding, and this would not occur for another year and a half. Thus it does appear that VRMs are a means by which thrifts can eliminate their maturity-imbalance problem and thus have interest income and expense more in unison.

Table 5-7

The Combined Effect of Flexible Certificate Rates and the Existence of VRMs during a Period of Rising Interest Rates

	1973	1974	1975	Sum
Interest Rates (yearly average in basis points)				
New Issue certificate yield	140	79	25	
Average yield on SLA certificates	58	98	75	
One-year treasury bills	85	−26	−110	
Home mortgage	−21	−36	−26	
Tax-exempt bonds	4	20	89	
Corporate bonds	40	17	−38	
Deposits and Other Items (end of third quarter, billions of $)				
Deposits at CBS	12.0	26.2	36.2	
Deposits at SLAs	11.3	24.1	32.4	
Deposits at MSBs	3.8	9.2	13.3	
Commercial bank reserves	−0.1	0.8	1.2	
Commercial bank tax-exempts	4.9	−3.3	−23.6	
Retained Earnings (billions of $)				
CBs	0.26	−0.23	−1.12	−1.09
SLAs	−0.44	−0.54	0.07	−0.91
MSBs	−0.18	−0.32	−0.24	−0.74
Other	0.36	1.09	1.29	2.74
	0	0	0	0
Nonfinancial Investment (billions of $)				
1-4 family housing	0.55	1.43	1.26	3.24
Multifamily housing	−0.26	−0.86	−0.67	−1.79
State and local structures	−0.04	−0.12	−0.75	−0.91
Other	−0.25	−0.45	0.16	−0.54
	0	0	0	0
Single-family sales (thousands)	28	48	34	110

Regulated Deposit Rate Ceilings when VRMs Exist

Experience of the last decade suggests that removal of deposit rate ceilings is easier said than done. Commission after commission and expert witness after expert witness have called for the removal of rate ceilings, but prospects seem no better now than five years ago.[22] The main obstacle is possible declines in thrift earnings of the nature described in the earlier simulations without VRMs. An alternative tack to simply removing restrictions against VRMs and ceilings on deposit rates would be to allow VRMs and then manipulate the rate ceilings so as to pass any resultant thrift income gains through to depositors.[23] This would, of course, eliminate the risk of large thrift losses and succeed in raising returns to depositors. In addition, the quarter-point advantage for thrifts could be maintained.

In this section a simulation is run over the 733-754 period where half of all home mortgages are assumed to be VRMs. The income VRMs would generate for SLAs is assumed to be paid out on certificate accounts. In the model simulations, the expression for SAV—equation 5.2—for SLAs determines $Rcert$, and SAV is treated as exogenous (held fixed). The expression for $Rcert$—equation 5.3—for SLAs determines the required new-issue certificate yield, given the average certificate yield necessary to "absorb" the increased income on VRMs. Because MSBs and particularly CBs have smaller portions of their assets in home mortgages, the existence of VRMs during a period of rising interest rates benefits them relatively less—raises the average yield on their total asset portfolio less—than it would benefit SLAs. As a result, VRMs are not likely to provide CBs and MSBs with enough income to match the increases in the SLA new-issue certificate yield. Nonetheless, we shall assume that they do match the increases and suffer net income losses (declines in retained earnings). In the model simulations, the CB and MSB new-issue certificate yields move with the SLA yield, the average-certificate-yield equations generate the resulting changes in the CB and MSB average certificate rates, and their savings equations measure the declines in retained earnings. Competition among institutions would likely produce this scenario of equally rising new-issue certificate yields if regulatory authorities raised ceiling yields on certificates in response to the increased income of SLAs. Treasury and household saving move in the manner described earlier so as to maintain total nonfinancial saving at its observed level.

Simulations were run with deposit-demand equations having low and moderate interest rate elasticities. The results with the higher elasticities are reported in detail; a few key results for the low elasticity simulation are referred to in footnotes. As in the earlier VRM simulations, California-type dampers have been approximated by simply setting $\Delta Rcf = 0.125$ per quarter.

The Results

The simulations begin in 733 (third quarter of 1973), the quarter in which the cost of funds of depository institutions began to rise significantly. For many interesting variables, the impact of VRMs differs notably between 1974 and 1975. For this reason data for these two years are listed separately in table 5-8, and the hypothetical effects of VRMs during each of the years is discussed separately.

1974. The increased income generated by VRMs during a period of rising cost of funds leads to higher certificate yields by assumption. The new-issue yield on all certificates rises by 72 basis points, and the average certificate cost to SLAs rises by 40 basis points. The rise in the certificate rate channels funds from the market for taxable securities to thrifts who invest relatively heavily in home mortgages. The result is a decline in the yield on home mortgages (13 basis

Table 5-8
Impact of VRMs on Interest Rates and Nonfinancial Investment and Saving

	1974	1975	Sum
Interest Rates (basis points)			
New Issue certificate rate	72	100	
Portfolio certificate cost (SLAs)	40	76	
Home mortgage	−13	−25	
Corporate bond	23	21	
One-year treasury bill	36	11	
Long-term tax-exempt	−3	15	
Nonfinancial Saving (millions of $)			
CBs	202	−141	61
MSBs	−70	−208	−278
Treasury	97	−93	4
Households	−229	442	213
Σ	0	0	0
Memo: CB demand for tax-exempts (end of year in billions of $)	3.6	−1.3	
Nonfinancial Investment (millions of $)			
1-4 family housing	493	1049	1542
Fixed business nonresidential	−98	−157	−255
Multifamily housing	−283	−653	−936
State and local structures	25	−99	−74
Net consumer durables	−137	−140	−277
Σ	0	0	0
Memo: Member bank reserves (end of year in billions of $)	0.0	0.4	
Single-family housing starts	19,000	34,000	53,000

points) and increases in the yields on other taxable securities (the corporate bond rate by 23 basis points and the one-year Treasury bill rate by 36 basis points). Offsetting forces operate on the tax-exempt yield. The yield tends to rise because households shift from tax-exempt securities to taxables in response to the rise in taxable yields, but it tends to fall because the rise in CB profits—CBs pay out less additionally on certificates than they receive on their short-term assets and VRMs—raises CB demand for tax exempts (by $3½ billion by the end of the year). The net result is a minuscule decline.

Looking more closely at changes in savings or retained earnings, MSBs suffer a $70 million loss; they pay out more on certificates than they receive on VRMs because they have a smaller proportion of their total assets in home mortgages, and thus VRMs, than do SLAs. (Recall that SLAs by assumption pay out all additional income generated by increases in the yield on their VRM portfolio to certificate holders.) Due principally to the gain in tax revenues from CBs, the Treasury experiences a $100 million increase in income. Households, in contrast, lose $230 million in net income; interest expense on VRMs rises by far more than does interest income on certificates.

Turning to the impact of the changes in market interest rates on the composition of nonfinancial investment, single-family housing responds positively ($490 million) to the decline in the home mortgage rate, while multifamily housing, consumer durables, and nonresidential business investment decline due to the increase in the corporate bond rate. The largest decline is for multifamily housing ($280 million). The impact on single-family starts is a gain of 19,000 units.

1975. The average yield on VRMs at SLAs continues to rise, as do the new-issue and average cost of SLA certificates. The accelerated flow of funds to depository institutions depresses the home mortgage rate even further relative to what it otherwise would be. The corporate bond rate remains down 20 basis points, but the tax-exempt rate now rises by 15 basis points owing to a decline in CB profits and thus demand for tax exempts. Bank profits fall because of the even further rise in interest expense on certificates and a reduction in the magnitude of the increase in short-term rates (the one-year rate is up by only 11 rather than 36 basis points) and thus in bank interest income. Retained earnings of MSBs are impaired further, and the Treasury now loses and households experience a $450 million gain; the Treasury participates in bank losses rather than gains, and households gain more on certificates than they lose on VRMs.

The impact on the composition of nonfinancial investment in 1975 is similar in direction to 1974 but about twice as large. One difference is that state and local structures join all other components in being pushed out by increases in single-family housing, although multifamily housing still bears most (60%) of the burden. Single-family starts are up by 34,000.

Another view of the likely impact of VRMs during a period of rising interest rates is given by data in table 5-9. These data relate to the changes in the combined balance sheets of households, nonfinancial businesses, and state and local governments. On the asset side, the rise in certificate and tax-exempt yields causes over a $44 billion shift out of taxable primary securities. Households purchase most of the $1.3 billion reduction in tax-exempt demand by CBs (the other half billion is a reduction in net issues). Intermediary claims rise by $54 billion. On the liability side, businesses and state and local governments issue slightly fewer securities due to the decline in their nonfinancial investment and rise in borrowing costs, while household net issues of home mortgages rise by $12 billion. Less than a billion and a half of this is to finance new sales. The remainder is refinancing of existing homes; sales of existing as well as new homes increase in response to the easing of conditions in the home mortgage market.

Table 5-9

Impact of VRMs on Holdings and Outstandings of Private Domestic Nonfinancial Sectors, End 1975

(millions of $)

Assets	
Money, credit union shares, and consumer credit	−657
SLA shares	22217
MSB deposits	8382
CB deposits (excluding DD and CDs)	24507
Tax exempt securities	803
Taxable securities	−44399
Total	10853
Liabilities and Net Worth	
Home mortgages	11872
Other	−1179
Cumulated household saving	160
Total	10853

Conclusions

The prohibition against federally chartered institutions holding VRMs has a significant impact on the well-being of households, firms, and businesses during periods of sharply rising interest rates. The most obvious gainers from the prohibition are existing homeowners whose mortgage payments do not rise. The most obvious losers are depositors who receive a below-market rate of return due to the deposit rate ceilings that are imposed so as to prevent thrift earnings from falling too far; potential home buyers (both new and existing) who find new mortgage loans expensive and difficult to come by; and builders of single-family homes who find the downturn in starts to be greater than it otherwise would be.

The simulations provide estimates of the magnitudes of these gains and losses. The prohibition against VRMs costs depositors about $3½ billion in extra (before tax) income and saves existing homeowners a like amount in (before tax) mortgage interest. Regarding the impact on home builders and new homeowners, housing starts would have been 19,000 units greater in 1974 and 34,000 greater in 1975.[24] The impact on the building cycle is best viewed by contrasting the observed building recession with that which would have occurred in a world with VRMs. If a normal building year is considered to be 1,225 thousand single-family units, then the observed shortfall in 1974 and 1975 was 300,000 units. The existence of VRMs would have offset nearly 10% of the shortfall. On the other hand, if 1,075,000 units was viewed as normal for that period (in no year in the 1960-1970 period were starts as great as 1,075,000 units), then VRMs would have offset nearly 20% of the shortfall. Existing homeowners, wishing to trade upward or change locations, would also have benefited from VRMs. Not much more than a billion of the $12 billion hypothesized increase in mortgage credit is to finance sales of new homes; the remainder is extended on existing homes.[25]

Summary

There is one particularly straightforward implication of the analysis and simulation experiments. Increases in deposit rate ceilings during a period of sharply rising open-market interest rates would have a quite favorable impact on single-family housing activity, especially if thrifts held a significant portion (say, half) of their mortgage portfolios in VRMs. Our estimates suggest a 10-20% reduction in the shortfall of single-family starts during the production trough. This reduced volatility in housing activity would make the building of single-family houses a less risky business and could result in both lower housing prices and higher share prices for companies that build single-family homes (the risk-adjusted profit rate would rise). How striking these changes would be is unknown, but the direction of the change is certain. Why home builders and consumer groups do not lobby for such a deregulation is unclear.

Consumer groups should also be impressed with the substantial gain in interest income of depositors that comes at the expense of existing homeowners and shareholders of CBs. The greater expense of existing homeowners would simply balance the significant housing capital gains they generally reap during periods of rising inflation and interest rates. Those concerned with equity would certainly have to applaud cessation of the present income transfer from lower income depositors to middle income homeowners.

Another aspect of the simulations has less appeal: the relatively sharp rise in the borrowing rate of state and local governments owing to the reduced demand for tax exempts by CBs. However, another "deregulation" currently being considered, the subsidized taxable bond option, would mitigage the rise in tax-exempt yields by tying them to taxable yields. (The fact that "relative security supplies" in the two markets would no longer matter leads me to classify this option as deregulation.) While a 40% taxable bond option might not save state and local governments much expense today (early 1978), placing a ceiling on the ratio of yields on equally risky tax-exempt and taxable securities might be quite valuable at some future date, especially if reforms in the banking system lead to greater competition and reduced CB profits.

Notes

1. The most outspoken proponent of this view seems to be Meltzer (1970, 1974). For a rebuttal to some of Meltzer's empirical evidence, see Edelstein and Friend (1975, pp. 25-27).

2. Thurow (1972) takes the most extreme position; for rebuttals here, consider the Kane and Shapiro comments on Thurow's paper in the same publication. Maisel (1973) also appears to view credit allocation as having great potential.

3. For a full and nonpolemic discussion of selective-credit policies, see Kaminow and O'Brien (1975, chapter 1).

4. For an early discussion of this relation, see Anderson and Eisenmenger (1970).

5. See Jaffee (1976) for an especially enlightening discussion of this problem.

6. Kane argues, less persuasively, that SLAs would be better off without deposit rate ceilings (1976, 1978). See Hester (1977, pp. 656-657) for citations of thrift and related testimony against removal of deposit rate ceilings.

7. This legislation was dropped when the FHLBB agreed not to issue regulations permitting VRMs. A discussion of congressional views on VRMs is contained in *Hearings* (1975, pp. 1-4). More recent *Hearings* (1977) suggest that the sentiment against VRMs has decreased greatly.

8. The adjusted rate R_c^*, is calculated from the observed rate, R_c, as

$$R_c^* = 2 \left[\left(1 + \frac{R_c}{365}\right)^{\frac{365}{2}} - 1 \right]$$

This adjustment raises the certificate rate by 8 to 15 basis points.

9. Two-year certificates were offered with higher yields in 1970, but except for the first quarter the difference between two- and one-year certificate yields was matched by the difference between two- and one-year Treasury yields.

10. FDIC insurance makes default risk equal for certificates and treasuries, but the possible delay in obtaining one's funds if an institution experiences difficulties would also make certificates less attractive.

11. Kane's evidence [1978, table 2] is consistent with a general willingness of institutions to pay rates exceeding the four-year Treasury rate (the bill rate in Kane's table is not comparable to the four-year certificate rate), but not rates 2 percentage points above the Treasury rate, as some have suggested CBs generally did.

12. See the estimates provided by Gramlich and Hulett and Modigliani in Gramlich and Jaffee (1972) and by Hendershott and Lemmon (1975), for examples.

13. Errors exist in both the quantity and yield data. The deposit data should be partitioned into passbook and time or certificate accounts, and the latter should exclude accounts of over $100,000 that are not subject to deposit rate ceilings. Currently over half of large CDs at commercial banks—those at

nonweekly reporting banks—are included in regular time-deposit accounts [on this point, see Cook (1978)]. The yields on certificates at any point in time should be measured as those on the highest paying certificate relative to the same maturity Treasury securities; they should be compared with the yield on that maturity Treasury security; and the method of compounding the interest received on the alternative instruments should be identical.

14. The most prominent of these are Fair and Jaffee (1972), Jaffee (1973), and Jaffee and Kearl (1975).

15. An earlier version of the underlying financial model is described in detail in Hendershott (1977a).

16. The different equations were estimated on various subsets of quarterly data from the 1956-1976 period.

17. For an extended defense of this assumption and an illustration of how it is imposed on model simulation experiments, see Hendershott (1977b).

18. The income statements for SLAs and mutual savings banks are presented in Hendershott, Scott, and Winder (1977).

19. See Hendershott and Koch (1977, chapter 3) for a discussion of the demand for tax exempts by financial institutions.

20. To test how important the fall in state and local outlays (in response to the sharp increase in tax-exempt yields) is to the results, simulations were run assuming no response of these outlays. When STL outlays did not fall off, the mortgage and bond rates were 5 to 10 basis points higher. The stimulus to owner-occupied housing was about 20% less (outlays rose by $2.6 billion and starts by 82,000 units), and most (75%) of this was at the expense of multifamily housing.

21. Taggart (1978, p. 154) estimates that declines in other expenses of MSBs in Massachusetts would have offset 40% of the increase in interest expense in 1975 in the absence of deposit rate ceilings.

22. My favorite analysis and interpretation of this history and the issues involved is Hendershott and Villani (1978).

23. This tack is advocated by Hendershott and Villani (1978).

24. In the simulation with low certificate interest elasticities, the inflow of funds to SLAs is less, the mortgage rate falls by less, and the impact on starts is only 7,000 in 1974 and 11,000 in 1975.

25. The comparable figures in the low elasticity simulation are a $3.7 billion increase in mortgage credit with less than a half billion financing new home sales.

References

Anderson, Paul S., and Eisenmenger, Robert W. "Structural Reform with the Variable Rate Mortgage," *Housing and Monetary Policy,* Conference Series No. 4, FRB of Boston, 1970.

Cook, Timothy Q. "The Impact of Large Time Deposits on the Growth Rate of M_2," *Economic Review,* FRB of Richmond, March/April 1978.

Cook, Timothy Q. and Hendershott, Patric H. "The Impact of Taxes, Risk, and Relative Security Supplies on Interest Rate Differentials," *Journal of Finance,* 1978.

Edelstein, Robert H. and Friend, Irwin. "The Allocative Efficiency of the Private Housing Finance Sector," *Resources for Housing,* First Annual Conference, FHLB of San Francisco, 1975.

Fair, Ray C. and Jaffee, Dwight M. "The Implications of the Proposals of the Hunt Commission for the Mortgage and Housing Markets: An Empirical Study," *Policies for a More Competitive Financial System,* Conference Series No. 8, FRB of Boston, 1972.

Gramlich, Edward M., and Jaffee, Dwight M., eds. *Savings Deposits, Mortgages, and Housing,* Lexington, Mass.: Lexington Books, D.C. Heath, 1972.

Hearings on Variable Rate Mortgage Proposal and Regulation Q, 94th Cong., 1st sess., April 1975.

Hearings on Alternative Mortgage Instruments, 95th Cong., 1st sess., October 1977.

Hendershott, Patric H. *Understanding Capital Markets: Volume 1: A Flow of Funds Financial Model.* Lexington, Mass.: Lexington Books, D.C. Heath, 1977*a*.

_____. "Model Simulations of the Impact of Selective Credit Policies and Financial Reforms: The Appropriate Monetary Policy Assumption," *Journal of Banking and Finance,* September 1977*b*.

Hendershott, Patric H., and Koch, Timothy W. *An Empirical Analysis of the Market for Tax-exempt Securities,* Monograph Series in Finance and Economics, NYU GBA Center for the Study of Financial Institutions, 1977-3.

Hendershott, Patric H., and Lemmon, Richard C. "The Financial Behavior of Households: Some Empirical Estimates," *Journal of Finance,* June 1975.

Hendershott, Patric H.; Scott, Jonathan A.; and Winder, James P. "Endogenizing Income Statements of Thrift Institutions," *Institute for Research in the Behavioral, Economic and Management Sciences,* Krannert Graduate School of Management, Paper No. 628, September 1977.

Hendershott, Patric H., and Villani, Kevin E. *Reform of the Housing Finance System.* Washington, D.C.: American Enterprise Institute for Public Policy Research, 1978.

Hester, Donald. "Special Interests: The Fine Situation," *Journal of Money Credit and Banking,* November 1977.

Jaffee, Dwight M. "The Asset/Liability Maturity Mix of S&Ls: Problems and Solutions," *Change in the Savings and Loan Industry,* Proceedings of the Second Annual Conference, FHLB of San Francisco, 1976.

_____. "The Impact of Removing Regulation Q Ceilings from Savings and

Loan Associations," *Journal of the Federal Home Loan Bank Board,* August 1973.

Jaffee, Dwight M., and Kearl, James. "Macroeconomic Simulations of Alternative Mortgage Instruments." In *New Mortgage Designs for Stable Housing in An Inflationary Environment* edited by Modogliani and Lassard, Conference Series No. 14. FRB of Boston, January 1975.

Kaminow, Ira, and O'Brien, James B., eds. *Studies in Selective Credit Policies.* FRB of Philadelphia, 1975.

Kane, Edward J. "Institutional Implications of the Changing Regulatory and Technological Framework for S&L Competition," *Change in the Savings and Loan Industry,* Proceedings of the Second Annual Conference, FHLB of San Francisco, 1976.

_____. "Good Intentions and Unintended Evil: The Case Against Selective Credit Allocation," *Journal of Money Credit and Banking,* February 1977.

_____. "Getting Along Without Regulation Q: Testing the Standard View of Deposit Rate Competition during the 'Wild-Card Experience'," *Journal of Finance,* June 1978.

Maisel, Sherman. "Improving Our System of Credit Allocation," *Credit Allocation Techniques and Monetary Policy,* Conference Series No. 11, FRB of Boston, 1973.

Meltzer, Allan H. "Regulation Q: The Money Markets and Housing-I," *Housing and Monetary Policy,* FRB of Boston, Conference Series No. 4, 1970.

_____. "Credit Availability and Economic Decisions: Some Evidence from the Mortgage and Housing Markets," *Journal of Finance,* June 1974.

Stigler, George J. "The Theory of Economic Regulation," *The Bell Journal of Economics and Management Science,* Spring 1971.

Taggart, Robert A., Jr. "Effects of Deposit Rate Ceilings," *Journal of Money Credit and Banking,* May 1978.

Thurow, Lester C. "Proposals for Rechanneling Funds to Meet Social Priorities," *Policies for a More Competitive Financial System,* Conference Series No. 8, FRB of Boston, 1972.

Comment

Michael A. Redisch

My comments address regulatory reform and the banking industry as they are perceived by Mr. Schotland in his presentation. He attempts to come to grips with broad methodological issues applicable to many aspects of regulation in our modern society; he then tries to relate these to the current regulatory framework and proposals for reform in the banking and securities industries.

I feel that he errs in suggesting that economic regulation of banks is simply a "panoply of techniques." It would be more instructive to view the current set of bank regulations as a series of governmental interventions into economic markets initiated with some specific ends in mind. An initial discussion of these presumed ends, or regulatory goals (that is, policy targets), will allow us to judge more rationally the effectiveness of specific regulations (that is, policy instruments). This is a particularly appropriate methodological framework with which to view regulation of financial institutions since the current patchwork regulatory framework was built up via an ad hoc process that resulted from the shock of the depression and the postdepression evolution in this country of markets and intermediaries. Different and often conflicting regulatory goals were typically not viewed as being part of a global system when individual regulations were designed and adopted. If the past excesses of this process are to be corrected through new regulatory reforms, then initially we must pay careful attention to the important matters of defining criteria for evaluating regulatory performance. This practice will allow us to specify more exactly just what it is we expect from regulators of our financial institutions.

Economists have traditionally justified regulatory intervention into economic markets when problems arise relating to issues of allocative efficiency or distributional equity. The latter are typically defined by politically determined distributional issues and broad-based social policies. The former involve four distinct types of "market failures": (1) natural monopoly, a declining cost industry; (2) externalities in production or consumption that private markets are not equipped to handle when individuals act as if their decisions affect only themselves; (3) inadequate information leading to poor decisions and wasted resources; and (4) that mythological creature, destructive competition (a situation arising where there are competing firms with high fixed costs, immobile capital, and low variable costs).

Mr. Schotland would prefer to view these not as examples of market failures but of inherent market weaknesses. He thinks of failures as events such as the 1971-1973 overexpansion in real estate investment trusts. Following a similar

Any views expressed in this paper are those of the author and do not necessarily reflect an official position of the U.S. General Accounting Office.

logic, many policy makers have reacted strongly to specific failures such as Penn Central, W.T. Grant, and Franklin National Bank.

An economist would turn this around and suggest that these are not examples of markets failing but of markets *working*. Perhaps these specific failures are the cause of a developing set of ambiguous public attitudes regarding unfettered competition and free markets. After all, the competitive process improves resource use in the long term in part by a process of social Darwinism that can destroy jobs, put firms out of business, or both. The threat of firm (not market) failure can help guarantee socially efficient resource use; actual firm failure can terminate misuse but at high cost to many individuals caught up, sometimes quite innocently, in the vortex.

Small wonder that more and more people are in favor of competition for everyone but themselves. Even members of our banking and securities industries, who view themselves as the guardians of the flow of capital into our so-called free-market system, have long been in favor of a government-run cartel to control behavior within their sectors.

Mr. Schotland joins this debate by noting that our nation's ideological commitment (our basic policy goal, so to speak) is toward free men. We have simply made the pragmatic judgment that free, competitive markets are a good means (that is, our policy instrument) of assuring this goal of free men and an open society. However, economists as a group seem to take this association more seriously than many others, and they make fewer cases for exceptions. While not all economists believe markets work perfectly, almost all economists think markets work more efficiently than other people think they do.

Evidence of their attitude is apparent in comparing the methodological biases of economists versus those of the lawyer class that legislates and implements most regulatory constraints placed on market behavior. Economists' systemic orientation leads them to search for general rules that may ensure global efficiency but often sacrifice individual equity. Lawyers, on the other hand, through the case-study approach are taught to discern the uniqueness of each situation. Economists note an unfortunate paradox: lawyers' searches for individual equity often lead to ad hoc case-by-case approaches in the regulatory arena. In the end the entire system may be corrupted.

I have found a succinct statement of the economists' case that is particularly appropriate to this conference, since it was written by lawyers and relates in context specifically to banking. The majority Supreme Court decision in *U.S.* vs. *Philadelphia National Bank* (which denied what was determined to be an anticompetitive bank merger) states: "Subject to narrow qualification, it is surely the case that competition is our fundamental national economic policy, offering as it does the only alternative to cartelization or governmental regimentation of large portions of the economy."

Let me now move on, as Mr. Schotland does in his paper, from generalities concerning economic markets, regulation, and the competitive process in our society to specifics concerning our banking sector. As noted earlier, when discussing prospects for bank regulatory reform, I felt there were more fruitful approaches than simply examining individual regulations as part of an ad hoc series of techniques. An alternative that I favor for an "overview" paper is to examine the regulatory process under the following headings:

1. What are the reasons for economic regulation? Discussion would entail both historical perspective and the current justification for a set of policy targets.
2. What economic regulations (the policy instruments) have in fact been adopted?
3. What has been the economic and social impact of those regulations?
4. What is the organizational structure that governs the regulatory structure? While this appears to be fertile ground in the banking area, it is often a red herring; to be successful, reformers must look into the "why" of regulation, not just the "how." Thus, I believe Mr Schotland is guilty of gross overstatement with his claim that recruitment of "good people" is the single key to better regulation.
5. What regulatory reform is appropriate?

In these brief comments I will state, without lengthy justification, how I would respond to the first of these queries. In order to comprehend the underlying rationale for any economic regulations, it is important to start by enumerating exactly what it is the firms in question do and what close substitutes are available. Banks perform three primary economic functions in our society:

1. They provide a payments mechanism (although the growth of electronic funds transfer threatens the monopoly commercial banks have had in this area) and in the aggregate help produce the nation's monetary base.
2. They provide a low-cost, zero-risk, small-denomination household asset that is more convenient and more divisible than savings bonds.
3. They (along with insurance companies, pension funds, investment banks, etc.) provide a series of financial intermediation services by tailoring the safety and maturity distribution of the stock of the community's assets and liabilities to meet the demands of borrowers and lenders.

With these functions in mind, let me state briefly what I believe to be the current and often conflicting rationales for and goal of economic regulation of banking activities:

1. soundness of the banking system (and the liquidity of the payments and intermediation functions);
2. safety for (small) individual depositors;

3. credit allocation (primarily housing but extending to other areas);
4. a smoothly functioning mechanism in place to carry out the nation's monetary policy;
5. promotion of competition and retardation of concentrated corporate power;
6. protection of the (small) borrower and other "proconsumer" concerns; and
7. privileged position of the status quo.

I will note in passing that the first two goals are provided for primarily through our system of deposit insurance. A central issue in regulatory reform is the extent to which the protective regulatory shields we have erected around banks are redundant methods of assuring these basic goals.

Society has chosen to attempt to achieve the third goal in an indirect manner through creation of a heavily regulated set of thrift institutions that are intended to transfer resources from the economy as a whole to the housing sector (without becoming a line item in the federal budget). Goal 5 is a reminder that while one set of regulations are intended to provide a protected environment within which banks can grow and prosper, there are other regulations to see to it that banks do not become too large or powerful.

Goal 7 is a catchall to denote two separate ideas. First, many believe it is not fair to disturb the value of charters created by our current regulations. Regulatory reform is likely to lead to windfall gains and losses to identifiable groups and will be opposed unless an equitable system of compensation can be devised. Second, there will always be risk adverse groups that prefer the certainty of our current system to the uncertainty of change.

Comment

Robert Lindsay

On Lee Pickard's paper, let me note chiefly that I am very sympathetic to his point of view. I sometimes get the feeling that the SEC has gone quite mad, and I am interested that Lee now seems to agree. He seems in fact one more good example of the famous dictum of Wilbur Cohen, who was secretary of HEW back in the 1960s. He said, "Where you stand depends on where you sit."

In trying to understand the SEC in recent years, I usually end up explaining to myself that the problem is all those damn lawyers—or, more precisely, all those lawyers *behaving* like lawyers. Then a news story I read this morning gave me the notion that the SEC may have been infiltrated by the CIA. The story said Chairman Williams had "asserted that the so-called right to financial privacy measure would, if enacted, delay agency investigations for months. . . ." This sounds like a national-security argument to me. Maybe the SEC wants to be the "National Security and Exchange Commission."

On Patric Hendershott's paper, I have a little more to say. It is an exceedingly useful undertaking and, without question, a high-quality piece of work. I must admit that simulations usually leave me disappointed. I know they are important to do because they are a terribly useful way to keep us all honest. Even so, the typical simulation paper, by its nature, first drags the reader through a set of numerical instructions, not too different from a maintenance manual for a ten-speed motorbike. The second half is then a kind of reading out loud of a printout, which usually leaves me, at least, with an uneasy feeling that the results may have been foreordained by a casual assumption in the earlier instructions that I missed because my attention was wandering.

Hendershott's paper has not escaped entirely these limitations of the genre, but it has stirred up, for me, a couple of lines of thinking that I find stimulating.

I am first interested in Hendershott's statement that: "If any inequities exist, they would seem to be in the current system. Existing homeowners reap substantial capital gains without even paying the going cost of funds . . . and potential first-home buyers and households wishing to change residences pay especially high yields or final mortgage funds unavailable altogether. . . ." (pp. 74-75).

I find this statement interesting as a general proposition about equity, and it is far from self-evident. It poses what might be called the early-settler issue. Should the people who arrive first at a land of milk and honey, and commit their resources to making a home there, be allowed no capital gains at all if later on the settlement grows and prospers? More generally, should real capital gains be taxed at rates well *above* those levied on regular income, perhaps all the way up to 100%? Put still differently, do all long-term contracts confer an unfair advantage, an unreasonable advantage, if elsewhere in the economy, rates or prices or wages of whatever rise thereafter?

There are probably two sub-issues here. The first is what we think is the appropriate return to dumb luck. Even if we could be sure of distinguishing between random good fortune and purposeful and perspicacious investment choice, we would still be reluctant, I think, to tax away or otherwise recapture all the gains from good fortune. This is a judgment, of course, about a social utility function, but I doubt that there is much support for taxing away *all* the early-settler gain even in the *transfer* of such wealth from one generation to another, much less the gain from continued possession by the early settler himself.

The second sub-issue is the appropriate reward for *off-peak* borrowing, and it is probably more a matter of efficiency than equity. Interest rates do rise and fall, even in the presence of general inflation, and inflation has not been with us always and will not be with us forever. Presumably in a market economy, the purpose of rising and falling rates is to encourage borrowing in the slack periods and to discourage it in tight-money times. Any investment demand that can be shifted into low-interest periods will help flatten out the roller-coaster of investment spending. Since this result is generally thought to be a good thing, maybe we should want to reward those who help make it happen. If we were to index away that interest rate effect, or some part of it—require borrowers to accept a floating mortgage rate—we would certainly diminish any tendency to postpone real outlays past a time of generally high demand for real investment resources in the economy.

Hendershott's simulations offer some evidence on this issue. He finds that the combination of VRMs with increases in the deposit rate ceiling during a period of sharply rising open-market interest rates would result in a "10-20% reduction in the shortfall of single-family starts during the production trough." The design of the simulation requires that this come at the expense of some other investment sector so that no overall shift between peak and off-peak can occur in the *total* volume of investment. Nevertheless, over the longer run, as he suggests, the narrowing amplitude of the building cycle would reduce business risk for builders and reduce housing prices. To be sure, this might not increase the total *resources* drawn into single-family-housing construction when the rest of the economy is also booming. It might simply mean a more efficient use of the same level of resources with less waste in the housing-construction industry. Still, the possibility remains—and I would think the probability—of a reduction in the rewards for off-peak borrowing, that is, an increase in congestion in the market for real capital resources.

The other line of noodling that was set off for me by Hendershott's simulation was triggered entirely by his results, as distinct from his statement about his own value system, but the two are related. In particular, I am thinking that for the cities, and especially the older cities, Hendershott's results are not good news. They are, in fact, bad news, *more* bad news.

One piece of ill-tidings is the encouragement his reforms would give to the building and buying of *new* single-family housing at the expense of owners of *existing* housing who had *not* planned to sell. There has been a lot of this already, in one form or another, and more of it is not what the older cities need at this point. Part of the problem of these urban centers has been suburbanization, part of it has been regional shift, and part of it has been the declining *national* rate of population growth, which has increased the chance that any given area will lose population in what is approaching a zero-sum game. These shifts are leaving in their wake, among other things, a much weakened market for existing homes in some parts of the older urban areas and a much weakened ability of some owners of those homes to maintain them, even those financed at the lower mortgage rates of earlier years.

A second piece of bad news for the cities is the "relatively sharp rise in the borrowing rate of state and local governments" (p. 95). On this point, let me end with two observations.

One is that many of the older cities, because of the troubles they already have in the municipal bond market—before Hendershott gives them still more trouble—have come to rely heavily on the temporary public-works programs of the federal government for their capital budgets—Pittsburgh, for example, for 65% of its capital budget in 1978 and Newark for 80% of its capital budget. And that program is now to end.

The second observation is on the capital spending for the maintenance of urban infrastructure that has remained *un*done, despite these federal monies. Engineering studies suggest, for example, that water mains should be replaced roughly every hundred years. In New York City, the current replacement rate implies an average useful life of 296 years. The repaving of city streets ought to occur every 15 to 25 years. New York City, which has 5,300 miles of city streets, has in recent years been replacing about 40 miles annually, which implies an average replacement cycle of something over a century and a half. I guess what I end up with is a call for a still bigger simulation. I hope when it is done, it will be as good as this one.

Comment

Lawrence J. White

Instead of providing specific comments on the papers in this session, I will try to provide a more general framework for interpreting much of the regulation that occurs in the financial markets. I offer three paradigms. In various forms these paradigms appear in the papers of this session and in many of the papers in the remainder of the conference.

As will be clear, I have strong views on these paradigms, and I shall not hesitate to air these views. However, my major purpose here is to set out these paradigms, expose them to scrutiny, and ask that readers of these papers think hard about them. I hope readers will ask themselves whether these paradigms are valid and provide a satisfactory basis for the kinds and extent of regulation that we find today.

Paradigm 1: Fragile Markets.

If unfettered competition is permitted, the large firms will drive out the small firms. The remaining large firms will "pull up the gates"; entry by small firms will no longer be possible. At the end of this process, monopoly-oligopoly will prevail in the market with the likely abuses of monopoly-oligopoly. Regulation is necessary to prevent this process from taking place.

This argument has been offered by defenders of regulation in virtually every regulated industry: banking, securities, airlines, trucking, water transportation, local transportation, insurance. One also hears it in industries that are currently unregulated such as retailing or services.

I would like to offer three comments on this paradigm. First, I seriously doubt that the economies of scale and the (nonregulatory) barriers to entry are very serious in the industries for which this argument is made.[1] In the absence of substantial economies of scale or serious barriers to entry, this kind of market concentration is unlikely to occur.

But second, suppose the economies of scale actually are substantial. In that case, perhaps we ought to allow the larger, more efficient firms to prevail. Why keep a group of small inefficient firms in existence artificially through regulation?[2] Artificial competition does not qualify for the same support that genuine competition receives from economists.

Finally, I would argue that usually it is not the large firms who "pull up the gates"; more often it is regulation and legal prohibitions that pull up the gates and prevent entry. It was CAB and British regulation that prevented Freddie Laker from offering his low-cost trans-Atlantic flights for many years. It is CAB regulation that is currently preventing World Airways from offering low-cost transcontinental flights. It is legal prohibitions that prevent anyone from competing with the U.S. Postal Service in delivering first-class mail. It is FCC regulation that has impeded cable-television and pay-television operators in their ability to compete with the existing networks. It was regulation that prevented entry for so long in telecommunications. It is Glass-Steagall that prevents the banking and securities industries from offering more competition to each other. And, as Pickard points out, it is a recent SEC regulation that has prevented new options markets from offering competition to the existing options markets (and perhaps reducing some of those options transactions costs about which Schotland complains). Unfortunately, the list could be extended much longer.

If I had to make the choice between unregulated concentrated markets in which entry is not legally impeded and regulated markets in which regulation forecloses entry, I would unhesitatingly opt for the former.

Paradigm 2: Widows-Orphans and Cheats-Charlatans.

On the demand side of markets are widows and orphans. They do not act in their own best interests. They are continually done in by the sellers. They never learn from their mistakes; they never acquire good advice; they never have any friends who can provide them with any useful help. And on the supply side are the cheats and charlatans who bilk the widows and orphans. These sellers do not worry about their long-run reputations, either because they are "fly-by-night" firms that do not expect to be in existence for the long run or, since the widows and orphans never learn, the sellers need not worry about reputations.

Well, maybe there are a few widows and orphans and a few charlatans and cheats in markets. But do we want to regulate and structure entire markets on the basis of this paradigm? Here, Pickard's call for cost-benefit analysis before regulation is imposed or extended should be heeded. I would argue that in financial markets, and especially in securities markets, we are dealing with relatively sophisticated demanders who largely can take care of themselves, who can acquire advice, and who can learn from their mistakes. Accordingly, we need to ask hard questions about the real costs of saving people from their own mistakes.[3]

In this context, I heartily endorse the Lorne-Mendelson call for a reexamination (and, I would argue, an abandonment) of the fiduciary obligations of the brokerage industry. I am struck by the large costs and serious delays in the development of a central market system that seem to be due to the fiduciary obligations of securities firms. There is a joke on Seventh Avenue that has the punch line, "Sam, you made the pants too long." Unfortunately, I have never learned the main body of that joke. But I do know the sequel: If Sam continued to make the pants too long, people would soon take their tailoring business elsewhere. Similarly, in the securities industry, if "Al, you sold the stock too short" were heard very often, people would soon take their securities business to someone other than Al. And that is the way it should be.

Paradigm 3: Investor Confidence

If someone in the securities industry does something of a dubious nature to an investor, the investor will pull his money out of the financial markets and probably put it in a pillow. And that investor will tell all of his friends, and they too will withdraw their money from the financial markets and put it into their pillows. In sum, investor confidence will be impaired generally because of the original dubious act.

Note immediately that this paradigm is quite different from the second paradigm. Here, demanders do learn, they do have memories, they do have friends, and they do give and receive advice.

This paradigm does offer something that an economist can sink his teeth into: This is an externality problem. The dubious act of securities firm X affects firms Y and Z in an uncompensated nonmarket fashion. But again we have to ask whether this problem is serious enough to warrant all the efforts that have been devoted to building up and maintaining investor confidence. How big is the problem? What does it take to impair or improve investor confidence? I do not know the answer to these questions, and unfortunately, I do not think that anyone knows. We all have "stories" concerning this confidence factor. But these "stories" are a far cry from the hard evidence that is necessary here.

One or more of these three paradigms frequently appear in discussions of financial regulation. They appear in many of the papers of this conference. I hope they will receive careful scrutiny.

Notes

1. For a number of studies of regulated industries that also include estimates of economies of scale and barriers to entry, see Phillips (1975).

2. There is only one economic reason that might be offered to justify preserving a large number of firms under these circumstances: preserving a large number of centers of initiative so as to encourage more rapid technological change.

3. A friend has suggested that "the SEC spends far too much of its time saving the doctors and dentists from their own greed."

Reference

Phillips, Almarin, ed. *Promoting Competition in Regulated Markets.* Washington, D.C.: Brookings Institution, 1975.

**Part II
The Securities Industry**

6 The Scope of Deregulation in the Securities Industry

Michael Keenan

The Meanings of Deregulation

Economic deregulation is a phenomenon so rare that economists in most countries may never experience it in their lifetimes. It is not surprising, therefore, that there seem to be no accepted theories about economic deregulation or even a precise definition of what the phrase means.[1] The lack of a model framework notwithstanding, our country has embarked on a grand series of experiments in deregulation this decade. The securities industry has been made one of the prized experimental subjects in this process, and like most guinea pigs, the industry is not exactly enthralled by some of the immediate consequences of the experiment.

The task of this paper is to describe the scope of deregulation in the securities industry. We begin in this section by reviewing possible meanings of "economic deregulation" as it might apply to the securities industry. The next section examines some of the issues in any theory of deregulation. It seems very doubtful that removal of a regulation on an industry has effects symmetrical (but in the opposite direction) with the effects associated with imposition of the regulation. The third section looks at price deregulation as it has occurred in the securities industry. While the consequences in this area have been dramatic and widely discussed in recent years, this area of deregulation may not have the greatest long-run consequences. The fourth section looks at changes in the regulation of securities products, and the fifth section examines structural deregulation that has taken place in this industry. That structural change is likely to have the greatest long-run consequences for the structure of the industry.

In a narrow technical way the concept of economic deregulation is easy enough to define. It is the abolishment by a government agency of a binding law or administrative regulation that affects economic decisions made by firms. Thus there are three critical elements in the process: (1) previously imposed regulations by a government entity (2) that are binding so that there is positive economic cost and (3) that when relaxed would lead firms to make other economic decisions.

The government agencies imposing regulations on the securities industry include the Securities and Exchange Commission with direct primary regulatory responsibility and a host of other agencies such as the Federal Reserve System, the Securities Investor Protection Corporation, the Justice Department, the

Attorney General offices of major states, and others. But this definition is too narrow for our purposes. The securities industry is almost unique in that primary day-to-day regulation is imposed not by government entities but by industry self-regulatory organizations.[2] These organizations include the National Association of Securities Dealers, the New York Stock Exchange and other exchanges, the Chicago Board of Trade and other commodity exchanges, and several professional associations imposing their own membership standards within the industry. Some of the most binding economic regulations have come from these groups, not government agencies, and the relaxation of their rules has been a major impetus for change.

It would be possible to go even further. There are informal traditions within the securities industry that are just as binding as government-imposed regulations. Examples include the way securities research is sold and paid for, the way investment-banking syndicates are formed and the type of display advertising such syndicates do, the fractions in which particular security types are quoted. Whenever one of these traditions is altered, wherever there is a new market innovation, wherever there is a structural change in the way a process in the industry is handled, are we to assume it to be economic deregulation? Such a broad interpretation would make almost any industry change or innovation a type of economic deregulation.

Traditions are breaking down in the securities industry, and some of these changes may have important economic consequences. However, in this paper we shall ignore these informal social shifts and focus on the formal instances of deregulation by government agencies or self-regulatory groups that have had, or may have, major impact on the firms in this industry.

Some Issues in the Theory of Regulation

Most attempts to look at regulation treat it as a goal or end rather than as an ongoing adaptive process.[3] Thus the measure of regulatory worth is apt to be how close it comes to some ideological extreme, where the particular characteristics of the extreme are set by whoever desires to possess the regulatory power. Social systems cannot be molded easily to the simple extremes one is likely to postulate so that direct attempts to devise regulatory mechanisms to achieve the desired ends may often have unanticipated consequences.

If regulation were more often viewed as a process for modifying some powerful ongoing system, certain advantages might obtain: (1) the goals one sets would more likely be "improvements" in the existing state or the damping down of undesirable characteristics rather than some simplistic idealization; (2) the costs of regulation and the modification of regulations would be more carefully considered; (3) the direct and indirect reactions of the system to new constraints or relaxation of existing constraints would be studied more carefully rather than waiting in hope for the new equilibrium. What we have said about regulation in general applies with even greater force to "economic regulation." Regulation of economic conduct is almost wholly means-ends regulation with little consideration of the transformation process or possible feedbacks of the promulgated rules. Simplistic economic regulation thrives on uniformity and constancy of behavior. Without great care, such regulation becomes an absolute deterrent to innovation; thus short-run economic efficiency is achieved at the expense of living with very great, longer-run inefficiencies.[4]

What are some of the pressures that have been alleged to create the need for strict regulation within the securities industry? One suggested pressure is that high profitability and easy capital mobility would attract a large number of dishonest firms that must be carefully excluded from the business. A second related pressure is that personal customer greed would lead individuals to make "irrational" decisions, so markets must be designed to prevent excessive speculation, gambling, or other types of chance-rewarded behavior. A different type of pressure arises from the historical production function forms in this industry. The complex transaction process for securities requires codification and standardization of procedures if the system is to operate smoothly. Another type of pressure comes from preconceived notions about what is the best industry structure for our economy. Thus some argue that for efficient capital raising in this country we need a securities industry with many firms, and competition would substantially reduce the number of firms in the industry.[5] A final illustration of felt pressures is the attempt to create regulations so that certain types of risks will appear to be absorbed by industry firms rather than transferred directly to customers. Thus customers are protected by market makers from abrupt stock fluctuations and by regulations on firms' capital structures from bankruptcy risk for funds and securities left on deposit.

The regulation that has occurred in the securities industry has thus had twin objectives: (1) regulation of ethical conduct and (2) regulation of economic conduct. Government regulation by the SEC has traditionally focused on ethical conduct. The focus has been on the prohibition of fraudulent activities and the curtailment of dishonest business practices. Thus in addition to preventing fraud, the regulators have discouraged brokerage firms or corporations offering to sell or purchase securities from offering misleading impressions, incomplete information, or high-pressure sales tactics. Ethical regulation also involves prescription of standards of conduct and professionalism. There are regulations on hiring (in terms of criminal and educational backgrounds), on training requirements (in terms of industry-wide tests), and on advertising practices. The intent and effect has been to put out of business those brokerage firms, those exchanges, those private corporations, those types of securities through which there has been more than minimal chicanery, hype, or gambling-type risk involved.

Regulation by the industry self-regulatory groups, particularly the exchanges, has constrained economic conduct as much as ethical behavior. Four areas are usually considered in evaluating the economic impact of regulation on the securities markets: (1) *allocative efficiency*—raising and allocating new capital and redistributing and revaluing existing capital in the secondary markets; (2) *operational efficiency*—the cost effectiveness of firms, production functions, the ability profitably to produce and market new securities industry products; (3) *market-stabilizing effects*—the ability of exchange and other trading arrangements to damp random order and price fluctuations; (4) *industry structure objectives*—the desire to maintain a given number of firms in the industry, to control entry and exit conditions in a particular way.[6]

Economic regulation in most industries is used to assert some public control over monopoly power. Most researchers believe that regulation in the securities industry was traditionally designed to promote cartel-like arrangements that preserved monopoly benefits for members of the industry.[7] The results of this regulation have been widely discussed elsewhere, so we will merely enumerate some of the major consequences: (1) non-price competition for customer business; (2) a large number of relatively small firms in a capital-intensive industry with apparent scale economies; (3) high hidden profitability, with most firms maintaining secrecy about their financial condition; (4) more exchanges than scale economies warrant; (5) market stabilization of small orders and of more securities than would occur in free markets; and (6) limited innovation in production technology or new marketing strategies.

Most of this is history and need not concern us here, for it is being swept away by the impact of deregulation decisions to be described in subsequent sections. Its only importance is that it provides the "state of the world" from which change is now taking place. Under a different scenario in which the industry might have been more public with less direct regulation by the self-regulatory groups, the changes now taking place would have seemed less dramatic.

If deregulation has any significant impact, it must be because the prior regulation had a significant impact as a binding constraint on the economic decisions that would have been made. And this is not a symmetrical relationship. For example, take the number of firms in the industry. As industries evolve, they go through transformations in the number and concentration of firms. A typical pattern might find the industry in the first third of its existence with a growing number of competing firms and relatively low concentration. By the time the industry reaches maturity, the number of firms may have been substantially reduced through merger or other forms of corporate death, and relative concentration may be considerably higher.[8] Suppose that at the end of the industry's first third of existence, regulations are imposed that act as stopping rules on industry evolution. The regulations might take the form of fixing minimum prices to protect the profitability of cost-inefficient firms; this would transfer revenues to smaller firms on the basis of special services provided (say, "research") that have minimal economic value; and entry into the industry would be constrained at key points with segregationist arguments (say, all insurance companies are unwelcome as stock exchange members).

These regulations might be imposed on the industry with minimal immediate impact. They preserve the status quo by slowing down (but never completely stopping as long as there are profits in the system) industry evolution. When deregulation occurs, there will be an impact as natural evolution proceeds. The change may even take place at an accelerated pace if long-embedded inefficiencies must suddenly face aggressive profit-seeking management. There should be no surprise that a number of smaller Wall Street partnerships managed by principals near retirement have decided to close down their firms now or that mergers are very active in this industry.

Existing theory concerning regulation is sufficiently detailed to indicate likely directional impacts of deregulation. Abolish binding minimum-price constraints, and you are likely to have price competition at prices below those minimums and changes in the form of previous non-price competition. Abolish requirements that brokerage firms be private partnerships, and you will get brokerage firms that are public corporations. The implications of such a shift for firm goals, firm capital sources, firm opportunities to engage in mergers and acquisitions may be dramatic. Abolish requirements that firms expose all their buy-sell orders to other firms in a central auction, and you will probably get some firms internalizing part of their order activity. While we can indicate directional impacts of deregulation, the existing theory does not seem rich enough to specify the rapidity of change or the magnitude of that change. We cannot guarantee that, left to itself, the securities industry would not be converted into a three-firm, no-exchange industry by the end of this century, for example. Nor do we know how the disruptiveness of the transitional process might affect the functional capital-raising and pricing roles of the securities industry.[9] Such uncertainties scare many inside and outside the industry. Better to have an existing regulated environment with cost inefficiencies already distributed than a possibly more efficient industry environment whose future benefits would not match the costs of getting there.

Given the known inefficiency of an existing regulated environment and the possible unknown destabilizing impact of an abrupt change to a deregulated environment, many opt for a policy compromise of limited deregulation over an extended period of time—the "let's all work together to make reasonable changes as they are developed and truly ready to implement" syndrome. Unfortunately, this fine tuning may produce the most inefficient process of all. There are a great many externalities in the production and distribution of securities. The success of any firm depends on the system in place and the efficiency of other firms. If there is a "best production technology" in terms of the way securities are marketed, or transferred, or brought to an exchange, that best system is unlikely to evolve from a compromise among existing inefficient firms operating under regulation. Meanwhile, the continuing attempts to compromise and arrange an acceptable new system could drain enormous managerial talent from already strained industry resources. The costs of swift deregulation may prove to be very high, but at least they are short run and borne mostly by stockholders in the industry involved. The longer-run costs of compromise regulatory change would fall heavily on the industry and its clients. Unfettered deregulation after years of binding regulatory constraints is likely to be a bloody, unpredictable, unprofitable struggle for those directly involved, but the weight of history and economic theory both suggest the eventual outcome may be closer to the best possible system than the system evolving from any other process.[10]

Thus the issues in any theory of deregulation must be the relative costs of (1) the existing system and (2) the process of transferring to a new system when compared to the benefits of such a change. Both the cost-benefit patterns for firms in the industry and for customer groups must be considered. Existing theories of regulation are static equilibrium theories focusing on limited-parameter-variable differences between a regulated state and a perfectly competitive model industry. Since deregulation may not be symmetrical with imposing regulatory constraint and since the process of deregulating an industry may impose costs on customer groups as well as industry firms, our existing theory for predicting outcomes is very weak. Deregulation in the securities industry is not so much a datum that supports existing theory as it is an experiment that will supply evidence for new theory.

Pricing Deregulation

To understand the scope of price deregulation in the securities industry, one must go back to its roots in the 1950s. Three things contributed to a fundamental change in the nature of the securities business. First, the postwar increase in the dollar magnitude of individuals' savings and the regulatory-imposed low rates on bank-type savings accounts made households more receptive to mutual funds as an investment than was true in earlier decades. (Note how regulatory constraints in one industry led to an "artificially high" demand in another industry. As the interest ceiling constraint on bank savings accounts and on government savings bonds was relaxed, we would expect relative demand to shift so that mutual funds would get a smaller share of total saving.) Second, through labor negotiations and competitive pressures to acquire and keep a good work force in a tight labor market, employee pension funds became a widespread pension benefit. Third, relatively low inflation rates and stable economic conditions led to a rather low interest rate structure. Developing financial theory and empirical research suggested that there were ways to obtain moderate risk levels and relatively higher returns than seemed to be available on bonds by investing in the equity markets.

By the late 1950s institutions were beginning to be an important source of business for trading in the already-issued shares of large corporations. Brokerage rates had for some years been fixed at a minimum price scale (high enough to be the prevailing commission rate) per unit of sales—usually a 100-share lot. Since an institution might buy several hundred 100-share lots at a time in any order and place many orders each month, this customer relationship became extraordinarily profitable to develop. Since direct price cutting by exchange member brokerage houses was not possible, familiar patterns of non-price competition developed. These included (1) fee splitting for bringing in revenues, (2) payment of customer bills for research or other support activities, (3) fancy meals, gifts, educational seminars in Bermuda for client groups, (4) inside tips or special allocations of new issues, (5) direct under-the-table cash bribes or rebates. Much of the 1960s was spent trying to design laws or industry standards to end these practices. The more successful such efforts became, the greater the pressures from customer groups for direct price competition.

Institutions had experience with a highly competitive, price-conscious dealer market in that many of them dealt in the government bond markets. If they could not get that kind of market for stocks from the exchanges, perhaps they could set up their own market. Since insider commission fees were lower than regular customer fees, institutional pressure developed in the late 1960s to allow them to become stock exchange members. When the NYSE refused, other exchanges actively sought such groups to enhance their own standing. And various types of third-market and institution-to-institution arrangements were created to effect high-volume transactions at lower unit costs. Thus well before 1970, before most firms even considered the possibility of direct price competition in the securities industry, there was in fact increasing price competition for institutional business in the securities industry.[11]

Of course, the principal exchanges and their member firms were aware of this process since they were the targets. Attempts to solve the problem and get back to the orderly, profitable, price-regulated days included attempts (1) to promote legislation to forbid any direct trading by institutions for their accounts; (2) to forbid member firms and specialist firms from participating in some of these new market arrangements; and (3) to persuade exchange-listed firms to refuse to transfer on their books any securities that were not bought or sold through the exchange. These attempts obviously failed and in retrospect may have been counterproductive. Activity of this type in addition to complaints from institution and smaller exchanges roused the curiosity of the Justice Department and Congress, who finally forced an extremely reluctant SEC to take direct action in the area of commission price regulation in the early 1970s.

Beginning in a limited way in 1971 and slowly increasing to 1975, negotiated commission rates became a fact of life for the exchanges and their member firms. Legislatively mandated deregulation of all brokerage commission charges occurred on May 1, 1975. Within two years price competition for institutional business had forced some brokerage firms to offer to transact large orders at less than 10¢ a share, where they might have been getting more than 30¢ a share three years earlier. Price deregulation seems to have already had the following consequences: (1) sharply lower brokerage prices for institutional customers; (2) a market of commission-price-offer uncertainty as commission rates have not found a new stable level; (3) fewer non-price benefits to customers as firm search for ways to cut costs to match the relatively lower revenues; and (4) cost-based-pricing schedules, as some firms have raised prices by charging smaller customers for unbundled services and infrequent trading.

Vigorous price competition for institutional business has almost wiped out pressures from institutions for direct access to exchanges. Now the pressures have almost been reversed. Some member firms and specialist groups of the NYSE would like to be able to handle in-house selected orders rather than bringing them to the Exchange. The fixed fees (exchange-related costs) would be saved, and the firms would have more of an opportunity to handle both sides of the transaction—important considerations in an era of reduced commission-rate structures.

Competition for individual customer business has led to generally increased brokerage rates for this customer group.[12] What were once joint products have now been unbundled, with separate custodial, research, and transactions charges.[13] One of the more curious things about the securities industry is that most firms have been extremely secretive about these price increases—most firms not telling customers about commission-rate increases until after a trade has occurred and several firms refusing to send written documentation of the new schedule when a direct request is made. This type of marketing immaturity is unlikely to persist for very long in a competitive environment.

Most brokerage houses claim they have had to raise prices to individual customers because the costs of handling these orders have increased, and some of the costs were supported by institutional business before May Day 1975 anyway. There is evidence to support these assertions. There is also an additional factor: since commission-rate schedules are mostly a stated percent of the value of the transaction with a smaller fixed charge added on, the stock market decline has reduced revenues from each unit of transaction. Still, it is possible for individuals to obtain lower commission prices. A few brokerage houses are setting themselves up as telephone-order centers. They do not pay their registered representatives to be financial advisors but only to be order takers getting a straight salary. Fees charged customers are about one third below the 1975 schedule. Customers who are long-term investors have another way to get low brokerage fees. For most large corporations, banks have now set up dividend reinvestment plans that permit the periodic purchase of additional shares. Customers for whom day-to-day timing is not critical can send their money for quarterly pooling with other funds, and the bank will buy the stock for commission rates that are the negotiated institutional rate plus about a $2.00 "service charge" to the customer.

Price deregulation in the securities industry thus began before 1975 (table 6-1) as some institutions and some banks found ways to bypass the Exchange rules. These initial steps benefited very large institutional customers and very small odd-lot customers (where eventually the pressure to reduce odd-lot fees forced the specialist firms handling that business out of existence). May Day 1975 had two effects: (1) In the short run it forced every firm to react immediately to the new environment. Despite the forewarning, most firms in the securities industry had done no planning to handle this new state of the world, so they were not prepared to service the intense competition, the increased capital requirements, the reluctance of institutions to pay in transactions volume for ordinary research. (2) In the longer run May Day may have saved the NYSE as an institution. Some major brokerage firms had given serious consideration to leaving the Exchange if the conditions of the early 1970s prevailed and business continued to drift away. As the Federal Reserve System is finding out with system banks, in the very long run if it is more profitable for firms to drop out of the system (especially if there are firms already outside competing), they will do so.

Securities Products Deregulation

Even more important in the long run to the health of the whole securities industry than deregulation of commission-rate prices is the relaxation of constraints on products that may be offered for sale. In several instances brokerage firms, narrowly defined, have not taken advantage of these new product opportunities or the opportunity to provide expanded services to the customers attracted by these products. In some cases new products have become available as a result of an explicit change in law. More often products that were already existing have had their demand expanded by an order of magnitude because of an administrative ruling that facilitated product standardization or a more readily available trading mechanism for trading outstanding issues.

Table 6-2 summarizes selected product developments related to the securities industry over the past decade. A few of the products result from direct

Table 6-1
Evolution of Price Competition

1. Give-ups, special services for institutional business (1950s)
2. Load and no-load fund competition (1960s)
3. Institutional off-board trading (1960s)
4. Direct discounting of very large orders (1971)
5. Dividend reinvestment plan extensions (1970s)
6. Reduced odd-lot fees (1970s)
7. Competitive commission rates (1975)
8. Discount brokers and other noncommissioned-salesmen-type firms (late 1970s)

Table 6-2

Selected Securities Industry Related Products With Rapidly Growing Markets over the Past Decade

1.	Standardized call options on American stocks
2.	State lottery tickets
3.	Gold coins and futures contracts
4.	Tax exempt revenue bonds
5.	Real estate trust certificates and other standardized mortgage instruments
6.	Futures contracts in government securities
7.	Small bearer bonds
8.	Dividend reinvestment plans
9.	Several new financial magazines and research journals
10.	Computerized investment advisory and portfolio strategy services, including hand-held financial calculators
11.	ERISA and Keogh pension plan services
12.	European option exchanges for American securities

legislative changes (for example, gold coins or lottery tickets), while most of the others are the result of administrative rulings that eased apparent roadblocks in their development (for example, call options or dividend reinvestment plans). No deregulation was necessary, of course, for someone to start publishing a new journal in portfolio management or selling a computer that would calculate optimal warrant-purchase prices. These products are on the list as indicators of the type of secondary fallout product that might be in demand once deregulation creates new investment-packaging opportunities.

The listed investment opportunities in table 6-2 will seem peculiar to some in the securities industry for two reasons. First, more than half these innovations came from outside the industry as narrowly defined (say, the larger brokerage houses around the country). Second, several items look rather risky as securities (without even listing the presently banned commodity futures options contracts). What does a lottery ticket have to do with the securities industry? I would argue, more than the industry cares to admit. High public demand for securities has always been, and will likely continue to be for several more decades, a demand for risky opportunities—a chance in a lifetime to get rich quick or beat the other fellow. In the decades after the market collapse in 1929, the industry regulated out of existence high risk taking (or at least tried to do so). Mining exchanges were closed down, borrowing power reduced, floor-trading activity curtailed, blue sky securities outlawed, boiler room sales strategies curtailed. Securities became an "investment" as defined by the industry and government regulators, not by individual customers.

The public managed to have a bit of fun in the mid-1960s (and they paid for it, as people usually do, with a seven-year hangover afterwards), but by and large, they have had to turn to new exchanges or new marketing channels to find the risky products they seek. Lottery tickets now gross hundreds of millions of dollars around the country. As a security, a lottery ticket has the basic characteristics of a low-priced option—a high probability of being worth zero in a finite time period with low probabilities of a small, or in a few cases extremely high, payoff. Why hasn't the securities industry been involved in raising this capital? Because the industry is absolutely opposed to gambling-type securities? Nonsense![14] Because industry firms cannot design marketing channels as cost efficient as each state can do on its own? Nonsense! Because brokerage firms have not truly examined demands of different types of customers or the scope of product innovation possible once certain regulations are relaxed? Probably. There is every reason to believe that with a well-designed lottery-ticket system, brokerage firms could easily raise large amounts of capital for new or small growing firms who do not now have direct access to the capital markets. The fact that it is now illegal should be of minor consequence to a real industry innovator. Some state wanting to attract new business might be persuaded to experiment, and federal regulators would soon be forced to consider seriously the merits of the proposals.

Regulation in the securities industry has increasingly taken on the task of protecting customers from fraud or unethical practices by those in the industry, and the additional task of protecting customers from themselves—from their individual greed, speculative enthusiasm, or attempts to balance otherwise conservative portfolios of owned homes, savings accounts, and government bonds with some very risky speculation. And so individuals have increasingly gone outside the traditional securities industry to find such high-risk opportunities.

It is not obvious that American capitalism is better served by encouraging people to take their money to Atlantic City or the Off Track Betting Corporation than to buy a $10 ticket on a new-firm pool. Nor is it obvious that the capital markets are made more efficient by designing securities products, marketing techniques, commission-pricing schedules, as we have done, that have the effect of significantly reducing the number of potential customers. In a market of informed participants where brokerage transactions occur on an honest open basis, why should the price of American Telephone be affected by the fact that the same exchange also permits trading in $5 mining speculations (or options, for that matter)? It should not, of course, except to the extent the mining speculations permit customers to rebalance portfolios in ways more desirable to them or society as a whole changes its preferences with regard to risk-return tradeoffs.[15] The sooner the securities industry and its regulators decide to get out of the business of prescribing "suitability standards," the sooner securities industry products and clientele can be broadened to capture savings for direct investment in private industry and government projects on a much larger scale.

Structural Deregulation

In the long run we suspect that the most important changes in regulations for the securities industry will be those changes that affect organizational paradigms within the industry. Such changes have occurred at the firm level, at the exchange self-regulatory association level, and even at the federal regulatory level. While the changes may seem to be legalistic and rather innocuous, they will have a fundamental impact on long-run goals and the way own capital is raised for securities industry firms.

Throughout most of their history, major brokerage firms and the exchanges were organized as private partnerships. Additional capital for expansion came from new partners being allowed to buy into the firm at book value (or old partners increasing their ownership on the same value basis), and by the supplying of subordinated debt capital by the partnership groups. As long as brokerage firms remained small, rich men were attracted to the securities industry, and personal liability risks were not excessive, the system seemed to work. The presumed advantages of the system were that it exposed partners to personal liability for the actions of their firms and permitted careful screening and control of those becoming partners so that "undesirables" (defined as crooked individuals or institutional clients trying to gain direct access to the exchange) could not gain a foothold in the industry.

By the early 1950s pressures for capital expansion and some tax advantages of incorporation were such that the NYSE governing body relented and permitted member firms to incorporate as long as they remained closely held private firms (essentially, the partners held the stock). By 1959 about 10% of the NYSE member organizations were incorporated, and a decade later almost 35% had chosen this form of firm organization. But these firms were still closely held, responsible only to the "partners" owning shares and not to public shareholders.[16]

At the beginning of the 1970s the Exchange approved public ownership of member firms, with side restrictions that attempted to ensure that financial institutions would not be able to obtain NYSE seats for direct trading of their managed portfolios. Now more than half the member firms are corporations, and about 20% of those incorporated might be considered public firms. The exchanges themselves incorporated in the early 1970s and one may expect most future firms in the industry to incorporate unless they are so small that there are tax or reduced form-filing advantages to remaining a partnership.

Becoming a public corporation or exchange has been a very unsettling experience for most of those involved in the process. Most of those brokerage firms who went public in the early 1970s by offering a combination of new shares and the shares of retiring partners saw the price of their stock drop sharply—often below book value—within two years. Thus at the time some brokerage firms found they needed additional capital, it was almost impossible to raise that capital (this is one of the reasons for mergers among brokerage firms). Just as important, a corporation needed a board of directors and officers, with clearly defined lines of responsibility. The old informal arrangement, by which all partners after the top two or three were more or less equal in status and where one person would cover for another who was not doing the job right, were no longer possible. At the beginning of the 1970s, a lot of partners got out of the industry, with its new rules they did not understand, and they took their capital with them.

As public corporations, brokerage firms find they are subject to the same pressures as any other corporation. Profits, and short-run trends or fluctuations in profits become important. Since the brokerage business is very cyclical and price competition has reduced the profitability of the most highly profit-margined lines of business, some firms have restructured themselves as holding companies to branch out into other lines of business. As these firms diversify with subsidiary corporations both domestically and internationally, they create regulatory problems existing agencies are not structured to handle; even more interesting are the problems created by foreign corporations setting up American subsidiaries to engage in some phase of the securities business. Who is going to regulate the banking activities of a brokerage firm (or the brokerage activities of a banking firm)? So we may be having deregulation by organizational complexity. Even the exchanges have found the transition unsettling. The NYSE and ASE created boards of directors with public (non-exchange-community) board representation. Even though the public members were obviously screened for their sensitivity to industry issues, a few of these members publicly disavowed some of the proposals and practices of exchange officers. And other potential board candidates declined to serve on the boards when it became clear they would not have direct access to independent counsel or outside auditors. Attempts have been made to keep board seats allocated on the basis that specialists and floor traders would have significant representation compared to the large brokerage firms bringing most of the business to the exchanges (and who control the largest number of seats or votes). The result has been a continuing stalemate on both exchanges as to the best future direction for the exchanges and the way to implement plans that may be accepted.

As every corporate officer must know, if you have people in fundamental conflict and what seems to be the best solution will destroy the power of one group or another, you cannot use a committee of all to make the decision. All planning to date for reorganization of the exchanges has been done with committees of all factions. It will not work in the end. By now, almost everyone but those directly involved in the negotiations believes that an exchange can eventually (this century) be organized that will effectively put the regional exchanges out of business and significantly reduce specialist profits and perhaps cut by an order-of-magnitude non-sales transactions costs. At some point a stockholder in one of the major public brokerage firms may get up at the annual meeting and ask, "Why is our firm still a member of the Exchange? Wouldn't it be more profitable if the firm left the Exchange (there is a high probability it would under existing conditions), or if the firm and other large firms exercised their voting power to nominate a board of directors slate who would take charge of building a cost-efficient exchange regardless of the consequences to other exchanges or firms in the industry?" Brokerage firms that become public corporations must respond to such pressures: the firms must publicly display financial statements (unlike most firms in the securities industry). This type of situation will put additional pressure on the exchange structures. That pressure is already there, for in the past several years the exchanges and their subsidiary firms have had an extraordinary turnover in executive personnel.

Even the SEC has not escaped the impact of organizational change. It has gone through a modest reorganization itself and has seen other agencies spun off to handle some of the regulatory problems for options, commodities, municipal bonds, and insurance of customer accounts. And the Justice Department, the Treasury Department, and the Federal Reserve Board have all formed specialist groups to examine some facet of the securities industry in recent years. Some feel the SEC is still improperly organized, with the wrong type of personnel, to provide oversight for the real regulatory issues of the next two decades.

One of the results of being caught with the wrong structure and personnel is that some believe the SEC has begun to exhibit the most invidious type of regulation-deregulation possible in a free economy. It is what we might call "Ping-Pong" regulation. Ping is "go" to develop in a relatively unregulated environment a market for a new product line. Because the product line is attractive and rapidly growing, new personnel enter that business line. Some of them are not properly screened and turn out to be liars and cheats. In most cases their ethical conduct turns out to be so bad it is obviously illegal under existing securities and tax law. Rather than have the individuals involved arrested and their firms suspended from business, the SEC has decided that until it "fully understands the market and can put in place suitable regulatory safeguards," it is better for customers (and the SEC) if the whole market is "ponged"—stopped dead in its tracks for some indeterminate sentence (but which may turn out to be longer than any time the crooks get). In recent years the SEC has ponged individual securities, an exchange, the whole development of the options markets, and certain forms of commodity futures trading.

In the case of the options markets, the economic costs of the SEC's throwing the go-stop switch may be enormous. Dozens of memberships were sold on exchanges two years ago at prices that incorporated expectations that increased call lists, and put lists, would soon be available. The lack of volume from the limited existing lists has almost put some of those new firms out of business. The inability to expand the list has directly reduced employment at two or more exchanges. Tens of millions of dollars of revenues have been lost forever by the delay in the development of this market. The SEC claims to be acting in the public interest, of course, but no cost-benefit analysis has been forthcoming. Safety at any cost may be an appropriate criterion for the Food and Drug Administration (although there is mounting evidence that even here it is not the right goal), but it is absurd in a securities market dominated by relatively sophisticated traders. As presently structured, the SEC does not have the agency goal orientation or the technical capacity to provide oversight for complex securities markets.[17] Unless conditions change, we may expect more Ping-Pong regulation of this sort in the future. That does not make it any easier for firms in the industry to do any long-range planning.

Abrupt changes in government regulatory policy for an industry can create major economic fluctuations that may take a decade to correct. This is true whether those regulatory changes involve price control-decontrol (example, the gas industry); a switch in product acceptability (example, diet soft drinks); go-stop development of a new market (example, cable television); permitted switch in organizational structure and implied strategic planning changes (example, bank-holding companies); or a change in the focus of the regulatory body itself (example, public accounting regulation). In all these instances it has or will take several years to work out the dynamics of the reversal in regulatory policy.

In the securities industry *all* the regulatory reversals described here have occurred within the past decade. All have affected a major segment of the industry, if not the whole of the industry. The scope of deregulation experimentation in the securities industry has caught up all participants—industry firms, exchanges, government regulators, even customer groups. That an industry can remain viable in the face of such perturbations is a remarkable testament to the power of profit motivation and the vitality of private enterprise.

Notes

1. For a survey of the theories of economic regulation, see Posner (1974) and the references he cites.

2. From the viewpoint of American industry as a whole, this situation is relatively unique. It has been something of the custom in professional, service-sector industries ranging from baseball to the legal profession.

3. For an elaboration of these issues, see the papers by Demsetz and by Williamson in Manne (1969).

4. We think it no accident that most of the interesting product innovations in "securities-type" products have come in recent years from outside the New York Exchange community.

5. Since this is a relatively easy industry to enter, we do not really know whether competition will reduce the number of existing firms in it. In any event, the industry is probably not dynamically stable with as many firms as currently exist (except under monopoly price protection conditions) (see Keenan 1977). Finally, it is not obvious that the economy would be better off with many small brokerage firms (or auto manufacturers, or telephone companies) than with a small number of competitive large firms.

6. See, for example, the discussion in West and Tinic (1971).

7. See Shepard (1975) and the literature he reviews.

8. For a basic discussion of some of these issues, see Scherer (1970).

9. Most existing theory is couched in terms of partial equilibrium shifts under the presumption that the transition is very short and of only second order consequence, and the new equilibrium is long and where the major impact will be revealed. As some countries have already found out, the economic transition to the new desired state may prove to be so disastrous that the new state is never reached.

10. Think back to the periods of turmoil in the economy after general price decontrols. It was not a pleasant process for firms or politicians, yet few would argue we should have kept the price controls.

11. There was even some price competition for individuals' business in the form of arguments over whether load or no-load mutual funds were the more desirable and exactly how high a loading charge should be.

12. See, for example, announcements by Merrill Lynch this past year about increased brokerage commission-rate schedules for small orders (in part to cover higher salaries to registered representatives) and fees for custodial services.

13. Some brokerage houses have tried selling research reports that they formerly gave away to selected clients.

14. The notion that securities industry firms and employees are professionals interested in "investing in the future" rather than speculating from time to time is a hypocrisy. Last year after strong publicity from the *New York Post* and other local news media, the NYSE was forced to temporarily stop the traditional high stakes gambling ring operating on the floor of the Exchange during business hours. As for the good old days, see the comments by Robert Sobel (1977), particularly pp. 22-43.

15. That is, the market would be extended for most customers so that they could buy directly covariance possibilities that can now be obtained only indirectly if at all.

16. For summary data, see *New York Stock Exchange Fact Book* (1976).

17. Some have argued that the SEC and the securities industry would be much better off now if the SEC were run by an officer of IBM. Whatever the merits of that argument, it is clearly true that the SEC is not, as it continually argues, so much "understaffed" as it is probably grossly overstaffed with the wrong kind of expertise.

References

Bloch, E., and Sametz, A.W. *A Modest Proposal for a National Securities Market System and Its Governance,* Bulletin 1977-1. New York University Center for the Study of Financial Institutions.

Chicago Board of Trade. *Annual Reports* (1975-76).

D'Ambrosio, Charles A., ed. "Wall Street, Government Regulation, and Market Efficiency," *Journal of Contemporary Business,* Summer 1976.

Keenan, Michael. *Profile of the New York Based Securities Industry,* Bulletin 1977-3. New York University Center for the Study of Financial Institutions.

Manne, Henry G., ed. *Economic Policy and the Regulation of Corporate Securities.* American Enterprise Institute, 1969.

New York Stock Exchange. *Fact Books,* Annual Reports (both yearly).

New York Times.

Posner, R.A. "Theories of Economic Regulation," *Bell Journal of Economics,* Autumn 1974, pp. 335-358.

Scherer, F.M. *Industrial Market Structure and Economic Performance.* Chicago: Rand McNally, 1970.

Schwert, G. William. "Public Regulation of National Securities Exchanges: A Test of the Capture Hypothesis," *Bell Journal of Economics,* Spring 1977, pp. 128-149.

Securities Week.

Shepard, L. *The Securities Brokerage Industry.* Lexington, Mass.: Lexington Books, D.C. Heath, 1975.

Sobel, Robert. *Inside Wall Street.* New York: Norton, 1977.

Stigler, George J. "Theory of Economic Regulation," *Bell Journal of Economics,* Spring 1971, pp. 3-21.

U.S. Department of Justice. "Memorandum on Fixed Minimum Rate Structures of Registered Exchanges," 1969.

U.S. Securities and Exchange Commission. *Hearings on Fixed Minimum Rate Structures, a National Securities Exchange Market System, and Related Matters,* Hearings and Exhibits, 1968-1972.

Wall Street Journal

West, R., and Tinic, S.M. *The Economics of the Stock Market.* New York: Praeger, 1971.

Wiesen, Jeremy L. *Regulating Transactions in Securities,* West Publishing, 1975.

7 In the Middle of the Regulation-Deregulation Road

Edward I. O'Brien

It is one of the anomalies of our time that we talk so often of our "free enterprise" economy when in fact it is one of the most closely regulated and supervised in the world. If that observation is true for the economy as a whole, it goes in spades for the securities industry. As one who thinks of himself as a believer in "free markets," I am bothered. We have all become familiar with the effects of the clutching hand of government on our affairs. Vigor and innovation are sapped by paternalism and bureaucratic red tape. Important decisions with vast economic consequences are made by federal officials lacking even rudimentary knowledge of the workings of the businesses they regulate.

Whether these or other stereotypical views of government regulation are an adequate assessment of the problem, however, remains to be seen. I would propose this afternoon to look at several different categories of regulation in the securities industry in order to illuminate the extent and effects of regulation and in the course of that analysis, to offer some observations as to the desirability and practicability of loosening some of those constraints in the future.

To begin, I will describe five separate, if not always mutually exclusive, categories into which much regulation of the securities industry falls. It should be noted that in the context of this industry, regulation subsumes not only that supplied by the federal government and the several states but also the comprehensive scheme of self-regulation originating from the stock exchanges and the NASD, which are themselves subject to the federal regulatory authority.

The first category of regulation covers the financial responsibility and operational capability of broker-dealer firms. Its classical instrument is the net capital rule, which since 1975 has been based on a uniform standard supplied by the SEC and only peripherally supplemented by the self-regulators. Other examples of this application include the SEC's rules respecting the custody and use of customer free-credit balances and securities, FOCUS, and other financial and operational reporting requirements.

The second broad category relates primarily to the handling by broker-dealers of customers' accounts. These include the multitudinous requirements for the registration of salesmen, confirmation requirements, and the "know your customer" rule, to name only a few.

I wish to acknowledge with deep gratitude the general contribution to the substance of this paper by Mr. Richard O. Scribner, senior vice president and general counsel of the Securities Industry Association.

The third category is what I will call the trading rules, rules designed essentially to prevent fraud, manipulation, or the taking of unfair professional advantage in the trading process itself. Rule 10b-5 is the glittering gem in this particular regulatory tiara, although most of its luster has been added by the courts, which at least until recently wielded it as a remedy for virtually every imagined wrong. Other examples of trading rules are SEC Rules 10b-4 relating to the short tendering of securities, 10b-6 prohibiting certain trading by those interested in a distribution, and 10a-1, the short-selling rule.

Related to and often barely distinguishable from the trading rules is the fourth category, regulation that by design or otherwise establishes or maintains structural patterns with the securities industry itself. Obviously, here we are talking about such items as NYSE Rules 390 and 113; Section 11A of the 1934 Act, the national market system provisions added by the 1975 amendments; and Section 11(a), another provision tailored by Congress in 1975, in this case to deal with the questions of institutional membership and the combination of brokerage and money management. In the past, of course, the most important of these economic or structural rules were those of the exchanges that established the fixed minimum rates of commission that members charged to their customers. As we all know and as some in my industry deeply regret, these ancient rules were sent to their grave in 1975.

My fifth, and last, category has to do with new-product regulation. In this category, of course, we have the regulation of options and of the markets that have sprung up to service that product. Another is commodity futures. Noting recent developments in both those areas, we should recall that the ultimate logical extension of the ability to regulate is the ability to outlaw altogether.

Let us go back over each of the categories to see whether regulation has been beneficial or detrimental and to gauge the possible effects as well as the practicability of a dose of deregulation.

I believe we can consider the first two categories—those relating to financial responsibility and operational capability and those covering the conduct of customer accounts—as a single analytical unit. The securities business rests on public confidence, confidence that the brokers and dealers with whom the public transacts business are properly qualified and held to standards of fair dealing, and confidence that customers' funds or securities are safe and will be handed over at the proper time. Public confidence is clearly enhanced by rules ensuring that brokers are financially responsible, that securities will not be lost or stolen, that a firm's books and records are accurate, that brokers are required to "know" their customers and to make only those recommendations that are suitable for those customers, and so forth.

The banking industry too found many decades ago that public confidence in the banking system required public confidence in the soundness and integrity of individual institutions. As a result, the elaborate program of reports and examinations was developed, then overlayed with the Federal Deposit Insurance

Corporation guarantee. Although one may always be concerned that regulators will be too protective of their flock, so concerned with preventing the failure of any institution that they draw their regulatory net too tightly thus causing stagnation throughout the system, it is hard to imagine that both banking and the securities industry have not benefited greatly from this sort of regulation and the "Good Housekeeping Seal of Approval" that goes with it. Thus I for one would not be willing to advocate significant deregulation in these areas.

There is something to be said, however, for the elimination of duplicative regulation. As you know, many broker-dealer firms are subject to similar sets of regulations imposed by, for example, the SEC, one or more stock exchanges, and the NASD. It is difficult enough simply to keep up with multiple sets of regulations, much less to comply with them. The burden on smaller firms can be overwhelming and a discouragement to this vital segment of the securities industry that is trying to remain in business. In the 1975 amendments Congress sought to address this problem. In Sections 17(d)(1) and 19(g)(2), Congress described a framework for the allocation of self-regulatory responsibility and oversight among the existing organizations so that the entire system could function more efficiently and with less duplication. Over the past 18 months, the various self-regulatory agencies have reached a number of bilateral accords whereby one or the other will be the exclusive agency to perform certain regulatory tasks with respect to dual members. From the point of view of the members, this is a desirable and a cost-saving move.

There have also been suggestions for more fundamental restructurings of the patterns of self-regulation. As many of you know, the NASD proposes that a single self-regulator—presumably the NASD—replace the existing multiplicity of self-regulatory organizations. In my judgment, whether the single self-regulator concept or some other system is more appropriate will depend on the configuration of the national market system as it reaches a more mature stage in its evolution. In other words, if the national market system consists of multiple competing marketplaces, that would seem to dictate the presence of multiple, but (let us hope) not competing, self-regulators. Then it will be necessary to continue the difficult but essential task of assuring that regulatory responsibilities are allocated among them to minimize overlap. On the other hand, if a national market system evolves into essentially a single marketplace such as the fabled "black box," then it would seem to me altogether appropriate that we have only one self-regulatory organization performing all the regulatory functions included within these first two categories.

Next we come to the category of trading rules. Here again it can hardly be denied that rules designed to prevent fraud in the marketplace or the over-reaching of customers operate in the interests of the securities industry since at a minimum they enhance public confidence. Moreover, many of these rules were originally conceived in response to specifically identified problems or abuses, and it is difficult to imagine that those problems or abuses would not reappear if such rules were "deregulated" out of existence. Let us take, for example, the short-selling rules, which the Commission has proposed be eliminated. The short-selling rules were, of course, invented to curb the abuse of the bear raid, which was a favorite technique of manipulators in the 1920s and before. Apparently the rules worked, because we no longer have the phenomenon of bear raids. Nonetheless, the SEC from time to time has looked at the short-selling rules and wondered whether they did not constitute an inappropriate interference with the operation of the free market. The SEC also questioned how they worked functionally and whether things would operate just as well without them. I would agree that rules of this sort should be subject to periodic reappraisal. However, I think that public-confidence rules of this sort should not be cast aside unless we can be pretty certain that the abuses they were originally intended to cure will not reappear, and I do not believe that we have that sort of reassurance in the case of the short-selling rules.

Having staked myself out in favor of trading rules that protect against actual abuses, I will hasten to add that we should not countenance regulation that jousts at theoretical abuses. As an example of this sort of overregulation, I give you the SEC's recently proposed amendment to Rule 10b-4. As you may know, this rule was originally adopted shortly after passage of the Williams Act to eliminate the practice of short tendering. The commission's proposed amendments are designed, according to the accompanying release, to prohibit a variety of additional strategies or practices relating to the tending of securities. Nowhere in its long release does the commission attempt to estimate the prevalence of these activities or practices or to document any abuses actually arising from them. Indeed, some of the practices very much facilitate the normal process by which arbitrageurs maintain markets, servicing those shareholders who do not wish to incur the risk of proration and who wish to realize prices closely approximating the tender price. Nevertheless, the commission, without any attempt at analyzing or quantifying the potential harmful effects of its proposals, put them forth for comment as if it were prepared to proceed blithely with their implementation. While this example certainly does not state the case for deregulation, it is most eloquent testimony for the need to subject new regulation to rigorous cost-benefit analysis.

The most difficult category to deal with in the regulation-deregulation debate covers those rules that, although ostensibly trading or conduct rules, are actually rules that fundamentally affect the structure of the securities markets or the securities industry itself. I mentioned fixed minimum-commission rates at the outset of my remarks. When Congress and the SEC decreed the deregulation of commission rates, it was apparent that they had in mind that the forces of competition would adjust rates to more economic, and presumably fairer, levels. Well, rates have come down dramatically for institutional investors and stayed about the same or gone up slightly for individual investors. I suppose these adjustments reflect "true" economic forces at work. At least they show that large buyers and sellers can trade more cheaply than smaller ones. But there have been effects on the securities industry, on the markets, and on the distribution system that may not be healthy. Securities research is less available today, and the range of companies covered is not as broad. Market liquidity has been impaired in a way that may not be measurable to economists but that is palpable to those in the marketplace. Numerous securities firms have been forced out of existence. These firms were not necessarily "inefficient" in the classic economic sense. They just happened to be in the wrong business at the wrong time. Although many of them were absorbed by other firms, it can fairly be argued that there has been a real diminution in the capacity of the broker-dealer community to distribute new issues. If nothing else, we have witnessed a continuation of the disturbing trend toward concentration in the securities industry, a trend that threatens to accelerate the occurrence of the adverse consequences recited a moment ago. Let me make it plain that I am not urging a return to fixed rates. That ship has sailed. The example, however, should serve to make us cautious when taking other fundamental steps in the future.

That brings me to a subject of more current interest in the deregulation debate, the establishment of a national market system. Essentially, the question is, can that form of structural change best be accomplished by simply eliminating rules that in some respects hamper competitive interplay such as NYSE Rule 390 or by the establishment of some grand design, whether conceived by the government or by the private sector or by some combination of the two, into which mold all the participants will be forced whether they like it or not. We have all heard a good deal about dealer markets and auction markets, their virtues and their vices. I do not propose to rewalk that ground. I observe, however, that we have a system that appears to work reasonably well. It may not work perfectly for everybody. But the trading markets, and particularly the exchange mechanisms, seem to be providing the kind of secondary markets that support capital formation to the degree required by the corporations who shares are traded there. Investors seem to be tolerably happy with their treatment, and as previously noted, a rather elaborate framework of regulation has developed to ensure that they are treated fairly.

Clearly, the objective that Congress, the SEC, and the industry have had in mind for some time is the creation of a *better* marketplace, one that will more perfectly fulfill its overall responsibilities to this nation's economy. The specific objectives for that improved system were spelled out by Congress in new Section 11A. Few would quarrel with that congressional enumeration. The real unanswered question, as I mentioned a moment ago, is whether those objectives can best be attained simply by eliminating certain existing "barriers to competition," that is, by deregulation, or through the process of planning and concerted conduct by the various overseers of the system, that is, by regulation. Section 11A does not provide an unequivocal answer to that question.

The dilemma I envision is that rules such as 390 and 113 become after a time structural pillars of the system itself. To remove them, without more, may, and I would emphasize the word *may*, cause the structure to collapse. Still, this is simply too serious a risk to run, and we should be reasonably certain that the worst will not in fact occur. Moreover, while removal of structural rules such as these may promote competition and innovation, their removal could also lead to greater concentration or even a monopoly in the trading function. Wouldn't it be ironic if the result of such structural deregulation was the aggrandizement of the NYSE's power? As a consequence of these considerations, I for one would be very reluctant to remove rules such as 390 and 113 until we can see pretty clearly, at least more clearly than today, the nature of the changes that will result.

But what I have just said does not necessarily make the case for the "grand design" approach that is embodied, for example, in the SEC's composite limit order book proposals dating back to 1976. That approach, which seems to involve a rather high degree of regulatory coercion, presents a number of shortcomings all its own. First, we have the not inconsiderable expense of the system's construction and operation. Who is to provide these funds? Second, such a system would require a new and evidently extensive network of rules to police activities within its confines. Third, such a regulatory system would itself become a structural pillar, possibly inhibiting or predetermining the direction of future evolutionary development. Thus while it is clear that a national market system meeting the congressional specifications will not simply evolve by itself and that its development will require a high degree of purposeful encouragement, I would hope that in formulating the program for this system, the SEC *and the industry* would minimize the creation of new structural pillars. Similarly, there should be a forebearance from regulation except in those areas where we are consciously seeking structural change and then only when we know with some exactitude the direction and the consequence of the change sought to be achieved.

Let me turn now to some major statistics that bear upon the securities industry and indicate to you eight major conclusions that flow from these statistics.

1. It is quite clear that the securities industry is a highly volatile industry, and this applies to both overall revenues and expenses.
2. Return on capital shows a persistent seesaw pattern with extreme highs and lows, and the interesting point is that over the last several years the return on capital at its high point is lower each time such a high is reached. In other words, the return on capital in the industry is not improving.
3. There has been a major shift in sources of revenue, primarily away from commissions and into more risk. There are reasons for this, which relate in great measure not only to the appetite of clients for different types of investments but also to the need for the industry itself to diversify in order to survive.

4. There has been a major decline in stockholding by various institutions. This is particularly notable in the case of mutual funds, but overall the holding of equities by institutions has declined across the broad range of institutional clients.
5. Foreign investors, as the percentage of total purchases of U.S. securities, has truly skyrocketed. The statistics are available, and they show that foreign investment is now a major factor in the U.S. securities industry.
6. There has been a significant increase in principal trading by firms. This increase also reflects the appetite of clients and a shift in the risk-taking concepts.
7. There has been a decline of major proportions in the number of NYSE firms dealing with the public, from a high of 476 firms in the year 1973 to 364 firms in 1977.
8. Concentration has increased greatly in the securities business so that now the business is increasingly concentrated in the largest 10 and the largest 25 firms. This concentration applies to commissions, to revenues, and to capital. In other words, it is across the board, and it means that the big are getting bigger.

What is the meaning of these statistics? I think there are several. As seen by the firms themselves, it is the perception of the firms that the industry has done its job quite well since the problem days of the late 1960s. Many new products and financial services have been brought into effect. Operations have been greatly strengthened to the point of great reliability. Capital has at least been held in the industry, even though it has not increased; and there has also been a significant increase in management consciousness and performance. The interesting point, however, is that all of this has taken place while the industry has been squeezed in at least two ways. First of all, the industry has been squeezed by regulators, not only by the SEC but also by others, and there has been an inhibition, directly or indirectly, on the ability of the industry to develop or market new products and services. Some examples are the marketing of options, which is now under a moratorium from the SEC, and significant regulatory impediments to the issuance of stock in smaller corporations. Naturally, these inhibitions have direct impact on gross revenues of the industry, to say nothing of the impact on our clients. Second, the industry has been squeezed on the expense side. When an industry is under cost pressures, as well as pressures on revenue sources, it is crucial that the industry have every opportunity to reduce its expenses. This need has not always been filled. For example, it is important that clearance costs be kept under control and in fact that they be brought down as much as possible so that profitabiity can be brought to the bottom line. The fact is, however, that we are completely in the dark as to the costs that may be involved in the building of a national market system, and furthermore, some of the clearance facilities have tarried for so long that it is costing the industry a fair amount of money and, therefore, has an impact on profitability.

Overriding the entire securities industry is the question of national economic policies. The position of the industry is that these policies have been consistently poor and against the interest of investors, savers, and capital formation. It is simply not possible for a country to continue running large budget deficits and have a tax bias against capital investment, which has been the clear philosophy of our government for the last 30 years. The interesting conclusion from this latter point is that even if the industry were able to do everything appropriate to increase its revenues and reduce its costs, these national economic policies have a direct and significant impact on the industry's future.

The securities industry has an attitude, therefore, with respect to regulation. We are obviously quite anxious to retain regulation that maintains confidence. However, it is important that we clear out those regulations that inhibit our ability to add to our revenues, to service our clients with new products and services, and that help us reduce our expenses. These principles will apply to the industry's evaluation of progress, toward clearance and settlement, and toward a national market system.

Summing up, let me offer these overview thoughts on deregulation of the securities business. The history of the securities industry does not support the classic case for deregulation. Many regulations are justified on the basis that they were designed to and in fact operate to prevent identified abuses. Those regulations that enhance public confidence in the securities industry and the securities markets should be retained. This is not to say that further regulation should be imposed willy-nilly. Regulation should occur only when there is a specific evil to be remedied, and then the regulation should be carefully contoured to cover only that situation. On a structural plane, a theoretical case can be made for deregulation, but we face two problems right at the outset. First, certain regulations have become structural pillars of the system itself, and they may be removed only at great risk. Second, deregulation in certain areas, rather than promoting innovation and competition, may only inhibit it. We should be very reluctant to impose new regulation of a structural character. In effect, it might be said that we should favor a policy of prospective deregulation.

If all of the foregoing seems to put me right in the middle of the road in the regulation-deregulation debate, that is exactly where I want to be.

8 The Semantics of Securities Industry Deregulation

Robert C. Hall

People who take sides on controversial public issues often develop a knack for using standard words and phrases to suit their own philosophies and objectives. A generation ago, for example, conservative lawmakers proclaimed "the right to work" as an indisputable eternal truth. To labor leaders, on the other hand, the same words were like a red flag. Similarly, "environmental protection" does not mean the same thing to social activists who can hardly get enough of it as it does to the business community that is expected to foot the bill within the constraints of sound fiscal management.

Much the same semantic dichotomy applies to "deregulation." It has a broad spectrum of both positive and negative connotations depending on who uses it, who hears it, and the specific condition to which it refers.

Some of those who embrace the concept of deregulation seem to believe, as former President Gerald R. Ford once suggested, that the business environment would be much improved by getting government out of the businessman's hair. Removing layers of regulatory encumbrances that have accumulated over the years and that no longer serve any discernible public benefit should simplify the businessman's lot and allow him to devote a greater proportion of his efforts to improving his product or service.

Some who espouse deregulation stress eliminating regulatory strictures that they view as interfering with free competition, while others decry the evils of rampant competition.

Anyone unfamiliar with the structure of government regulation of business in this country might be pardoned for assuming that "deregulation" would necessarily result in a net reduction in government-administered rules and regulations to give business a freer hand in determining its destiny.

However, as Professor Irving Kristol pointed out in an article in *The Wall Street Journal* some time ago, unfettered competition in some industries can be a euphemism for the survival of the fittest. And if the fittest are also the biggest, deregulation is unlikely to be the road to less government control over business and the economy.

To the extent that "deregulation" may produce more concentrated industries, it may very well lead to more real or imagined abuses—and more stringent regulatory controls in the future. Thus a move toward "deregulation" today could turn out to be a transition between self-regulation or cooperative regulation now and more pervasive government control in the future—unless care is taken.

The Securities Industry Experience

In the securities industry today, deregulation is closely tied to the development of a National Market System. In 1975 Congress enacted legislation calling for such a system and gave the Securities and Exchange Commission (SEC) responsibility for overseeing its implementation. Although Congress did not provide detailed specifications for the system, one of the major guidelines was the elimination of inappropriate burdens on competition. Yet it was clear from the outset that major structural changes and innovations would require comprehensive new rules and regulations.

As progress toward a National Market System accelerates—and as government and industry views about the essential components of the system take more definitive shape—it seems increasingly fanciful to characterize what is going on in the securities industry today as "deregulation."

But all of us would be much better advised to push forward the evolution of the kind of system that will achieve the goals set by Congress—without concerning ourselves with semantics.

The Congressional Goals

Just what did Congress have in mind in giving the force of law to its call for a National Market System? The 1975 legislation specifically states that "the securities markets are an important national asset which must be preserved and strengthened."

Congress noted particularly that "the linking of all markets . . . through communications and data-processing facilities" should produce a number of benefits. It should foster efficiency. It should enhance competition. It should increase the availability of market information. It should facilitate the offsetting of investors' orders. And it should contribute to best execution of such orders.

Obviously these expectations look toward major changes in the securities markets—changes that most will agree are both desirable and achievable. The great challenge to the industry and regulatory authorities has been to define, chart, and pursue the development of a National Market System that can achieve the congressional goals without jeopardizing the fundamental strengths and integrity that have made the U.S. capital markets the subjects of worldwide admiration and envy.

At the New York Stock Exchange (NYSE), we have consistently stressed an approach to key changes through an orderly process of evolution that builds on the strengths of the existing system to create a better one. We have been heartened by recent evidence that while the SEC is understandably eager to expedite the implementation of a National Market System, the regulators also recognize the dangers of fragmentation inherent in acting precipitously. On 26

January, 1978, the Commission issued a major statement, "The Development of a National Market System." After tracing the progress to date toward a national system for trading securities and outlining in some detail the Commission's future plans for facilitating its establishment, the document concludes by stressing the importance of an evolutionary approach to a National Market System. To quote from the release, it is the SEC view that, "as each step of the process of fusing the existing markets into a National Market System is completed, and as the effects of each such step become realities, refinements and adjustments in succeeding steps will suggest themselves."

Key Components of a National Market System

The Commission's review of progress to date makes clear that more has already been accomplished than is generally recognized. For example, one key component of a National Market System—the consolidated tape—has been in full operation for well over two years and is functioning efficiently.

The SEC has set 1 August, 1978 as the start-up date for the Composite Quotation System characterized as "a fundamental building block of a National Market System."

Another essential component of a National Market System is a national clearance and settlement system. It too is up and running although resolution of a few legal snags and approval of a final plan by the SEC are still pending.

The Intermarket Trading System

As this is being written, six of the nation's leading marketplaces—The American, Boston, Midwest, New York, Pacific, and Philadelphia Stock Exchanges—are preparing to implement an electronic trading linkage that will greatly expand trading and intensify market-making competition among the markets in which many corporate stocks are dually or multiple listed and traded. On 17 April, the New York and Philadelphia Stock Exchanges began a pilot operation with eleven stocks. And the four other exchanges are moving with all due speed to come on line.

This Intermarket Trading System (ITS) permits orders that are received in any of the participating marketplaces to interact almost instantaneously with orders in the same stocks in any or all of the other marketplaces.

The ITS linkage consists essentially of a central computer facility and a network of interconnected terminal devices in the participating market centers. It operates in conjunction with automated quotation displays in each market center. These displays show the current quote for each stock traded in that market plus—at the option of each market—either the current quotes in all other markets in the system or the best quote currently available systemwide.

In general, the system enables a broker or market maker in any participating market center to reach into any of the others within a matter of seconds—whenever a better execution may be shown to be available there.

The SEC's willingness to have a pilot ITS operation begin before their giving formal approval to the system is a measure of the SEC's commitment to encouraging the securities industry to develop the essential components of a National Market System.

During the pilot phases, of course, the participants will be monitoring the ITS operation very closely. And we all assume that we will be making improvements or modifications, as experience may suggest, before moving on to additional applications in an orderly sequence.

While it is too early in the pilot phase to predict with any certainty how fast we may be able to move ahead, we hope to expand the operation to include some 150 to 200 of the most actively traded stocks by the end of summer. And if everything goes smoothly, all NYSE-listed stocks that are traded in at least one other market could be in the system within a year.

We believe ITS represents a major step forward in meeting the competitive and technological challenges of the National Market System concept. It should be stressed, however, that ITS will not revolutionize securities trading in the United States. It will not create a mysterious or intimidating "black box" system where all trading might be forced into a single computer mold. On the contrary, ITS will use computer technology to support the exercise of human judgment in determining how a broad range of trading strategies can best be used to serve the particular needs and wishes of all types of investors.

Some Unresolved Questions

Significantly, the SEC's policy statement noted that the Intermarket Trading System could become a central element of the evolving National Market System—if all qualified markets, including those supervised by the National Association of Securities Dealers (NASD), become active participants. And that is one of the goals of the six exchanges that have developed ITS.

Still unresolved is the question of what securities will qualify for trading in the National Market System. The SEC has indicated that it will be addressing that issue within the next few months. There appears to be a strong possibility that certain issues that are now traded only over the counter may be included—in which case, trades in those issues would have to be reported on the consolidated tape.

In other areas the thrust of SEC policy is less clear. For example, while disavowing the intent to create a single automatic execution-type system, the Commission has called on the securities industry to present by 30 September, a plan for developing a central limit order file. We are frankly concerned that such a file could quickly take on the salient characteristics of an electronic market, to the exclusion of all others, eliminating existing alternative trading strategies for investors and stifling innovation.

The Commission also set 15 April as a deadline for the industry to propose an order and message-routing system that would enable brokers to send orders directly from their offices to any market center. The NYSE has agreed, subject to concurrence by the American Stock Exchange and negotiation of equitable compensation, to modify the NYSE/AMEX-owned common message switch to serve this purpose. However, we question the need for such a facility in view of the variety of message switches already developed by other securities exchanges and data-processing service bureaus. We also believe that the linking of market centers to each other rather than the unitary linking of individual broker-dealers to individual market centers is the key to promoting healthy competition in a National Market System.

Striving for Competitive Excellence

In the securities industry, we have seen many times in the past how striving for competitive excellence can lead to innovations that ultimately benefit the entire industry and its constituents. One prominent example is the Pacific Stock Exchange's development of the continuous-net-settlement system that was subsequently copied by the rest of the industry.

Similarly, the NYSE's pioneering work in perfecting the automated securities depository concept succeeded in virtually immobilizing the stock certificate and in lifting a tremendous burden of paperwork from the industry. And this innovation too was emulated by others.

More recently many exchanges have developed different types of automated execution techniques that are aimed at capturing order flow from their competitors. And the exchanges are constantly working to improve and expand their individual systems, trying to keep a competitive step ahead of one another. The new result of these efforts, which obviously should be encouraged, has been a significant industry-wide reduction in execution costs.

Competition in the securities industry is multifaceted, and at least three levels of competition must be realistically addressed in terms of the emerging National Market System. In addition to strengthening competition among the various market centers, we must maximize competition among exchange stock specialists and other market makers who handle the same National Market System stocks. We must also maximize competition among orders; that is, we must find ways of enabling all orders in National Market System stocks to meet and interact, so that they can compete to obtain the best available purchase or sale price.

Overall, if a National Market System is to achieve the objectives outlined by

Congress, vigorous industry-wide competition must be the prime stimulus for quality, innovation, cost-effectiveness, efficiency, technological excellence, and all the other characteristics that will attract public participation in the market.

Regulation's Role in a National Market System

We cannot, however, realistically expect unfettered competition alone to produce the ideal securities trading environment. There must be carefully considered, detailed, comprehensive rules to ensure that competition will be fair as well as vigorous. There must be regulatory—and responsible self-regulatory—oversight to ensure that all participants are qualified to compete and that they compete according to the rules. Inherent in the quest for a better market system is the almost certain prospect of more regulation—not less.

The real challenge is not to find ways to deregulate the securities industry but to devise a fair and workable new regulatory scheme to govern the structure and operation of a National Market System and protect the interests of investors—without imposing costly or unnecessarily burdensome requirements on the industry.

The industry should not look on regulation or self-regulation as a necessary evil, however. Regulation has an affirmative role in the operation of the industry. It is the basis for the financial confidence among securities firms so necessary to support free intermember trading. It is also the indispensable foundation of public confidence in the industry. The public has a right to the assurance that the funds investors put at risk in the ownership and trading of securities are handled by qualified professionals whose activities on their behalf are constantly subjected to responsible oversight.

Streamlining Self-Regulation

Over the years the self-regulatory organizations have not invariably discharged their responsibilities with maximum efficiency. Particularly, the proliferation and retention of many rules, regulations, and requirements—often duplicated from one self-regulatory organization to the next—have sometimes seemed designed to make it as difficult as possible for securities firms to operate efficiently.

The NYSE recognizes that it has not been entirely blameless in this regard. But we have launched an ongoing program to streamline our self-regulatory mechanisms. Our goal here is to strengthen those rules and regulations that are necessary and to relax or eliminate those that are not.

Our reduction of certain controls over the activities of members and member organizations are, in the purest spirit of deregulation, designed to simplify procedures for member organizations.

Some of these changes were clearly suggested by the 1975 amendments, which specify that the Exchange must not impose unnecessary burdens on competition in connection with carrying out its responsibilities to enforce member compliance with the provisions of the securities laws, the rules of the SEC, and the rules of the Exchange itself. In addition, the new competitive climate places Exchange members in competition not only with one another but also with nonmember broker-dealers and to some extent with banks.

One of the earliest examples of deregulation by the Exchange was the elimination of rules that limited the sale of stock by member corporations whose stock was not freely transferable. The thrust here was to eliminate competitive advantages enjoyed by nonmember firms that had elected to issue publicly traded stocks.

In another area the Exchange has eliminated numerous rules that restricted the ability of members and member firm employees to be associated with more than one firm or to engage in non-securities business activities while also employed in the securities business.

With respect to advertising by member organizations, the Exchange no longer requires prepublication submission and approval—although it may be noted that the SEC indicated some dissatisfaction with this deregulatory step when it was taken.

Eliminating Duplicative Regulation

Duplication of regulatory requirements, enforced by the various self-regulatory organizations, the SEC and state regulators, has long been one of the most frustrating and costly aspects of regulation for securities firms. Since December 1976 SEC rules have permitted self-regulatory organizations to enter into voluntary agreements to reallocate self-regulatory responsibilities—and many such agreements are now in force.

For example, the Exchange and the NASD now conduct joint financial and operational examinations of firms that are members of both organizations, effectively cutting in half the number of such examinations to which dual members were formerly subjected.

Virtually all duplicative upstairs regulation of firms that belong to more than one exchange has been eliminated under a system of report sharing among the New York, American, Boston, Midwest, Pacific, and Philadelphia Exchanges.

In other areas such as testing and registration of sales personnel, uniformity of qualifying examinations has become the rule rather than the exception, both simplifying the tasks of the self-regulatory organizations and vastly reducing the compliance burdens formerly imposed on member organizations.

Major changes have also streamlined financial regulation of securities firms. A key innovation here has been the SEC's adoption of Uniform Net Capital Rules and Alternative Methods for computing net capital. These are effective throughout the industry and have taken the self-regulatory organizations out of the business of maintaining and enforcing their own capital requirements. This enables the self-regulatory organizations to focus more intently on preventive-regulation techniques aimed at identifying potential financial difficulties before they can develop into serious problems. At the NYSE, for example, close attention to profit-loss ratios and intraindustry comparisons permit us to catch early signs of trends that might eventually lead to capital violation or other financial trouble. Detection of such early-warning signs triggers specific programs to assist firms in taking appropriate steps to shore up their financial positions at a time when that can be done without excessive disruption of their operations.

In a sense, of course, this is a more specific example of how "deregulation" can lead to better regulation—constructively and in the best interests of both the securities industry and the investing public.

Conclusion

In the final analysis, it matters little whether we describe as deregulation, or streamlined regulation, or more effective regulation, the ongoing evolutionary changes that all of us hope will produce a more competitive, more efficient, more cost-effective securities market system in this country.

What does matter—to the regulatory authorities, to the self-regulators, and to those who are regulated—is the assurance that the changes that are now being implemented, and those that may occur in the future, will build creatively on the existing market structure—and not dismantle it.

> The securities industry and the SEC must not forget that our primary mutual objective is a secondary trading market of sufficient excellence to warrant investor confidence, and to give investors the incentive to purchase securities with their capital savings.

At the NYSE, we believe that implies an urgent industry-wide responsibility to use cooperatively the vast pool of talent that exists in every area of the industry to improve what we have—in ways that, together with other initiatives from both the private sector and government, can give strong new impetus to public confidence and participation in the securities markets.

References

Karmel, Roberta S. "The Resolution of Broker-Dealer Conflicts of Interest in Market Execution." Address to Compliance and Legal Seminar sponsored by the Securities Industry Association, Sarasota, Florida, 20 March, 1978.

Kristol, Irving. "Some Doubts about 'De-Regulations' ", *The Wall Street Journal,*
    20 October, 1975.
Securities and Exchange Commission. *Development of a National Market System*
    Release No. 34-14416, 26 January, 1978.

Deregulation of Fixed Commission Rates in the Securities Industry

Dan Roberts, Susan M. Phillips, and *J. Richard Zecher*

Medical science has long suffered the criticism that a disproportionate amount of its time and resources is spent studying exotic diseases or rare abnormalities. A similar charge can be leveled with considerable justification against economists who study the relatively infrequent instances of deregulation such as the unfixing of commission rates in the securities industries. The reason for the paucity of examples of deregulation is simple: The regulation industry is not only large but apparently has one of the strongest growth records in the country over the past twenty years.

Since the Commerce Department has not yet defined regulation as an industry, no precise measures of the income and product generated by regulatory activity are currently available. However, some rough measures of the growth and size of this industry can be made and are worth mentioning in order to put the discussion of deregulation into perspective. One indication of the growth of regulatory activity is suggested by the number of pages published annually in the *Federal Register* (the daily compilation of federal regulation). Just over 10,000 pages were published in 1955 while over 60,000 were published in 1975. The compound annual growth rate of pages published was 5% from 1955 to 1970, and from 1970 to 1975 the regulation reporter's pages grew by 25% annually.[1]

When a new regulation is approved, it typically affects resource allocation and income distribution in both the government and the private sectors. In government, staff and other resources must be provided to interpret, administer, and enforce the regulation. One estimate of federal budget expenditures for business regulation in 1976 is $2.9 billion, which reflects an annual growth rate of nearly 22% from 1974.[2]

However, the evidence suggests that the lion's share of the cost of regulation is borne by the private sector. Although no complete measures are available, major components of these regulatory costs are associated with providing information to the federal government through its more than 5,000 approved forms. The Federal Paperwork Commission (1977) has estimated that over $33

The authors gratefully acknowledge the extensive assistance of William Dale and the constructive and thoughtful suggestions of Lawrence J. White as well as the comments of the other participants in the Deregulation Conference and absolves them from guilt for any remaining errors.

billion was expended by the private sector in 1975 alone to fill out these federal reports. In addition to these reporting costs, the private sector expends substantial, but as yet incompletely measured, resources on complying with regulation and in "dealing with" the regulators. These expenditures include, among other things, retaining "experts" (lawyers, accountants, economists, lobbyists, etc.). The expenditures on experts might also be viewed as an effort to reduce total compliance costs.

This recent vigorous growth in the regulation industry has been interrupted only occasionally by the removal of an existing regulation. The unfixing of minimum-commission rates on the New York Stock Exchange (NYSE) is perhaps the premiere example of such deregulation to date. Trying to better understand this aberration on the regulatory landscape is the major focus of the present paper.[3] The interpretation of the unfixing of commission rates offered here stems from some recent work in the economics of regulation, which views regulation as primarily a device to effect wealth transfers.[4]

The main part of the paper presents estimates of the size and incidence of the regulatory tax imposed by fixed commission rates over the period 1961-1974. Readers wishing to review the chronology of major events relating to fixed commission rates are referred to appendix 9c.

Fixed Commission Rates as a Regulatory Tax

Price regulation can operate to protect the status quo. For example, fixed commission rates protected participants in the brokerage industry from effective price competition. Firms were not encouraged as they otherwise might have been to introduce cost-reducing measures because they could not reap the full benefits of their innovations through cutting prices and attracting new customers. In this sense, fixed commissions were a tax on innovation.

Regulation can also result in direct wealth transfers among various groups, creating a transfer tax (or subsidy) levied on different groups. Many federal reporting requirements, for example, may have the effect of transferring wealth from issuers, brokerage firms, and investors to the securities law and accounting groups. Fixed commission rates could similarly provide a transfer if they were set either above or below the competitive price of supplying brokerage services.

We estimate that the government-sanctioned structure of fixed commissions, at least until the mid-1960s, predominantly produced a tax on innovation rather than a transfer tax. Beginning in the mid to late 1960s, however, the transfer tax effect becomes evident, and as the tax burden increased over the period, continuous adjustments to the structure were initiated.

Figure 9-1 shows the fixed commission rate structure that was in effect prior to December 1968, and the one in effect in late 1974 for trades of 300 shares. Several rate-structure changes occurred between 1969 and 1974, each of

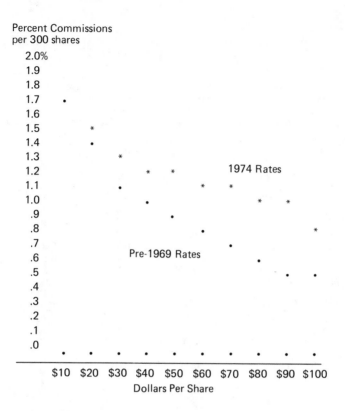

Percent Commissions
per 300 shares

aBased on trades of 300 shares.

Figure 9-1. Fixed Commission Schedules for 1947-1968, and for 1974[a]

which would have produced a commission schedule between the two shown. Each schedule shows a rapid decrease in commission rates, as the value of the share (or trade) increases, and similar scale economies are evident in the competitive price structure that has existed since 1975.

To examine further investor trading patterns and associated commission costs, representative dollar trades for two classes of investors, individuals and institutions, were estimated using average trade size and price per share for the years indicated.[5] Table 9-1 displays the principal amount of such trades from 1961 to 1977. In the years 1961 to 1974, we have calculated the fixed commission on typical trades using the appropriate fixed rate for each year. In 1975 through 1977 the commissions paid are from negotiated commission rate data for typical trades for each of these years. The "effective commission rate" is commission paid as a percent of the principal amount of the trade.

Between 1961 and 1977 both the relative importance and absolute size of

Table 9-1
Individual and Institutional Commission Rates for Representative Trades;
Fixed Rates 1961-1974; Negotiated Rates 1975-1977[a]

	Individuals			Institutions		
Year	Average Trade Size (000$)	Commissions ($)	Effective Commission Rate (%)	Effective Commission Rate (%)	Commissions ($)	Average Trade Size (000$)
1961	7.5	75.54	1.0	0.9	88.10	10.1
1962	7.6	76.83	1.0	0.8	89.00	11.0
1963	8.1	77.62	1.0	1.0	119.00	12.4
1964	8.1	78.47	1.0	0.9	128.00	14.2
1965	7.9	77.47	1.0	0.8	133.00	16.0
1966	9.5	85.29	0.9	0.9	176.20	20.2
1967	9.3	84.29	0.9	0.8	177.40	21.4
1968	9.5	85.58	0.9	0.9	215.00	24.0
1969	9.0	101.91	1.1	0.9	218.00	24.6
1970	7.0	105.96	1.5	1.1	240.50	22.3
1971	7.5	109.26	1.5	1.0	285.50	27.5
1972	7.7	108.99	1.4	1.0	318.00	32.0
1973	7.3	116.30	1.6	1.1	370.10	33.7
1974	5.6	99.92	1.8	1.3	394.10	29.2
1975	5.8	117.10	2.0	1.0	330.60	34.8
1976	6.4	121.30	1.9	0.8	356.80	44.6
1977	5.9	113.00	1.9	0.8	343.40	44.6

[a]See appendix 9A for an explanation of the calculations.

institutional trading grew rapidly. At the beginning of this period, the total dollars paid in commission on a representative trade, the principal amount of the transaction, and hence the effective commission rate on the transaction were very similar for both individuals and institutions. Over the period while the dollar value of a representative institutional transaction grew by over 340%, the value of a representative individual order declined by about 22%. Additionally, while in the early 1960s individuals' dollar amount of trading dominated public exchange trading (that is, nonmember trading), we estimate that by about 1965 the value of institutional trading surpassed individual trading. Importantly, we believe that the typical dollar trade size for institutions has risen rapidly since the early 1960s at an annual compound growth rate of nearly 10% between 1961 and 1977. Over the same period the same measure for individual trades declined annually by 2%. Thus the disparity between the patterns of individual trading and institutional trading has widened over the period.

In the early 1960s an individual trade was likely to represent about 70% of the dollar value of a typical institutional trade. By 1977 the value of a typical individual trade had dropped to less than 15% of an institutional trade. This changing relationship is reflected in the fact that while the number of shares per individual trade grew at an annual rate of about 3% over the period, the value of the average share traded by individuals declined by a little more than 4% annually.

Both institutional and individual commission effective rates increased quite rapidly in the late 1960s and early 1970s as the fixed rate structure was shifted higher. Subsequent to the unfixing of commission rates (1975), individual rates advanced slightly and appear to have stabilized, while institutional rates fell sharply before (apparently) stabilizing. We have observed that in the early 1960s effective commission rates paid by individuals and institutions for their respective representative trades were quite similar. However, successive changes in the fixed rate schedule (combined with the diverging trading patterns that were emerging between groups) appear to have resulted in diverging effective commission rates for the two classes of investors. The variance between individual and institutional rates appears to grow more rapidly beginning in about 1969.[6] From 1969 to 1974, the effective rate on the representative institutional trade increased from .9 to 1.3%, an advance of about 44%. During the same period the effective rate on a typical individual trade grew from 1.1 to 1.8%, or an increase of 64%. Stated another way, the spread between the individual effective rate and the institutional effective rate widened from 0.2 to 0.5% and by 1977, that spread had widened to 1.1%.

The divergence between commissions actually paid during the fixed-rate period, as given by the fixed-rate schedules, and the competitively determined rates that would have been paid in the absence of fixed rates, provides an estimate of which trades (if any) were being taxed or subsidized. Our estimates of this divergence between fixed and competitive rates are based on the assumptions that (a) the fixed rates on 100 to 200 share individual orders were always set so as to yield no excess profits,[7] and (b) the competitive discounts from that rate for larger orders would have been proportionately the same throughout the period 1961-1974 for both institutions and individuals as the actual discounts available during the negotiated rate period 1975-1977.[8]

These assumptions lead to the estimates of the tax on typical institutional and individual trading presented in Table 9-2, for the period 1961-1974. Starting in the mid-1960s, institutions began paying a regulatory tax that rose sharply in dollar terms and as a percentage of commissions paid through most of the period. For individuals the tax rate was lower, and the total dollars taxed was much smaller than for institutions. By our estimates the *typical* individual trade paid no regulatory tax until 1967, and thereafter paid an increasing tax rate and total dollar tax until rates were unfixed in 1975.

Indirect evidence that fixed commissions were imposing an increasing tax burden on investors during the period 1961-1974 is provided by the various schemes that were developed to avoid the tax. One well-documented method was trading away from the NYSE floor so as to avoid the NYSE fixed commission and other requirements. By 1975 regional exchanges, the third and fourth markets, and foreign trades accounted for between 15 to 20% of volume in NYSE-listed stocks.

Table 9-2
Estimated Tax Effects 1961-1974[a]

| | Institutions | | | Individuals | | |
Year	Effective Commission Rate (% of principal)	Estimated Competitive Rate (% of principal)	Tax ($mm)	Tax ($mm)	Estimated Competitive Rate (% of principal)	Effective Commission Rate (% of principal)
1961	0.90	0.90	0	0	1.00	1.00
1962	0.80	0.80	0	0	1.00	1.00
1963	1.00	1.00	0	0	1.00	1.00
1964	0.90	0.90	0	0	1.00	1.00
1965	0.80	0.80	0	0	1.00	1.00
1966	0.90	0.86	38.0	0	0.90	0.90
1967	0.80	0.77	40.0	8.0	0.90	0.89
1968	0.90	0.83	120.0	10.0	0.89	0.90
1969	0.90	0.82	130.0	24.0	1.09	1.10
1970	1.10	0.96	166.0	10.0	1.49	1.50
1971	1.00	0.88	233.0	14.0	1.48	1.50
1972	1.00	0.87	277.0	27.0	1.37	1.40
1973	1.10	0.96	258.0	29.0	1.57	1.60
1974	1.30	1.12	219.0	42.0	1.75	1.80

[a]See appendix 9A for an explanation of the calculations.

A second method of attenuating the tax burden was to engage in non-price competition. Familiar examples of this phenomenon include the provision by brokers of extra services to clients (research, etc.) and the give-up arrangements described in appendix 9C, whereby a client directs part of the commission to third parties who supply other services.[9] However, barter and non-price competition are not a perfect substitute for price competition. Barter is less efficient since it requires negotiating in each case the mix of services of a given market value that are of the highest value to the recipient. This inefficiency could become a major consideration if there is very effective non-price competition among brokers (as seems likely) and the proportion of the commission to be bartered, given up, or "returned" becomes large.

A third method of dealing with a regulatory tax structure that is not in equilibrium is for the regulator to change the tax schedule. Various attempts were made to change the tax structure in the late 1960s and early 1970s. Discounts on very large share transactions were first allowed in 1968. Later, other efforts were made to change further the tax rates faced particularly by institutions. The pre-1975 changes put the SEC in the awkward political position of mandating (or as it was called during this period, "not objecting to") relatively high percentage commission rates on individual or small orders, and at least "condoning" negotiated and deeply discounted commission rates for very large or institutional transactions. In 1971 the commission on transactions larger than $500,000 was made negotiable, and that breakpoint was dropped to $300,000 in 1972. In 1975 all commissions were made negotiable. With respect to smaller transactions, in 1970 a surcharge was approved for orders of 1,000 shares or less, and in 1974, commissions on orders below $5,000 were made negotiable.[10]

Based on the indirect evidence just described, we assume that in the early 1960s the fixed commission schedule reflected the shape of the underlying industry cost curves fairly closely so that, typically and with the exception of the tax on innovation, the commission rate charged was very close to a competitive price. Thus during this period the major effect of fixed rates was to preclude innovation and price competition and not to tax or subsidize customers by over- or undercharging them.

By contrast, as the representative value and share size of trades increased during the 1960s, the fixed commission charged deviated more and more from the implied competitive rates. We estimate that beginning in 1966 for institutions and 1967 for individuals, a positive regulatory tax was imposed that rose sharply over most of the next decade, despite (in some cases as a result of) the numerous efforts to revise the fixed price schedule.[11]

The large and increasing regulatory tax on individual investors, which incidentally we estimate was rapidly approaching the size of the annual SEC budget by 1974, is likely to have increased the opposition of individual investors to the fixed commission structure. These views may have contributed to the growing political opposition, both from Capitol Hill and the administration, to fixed rates over the period 1965-1975.

Changes in the economic interests of institutions and the fixed commission rate structure over the period 1961-1975 are more difficult to assess and are complicated by the fact that many institutions are regulated to some extent by the SEC. The reduction in the regulatory tax rate on very large orders through discounting surely benefited institutions and thereby somewhat reduced their opposition to fixed rates. However, in our judgment total taxes implicit in the fixed rate structure increased sharply through 1972 (see Table 9-2), which would have operated to increase the opposition of institutions to a continued fixed commission structure.

On the supply side of the market, securities firms, exchanges, and other marketplaces had various degrees of economic interest in maintaining a fixed commission structure. However, this is not to say that all of these diverse organizations were earning excess profits due to fixed commissions by the early 1970s. For example, much of the potential profits associated with the implied taxes shown in Table 9-2 were probably returned to customers through non-price competition.

It seems clear that the amount of support that any group gives to maintaining fixed commission rates should be greater, the greater the economic benefits they receive from fixed rates. While this seems almost a truism, it raises the question of why some securities firms, particularly the larger publicly owned ones, either gave little support to maintaining fixed rates in the early seventies or actively opposed fixed rates. We are left with two alternative explanations: (1) They were not acting in their own self interest, or (2) they had no positive economic interest in fixed rates.

There is at least some indirect support for the notion that publicly traded securities firms had little economic stake in the fixed commission system.[12] This is provided by the movement in publicly owned securities firm share prices, relative to a general market index, over the period when fixed rates were removed. Despite large deviations from market performance over recent years, a casual reading of brokerage firm share prices reveals no apparent permanent drop below average market performance, as there would be in the case of a permanent loss of a monopoly profit stream. This observation is consistent with the notion that these firms were earning little or no monopoly profits from the existence of fixed commissions.

Many other securities firms were harmed by the unfixing of commission rates, and some either went out of business or were merged with larger and/or more diversified firms. Even these firms, however, may not have been earning monopoly profits. The harm they sustained from the unfixing of commission rates may have been due largely to their specialization of capital and personnel in servicing the "large-tax" or institutional orders.

Exchanges were much more uniform than firms in their opposition to the removal of fixed commissions, suggesting that some exchange members and exchange employees had a substantial interest in maintaining the fixed-rate structure. And the market evaluation of the future of exchanges, as reflected in seat prices, confirms that exchanges suffered a large deterioration in their economic prospects over the period when rates were unfixed, a deterioration that has continued to the present time.[13]

NYSE seat prices, for example, peaked in 1969, and since then have declined by about 85% to their February 1978 level of $64,000.[14] This decline has continued unabated throughout the period, in what were historically both good times and bad for exchanges.[15] Reductions in floor brokerage rates on the NYSE, estimated at about 20% from the fixed rate by 1977, surely accounted for some of this decline in seat prices. But it seems likely that other factors that may have diminished the profit prospects of NYSE membership also played a role.[16]

As noted earlier, both regional exchanges and the OTC market may have benefited somewhat from the NYSE fixed commissions by engaging in moderately successful non-price competition. In addition, although the American Stock Exchange (Amex) did not list the same stocks as the NYSE during this period, since many of the Amex stocks are in similar risk-return classes as NYSE stocks, Amex can be said to be an indirect competitor to the NYSE. Over the period since 1969, the economic prospects for all these competing exchanges appear to have deteriorated proportionately even more than those for the NYSE. Amex seats have declined over 90% to $25,000, and most regional exchange seats are now essentially free. Again the unfixing of commission rates played a contributing but indeterminate role in these declines.[17]

The third market and the unlisted over-the-counter (OTC) market did not have fixed commissions, but both markets were providing services in competition with the NYSE and other exchanges; that is, the third market traded NYSE-listed stocks, and the OTC market traded many stocks that were in the same risk-return classes as listed stocks. In this sense, both markets competed with the NYSE and were partially protected from unfettered price competition by the fixed commission on exchanges. That is, although they did engage in limited price competition and in non-price competition, the effective price of the services offered by the OTC markets may still have been higher than would have been available in an unfettered price-competitive environment.

Evidence that the third market has suffered in line with the exchanges over the 1969-1978 period is provided by the diminishing resources committed to that market. By early 1978 the third market had virtually disappeared. In January of 1978 Weeden and Co. announced that it was going to reexamine its commitment to third-market operations and, it is understood, has considerably reduced its activity in that area. Since the third market was developed largely as a result of the fixed commission structure, its demise could well be anticipated when fixed rates were eliminated and off-board principal trading restrictions for exchange members were left in place.

The effect on the OTC market of the unfixing of commission rates is difficult to measure, but some reorganization of that market is evident by observing market-making activity in NASDAQ securities. As is indicated in table 9-3, the NASDAQ marketplace, which encompasses most OTC securities, has seen a decline in the number of market makers and an increase in the number of stocks in which the average market maker deals. Since the number of securities traded through the NASDAQ system has not decreased significantly while the number of market makers has decreased by nearly 40%, we can surmise that the organizational structure of OTC market making has changed. On average, in 1971 OTC market makers were making markets in approximately five securities, but by 1977 that number increased to over seven securities. The increased scale of operations in this industry does not mean, however, that competition or the quality of services offered has been reduced. This observation is supported by the fact that the number of market makers per security increased over the period.

In sum and in a manner similar to the increased scale of operation observed in the brokerage industry, OTC market making has become more concentrated over the period of the unfixing of commission rates. In both cases the unfixing of commission rates provided brokerage firms and market makers (which in some cases may be the same firms) with the competitive incentive to experiment with different firm sizes in order to locate economies of scale.

Conclusions

This paper represents an effort to begin to meet the challenge presented by Peltzman to test the developing general theory of regulation.[18] In particular, in this paper we have examined fixed commissions rates as a regulatory tax, either a tax on innovation or a transfer tax. Since commission rates have been

Table 9-3
NASDAQ Market Making, 1971-1977

31 December (1)	Number of Securities (2)	Active Market Makers (3)	Average Market Makers per Security (4)	Mean Number Securities per Market Maker (5) = (2) − (3)
1971	2,969	578	N/A	5.1
1972	3,454	628	5.6	5.5
1973	2,900	491	4.7	5.9
1974	2,564	387	5.0	6.6
1975	2,579	369	5.6	7.0
1976	2,627	365	6.5	7.2
1977	2,575	353	7.6	7.3

Source: *NASDAQ Factbook,* 1977, p. 8. (NASD 1978, Washington, D.C.)

deregulated only since 1975, the estimates made here must be considered as preliminary, and much remains to be done to test all of the implications of regulation theory.

Briefly, we believe that in the first half of the 1960s fixed commission rates were set at levels that, with the exception of the tax on innovation, closely approximated the rates that would have been paid for typical trades in a competitive environment. If our interpretation is correct, then a major effect of fixed commissions prior to about 1965 was to preclude price competition and thereby place a regulatory tax on innovation.

After the mid-1960s, fixed commissions rose above our estimates of competitive rates for typical trades by both individuals and institutions, thereby creating significant transfer taxes. This implied regulatory tax continued to increase into the 1970s, during the period when numerous adjustments were made to fixed commissions. By our estimates, the total implied annual tax rose from close to zero in 1965 to annual rates of more than $200 million in the early 1970s.

Whatever the precise size of the tax implicit in fixed rates, we feel confident that it increased dramatically over the 1965-1974 period. It also seems clear that at least the large publicly traded firms derived little benefit from fixed rates, a conclusion that is supported by their attitude toward freeing commission rates. Most of the benefits of the tax to these firms seem to have been bid away through non-price competition. By contrast, negotiated rates may have contributed substantially to the overall lowered economic prospects of exchanges as measured by the severe drop in seat prices over the past decade. By the time commission rates actually were unfixed, the regulatory tax had become so onerous that little effective opposition to the deregulation of the fixed commission structure remained.

If our estimates are correct, then, freeing commission rates is best understood not as part of a general deregulation trend in Washington but rather as the result of changes in the economic interests of various groups affected by fixed commissions.

Notes

1. For a discussion of the growth of regulation, see Miller (1977).
2. See Weidenbaum (1976).
3. In this paper we beg the fascinating and closely related questions of: (1) why regulation is growing so fast, and (2) who benefits from this growth.
4. See, for example, Peltzman (1976) and Stigler (1971).
5. For an explanation of the calculations described in this section, refer to appendix 9A.
6. In 1969 a surcharge was placed on commissions, which appears to have

affected the effective rate for individual trades to a greater extent than similar measures of institutional rates. (Refer to appendix 9C.)

7. This assumption is supported by three observations: (1) Executions involving less than 100 shares were charged a commission surtax, called the "odd-lot differential"; (2) there was no competition in the over-the-counter market for smaller orders, indicating that there was little excess profit being made on these orders; and (3) 100 to 200 share orders were competitively priced apparently because rates on that trade size have not decreased since the deregulation of commission rates.

8. See appendix 9A for an explanation of how these assumptions were implemented.

9. To the extent that give-ups were directed to affiliates of investors, they more closely approximate a rebate and thus price competition.

10. In addition, general rate increases to reflect inflation were allowed in 1971 and 1973. For a detailed discussion of the changes in fixed rates over the period, please refer to appendix 9C.

11. See appendix 9C for a discussion of the attempts to bring fixed commissions back into line with competitive prices.

12. This may be due to the importance of the lightly taxed individual business to publicly owned firms. In fact, fixed rates may have discriminated against retail firms to the advantage of institutional firms.

13. See appendix 9B for a documentation of seat prices for all U.S. exchanges and boards of trade and selected foreign exchanges.

14. This $64,000, of course, reflects the expected liquidation value of a seat (pro rata shares in real property, etc.) as well as the expected discounted profit stream of being a member. Thus the portion of the $64,000 that reflects the value of the NYSE as an ongoing business may be small or even zero since equity per member totaled $56,314 at year end (1977) [see NYSE (1978, p. 33)].

15. The seat-price experience should be distinguished from the evidence cited regarding stock prices of publicly traded firms. Exchange seat price experience and brokerage firm price performance may be independent since brokerage firms utilize both exchange and nonexchange trading facilities. Seat prices therefore may not be used to measure the economic welfare of public firms.

16. Using NYSE seat prices as a measure of brokerage profitability, Schwert (1977) has tested the hypothesis that the SEC is captured by the industry it regulates. Based particularly on the decline in seat prices since the unfixing of commissions, he rejects that conclusion.

17. As an aside, it is interesting to note that Canadian stock exchanges have fared no better than American regional exchanges over the past ten years, as measured by seat prices. These exchanges trade stocks that are similar in risk-return characteristics to American stocks and thus compete with American

exchanges in the international market. Those exchanges therefore were to some extent insulated from price competition by the fixed commission structure.

In direct contrast to the stock exchange seat-price experience, the commodity exchange seat prices have been continuously bid up. Those exchanges have experienced a gradual unfixing of their minimum commission rate structure similar to that experienced by the stock exchanges. The Justice Department brought an antitrust action against the Chicago Board of Trade in 1972, which led to class-action suits against other exchanges and commission houses. In 1973 an agreement was made to phase out the fixed commission structure, and in March 1978 all commissions for future contracts were made negotiable. A similar argument can be made for commodities that was made for stocks. That is, the fixed structure was set approximately to offer competitively priced executions until the cost structure of the industry changed. At that time there was enough dissatisfaction with the fixed-rate structure to force its demise and/or provide discounts from the fee structure. The commodity commission rate structure may not have had as large a tax and subsidy built in as did the stock commission rate structure so that the unfixing of commodity commission rates may not have shown up as forcefully in seat prices. In any case, the recent increase in commodity contract volume, particularly since 1972, may have had an overwhelming effect on commodity exchange seat prices, masking any effect that may have been felt by the unfixing of commission rates.

18. See Peltzman (1976, p.240).

References

Bank and Stock Quotation Record (March 1950, 1955, 1960, 1965-1978).

Federal Paperwork Commission. *A Report of the Commission on Federal Paperwork;* Final Summary Report (3 October, 1977).

Mann, Michael. "A Critique of the New York Stock Exchange's Report on the Economic Effects of Negotiated Commission Rates on the Brokerage Industry, the Market for Corporate Securities and the Investing Public." Prepared for the U.S. Department of Justice (October 1968).

Miller III, James C. *Regulatory Reform: Some Problems and Approaches.* A.E.I. Reprint No. 72 (August 1977).

NASD. Letter from Richard B. Walbert, President, NASD to U.S. Securities and Exchange Commission (1 April, 1968).

NYSE. *1977 Annual Report of the NYSE* (1978).

_____. Economic Effects of Negotiated Commissions on the Brokerage Industry, the Market for Corporate Securities, and the Investing Public" (August 1968).

_____. "The Economics of Minimum Commission Rates" (1 May, 1969).

_____. *NYSE Factbook* (various years).

_____. *Public Transaction Study* (1976).

_____. Letter from Robert W. Haack, President, NYSE (2 January, 1968).

Peltzman, Sam. "Toward a More General Theory of Regulation." *Journal of Law and Economics* 19, no. 2 (August 1976):211-240.

Rowen, H.A. "The Securities Acts Amendments of 1975: A Legislative History." *The Securities Law Journal,* (Winter 1976).

Schwert, William G. "Public Regulation of National Securities Exchanges: A Test of the Capture Hypothesis." *Bell Journal of Economics* 8 (Spring 1977):128-150.

Silver v. *New York Stock Exchange.* 393 U.S. 341 (1963).

Stigler, George J. "The Theory of Economic Regulation," *Bell Journal of Economics and Management Science* 2, no. 3 (1971).

Weidenbaum, Murray. *The New Wave of Government Regulation of Business.* A.E.I. Reprint No. 39 (August 1976).

U.S. Congress, House Subcommittee on Commerce and Finance, Securities Industry Study, *Report of the Subcommittee on Commerce and Finance of the Subcommittee on Interstate and Foreign Commerce,* 93d Cong., 1st sess., February 1973.

_____. Senate, Subcommittee on Securities. *Securities Industry Study. Interim Report of the Subcommittee on Securities of the Committee on Banking, Housing and Urban Affairs,* 92d Cong., 2nd sess., 4 February, 1972.

_____. *Securities Industry Study. Final Report of the Subcommittee on Securities to the Committee on Banking, Housing and Urban Affairs,* 93d Cong., 1st sess., February 1973.

U.S., Department of Justice, Comments submitted in response to SEC Release No. 8239 (1968).

_____. "Memorandum of the United States Department of Justice on the Fixed Minimum Commission Rate Structure." Statement Submitted to the U.S. Securities and Exchange Commission (17 January, 1969).

U.S. Securities and Exchange Commission. *Institutional Investor Study Report.* Summary Volume (March 1971).

_____. Release No. 8239, 26 January, 1968.

_____. Release No. 8324, 28 May, 1968.

_____. Release No. 8860, 2 April, 1970.

_____. Release No. 9007, 22 October, 1970.

_____. *Report of Special Study of Securities Markets* (17 July 1963):347, 350.

_____. *Report to Congress on the Effect of the Absence of Fixed Commissions* (1 December, 1975; 29 March,1976; 10 August, 1976; 28 January, 1977; 26 May, 1977).

_____. Directorate of Economic and Policy Research. *Staff Report on the Securities Industry in 1977* (22 May, 1978).

Appendix 9A
Commission Rate
Calculations

To assess the importance of fixed commission rates to market participants, we have constructed two tentative series from 1961 to 1977, which attempt to identify effective commission rates for the two classes of public trades—institutions and individuals. Given the relative market share of trading for these groups by shares traded and by dollar value of trading,[1] we were able to estimate the dollar value of the average shares traded. From recent data available on shares per trade by group for 1977 and by assuming that earlier in the period individual orders averaged 200 shares per trade,[2] we constructed an implied series for average shares per trade for both groups. By combining share price and trade-size information, we developed a "typical" trade series for the two groups of traders.

Because of the importance of round lots both to trading in securities and, not incidentally, to computing commissions, we then adjusted the dollar amounts of typical trades to the nearest round lot. For example, in 1977 a typical institutional trade of 1,357 shares (at $32.84 each) was adjusted to 14 round lots with a value of $3,190 each.[3] Then for each year 1961 through 1977 we identified the applicable (and often changing) commission rate payable, whether as fixed by NYSE rule[4] or as incurred after the abolition of fixed commissions.[5] We then estimated the effective commission rate by dividing the total amount of commissions paid for each typical trade by the respective principal amount of the transaction.

To estimate the amount of the regulatory tax on commissions during the period of fixed commission rates, we estimated what the commission would have been under competitive conditions by extrapolating from the observed commission structure since the deregulation of the fixed commission structure. Specifically, we assumed that the commission rates charged on the 200-share trade throughout the period were set very close to what the competitive rate would have been. This observation is supported by the fact that there has been no significant change in those rates after the introduction of competition. Then from the data available during the competitive period, we calculated the discount rate that would have been obtained on representative trades for both classes of investors during the period of fixed commissions. This assumes that while the cost structure of the industry may have been shifting upward (1968-1974) that the slope and shape of the supply curve remained essentially unchanged. We then multiplied the relevant rate of discount, which represents the regulatory tax rate by the dollar value of trading for institutions and individuals for each year to obtain the dollar value of the tax, which is presented in table 9-2.

Appendix 9B
Exchange Seat Prices:
Last Sale for Month
of February

Table 9B-1
Primary Security Exchanges

Year	NYSE No. Seats	NYSE Last Sale	Amex No. Seats	Amex Last Sale	CBOE No. Seats	CBOE Last Sale
1950	1,375	$ 52,000	499	$ 10,000		
1955	1,366	90,000	499	20,000		
1960	1,366	156,000	499	60,000		
1965	1,366	200,000	877	55,000		
1966	1,366	250,000	880	95,000		
1967	1,366	275,000	883	145,000		
1968	1,366	475,000	883	260,000		
1969	1,366	480,000	889	320,000		
1970	1,366	300,000	880	165,000		
1971	1,366	300,000	885	135,000		
1972	1,366	240,000	881	100,000		
1973	1,366	155,000	857	100,000		
1974	1,366	85,000	827	35,000	750	$15,000
1975	1,366	95,000	818	50,000	750	39,000
1976	1,366	97,500	804	47,000	1,020	88,000
1977	1,366	75,000	772	49,000	1,020	65,000
1978	1,366	64,000	777	25,000	1,020	51,600

Source: *Bank and Stock Quotation Record.*

Table 9B-2
Regional Exchanges

	Boston		Cincinnati Regular		Cincinnati Limited		Pacific (Los Angeles)[a]	
Year	No. Seats	Last Sale	No. Seats	Last Sale	No. Seats	Last Sale	No. Seats	Last Sale
1950	120	1,250	16	4,497	10	1,000	59	9,500
1955	109	1,200	12	4,497	9	1,000	60	11,500
1960	102	1,200	12	8,000	7	1,000	76	12,000
1965	91	2,000	12	8,000	11	1,000	160	7,500
1966	100	11,000	14	5,700	14	1,000	160	37,500
1967	100	12,800	27	5,500			160	37,500
1968	101	24,750	26	5,500			175	65,000
1969	152	14,000	25	8,500			184	55,500
1970	178	14,000	35	8,250			206	70,000
1971	187	10,000	30	8,000			206	52,500
1972	192	5,000	30	4,000			207	33,000
1973	196	3,800	60	4,000			214	23,000
1974	214	1,400	60	2,500			214	10,000
1975	214	800	60	1,000			214	6,500
1976	204	500	60	1,000			214	12,000
1977	204	200	60	3,333			214	4,200
1978	204	350	60	3,333			214	250

Source: *Bank and Stock Quotation Record.*

[a]The Los Angeles and San Francisco Exchanges merged in 1955 to become the Pacific Coast Stock Exchange. Two divisions remained until 1965, and in 1973 the name was changed to the Pacific Stock Exchange.

Table 9B-2 continued

Year	Midwest		Philadelphia Regular[b]		Philadelphia Options		San Francisco[c]	
	No. Seats	Last Sale	No. Seats	Last Sale	No. Seats	Last Sale	No. Seats	Last Sale
1950	400	3,000	200	250			67	7,000
1955	400	4,500	200	1,100			80	4,000
1960	400	9,500	200	5,500			80	8,200
1965	400	9,750	200	5,000				
1966	400	15,500	201	11,000				
1967	406	17,500	212	17,000				
1968	422	36,000	217	27,000				
1969	429	55,000	461	16,500				
1970	434	40,000	515	16,500				
1971	435	45,000	473	33,400				
1972	435	15,000	505	9,000				
1973	435	15,000	505	7,000				
1974	435	7,000	211	4,000				
1975	435	4,600	505	2,000				
1976	435	5,000	208	500	223	3,000		
1977	435	6,500	208	na	213	6,500		
1978	435	150	208	100	223	4,000		

[b]Prior to 1966 called the Philadelphia-Baltimore Stock Exchange. In 1966 the name was changed to Philadelphia-Baltimore-Washington Stock Exchange (PBW), and in 1976 the name was changed to the Philadelphia Stock exchange (Phlx) and Options memberships were added in that year.

[c]The Los Angeles and San Francisco Exchanges merged in 1955 to become the Pacific Coast Stock Exchange. Two divisions remained until 1965, and in 1973 the name was changed to the Pacific Stock Exchange.

na: Not available

Table 9B-2 continued

Year	Detroit No. Seats	Detroit Last Sale	New Orleans No. Seats	New Orleans Last Sale	Pittsburgh No. Seats	Pittsburgh Last Sale	Salt Lake City No. Seats	Salt Lake City Last Sale
1950	49	700	30	75	65	600	34	1,000
1955	40	1,100	30	75	65	400	39	2,000
1960	40	1,600			59	500	42	1,200
1965	60	15,000			59	500	39	700
1966	60	5,000			59	475	45	600
1967	60	4,250			53	500	45	650
1968	60	8,000			54	2,500	38	1,000
1969	63	11,000			54	2,500	37	1,100
1970	63	6,300					37	150
1971	59	5,000					37	5,000
1972	60	2,750					na	na
1973	55	1,500					na	na
1974	52	1,500					45	800
1975	47	1,500						
1976	46	1,500						
1977								
1978								

na: Not available.

Table 9B-2 continued

	Spokane		Intermountain	
Year	No. Seats	Last Sale	No. Seats	Last Sale
1950	18	750		
1955	14	450		
1960	12	425		
1965	13	1,000		
1966	13	1,000		
1967	13	1,500		
1968	15	1,200		
1969	15	2,500		
1970	15	2,500		
1971	15	5,000		
1972	13	5,000		
1973	14	3,000		
1974	14	3,000		
1975	14	1,500	39	850
1976	13	1,500	34	700
1977	13	1,500	34	1,200
1978	13	1,000	34	1,550

Table 9B-3
Commodity Exchanges

Year	N.Y. Cocoa		N.Y. Cotton		N.Y. Coffee/Sugar		Commodity	
	No. Seats	Last Sale	No. Seats	Last Sale	No. Seats	Last Sale	No. Seats	Last Sale
1950	183	3,200	450	5,100	344	3,700	632	500
1955	183	10,000	450	8,500	344	2,200	545	500
1960	183	15,000	450	2,500	344	2,900	408	2,750
1965	183	7,400	446	750	337	4,000	402	500
1966	183	20,000	450	1,900	337	6,500	382	1,400
1967	183	20,000	450	1,800	337	6,500	378	1,050
1968	183	21,000	450	6,800	337	8,100	386	9,000
1969	183	24,000	450	6,500	337	7,900	386	11,500
1970	183	20,000	450	3,100	337	7,000	386	10,000
1971	183	14,500	446	4,200	337	7,000	386	8,350
1972	183	16,000	450	4,800	337	8,500	386	8,000
1973	183	20,000	450	4,800	337	10,500	386	14,000
1974	183	17,500	450	6,400	337	14,500	386	20,000
1975	183	15,000	450	6,300	344	13,000	386	17,000
1976	183	11,000	450	9,900	344	25,000	386	30,000
1977	183	22,000	450	12,000	344	38,000	386	38,000
1978	183	21,000	450	16,500	344	24,000	386	36,000

Source: *Bank and Stock Quotation Record.*

Table 9B-3 continued

Year	N.Y. Mercantile No. Seats	N.Y. Mercantile Last Sale	N.Y. Produce No. Seats	N.Y. Produce Last Sale	Chicago Board of Trade No. Seats	Chicago Board of Trade Last Sale	Chicago Mercantile No. Seats	Chicago Mercantile Last Sale
1950					1,422	2,200	494	2,100
1955					1,422	6,750	500	5,300
1960					1,422	6,000	500	3,225
1965	401	2,800	513	550	1,402	12,950	500	6,500
1966	401	3,000	503	1,000	1,042	17,300	500	12,100
1967	401	6,600	473	1,500	1,042	20,000	50	5,500
1968	403	18,500	473	2,500	1,402	18,500	500	25,000
1969	407	41,000	473	5,000	1,402	21,050	500	40,000
1970	406	34,000	473	8,000	1,402	36,000	500	75,000
1971	408	11,600	473	na	1,402	34,000	500	66,000
1972	408	7,500	473	5,000	1,402	31,500	500	85,000
1973	408	8,500	473	7,200	1,402	40,000	500	112,000
1974	408	12,000			1,402	71,500	500	105,000
1975	408	9,000			1,402	85,500	500	87,000
1976	408	9,000			1,402	132,000	500	150,000
1977	408	9,800			1,402	120,000	500	145,000
1978	408	13,500			1,402	150,000	500	165,000

na: Not available.

Table 9B-3 continued

Year	International Monetary Mkt. of Chi. Merc.		Ft. Worth Grain & Cotton		Kansas City Board of Trade		Memphis Cotton	
	No. Seats	Last Sale	No. Seats	Last Sale	No. Seats	Last Sale	No. Seats	Last Sale
1950			44	1,300	211	10,000	175	9,500
1955			44	750	211	5,000	175	9,000
1960			41	1,500	211	5,000	175	3,500
1965					211	4,500	175	3,000
1966					211	6,750	175	2,500
1967					211	7,750	175	1,500
1968					211	12,000	175	2,000
1969					211	9,000	175	1,000
1970					211	6,000		
1971					211	8,500		
1972					211	7,000		
1973					211	9,000		
1974	650	27,500			211	16,500		
1975	650	23,900			211	27,000		
1976	650	25,900			214	49,250		
1977	650	49,800			214	45,000		
1978	650	72,000			214	42,500		

Table 9B-3 continued

Year	Milwaukee Grain Ex.		Minnesota Grain		New Orleans Cotton	
	No. Seats	Last Sale	No. Seats	Last Sale	No. Seats	Last Sale
1950	142	200	522	2,000	500	1,050
1955	114	200	522	1,500	500	1,075
1960	84	200	514	600	na	na
1965			426	100	480	200
1966			409	50	480	200
1967			409	1,000	480	200
1968			409	600	480	175
1969			409	250	480	175
1970			386	50	480	150
1971			370	1,000	480	125
1972			420	3,000	480	125
1973			420	250	480	125
1974			420	1,500	480	125
1975			420	3,300		
1976			420	3,330		
1977			420	4,000		
1978			420	2,250		

na: Not available.

Table 9B-4
Canadian Exchanges
(Canadian dollars)

	Canadian Stock Ex.		Montreal Stock Ex.		Montreal Curb Ex.		Toronto Stock Ex.		Vancouver		Winnepeg Grain	
	No. Seats	*Last Sale*	*No. Seats*	*Last Sale*	*No. Seats*	*Last Sale*	*No. Seats*	*Last Sale*	*No. Seats*	*Last Sale*	*No. Seats*	*Last Sale*
1950	33	1,000	463	2,400			80	6,000	100	6,000	113	36,000
1955			463	1,900	109	6,500	80	28,000			113	75,000
1960			462	750	100	9,500	80	29,000			113	140,000
1965			410	250	92	10,000	80	20,500			113	71,000
1966			396	500	98	14,000	70	45,000			113	105,000
1967			383	700	96	5,500	80	43,000			113	85,000
1968			380	850	94	3,000	77	14,000			113	92,000
1969			374	900	94	5,250	79	15,000			113	125,000
1970			354	2,750	93	15,000	79	30,000			126	126,000
1971			354	2,100	93	10,000	na	30,000			126	125,000
1972			354	2,400	93	9,000	81	36,000			126	na
1973			333	3,000	89	5,000	79	27,000			126	90,000
1974			na	2,800	88	1,000	82	18,000			126	86,000
1975			339	6,500			85	18,000			126	34,500
1976			339	3,000			85	3,000			126	27,500
1977			338	1,000			85	2,000			126	20,000
1978			338	1,100			85	1,000			126	20,000

na = Not available.
Source: *Bank and Stock Quotation Record.*

Appendix 9C
Pressures Leading
to Negotiated
Commission Rates

The events that led to the 1975 actions, both regulatory and legislative, removing the NYSE-fixed commission rate structure are in some respects surprising. The SEC, created in 1934 as the "watch dog" of the securities industry and the protector of investor interests, did not initiate the action. In fact, on one occasion, the SEC testified on behalf of the NYSE defending the Exchange's immunity from the Sherman Antitrust Act, and that defense of the NYSE did not elicit any investor dissatisfaction.[6] Ironically, it was the bookkeeping problems associated with record volume and the Justice Department's criticism of NYSE efforts to dominate the market and erect barriers to entry that brought the fixed commission structure to the attention of Congress and the Commission and that led to the collapse of fixed-rate commissions and the inauguration of the national market system legislation.

The Stimulus Provided by the NYSE for Fixed-Rate Removal

The *Special Study of the Securities Industry* completed by the SEC in 1963 stated that the practice of "give-ups"[7] was questionable at best and should receive a thorough investigation by the Commission.[8] However, the SEC did not act on the give-up question until a proposal to limit give-ups was made to the Commission in January 1968 by Robert Haack, president of the NYSE. The NYSE proposal was prompted by concern about the erosion of the NYSE's market share to the regional exchanges. From 1961 to 1966 regional exchanges increased their dollar volume almost 250% and their market share (dollar volume) over 14%.[9] Regional firms had a competitive edge because they allowed give-ups not only to members of other stock exchanges but also to members of the National Association of Securities Dealers or any registered broker-dealer, while NYSE members were allowed to give up commissions only to other NYSE members.[10] Mutual fund and institutional investors, desirous of getting more for their fixed commission costs, would direct their transactions to the regional exchanges and authorize that part of their fixed commission be given up to other broker-dealers who, for example, sold their fund shares or who provided them with research.

The NYSE foresaw further erosion in their market share as institutional participation expanded. In their letter to the Commission, the NYSE Board of Governors asked for approval of rule changes that would not only make the

NYSE a more competitive exchange and therefore stop the NYSE commission "leakage" to other exchanges and the over-the-counter markets[11] but would also force regional exchanges to eliminate the rules that were affording them a competitive advantage. On 26 January, 1968 the SEC requested comment on the NYSE proposals.[12] Comments were submitted from the NYSE, American Stock Exchange (AMEX), the regional exchanges, trade associations, institutional investors, broker-dealers, law firms, individuals, and the Department of Justice.

The Department of Justice submission directly challenged the continuance of a fixed-rate commission structure. It suggested that the SEC: (1) determine the extent to which commission rate fixing is required in fulfillment of the purposes of the Securities and Exchange Act of 1934; (2) eliminate all rate fixing that is not found to be so justified as inviolative of the antitrust laws; (3) develop standards governing the extent to which rate fixing can be justified; and (4) determine the proper means for assuring equitable and nondiscriminatory access by nonmember broker-dealers to the NYSE.[13] In response to the Justice Department's submission, the SEC announced that it would commence hearings in July 1968 into the rate structure of the national securities exchanges.[14] In that same release, the SEC requested that the NYSE either provide for an interim commission rate schedule that would reduce rates for the portion of any order in excess of 400 shares or eliminate minimum rates of commission on orders in excess of $50,000.[15] The NYSE submitted an alternative proposal on 8 August, 1968 providing for reduced rates on the portion of a transaction that was in excess of 1,000 shares and prohibiting customer-directed give-ups.[16] The SEC approved the revision in a 30 August, 1968 letter from SEC Chairman Manuel Cohen to Robert Haack. The NYSE membership voted on the change, and it went into effect 5 December, 1968.[17]

The Stimulus Provided by the Brokerage Industry for Fixed-rate Removal

During the period 1960 to 1968, average volume on the NYSE more than tripled. This threefold increase was a result in part of increasing institutional volume.[18] Institutional share volume on the NYSE as a percent of total share volume increased from 25.4% in March 1956 to 33.8% in September 1961, 39.3% in March 1965 and 42.9% in October 1966.[19] Because of this significant increase in the volume generated by institutional investors, Congress requested that the SEC conduct a study outlining the effects the increase in institutional investor volume had and would have on the securities markets.[20]

In response to the increased volume, brokerage houses allocated resources to opening new branches and attracting sales.[21] The clearing, bookkeeping, and operational aspects of their business, referred to as the "back office," appear to have been neglected. During 1968 and 1969 in an effort to offer relief to their inundated back offices, brokerage houses "raided" each other for qualified people with back-office experience and hastily acquired data-processing equipment that was sometimes inadequate to the task.[22] Operating expenses rose sharply in the latter part of 1969 and early part of 1970. The number of shares traded and dollar volume of shares traded for that same period declined rapidly.[23] Firms found themselves without adequate working capital to meet day-to-day operating demands, while an excessive amount of their capital was tied up on uncompleted transactions.[24] Many were forced into liquidation, among them over 100 brokerage firms were forced to liquidate between 1969 and 1970.

At the same time that customers of these liquidated firms and others realized that their cash and security balances could be at risk, Congress enacted the Securities Investor Protection Act (SIPA) of 1970. This established the Securities Investor Protection Corporation (SIPC) to act as an insurer of last resort for the customers of brokerage firms. SIPC was given the authority to borrow as much as $1 billion from the U.S. Treasury to cover catastrophic losses.[25] Finally, numerous members of the Senate and the House specifically called on the appropriate congressional oversight committees to complete a study identifying the causes of failure in the brokerage industry and to propose corrective legislation.[26] The SEC was requested in the SIPA itself to collect a list of unsafe and unsound practices within the brokerage industry and recommend corrective legislation.[27]

Results of the Studies by Industry Participants, Governmental Agencies, and Congressional Subcommittees

By 1968 both the SEC and Congress had become involved in the fixed commission rate controversy. Concerned by the April 1968 memorandum from the Justice Department to the SEC calling for the abolition of fixed-rate commissions, the NYSE responded with a study submitted to the SEC in August of 1968 listing eighteen major problems caused by the foreseen "destructive competition" that would result in the absence of fixed commission rates.[28] The major points made by the NYSE in its study may be summarized as follows. First, they contended that the demand schedule for transactions is relatively price inelastic so that any changes in demand caused by commission rates would not significantly affect the demand for transactions.[29] Second, the smaller, more efficient firms would be eliminated by the larger, more inefficient firms. In the study's view, the larger firms would survive because they were diversified. Therefore increased concentration would occur without greater industry efficiency. Third, greater "fragmentation" would result in securities trading markets that would seriously weaken the primary auction market. Finally the existing system of trading stocks, including the minimum commission structure, had led to investor confidence, which could be destroyed if price competition were introduced. Indeed, it was stated that "chaos in the financial markets" could result.

On 30 October, 1968 the Justice Department invited a group of economists to present their views on the advisability of fixed-rate commissions. The Justice Department also commissioned Michael Mann to write a formal criticism of the NYSE's report and his paper was entitled "Economic Effects of Negotiated Commission Rates on the Brokerage Industry, the Market for Corporate Securities and the Investing Public." Dr. Mann addresses each of the contentions of the NYSE and summarizes by saying,

> I would anticipate the continued viability of the brokerage industry after the elimination of fixed prices, with the only major difference being that prices will move closer to the actual cost of providing the service.[30]

On 17 January, 1969, the Justice Department filed a memorandum with the SEC refuting the NYSE's economic and legal memoranda. In summary, the Justice Department argued that: (1) the *Silver* v. *New York Stock Exchange* case established that the Securities Exchange Act of 1934 did not exempt the NYSE from the Sherman Antitrust laws; (2) "fragmentation" would not occur in the securities markets if commission rates were unfixed since the NYSE would probably regain some of the market share that it had lost to the regionals and third market; (3) competition would eliminate the practice of give-ups and reciprocal business while lowering rates and improving accessory services; (4) establishing negotiated rates would eliminate apparent NYSE antitrust violations; and (5) the SEC should take further steps to abolish the restrictive practice imposed on members of the NYSE that preclude them from making off-board transactions and oversee rule changes that would increase direct access to primary exchange membership.[31]

In May 1969 the NYSE defended its earlier economic analysis by submitting "The Economics of Minimum Commission Rates" to the SEC. The testimony of the economists who appeared before the commission was criticized by the NYSE on several counts. Specifically, the NYSE charged that the economists did not offer any statistical evidence "bearing on the unique cost and demand conditions in the brokerage industry," were unfamiliar with the securities business, and relied heavily on general principles that were not applicable in the securities business. Moreover, the proposals and interpretations advanced by the economists were contradictory. The remainder of the paper offered rebuttals to the Justice Department's arguments and concluded by saying that the securities market "is not an area where one experiments, tries a new system and reverts to the old if the results are unsatisfactory."[32]

In March 1971 the SEC completed the *Institutional Investor Study,* outlining the then current and potential effects of institutional investors on the security markets. Among its recommendations the SEC proposed that all obstacles to competition, specifically the fixed-rate commission structure, should be removed[33] and that the interim schedule of fixed rates should be adjusted to reflect more the actual costs incurred and services received.[34] Alarmed by the recommendations of the *Institutional Investor Study,* the NYSE's Board of Governors asked William M. Martin to prepare a paper dealing with, among other topics, negotiated commission rates.[35] Martin's recommendations were submitted to the NYSE Board of Governors on 5 August, 1971. In his report, Mr. Martin suggested that the negotiated rates should be cautiously experimented with before any action was taken. Further, he generally agreed with the NYSE arguments regarding fragmentation.

As noted earlier, when SIPA was signed into law in 1970, the congressional committees charged with the oversight of the securities markets agreed to engage in comprehensive studies of such questions as negotiated commission rates and a centralized market system. The complete studies of both the Senate and the House Subcommittees were finished in 1973. Both subcommittees concluded that: (1) fixed commissions were a hindrance to competition and should be removed; (2) regional firms could compete with large national wirehouses in a negotiated commission environment; (3) the securities industry's ability to raise capital for its own use would not be affected by negotiated commissions; (4) negotiated commissions would lead to a more unified central market rather than causing fragmentation in that market; and (5) securities firms would be forced to focus more attention on costs and operating efficiency rather than solely on sales.[36] These two subcommittee reports formed the basis on which the amendments to the Securities Exchange Act were formulated and eventually passed by Congress in 1975.

NYSE's Requests for Increases in Commission Rates

During the early 1970s while Congress was exploring the merits of fixed-rate commissions, the SEC was holding hearings on the requests by the NYSE for increases in commission rates. In February 1970 National Economic Research Associates submitted a request on behalf of the NYSE to the SEC recommending a substantial increase in commission rates on orders of 300 shares or less but reducing commissions on orders of more than 300 shares. Because of the financial condition of the securities industry, in April 1970 the SEC approved a surcharge for the lesser of (a) $15 or (b) 50% of the applicable commission, on orders of 1,000 shares or less.[37] The SEC rejected, however, the initial proposal submitted by National Economic Research Associates to reduce the commission schedule for orders of more than 300 shares and concluded instead that the commissions charged for the portion of an order in excess of $100,000 should eventually be negotiated. To implement this decision, in April 1971 the SEC designated that commissions on transactions in excess of $500,000 were to be negotiable. In April 1972 the breakpoint was lowered to $300,000.[38] This gradual process of implementing negotiated commissions was used because industry participants had never traded in a negotiated commission environment.[39]

In the meantime the NYSE applied for further commission rate increases in 1971 and 1973, both of which were "not objected" to by the SEC.[40] In December 1974 the SEC approved an experiment in which commissions would be negotiated for orders below $5,000; for the portion of orders above $300,000 commissions continued to be negotiated.

Despite the continued allegations by the NYSE that negotiated rates would cause the demise of the regional firm, illiquid markets, chaotic market conditions, and market fragmentation, the Securities Act Amendments were signed into law on 4 June, 1975. In line with the intent of the act and regulatory initiatives, nonmember commission rates were made fully negotiable on 1 May, 1975, and exchange floor rates on 1 May, 1976.

Notes

1. NYSE (1976).
2. Sec-DEPR (1978).
3. $(1,357 \times \$32.84)/14 = \$3,190$.
4. NYSE *Factbooks* (various years).
5. SEC (1976-1978).
6. In *Silver* v. *New York Stock Exchange* (1963), Harold J. Silver sued the NYSE because the latter severed the direct-wire telephone connections, which were established between the two parties and necessary to the plaintiff's conduct of business.
7. Give-ups, an effective form of non-price competition, are arrangements whereby institutional customers directed that a percentage of their fixed commission rates be redistributed to third parties thereby nominally maintaining the fixed structure of commission rates.
8. SEC *Special Study* (1963), pp. 347, 350.
9. SEC Release No. 8239 (1968), p. 4.
10. SEC Release No. 8239 (1968), p. 4.
11. For a summary of the NYSE position on give-ups, see, Letter to the Commission from Robert W. Haack, president of the New York Stock Exchange, 2 January, 1968, reprinted in SEC Release No. 8239 (1968).
12. SEC Release No. 8239 (1968).
13. See the Justice Department's submission (1968).

14. SEC Release No. 8324 (1968).

15. SEC Release No. 8234 (1968).

16. Senate Interim *Special Industry Study* (1972), p. 54.

17. Senate Interim *Special Industry Study* (1972).

18. For a description of the events leading to the 1975 amendments, see Rowen (1976).

19. SEC Release No. 8239 (1968), p. 2.

20. Rowen (1976), p. 331.

21. Rowen (1976), p. 331.

22. Senate Interim *Securities Industry Study* (1972), p. 7.

23. For example, share volume declined 7.01% from 1968 to 1969 while dollar value of shares traded declined 11% for the same period. [Senate Interim *Securities Industry Study* (1972), p. 7.]

24. For example, the percentage of buy transactions made on the NYSE that actually cleared on settlement day declined from 65% in August 1969 to 20% in September of that same year. [Senate Interim *Securities Industry Report* (1972).]

25. In addition, "user charges" levied on brokerage houses were initiated in order to create loss reserves within SIPC.

26. Rowen (1976), p. 332.

27. Rowen (1976), pp. 332-333.

28. NYSE (1968).

29. NYSE (1968), p. 5.

30. Mann (1968), p. 57.

31. Department of Justice Statement (1969), pp. 9-14.

32. NYSE (1969).

33. Rowen (1976), p. 332.

34. *Institutional Investor Study Report,* Summary Volume (1971), pp. 104-105.

35. Rowen (1976), p. 332.

36. House *Securities Industry Study* (1973), pp. 131, 132, and Senate Final *Securities Industry Study* (1973), p. 44.

37. SEC Release No. 8860 (1970).

38. SEC Release No. 9007 (1970).

39. House *Securities Industry Study* (1973), pp. 136-143, and Senate Final *Securities Industry Study* (1973), pp. 44-61.

40. The SEC said that it did not "approve" the 1971 rate increase, but at most gave an "interlocutory nonobjection" [Senate Interim *Securities Industry Study* (1973), p. 58.]

Comment

H. Michael Mann

The papers of Michael Keenan and of Roberts, Phillips, and Zecher in different ways raise the question of the relationship between economic theory and the regulatory process. Keenan worries that there is no theory of deregulation and suggests that the brokerage industry will provide data by which to formulate such a theory. Roberts, Phillips, and Zecher articulate a theory of regulation based on a goal of wealth transfer. Each will be addressed in turn.

It is true that economic theory does not provide much on the paths that may be taken in the movement from an equilibrium of a regulatory regime to an equilibrium produced by a deregulated regime. It may be that in some circumstances the transition costs might be so substantial that even if deregulation improved static efficiency, that is, price closer to long-run marginal costs, one would hesitate to abandon regulation. The securities industry is not such a case, but in fact is an example that existing theory is well suited to analysis.

The argument of the New York Stock Exchange (NYSE) was that deregulation would generate destructive competition, the result of which could be a substantial increase in market concentration. (NYSE 1968). In order for the path from regulated equilibrium to a deregulated equilibrium to be characterized by destructive competition, certain conditions, well articulated by economic theory, have to be present. Although some are present, a critical one, inelasticity of supply, is not. (Mann 1975). Further, there is no evidence that economies of scale are present to the degree that calls for a natural oligopoly[1] (Ramsay 1975). Even if the transition process generated a level of concentration higher than that required for efficiency, entry is sufficiently easy that monopolistic pricing for more than a short period is highly improbable.

We have therefore no need for a theory of deregulation here. The brokerage industry's experience with deregulation has shown,[2] and will continue to show, that deregulation works when the circumstances are favorable, that is, the industry's market environment contains all the characteristics for vigorous competition. We now have prices that much more closely approximate the true costs of the provision of the brokerage service.

Roberts, Phillips, and Zecher's analysis indicates that fixed commission rates were a tax on innovation from 1961 to 1965 and a tax that transferred wealth from 1966-1974. Neither the theory nor the evidence offered for the former period is convincing. According to Roberts, Phillips, and Zecher, fixed rates coincided with competitive rates from 1961 to 1965, but since a brokerage firm could not cut its rate following a cost-reducing innovation to gain new customers, there was no incentive to innovate.

It is unclear exactly how these authors arrive at their estimates of the effective and competitive rates, but one can only wonder that if they coincided in the years 1961 to 1965, why was the give-up a common practice and why was there a third market, both of which are indications of rates substantially in excess of the costs of transaction and execution. Further, it strains credulity to believe that a rate structure that increased commission fees as a multiple of the number of round lots in an order tracked cost increases proportionately.

The theory that fixed rates were a tax on innovation is not persuasive. If an entrepreneur knows that he can reap the benefits of a cost-reducing innovation in increased profits, a strong incentive exists to innovate. This is particularly so because imitative innovation by others will not generate downward price movements to eliminate the profits gained from innovation. A more complex story occurred over the years 1961 to 1974 than Roberts, Phillips, and Zecher's "theory of regulation" implies.

Both papers leave unanswered a fundamental question: Why did the institutions not attack the regulated system directly, that is, challenge the SEC to use its jurisdiction over "the fixing of reasonable rates of commission . . ." (Memorandum 1969, pp. 18-37) rather than resort to tactics that bypassed the system, for example, the third and fourth markets? It is especially puzzling because these alternatives are arguably less efficient than use of the NYSE (Memorandum 1969, footnote 17, pp. 49, 50-53). What this experience may indicate is that the SEC made it more costly to contest than to bypass. This suggestion follows from a theory that emphasizes the political economics of the regulatory process[3] (Noll 1971, pp. 39-46). If subsequent research confirms this speculation, it will enhance our understanding of why an encouragement of competitive forces as a substitute for regulation comes so slowly, if at all.

Notes

1. Even if economies of scale dictated small numbers, we would probably be better off despite the likelihood of monopolistic pricing (Williamson 1968).

2. Michael Keenan's paper documents this quite thoroughly. Also see West (1978).

3. Michael Keenan points out that the SEC focused its energies on regulating ethical, not economic, conduct. The political-economic theory of regulation predicts such behavior, emphasizing such considerations as: Regulators will seek to minimize review of their decisions, a goal that in this case would lead them to prevent manipulation and fraud, highly visible events and if they occurred very often, would call into question the vigilance of the regulators; the losers from regulation are fragmented, raising the transactions costs associated with organizing against detrimental regulatory behavior; and it is difficult, given the indivisibility of the benefits from changing regulation, to overcome the free-rider aspects of a lobbying effort. In addition, Keenan surfaces the

important fact that the costs of the economic conduct permitted by the regulation were hidden, not obvious to the losers until they become so substantial that large buyers, institutions, found it in their interest to seek the benefits of competition (Mann 1976).

References

Mann, H.M. "The New York Stock Exchange: A Cartel at the End of Its Reign." In *Promoting Competition in Regulated Markets,* edited by A. Phillips. Washington, D.C.: The Brookings Institution, 1975.

————. "Deregulating the Brokerage Industry." *Challenge,* November/December 1976, pp. 48-51.

Memorandum of the United States Department of Justice on the Fixed Minimum Commission Rate Structure, SEC File 4-144, 17 January, 1969.

New York Stock Exchange. *Economic Effects of Negotiated Commission Rates on the Brokerage Industry, The Market for Corporate Securities, and the Investing Public,* August 1968.

Noll, Roger. *Reforming Regulation, An Evaluation of the Ash Council Proposals.* Washington, D.C.: The Brookings Institution, 1971.

Ramsay, Glen. "Statistical Estimation of Long-run Costs in the Brokerage Industry," Appendix to Mann 1975.

West, Richard. Letter to the Business Editor, *New York Times,* 30 April, 1978.

Williamson, Oliver. "Economies as an Antitrust Defense." *A.E.R.* 58 (March 1968):18-36.

Comment

Robert W. Swinarton

Deregulation in the securities industry is an intriguing subject and certainly out of context with the pervasive trend of expanding government intervention and involvement in all of our daily lives. Members of our industry, in particular, have decried the proliferating role of government regulation and championed the function of the marketplace in our free-enterprise system. The unprecedented opportunity to deregulate is with us today. It would be sad if we passed up this rare opportunity to remove ourselves from burdens of unneeded regulation and at that very moment become frightened of the system we believe in and one that has served our economic system so well.

Regulation can be viewed in two broad categories, namely, those rules and regulations that have taken the form of protection of the participants within the system and those which affect the securities industry's structure and behavior. We should not confuse the two types because I suggest that there is very little, if any, controversy over the need for adequate investor protection. The debate over regulation focuses mainly on those rules that have an impact on the structure of and behavior within the industry.

My comments will primarily address this second category. A great deal has been said with which I find substantial agreement so I will also pass over those areas so as not to be repetitive and zero in on the major subjects of disagreement. (It is interesting to note the apparent incongruity in positions taken by the speakers on this panel, academic and regulator representatives supporting deregulation and the two industry representatives taking a much more reluctant deregulation position.)

The most significant form of structural deregulation came in May 1975 when fixed commission rates were eliminated. We as a firm were advocates and supporters of this development. We anticipated it would have a major impact, but also a salutory one. The impact has obviously been deep and far-reaching, but this could logically have been expected considering the extended time period that fixed rates existed that allowed economic imbalances to be created within the industry. Prior to the demise of fixed rates, we heard all kinds of reactions from industry leaders. By some we were cautioned about terrible consequences to come including concern for the existence of the very system itself. To the contrary, I feel we are going through a transitional period that will produce a stronger, healthier, and more viable industry. This is not a beleaguered industry; at worst, it may be considered bewildered. For example, some spokesmen say securities research is less available today. On the contrary, I contend it is more available and achieving better quality under competitive rates. Suppliers of research have had to market their product more broadly to generate needed revenues; therefore a much broader spectrum of institutional clients are being solicited. Certain institutional research firms used to market their product to a few hundred major institutions, but this strategy would not succeed under today's level of rates. Even more important, for the same reasons institutional quality research is now being made available for the first time to the individual investor. This opportunity has materialized through mergers of institutional specialty houses with firms serving large numbers of individuals and via the shifting of research professionals to those firms providing full financial services.

Another concern expressed is that market liquidity has been impaired. My view of 28 years in the business is that market liquidity has never been deeper, greater, or more readily available. The size transaction that can be accommodated today is truly impressive.

A favorite strawman often espoused by the traditional investment banker is that the decline in the number of securities firms brought about by competitive rates has had a real impact on the capacity of the industry to distribute new issues. While the number of firms has declined, it is fair to say that underwriting capacity has expanded markedly, and distribution capability has been capable of processing larger and larger offerings of both equity and debt securities. This has been accomplished since May Day through an expanding universe of salesmen domiciled in an expanding number of branch offices. Industry statistics are:

12/31	Total Offices NYSE Number	Full-time RRs[a]
1977	3,633	39,072
1976	3,576	35,289
1975	3,425	34,643

Source: *NYSE 1977 Fact Book.*
[a]Estimated domestic full-time salesmen.

There are other reactions and views on the impact of competitive rates, but I have touched on the most frequently mentioned. In summary, I maintain that competitive rates are a most healthy development for this industry and in no way endanger its survival.

I believe the very same comment applies to removal of other structural rules such as Rule 390. Many of the same arguments used to oppose competitive rates are being similarly applied to this issue. Unfortunately, the voices lobbying for retention of 390 were much more organized in arousing the fears of corporate America who joined forces in pressuring the SEC and Congress to defer action and in so doing, may also have set back the entire cause of deregulation. I say this because I feel strongly that *the ultimate in pervasive government regulation* would be the step-by-step design by the SEC of a national market system with a *clob* as its centerpiece. We are very close to this reality and have been placed in this predicament because of the imagined fears of fragmentation and the related threat to the future of the NYSE. It is unfortunate that the exchange community does not foresee its real basis for existence and dismiss this obsession with Rule 390. To do this could defuse the present issue and perhaps head off the greatest threat to exchanges, namely, a computerized automated market facility.

Along with other objectives, the 1975 amendments called for the creation of a NMA. This system presumably was to materialize under industry cooperation. The facts are that no group, NMAB, NMA, or SIA, could develop a consensus because of the disparate economic interests. This predicament left the commission with two alternatives: Remove the remaining economic barriers and allow freely competing forces to gradually shape the system or design the key facilities under SEC staff direction and set various implementation dates. We are currently taking this latter path that has the SEC smack in the middle of economic regulation. However, it does not appear that the congressional act directed the SEC to "create" the NMS. Instead, the law simply directed that the SEC *"facilitate"* the establishment of the system. As an alternative, therefore, I would hope they could be persuaded to reconsider the elimination of 390 after the CQS is up and functioning. They could then rely on this important new dimension of disclosure along with the already existent expanded disclosure resulting from CTA and allow evolving industry forces to complete the development of an NMS.

Failing this course of action, consideration could be given to requesting Congress to clarify the 1975 amendments. In any event, in a competitive-rate environment such as exists today regardless of what regulations are swept away or what new regulations are conjured up, I ask that regulations apply equally and be administered evenly to all members of the industry and that existing or proposed regulations neither protect certain members from competition or prevent new entrants into that competition.

Comment

Joshua Ronen

The declared objective of the Roberts-Phillips-Zecher paper is to understand better the phenomenon of unfixing the minimum commission rates within the perspective that views regulation primarily as a device to effect wealth transfers. This is essentially the framework created by Stigler and formalized by Peltzman. By adopting this framework, Roberts, Phillips, and Zecher are ignoring a possibly significant explanatory variable in their attempt to explain the phenomenon of deregulation. This factor is the interregulatory agencies' conflicts and their differing objectives. Peltzman assumed a single regulator who wishes to maximize a voting majority in his support, which he needs for reelection. However, as Jack Hirschliefer points out in his critique of Peltzman, interagency conflicts and differing objectives can affect the regulation process. This could be a particularly significant factor in the case that we are discussing. Michael Keenan discussed in his paper the important role that the Department of Justice played in the evolution of the deregulation of fixed commission rates.

Nonetheless, Roberts, Phillips, and Zecher's attempt is interesting and commendable as a first step toward a positive theory of deregulation in the securities industry. But once they chose the Peltzman framework as a basis, I expected them to derive operational hypotheses and proceed to test some or all of them as they apply in the securities industry. Peltzman himself derives a few such empirical hypotheses that could perhaps be applied to the securities industries. Examples are the following: (1) Regulation will tend to be more heavily weighted toward producer protection in depressions and to consumer protection in expansions; (2) the incentive to regulate grows at the level of demand; (3) the income elasticity of producer protection is less than that of consumer protection; and (4) the tendency to change prices infrequently should be stronger when demand changes than when costs change.

I believe that at least some of these hypotheses could be tested carefully using data from the securities industry. Roberts, Phillips, and Zecher did not do this. Thus I will address myself specifically to what they did do.

The authors argue that commission fixing constituted primarily a tax on innovation rather than a regulatory transfer payment. Their argument is that firms were not as encouraged as they might otherwise have been to introduce cost-reducing measures since they could not reap the full benefits of the innovations through cutting prices and attracting new customers. But even if this view were true, no explanation is offered as to why any regulator, whether the government or self-regulators, would want to impose such a tax. If the price fixing did affect the incentive to engage in cost-reducing innovations, this must have been a by-product rather than the cause of the rate fixing.

Fixed commissions, of course, could be alternatively viewed as a private cartel feature as argued by Stigler (1964), Baxter (1970), and Doede (1967). In fact, the latter view seems to be borne out by the empirical evidence produced by Schwert (1977). Schwert's evidence suggests that exchange seat prices are at least partially attributable to rents, either monopoly rents or rents associated with superior efficiency in organizing security markets. Schwert's evidence that regulatory changes that gradually unfixed the commissions were associated with unexpected decline in seat prices is indeed more consistent with the view of the commission fixing being primarily a rent-producing device rather than a tax on innovation.

But I even doubt that the incentives to innovate in the area of cost reductions were affected by the fixed commissions. In support of their contention, Roberts, Phillips, and Zecher estimate the competitive commissions that would have been paid in the prederegulation period and compare these estimates with the commission paid under the fixed schedules in table 9-2. They estimate that until 1966, the commission rate charge was very close to the competitive price, and on the basis of that, they conclude that the major effect of the fixed rates in the early 1960s was to preclude innovation and price competition rather than to tax and subsidize customers. But if the estimates are correct and the divergence between the fixed rate and the competitive rate was zero in the early 1960s and this fact was known to the firms, why then would the incentive to innovate have been affected?

I have my doubts about the correctness of the estimates. The authors point out that the estimates were made under the assumption that competitive discounts for large orders were proportionately the same in the nonnegotiated rate period and the negotiated rate period. Since it is reasonable to assume that competitive discounts would be a function of the expected level of share trading volume, some bias is likely to have been introduced as a result of this assumption.

But I have another reason to feel uneasy about this assumed equality of the rates in the early 1960s. It is hard to reconcile equality of the rates with Schwert's findings that the post-1967 commission rate changes caused significant decreases in the NYSE seat prices. The seat-price decline implies decreased expectations of the rent attributable to the fixed commissions, included in the seat prices. While it could be argued that this attributable rent was based on anticipation of future divergences between the fixed commission rate and the competitive rate in the post-1966 period, it is more plausible to assume that it was based on existing (that is, in the early 1960s) gaps between the fixed rate and the competitive rate that were applied to anticipated trading volumes and level of share prices in order to obtain rent expectations. Thus I fail to see how the introduction of the tax on innovation further helps explain either the fixing or the unfixing of the commission.

Roberts, Phillips, and Zecher then move on to examine the effects of deregulation on security firms and presumably to deduce from these which groups had incentives to lobby for the deregulation. I do have a few problems with their analysis. By casually observing brokerage firms' share prices that reveal to them no apparent permanent decline below average performance, the authors conclude that publicly traded securities firms were earning little or no monopoly profits because of the existence of fixed commissions. Unfortunately, stock prices cannot be reliable measures of monopoly profits or other forms of rent. As Schwert indicates, the prices of stocks issued by security brokerage firms partially reflect competitive returns to production factors that are not specific to the industry and should not therefore be significantly affected by government regulation. Therefore, these prices are not likely to respond to changes in the regulation in as sensitive a fashion as seat prices.

Schwert concludes that the post-1967 rate changes had statistically significant negative effects on NYSE seat prices. Seat prices reflect the industries' specific factor of production—the economic rent—and therefore their use could be expected to increase substantially the power of the test of the regulatory effect. The effect Schwert observed was spread over the three months surrounding the change period. Specifically, seat prices fell unexpectedly about 5% on average during the three months surrounding changes in December 1976, April 1970, April 1971, and April 1972. These unexpected declines in the seat prices reflect the cumulative effect of reductions in the broker's expectations of future profitability associated with changes on the commission rate regulation. This in turn implies, contrary to Roberts, Phillips, and Zecher's conclusion, that economic rents did in fact exist prior to the regulatory changes. While Schwert's tests were not applied to the period after 1972, I would expect to observe similar results if his empirical tests were extended to include the effect of the unfixing in 1975.

Roberts, Phillips, and Zecher infer from the decline of seat prices the deterioration of economic prospects for the exchanges when the rates were unfixed. But wouldn't that observation be consistent with the deterioration of economic prospects of the exchange members themselves rather than merely the exchanges? After all, if seat prices are appropriately interpreted as equity of exchange members in the exchanges, then these prices would be indicative of expectations of these members regarding future flows of profits, which accrue to them as a function of their brokerage activities on the organized exchange. Thus the distinction that the authors seem to be drawing between exchange members—the securities brokerage firms—and the exchanges themselves is not clear to me.

In fact, Roberts, Phillips, and Zecher's casual observation of the time series of seat prices cannot be used without controlling for other variables as an indication of the effect of deregulation of the commissions. Unexpected changes in seat prices are a function of unexpected changes in share volume and unexpected changes in stock prices. This is so since the new information about the future levels of share volume and stock prices, which become available in a given period, would be contained in the unexpected changes of the seat prices. Indeed, Schwert found that in two major subperiods he observed, 1926-1945 and then 1946-1972, the regression model using unexpected changes in NYSE stock prices and unexpected share volume, as independent variables, explained about one third of the variation in unexpected changes in seat prices. But even though Roberts, Phillips, and Zecher did not extract from the changes in seat prices the effects of the share trading volume and the level of stock prices, I still agree with their conclusion that the deregulation of commissions since 1975 had a negative effect. In other words, if Schwert's tests were replicated to include 1975, I would expect to observe a negative effect due to deregulation.

To summarize the discussion of Roberts, Phillips, and Zecher's paper, I agree with their conclusions that the general deregulation trend occurred as a result of changes in the economic interests of the various groups affected by the fixed commissions. But since the analysis of seat price changes indicate that exchange members did not benefit from deregulation, they probably had little incentive to lobby for their unfixing. Perhaps a study of the institutions as a consumer group and the benefits they were likely to derive from unfixing the commission and of the costs of engaging in the political process could have led us to conclude that they are the ones who had the incentive to lobby for the unfixing. But even that would probably be too simplistic an answer. The complex relationship between the governmental agencies possibly could also contribute to the explanation of the deregulation phenomenon.

Discussion of Edward I. O'Brien's Paper

I will now make some brief remarks on Edward O'Brien's paper. O'Brien's paper is primarily prescriptive. Part of it is a classification of existing regulatory rules. The first two categories relate to the financial responsibility and the operational capability of broker-dealer firms and to the conduct of customer accounts. O'Brien sees these rules as necessary for building public confidence and favors retaining them. Basically, these rules fall into the traditional domain of regulation designed to prevent moral hazard. They are analogous to rules requiring corporations to provide information in annual reports and Form 10-Ks to the SEC and that require that a certain subset of this information be audited. Such rules could be viewed as means to minimize the negative effects of adverse selection on the incentive to trade in securities. Some argue that even though such regulation could be beneficial, its costs are likely to exceed the social benefits. But this is a difficult empirical question on which very little can be said a priori.

I cannot disagree with O'Brien's quest for the elimination of duplicative regulation. But if each regulatory body seeks to expand its regulatory activities so as to enhance its power and budget, this may prove to be a difficult proposition to implement.

O'Brien's treatment of the desirability of the trading rules category of regulation is similar to the previous two categories. He welcomes trading rules that prevent abuses of the kind that did occur, but opposes those designed to protect against theoretical abuses. This may not be a bad rule of thumb to apply. After all, the observation of an abuse leads us to expect a larger benefit from regulation than in the case where no such abuse is observed. In other words, the observation of a given kind of abuse would strengthen our belief that additional abuses of that same kind will occur in the absence of some regulation. It should be noted, however, that trading rules could adversely affect resource allocation in that they are likely to reduce the incentives to generate and reveal information relevant for consumption-investment decisions.

My major problem is with the second part of O'Brien's paper in which he expresses opposition to structural changes such as the deregulation of the commissions. For example, he argues that securities research is less available today after the deregulation. But he does not explain why the prederegulation amount of research was optimal. He argues that as a result of the deregulation numerous security firms have been forced out of existence that were not necessarily "inefficient" but just happened to be in the wrong business at the wrong time. But isn't this the essence of competition? That it weeds out firms that are in the wrong business at the wrong time in order to promote greater efficiency? In short, I have not been convinced that deregulation is undesirable. I am convinced that deregulation did affect wealth transfers, but this in itself doesn't shed any light on its desirability. Finally, it is not obvious to me that gradual removal of regulation of the kind that O'Brien characterizes as "structural pillars" is less socially costly and therefore less desirable than an immediate and once-and-for-all removal of unnecessary regulatory rules.

References

Baxter, W.F. "NYSE Commission Rates: A Private Cartel Goes Public." *Stanford Law Review* 22 (April 1978):672-712.

Doede, R.W. "The Monopoly Power of the New York Stock Exchange." Unpublished Ph.D. dissertation, University of Chicago, 1967.

Schwert, G.W. "Public Regulation of National Securities Exchange: A Test of the Capture Hypothesis."*Bell Journal of Economics* 8 (Spring 1977):128-150.

Stigler, G.J. "Public Regulation of the Securities Markets." *Journal of Business* 37 (April 1964):117-142.

Part III
The Banking Industry

10 The Deregulation of Banking?

P. Michael Laub

Introduction

The advance program for this conference gives an appropriate hint that perhaps the title of this panel, "The Deregulation of Banking," is inappropriate. The future course of banking regulation is hard to predict, and I think a proper focus for us today is to try to have a reasoned discussion of why this is so.

In certain policy-making circles and in academia, it is now well known that there is something akin to a "deregulation movement." Although bankers would certainly love to hop onto this bandwagon, I think we should recognize that those who are leading the band have little to do with banks. The Ford Administration had an extensive agenda for regulatory reform. The 12-page discussion of this item in the *1977 Report of the Council of Economic Advisers* discusses motor carriers, airlines, natural gas, electric power, and occupational health and safety regulations, but not banks. The typology or regulations listed in that report—those that keep the price too high, those that keep the price too low, and those that affect the cost of production—could certainly be applied to banks, but it is not. The Carter Administration's recent *Economic Report* also has an extensive discussion of regulatory reform, but again banking is deemphasized. The President's recent antiinflation speech mentioned the virtue of regulatory reform in certain industrial areas, but not in banking. This is not to say that there have not been at various times attempts to deregulate banking. The successful efforts in the holding-company area and the various unsuccessful attempts to deregulate deposit interest rates and restrictions on the powers of thrift institutions are good examples. The point is that banking, for better or for worse, is usually looked at differently, even though the same kinds of bad resource allocations occur because of unwarranted regulation.

Some clues to the future course of banking regulation might possibly be gleaned through a close examination of recent attempts to change the ways that banks are regulated. At least, that is the approach I will take. Three areas will be examined: attempts to change deposit interest-rate ceilings and the powers of thrift institutions, redlining and credit allocation. These three areas have been selected because the issues involved are very close to the guts of the banking business, the gathering of deposits and the lending of money.

The opinions in this paper are those of the author and do not necessarily represent those of the American Bankers Association.

Other issues could easily be discussed. Some that come to mind are the misnamed "Safe Banking Act" and the control of overdrafts and alleged insider dealings, the misnamed "Competition in Banking Act" and the alleged increase in banking concentration, and the various ups and downs in ways policy makers have viewed the holding company vehicle. But as one surveys the issues affecting the banking industry today, the only others that seem pervasive and basic to the business of banking are branching and electronic funds transfers. There have been some legislative discussions on the branching issue, but they have not gone very far in the legislative process. Despite all its detractors, the McFadden Act and the compromises associated with it seem firmly entrenched. EFT is, of course, very important. But, as I shall discuss, many of the forces propelling developments in this area are also evident in some of the issues just named. A related issue, which is probably too broad and complex for this discussion but very important to the future course of bank regulation, is the proper role of the various bank regulatory agencies.

Deposit Interest Rate Controls and the Powers of Thrift Institutions

The basic regulatory concerns in this area are the interest rate ceilings on checking accounts, and time and savings accounts, and the restrictions on asset and liability powers of thrift institutions. A tremendous amount of effort has gone into attempts to achieve a balanced comprehensive approach to deregulation in this area. The theory seems to have been that a balanced comprehensive approach would gain the support, or at least diffuse the opposition of powerful special interest groups that, allegedly, had a vested interest in preserving the status quo. All such attempts failed. A postmortem might prove useful.

Historical Background

The problem can best be examined by first reviewing some of the historical trends that created the problems these attempts at deregulation were trying to solve. Prior to the Interest Rate Control Act of 1966, thrift institutions did not have interest rate ceilings. Banks, however, have been under interest rate controls since the Banking Act of 1933.

Controls on banks were enacted at a time when the idea of price fixing was quite popular, and the public was horrified with the alleged abuses of unfettered competition. In banking, it was thought that excessive price competition for interbank balances precipitated many of the bank failures that wreaked so much havoc. Subsequent scholarship, however, has successfully challenged this claim. The prohibition of interest on demand deposits also seems to have been viewed as a useful way of offsetting the cost burden placed on large banks by newly imposed deposit insurance fees.

The important question, of course, is what happened after the interest rate controls were imposed. During the Depression, interest rate levels were so low that the prohibition had little significance. During and immediately after, World War II market interest rates were held at artificially low levels by the Federal Reserve, and the resulting inflationary finance produced a swollen, highly liquid banking system. The demands of war-time production precluded all but the most basic additions to the housing stock, and institutions specializing in housing finance did not grow very much.

In the 1950s the picture was quite different. A housing boom precipitated a significant growth in thrift institutions. These institutions offered higher deposit rates than banks, and the excess liquidity in the banking system prompted banks to give up a significant share of the consumer savings market to savings and loan associations and mutual savings banks. During this period, however, commercial development and increasing credit demands gradually dried up the liquidity in the banking system.

By 1960 banks were no longer content to take a passive role in competing for consumer deposits. Pressures of legitimate credit demands forced the Federal Reserve gradually to raise interest rate ceilings. For the first time policy makers were forced to mediate between the demands for mortgages, consumer credit, and commercial and governmental credit at banks and the demand for mortgage credit at specialized thrift institutions. The situation was aggravated when the exigencies of Vietnam war-time finance caused interest rates to rise to new heights. Disintermediation occurred at both banks and thrift institutions. Bank deposit rates were held down by controls. Thrift institutions had to perform a delicate balancing act. If deposit rates were raised too high, they would be caught in a profit squeeze because of their large portfolios of mortgages lent at relatively low rates. If rates were kept too low, deposits would be lost to the unregulated market. Accusations of "rate wars" between banks and thrift institutions were rampant. In addition, older thrift institutions had a competitive problem vis-à-vis newer ones that were starting up in developing areas and accumulating mortgage portfolios at rates that were closer to the market.

The result was the Interest Rate Control Act of 1966. For the first time ceilings were put on thrift institutions. A coordinating Committee of Federal Regulatory Agencies was established to regulate the ceilings. It was understood that there was to be a differential in favor of the thrift institutions. A bow was made to the legitimacy of credit demands at banks by permitting them to sell negotiable certificates of deposit in amounts over $100,000 with ceilings greater than those on smaller certificates. Eventually, these ceilings were lifted entirely. Small banks lost on two counts. Their larger bank competitors had access to the market for large negotiable CDs in a way they did not, and thrift institutions had been given an obvious advantage over them in competing for consumer time and savings accounts. The small saver was a general all-around loser.

The act was considered a temporary measure that would be allowed to expire when a more permanent solution was found. No one seems to have known in 1966 what form the solution would take. And, in retrospect, no one seems to know today.

The administration of the act has been marked by a series of episodes that repeatedly forced policy makers to mediate between conflicting pressures. Some inroads have been made on the size of interest rate differential, but in 1975 it was statutory for accounts that existed at that time. Further inroads on those accounts will have to be sanctioned by Congress. A short experiment with "wild cards," consumer certificate accounts with small denominations, no ceiling, and four-year maturity, was conducted in 1973. Thrift institutions generally offered higher rates than banks on these accounts and received a greater share of the deposits. Yet they did not like them, and the experiment was ended by Congress. Interest rate parity has been achieved on NOW accounts in New England and Individual Retirement Accounts nationwide. The system has survived further bouts with disintermediation. Structural changes in the thrift industry and, more importantly, increasing subsidization and support from Federal Credit Agencies and the Federal Home Loan Bank Board have made disintermediation less of an ogre today than it was in 1966. Congress, to its credit, has refused to extend a bad law for long periods of time. The act has expired several times and has always been renewed, sometimes with vigorous debate but never with the development of a consensus for a substitute.

It is this kind of very messy situation that produced the frustation that prompted proposals for more comprehensive, balanced financial reform.

A similar kind of mess has been developing in our payments system. The amount of checks written per year has been rising rapidly in the post-war period. Many of the same factors that precipitated the conflict between banks and the thrift institutions are also influencing this trend. The gradual drying up of liquidity and rising interest rates gave birth to a generation of corporate treasurers who were very sophisticated at managing funds. They became very adept at lowering balances held at banks and placing more and more excess funds in money market instruments. Consumers reacted likewise and gradually shifted a greater proportion of their balances into interest-bearing accounts. In addition, the prohibition of interest payments on checking accounts made it increasingly more difficult for consumers to earn an adequate return on their checking account balances. Service charges were lowered in many areas, and consumers responded by writing more and more checks. Banks tried to find ways of competing for balances through non-price means. Extra branches, expansion of hours, premiums, and advertising were typical methods.

As this trend continued, major technological developments in the area of electronic funds transfer began to occur. Both the private and public sectors, the latter through the Federal Reserve, began to develop such things as automated clearing houses, regional check-processing centers, and direct deposit of social security and payroll checks to alleviate the pressures of the burgeoning volume of paper checks. Automated tellers began to appear, which added more convenience features to bank checking and savings accounts. Remote terminals began to appear in retail stores and supermarkets for such transactions as check verification and in some cases withdrawal of funds from checking and savings accounts to make retail purchases. A very old form of electronic communication, the telephone, was brought into play as consumers were permitted to make telephone transfers from savings to checking accounts. A somewhat related development was the prearranged bill-paying plans that allowed both banks and thrift institutions to make regular recurring payments for their customers out of savings accounts. Many of these developments may have occurred without regulatory restrictions. But I think it is undoubtedly true that the prohibition of interest payments on demand deposits in a period of rising interest rates has accelerated the trend toward technological and regulatory developments that have enabled institutions to circumvent the prohibition and offer their customers more value for balances held.

The difficulties banks have had in satisfying their customers under the prohibition have prompted many of their non-bank competitors to try to get into the business. The advent of the NOW account, which extended interest-bearing checking account powers to bank and thrift institutions in New England, is the most well-known example. Many of the funds-transfer capabilities associated with remote terminals, the telephone, and prearranged bill-paying plans are available to thrift institutions who can offer customers the additional feature of making the transfers from an account that pays a higher interest rate than accounts at banks. Money market mutual funds, on which checks can also be written, have developed as a highly attractive investment vehicle during periods of disintermediation. More recently, Merrill Lynch has developed the "Cash Management" account. Excess balances in a margin account are put into a money market investment vehicle that offers relatively high returns. Account holders have access to the funds through a VISA card or check. In addition, customers who use up their excess balances have a line of credit equal to the margin value of their marginable securities. There is a relatively high initial-deposit requirement. But except for this requirement, the account is very hard to distinguish from interest on demand deposits with an automatic line of credit to cover overdrafts.

This kind of competitive alteration in the payments system is a second major trend that has prompted the several efforts at financial reform that have attempted to bring order to the process of change.

Attempts at Financial Reform

In the midst of all these changes, a movement for financial reform began to develop. The 1970 *Report of the Council of Economic Advisers* announced the formation of a presidential commission to study the role of financial institutions with a view toward formulating recommendations to make those institutions more responsive to changing economic conditions. The commission was headed by industrialist Reed Hunt and included several other representatives of the industrial and financial world, a few academics and consultants, one state legislator, and one union representative. The commission's report was submitted in December 1971 and covered a wide range of areas. It was recognized, of course, that the reason for the commission's existence was the responsibilities and privileges of thrift institutions vis-a-vis banks and the effect this had on the housing market. But several other issues, which always tend to surface in such commissions, were also discussed in this report. These issues included chartering and branching, the structure and role of depository institution regulators, and the role of life insurance companies and bank trust departments. Most of these issues are irrelevant to the problem being discussed and will not be considered further.

The most important recommendation of the commission was that rate ceilings on time and savings accounts were to be phased out gradually, and thrift institutions were to be given expanded lending powers and third party payment powers. The priority of housing and mortgage finance was to be satisfied through a mortgage interest tax credit to all lending institutions and, if this proved inadequate, a direct subsidy to home buyers. Equalization of reserve requirement burdens was to be achieved through mandatory membership in the Federal Reserve System for all banks and thrift institutions offering third party payment accounts, and the abolition of reserve requirements on time and savings accounts. Uniform tax treatment was recommended for all depository institutions. It was recommended that the prohibition of interest payments on demand deposits be retained. Intrastate branching restrictions were to be eliminated, and more liberal stock-mutual and state-federal charter conversion privileges were to be made available to thrift institutions.

Basically, the commission proposed to solve the problems that brought on the Interest Rate Control Act by making thrift institutions more similar to banks and by creating an incentive to get *all* institutions to invest more heavily in mortgages. Subsequent legislative efforts revealed some problems with the commission's approach.

First, many of the institutional participants did not fully understand, or perhaps completely believe in, what the commission was trying to do. Was it trying to make thrift institutions into banks, or was it trying to change the nature of all depository institutions? Whether or not there is a deficiency of mortgage credit at various times is perhaps arguable. If this deficiency does occur, at least the mortgage interest tax credit addresses the issue. But how could one say that there was an unmet demand for checking account services that thrift institutions could meet? After all, the interest prohibition on demand deposits was to be retained, and rate ceiling differentials on time and savings accounts were to be eliminated. This would tend to put thrifts on a par with banks who had had years of experience at handling the heavier lobby traffic and more burdensome transfer problems associated with checking accounts.

Also recent research by Alan Meltzer at Carnegie-Mellon University (1975) and the Economics Department of Citibank (1976) has demonstrated that our economy, at least in the long run, suffers not from a dearth but a glut of mortgage credit. The retreat from mortgage lending of the less restricted mutual savings banks in the Northeast tends to confirm this view. If this is true, the long-run future of specialized thrift institutions is perhaps rather bleak. In any event, I do not think the average thrift institution manager believes the answer to his problem lies in serving an unmet niche in the market that banks have forgotten about. If there really is an excess of depository institutions, perhaps the commission and subsequent efforts by various congressional committees should have dealt more directly with how consolidation was to be achieved.

There was a tremendous amount of mistrust about how the phase-out of the interest rate ceilings and differentials would occur. The commission recommendations, and subsequent bills, called for elimination of the ceilings after a rather long period of time, subject to approval of a congressional study, or standby authority to reimpose the ceilings being granted to regulators. Compared to the current system of relatively short extensions of the Interest Rate Control Act and continuing congressional debate, this seems a lot closer to more regulation, not less. Indeed, at one point savings and loan lobbyists were telling their constituents what a great legislative victory the proposed reforms would give them because of the proposed five-year extension of interest rate ceilings. Very little was said about the management of the ceilings during the proposed phase-out period. At several times during the relatively short extensions of the Interest Rate Control Act, ceilings have not reflected market conditions. Market participants had no assurances that the ceilings would be administered any better during a longer phase-out period. Recommendations were made about where the system should go, and how long it would take to get there, but not enough was said about how to get there.

The basic assumptions of the Hunt Commission received several challenges from various quarters during the legislative discussions that followed. Lane Kirkland, the AFL-CIO representative on the commission, did not sign the report. His minority report makes explicit a fundamental difference with the commission's philosophy. He believed the thrift institutions to be a justifiable mechanism for achieving an allocation of credit different from that which would occur in an unregulated market. If they could not fulfill this role properly, the answer was more interference with the credit-granting process, not less.

Thrift institutions themselves began to question the basic assumptions of the commission. Their fears about competing with banks and need for assurances on deposit rate ceilings have already been mentioned. A more fundamental problem appeared with the Financial Institution Act of 1975. In an attempt to gain the support of thrift institutions for the bill, the administration decided to scale the amount of the mortgage interest tax credit according to the proportion of mortgages held in an institution's portfolio. If this bill had become law, thrift institutions would have been tugged in opposite directions. They would be given consumer lending and checking account powers, which would give them an incentive to diversify, but the form of the tax credit would give them an incentive to specialize.

Before this scenario is summarily dismissed into the realm of irrationality, the reader would do well to consider the structure of the savings and loan industry. Many of these institutions are less than a generation old. They were formed during a time of high demand for home mortgages and implicit public subsidization of that market. Their managers know how to gether time and savings accounts and sell mortgages. They are much less familiar with other aspects of the banking business. Since the implementation of the Interest Rate Control Act, they have received a tremendous amount of support from other governmental credit and regulatory systems that have insulated them from disintermediation. If their markets are not threatened, they probably see little need to change.

Small banks, on the other hand, probably had the most to gain, at least if the commission's recommendations could have been implemented as intended. After all, they had been the big losers under the Interest Rate Control Act. The increasing ambiguity of policy makers over whether or not the undesirable features of that act would ever be ended began to give them second thoughts about the wisdom of reform. In addition, with the Financial Institutions Act of 1975 a new prospect entered the picture—interest on demand deposits. This was not even considered during the hearings on the bill but was tacked on during a mark-up session as members of the Senate Banking Committee suddenly became enthralled with the enthusiastic descriptions by Senators McIntyre and Brooke of the NOW account experiment in New England. Suddenly small bankers began to have fears of the types of wrenching changes that were bothering savings and loan executives.

Finally, there was criticism of the structure of the Hunt Commission itself. The one union representative had refused to sign, and the great majority of the commission's members had come from business organizations. This prompted Congressman Reuss, chairman of the House Banking Committee, to launch his own effort, the FINE (Financial Institutions and the Nation's Economy) study. The study was to be conducted by the House Banking Committee, which the chairman said would be more responsive to the nation's needs. It was conducted, and some rather interesting proposals were put forth. The problem arose when actual bills were introduced. Some bows were made to the need for more flexible interest rate ceilings and diversification of specialized lending institutions. But the bills were ambiguous in this respect and, in addition, carried an even broader array of provisions unrelated to the central problem. To most observers, this seemed to foretell more regulation, not less.

In 1977 the focus shifted back to the Senate and to the new administration in the White House. To many the time seemed ripe for a more narrowly focused, perhaps more reasoned reform effort. Market pressures for change were continuing unabated and seemed to point to the direction that potential reform efforts should take. Consumers in New England clearly liked NOW accounts. Also the early wrenching experiences that occurred in Massachusetts and New Hampshire were not repeated when the privilege was extended to the other four New England states. Savings banks in Connecticut and Maine got checking account powers about the same time they received the NOW account privilege and found the non-interest-bearing accounts more appealing. More importantly, all institutions learned the lesson of proper pricing from the early difficulties in Massachusetts and New Hampshire. Also credit unions now had their own interest-bearing transaction account, the share draft. And the tendency of thrift institutions to try to get into the payments business via the back door of EFT was continuing unabated. Thus the obvious question: Why not stop this continued "piecemealing" and regulatory disorder through nationwide NOW accounts?

Another development seemed to make the prospect of reform even more likely. The trend toward declining Federal Reserve membership was accelerating and the Federal Reserve was very concerned. The decline in membership had been particularly severe in New England, and the NOW account was shouldering part of the blame. Also the membership decline was clearly due to the excess burden of reserve requirements. A strategic decision was made to try to combine some form of interest on reserves with NOW accounts in an attempt to alleviate the membership burden and perhaps diffuse some of the banker opposition to the cost impact of NOW accounts.

A bill, S.1664, was constructed to attempt to do all these things. The bill was reported out of committee with some modifications as S.12055. It was not considered by the Senate as a whole because the leadership thought it was too controversial.

The source of the controversy should be analyzed dispassionately by proponents of bank regulatory reform. The banking industry, or at least the American Bankers Association, was supporting a substitute measure that, among other things, provided for a specific tradeoff between the usage of newly granted third party payment powers by thrift institutions and the elimination of the interest rate differential on all accounts offered by any institution that utilized third party payment powers. It also specifically provided for the payment of interest on reserves at a uniform rate to all institutions. The administration bill S.2055 provided for a two-year extension of the rate-setting authority granted under the Interest Rate Control Act of 1966. It did not say what would happen afterward, and the most the administration would promise was a task force to study the problem of ceilings and differentials. In testimony on S.1664 savings and loan industry spokesmen were lukewarm about the bill but suggested that their views might be made more favorable by extending the rate-setting authority five to ten years. The administration, concerned about the loss of Treasury revenues from depleted Federal Reserve earnings, did not provide a specific formula for the interest rate to be paid on reserves but instead provided a formula for the maximum amount that could be paid, which made it quite clear that the Federal Reserve would feel a need to discriminate against large banks in the payment of interest.

Banks did not like the way in which their problems were again put off to further study or undetermined regulatory action. Savings and loan representatives eventually opposed the bill and explicitly stated their reason for opposition to be their belief that it would eventually mean an end to the interest rate differential between banks and thrift institutions.

The strategy of the savings and loan industry can easily be understood by looking at what has happened to market shares of consumer accounts under the period of a regulated differential. Between 1970 and 1976 the bank share of consumer certificates of deposit decreased from approximately 56.6% to 44.6%. During the same period money held in these accounts grew 177.2%. The bank share of consumer savings accounts rose from 40.3% to 47.4%, but these accounts grew only 63% in that period. Thus in accounts that are held strictly for interest return and where deposit growth is highest, thrift institutions have made significant inroads. For savings accounts, where competition is on the basis of transfer capabilities and other convenience features as well as interest, banks have done well. Much of the competitive piecemealing that has gone on in recent years has been an attempt to increase the convenience features of thrift institution savings accounts so that they could combine added convenience with the interest rate differential to get an increasing share of this market as they have with certificates of deposit.

Without the differential, however, it is hard to see how they could implement this strategy.

At this point the combining of the ideas of nationwide NOW accounts and interest on reserves seems to have hurt more than helped. The argument that interest on reserves would help offset the cost impact of NOW accounts was not received enthusiastically by the large population of politically attuned nonmember banks who were most disadvantaged by the Interest Rate Control Act. Large member banks saw the possibility of some relief, but the bill seemed to be structured such that the bulk of the relief would go to small member banks. In addition, the position of the Federal Reserve and other policy-making authorities with respect to the pricing of Federal Reserve services, what services may be provided, and who has access to the services is very unclear at the moment. The possibility that the Federal Reserve might try to solve its membership problem by aggressively providing new free or underpriced services in competition with the correspondent banking system makes the issue even more complex. The issue remains unresolved.

Redlining

The genesis of this issue lies in the urban turmoil of the 1960s. The debate seems to have begun in Chicago, a highly industrialized city with many strong ethnic neighborhoods and a long history of racial problems. All the dismal features of modern urban life are evident there—disastrous public housing projects and urban renewal, the subsidization of suburbanization, crime and welfare problems, fear and prejudice, and business practices based on them. The antiredliners believe the most promising way of alleviating these problems lies in the regulation of the credit-granting process.

It is worth noting that debate on the issue did not start with concern about the availability of credit. It started with the strengthening of community groups who were upset with rapidly changing neighborhoods and had accused real estate firms and lenders of "blockbusting," a situation that while perhaps unfortunate, does not seem to connote the lack of credit availability for the purchase of homes. This is not quite as illogical as it would seem at first. The original redliner was the Federal Housing Administration. In the 1950s it apparently believed that redlining was the proper way to manage risk. As urban problems became more of an issue in the 1960s, FHA did a flip-flop. It promoted the granting of credit on excessively liberal terms, which in turn facilitated blockbusting and the mismanagement and abandonment of real property (see de Vise 1976 and FNMA 1976). Conventional lenders quite naturally were reluctant to lend in such areas.

The politics of this situation were such that it was eventually transformed into a much more general and dubious proposition—that the solution to urban problems lies in the availability of credit from private lenders. The National Training and Information Center, an anti-redlining group, has stated the view succinctly:

> Private sector lending institutions through their credit allocation policies have more power over the future of urban neighborhoods than any single force, *including government*. (emphasis added) (1978, p. 100).

The publication that this quote is from documents conclusively that in many cities private lenders have tended to place more loans in some areas than in others. The debate over redlining is in a sense a debate over the proper interpretation of this evidence. Former Mayor Alioto of San Francisco believes it means the lenders are the cause of the urban problem:

> A lender's decision to quit loaning in what he deems an undesirable neighborhood has inevitable consequences. Property values decrease, lawlessness increases, the already battered social structure is further weakened and soon more public services, rehabilitation programs and government involvement are required. The lender, in effect, has established public policy. (1975)

While such a blatant confounding of correlation with causation would not stand up to the methodological strictures of a decent Ph.D. examination, it has at times been highly influential in certain policy-making circles.

One hopeful sign is that the logic of economic analysis has begun to weave its way into the debate. HUD has made a distinction between irrational redlining and rational disinvestment that occurs because of neighborhood decline due to factors beyond the lender's control. "Irrational redlining" is really a euphemism for discrimination inspired by prejudice or fear. In competitive markets, this kind of discrimination should not occur. If a lender deserts a profitable market because of irrational fears, his competitors should take up the slack and gain accordingly. In addition, the history of the role of unfettered capital markets in promoting economic development was presented to policy makers and found to be quite compelling. The antiredliners did not abandon their view that bad lending policies were the cause of urban decline. But they were forced to attribute implicitly the alleged bad lending policies to a lack of competition in the marketplace.[1]

This led to the Home Mortgage Disclosure Act, an attempt to correct the alleged market failure. The legislative history reveals the theory behind the act. Its intent was not to interfere directly with the process of allocating credit. Rather, data on where institutions made their loans were to be collected and made available to consumers. Presumably consumers would then examine the available data and determine whether or not they liked where the money was being lent. If they did not, the threat of deposit withdrawal would force the deficient institutions to change their policies.

The law has been in effect for over two years, and there has been very little use of the data collected. Lenders have claimed that demand for mortgages does not exist in the allegedly redlined areas, and their depositors recognize this. The antiredliners would like stricter laws and regulations to attempt to measure demand and influence lending policies.

A second thrust of the antiredliners has been to force lenders to lend in the areas from which they draw their deposits. It is claimed that this is a responsibility of the institutions under the convenience and needs test that must be satisfied when a charter is granted. All depository institutions must to some extent meet the convenience and needs of their community. This has less to do with altruism than the nature of the banking business. The gathering of deposits, particularly from consumers, is a localized business in which a strong market presence is required; the lending of money, perhaps less so. However, at both the consumer and corporate levels, the association of loans with deposit services is still quite strong. I think most bankers would interpret the convenience and needs test as something which says they should be able to offer loans and deposit services to their communities when it is profitable. The granting of a charter implies that a regulator has found that there is a need for such services and has found an organization that will be responsible for offering them. The granting of the charter also implies the banking organization *should* offer these services on a basis that is expected to be profitable and not detract from the safety and soundness of the institution. The process does not imply that this is the only thing they are allowed to do or that they should do it on an unprofitable basis for certain types of communities. The unproved claim of the antiredliners is that banks are gathering deposits from local areas and not lending them back into these areas. It is further claimed that such lending would be profitable and that the loans and banks have made instead have been unprofitable. The alleged results are further urban decline and weakening of the banking system.

This discussion has led to the Community Reinvestment Act. This act would require the appropriate federal regulatory agency to assess the record of each depository institution it regulates in meeting its community credit needs. In connection with an application for a bank charter, deposit insurance, branch or terminal, office relocation, or holding company acquisition, the agency would be required to take the applicant's record in meeting its community credit needs into account while passing on the application. The theory behind the act is clear. The regulator is to make an assessment as to whether or not there is a market failure. If there is, the application's process, which is crucial to the growth and expansion of many institutions, is to be used as a tool to enforce the proper market behavior.

The legislative history of the act is an interesting commentary on how far the proponents of stricter regulations are able to go. The original provisions of the bill that was introduced by Senator Proxmire required every institution to define for its head office and branches its "primary savings service area," the contiguous surrounding market area from which 50% of the institution's consumer deposits were drawn. Each bank would then have been required to do an extensive statistical analysis of its "primary savings service area" and determine the extent to which credit need existed in the area and to make plans for meeting that need. The regulators would have been required to "provide for and encourage the involvement of community groups in the process." There seemed to be a clear implication of two things. First, substantial additional regulatory burdens were to be imposed on banks. Second, there was an obvious attempt to alter the allocation of credit. Banks would no longer be responsible for merely offering services on a profitable basis where a need existed. They would be responsible for measuring and meeting the needs by whatever means they had available to them. In order to get the bill passed, Senator Proxmire was forced to delete these more onerous provisions.

Currently regulators are holding extensive hearings to assist them in writing regulations to implement the law. It is clear that the proponents of the act would like the regulators to write into the regulations what they could not get into the law. The outcome remains to be seen.

Credit Allocation

Governmental programs to influence the allocation of credit are pervasive, and many have been with us for a long time. The discussion here concerns two specific legislative attempts that failed, H.R. 212, a bill to lower interest rates by maintaining an adequate supply and improved allocation of credit, and H.R. 6676, a bill to maximize the availability of credit for national priority uses.

The bills were introduced in the first half of 1975, a period of substantial economic instability. The country was in the process of coming out of a bout with double-digit inflation and plunging into the worst recession in the postwar period. Most of the previous programs for credit allocation had been dictated by war-time conditions or were responses to complaints from specific groups such as farmers or home builders. This time, the country was not experiencing a military emergency, and there was a general economic malaise. The response, at least by the chairman of the House Banking Committee, was a much more general attempt at credit allocation.

H.R. 212 was introduced first. It authorized the Federal Reserve to allocate credit toward national priority uses and determine what those priorities should be. It specified some of the categories that should be included in the Federal Reserve's list of priority uses. These included essential and productive capital investments, normal operations of established business customers to overcome a lack of adequate working capital, low- and middle-income housing, small business, agriculture, and local governments. The Board was to direct credit away from nonpriority uses that were considered inflationary. These were to include loans for such things as mergers and acquisitions, the repurchase of shares, or other "speculative" purposes. The Federal Reserve was given authority to use supplementary asset reserve requirements or any other means at its disposal.

It is worth noting that the credit allocation provisions of this bill were accompanied by a specific provision for a 6% growth in the money supply—an easy money policy relative to what the Federal Reserve was going at the time.

The problem and the response were different in both magnitude and kind from previous attempts at credit allocation. The economy had clearly gotten out of hand. It was more than a question of certain sectors being hurt by a tight-money policy. Everyone was hurting. Interest rates had been driven to unprecedented heights by severe inflation. The logic of the bill seemed to be that interest rates would be reduced by an easy money policy, and inflationary pressures would be controlled by direct interference in the credit-granting process. Congress did not buy it.

The monetary policies of 1972 and 1973 had taught policy makers an old and difficult lesson: An excessively easy monetary policy can hold interest rates down for a short period of time, but the ultimate inflation is inevitably worse than it otherwise would have been.

Also it was hard to see how direct credit controls would stop inflation, especially when the previous four years had been noted for extensive use of wage and price controls that failed to do so. It was also hard to see how such direct credit controls would actually influence the allocation of real resources.

Nonbank depository institutions, finance companies, insurance companies, and other segments of financial markets would not be covered. Many congressmen had been made acutely aware of the fungibility of credit by difficulties they had experienced in trying to support the housing market through interest rate ceilings and subsidies to specialized thrift institutions. This experience did not bode well for a much broader scheme of credit allocation.

The Federal Reserve opposed the bill as an obvious infringement on its independence. It also did not like the credit allocation provisions and viewed them as unnecessary and possibly counterproductive.

It should also be noted that the categories for priority uses were modeled after a statement of lending guidelines developed in September 1974 by the Federal Advisory Council, a group of bankers that advises the Federal Reserve. The difference between developing a set of advisory guidelines for banks to give to lending officers, and directing the Federal Reserve to make banks adhere to a set of priorities that it determines, with the burden of proof put on the banks, is quite evident to bankers, if not Chairman Reuss. The bill proposed to control economic instability by daily and continuous regulation of the myriad business judgments loan officers make every day. Congress rejected such a massive intrusion in the credit-granting process.

H.R. 6676 was Mr. Reuss's second foray in this area. The bill contained no credit allocation provisions. Once again, the Federal Reserve was to determine priority uses of credit and was to survey banks to see how their lending patterns fit into those uses. It was clear that the intent of the bill was to collect information to promote credit allocation measures. Otherwise, why collect the information? Essentially, the banks and the Federal Reserve would be asked to go through the exercises that could be used to allocate credit in the way Mr. Reuss wished, but the actual allocations were not to be made. The transparency of the proposal was evident to many congressmen who saw no reason to give authority to the Federal Reserve to impose extensive regulatory burdens on banks to collect information to support a proposal they had already rejected. This bill also failed.

Conclusions

I suspect most of you agree with me that regulation is a second-best solution, something that should be tolerated when a better solution is not available but something that should be minimized. After reviewing these episodes, I do not think one could conclude that policy makers are about to undertake a massive uplifting of the burden of bank regulation.

The credit allocation proposals were attempts to impose additional regulations on banks, and they were rejected. I believe they were rejected because Congress correctly perceived that the public blamed the government for the instability they were experiencing. Government economists tended to blame food shortages and oil price increases. The public might have accepted this to a certain extent, but they certainly did not exonerate Washington. In any event, I do not think they blamed banks. There was widespread concern over actual and prospective bank failures, and Congressman Reuss attempted to gain support from the alleged "unsound and speculative" lending policies of banks. But I do not think this characterization was widely accepted. Even if it was, there was also a fairly widespread recognition of the fact that many individuals and businesses were getting through those difficult times only through the forbearance of their bankers. Imposing additional and seemingly excessive regulatory burdens on banks just did not seem like the right thing to do, especially when the previous episode of controls in the nonfinancial sector had been so disastrous.

The Home Mortgage Disclosure Act and the Community Reinvestment Act have to be viewed as successful efforts to impose additional regulations on banks. Both laws are considerably less burdensome than their proponents would have liked. The Home Mortgage Disclosure Act imposes additional data-collection and disclosure burdens on banks, on the theory that the availability of such information will correct an alleged failure in the competitive marketplace. The Community Reinvestment Act, if my interpretation of it is correct, imposes additional burdens on regulators but not on banks. It does suggest the possibility that growth of particular banks will be restricted when regulators make a judgment that the benefits that should be achieved through competition have not been realized. Nevertheless, it is discouraging that the basic assumption underlying these laws—that the lack of available credit is a major cause of urban problems—was never seriously examined or tested in the policy debates.

The various attempts at financial reform and the lifting of deposit interest rate ceilings were attempts at deregulation that failed. Although the reasons for the failures are evident, the right solution is not obvious. Thrift institutions have been given certain competitive advantages over banks. In exchange for giving up some of these advantages, they were at first asked to accept regulations that would permit them to do what banks were already doing—a tenuous bargain. When the bills were changed to hold out the possibility that thrifts could keep their advantages and still get some of the things banks have, bank support waned. Adding additional and complex issues into the package, such as consolidation of regulatory agencies, the burden of Federal Reserve membership, or the regulation of foreign banks, has not helped. The result has been a continuation of the status quo.

Of course, the status quo does not imply absence of change. Piecemealing and small regulatory changes will continue to occur, as will the market pressures for more value for balances held. Also additional economic instability could further test the added support systems that have been created to mitigate the burden of disintermediation on thrift institutions. As of this date, however, the right combination of market pressures, technological innovation, and regulatory piecemealing needed to induce sensible financial reform has not occurred.

Notes

1. Lawrence J. White of New York University has suggested to me that another form of irrational redlining may take place even in competitive markets because of the "prisoners dilemma" problem. He hypothesizes that even though there may be profitable lending opportunities in a deteriorating neighborhood, an individual banker would not make such loans because he knows the amount of credit he has to lend will not solve the problem unless many other bankers also invest in the neighborhood. The uncertainty about what other bankers will do causes all of them to hold back. I do not believe this can occur because of the way market conditions encourage bankers to conduct their business. In addition to making judgments about the credit worthiness of individuals and businesses, loan officers are always evaluating the economic environments in which those individuals and businesses exist. If an individual loan can be made "bankable" only by additions of substantially larger amounts of credit to neighboring entities, bankers typically perform an entreprenuerial function and organize formal or informal lending syndicates to make the necessary credit available. This function has been undertaken in all kinds of lending activities including many successful urban revitalization efforts.

References

Alioto, Joseph. Statement to Donald E. Burns, Secretary of the Business and Transportation Agency, State of California, 23 June, 1975.

Citibank Economics Department. *Credit Allocation*. New York: Citicorp, 1976.

de Vise, Pierre. "The Anti-redliners." Chicago: University of Illinois at Chicago Circle, September 1976.

Federal National Mortgage Association. *Redlining*. FNMA, Washington, D.C.: January 1976.

Meltzer, Alan. "Credit Availability and Economic Decisions: Some Evidence from the Housing and Mortgage Markets." in *Government Credit Allocation*, Institute for Contemporary Studies, San Francisco, 1975.

National Training and Information Center. *Perceptions of Risk: The Bankers Myth*. Chicago, 1978.

11 Bank Holding Company Acquisitions, Competition, and Public Policy

Lawrence G. Goldberg

This session is entitled "deregulation of banking." But one may justifiably ask, what deregulation? There are a few areas where there has been a recent easing of regulatory constraints. A few states have relaxed branching restrictions. NOW accounts, in effect, interest-bearing demand deposits, are permitted in New England. Some interest rate ceilings have been increased, and some even removed.

However, movement has been overwhelmingly in the opposite direction. In the wake of several recent large bank failures, there has been increased public and congressional demand for a reevaluation of the adequacy of the regulatory structure and for tighter regulation of banks. The regulators themselves appear to be taking a more stringent look at bank capital and liquidity. There have been several presidential and congressional task forces[1] that have issued wide-ranging reports advocating deregulation of the banking environment, but no substantial legislative action has been taken.

The bank holding company is one area where significant changes have been made in the regulatory rules and environment. In one sense, the changes are a movement to more regulation, but in another sense, the development of the bank holding company has alleviated certain regulatory restraints. It is important to measure the consequences of regulatory change in order to guide future public policy. This paper examines this one particular aspect of banking.

What effect has the development of the bank holding company had? Several studies have attempted to assess the impact that bank holding company affiliation has had on bank performance. These studies have generally not uncovered effects with compelling public-policy implications.

The two major studies, Lawrence (1967) and Talley (1972), each examined the effect of holding company acquisitions on the performance of selected banks. Both studies yielded similar results. Talley summarizes his results as follows: "These banks tended to switch out of U.S. Government securities and into state and local government securities and loans, particularly installment loans. Such portfolio changes suggest that holding company acquisitions result in acquired banks making more credit available in their localities. Holding company acquisitions, however, did not result in statistically significant changes in the capital, prices, expenses, or profitability of acquired banks. Therefore, it appears that holding-company acquisitions do not have a broad impact on the performance of acquired banks."[2]

This study presents empirical evidence on the competitive impact of bank holding company acquisitions. We do not treat many other important issues such as the effect on bank safety of acquisitions. The results of the analysis have important policy implications. This will become apparent from the discussion of the changes and proposed changes in the regulatory framework and environment relating to bank holding companies.

The development of the bank holding company movement and with it the increase in bank holding company acquisition activity in the last decade has made it increasingly important that regulatory authorities be aware of the likely consequences of bank holding company acquisitions. Under current regulations, all bank holding company acquisitions of banks or nonbanking firms must be approved by the Federal Reserve Board. If a holding company acquires a bank in the same market as one of its banks or if it acquires a nonbanking firm that competes directly with any subsidiary of the holding company, existing competition is eliminated by the acquisition.[3] However, if the holding company and the acquired firm do not presently compete, any competitive effect in the acquired firm's market would depend on the effect of the acquisition on the performance of the acquired firm. If the holding company were to improve the performance of the acquired firm, it is likely that the acquired firm's market share would increase and consequently its market position improve. In the case of acquisitions that eliminate existing competition, that is, horizontal acquisitions, it is also relevant to consider changes in market share of the acquired firm since this effect may either augment or diminish the initial horizontal competitive effect.

It is recognized, however, that in some cases the competitive impact of a holding company acquisition might not be reflected in changing market shares, especially if the holding company entry is quickly countered by action of the other firms in the market. Nevertheless, in most cases there should be an effect on market share, and the change in market share, given data limitations, is still the best way to measure competitive impact.

Knowledge of what has happened to the market shares of firms acquired by bank holding companies would be very useful to the regulatory authorities in their analyses of the competitive implications of proposed acquisitions. In this paper a sample of banks that were acquired by holding companies has been collected and analyzed. In addition, evidence obtained by other researchers on the effect on market shares of holding company acquisitions of nonbanking firms is presented and evaluated. Before proceeding with the empirical evidence, it is necessary to first examine the changes in the regulatory environment that have occurred and to show how these changes have made the question analyzed here an issue of extreme importance for public policy.

The Development of the Bank Holding Company

The bank holding company has been in existence for many years, but it remained free of regulatory control until the passage of the Bank Holding Company Act of 1956. Bank holding companies until recently were formed primarily to enable banking organizations to circumvent restrictive state branching laws. Small banks saw the bank holding company as a competitive threat to their well-being, and in 1956 a law was passed which put the activities of the multi-bank holding company under the regulatory control of the Federal Reserve Board. In the act a bank holding company was defined as a company controlling at least two banks. This left bank holding companies controlling only one bank free of regulatory supervision, for at this point few observers were concerned with the omission of one-bank holding companies. Most one-bank holding companies had been formed by individuals or groups who controlled small banks to obtain tax advantages, or by large nonfinancial holding companies that would use their banks to provide banking services to employees and customers.

The Bank Holding Company Act was amended in 1966, but one-bank holding companies remained unregulated. A tremendous increase in the formation of one-bank holding companies occurred soon thereafter, as can be seen in table 11-1. Of the 1,318 one-bank holding companies that were registered on 31 December, 1970 with the Federal Reserve System, 891 were formed between 1966 and 1970. Of these 891 new one-bank holding companies, the Federal Reserve System determined that 455 were engaged in activities other than banking and activities closely related to banking.[4] This development inspired the fear that the United States would soon be dominated by large financial and industrial conglomerates similar to the Zaibatsu, common in Japan. These fears were compounded by the apparent desire of the largest banking organizations to form one-bank holding companies and to acquire large nonbanking firms. For example, First National City Corporation acquired leading firms in the following

Table 11-1
Number of One-Bank Holding Company Formations, by Date of Formation for Organizations Registering on 31 December 1970[a]

Before 1956	83
1956-1960	53
1960-1966	291
1966-June 1968	201
June 1968-31 December 1970	690

Source: "One-Bank Holding Companies Before the 1970 Amendments," *Federal Reserve Bulletin* LVII (December 1972):1001.

[a]Excludes 34 holding companies that submitted late registration statements.

industries: factoring (first acquired as a subsidiary of the bank); mortgage banking; management consulting; and credit cards (subsequently divested and reacquired). Justice Department opposition prevented acquisition of a major insurance company.[5] Diverse nonbanking firms such as Montgomery Ward, Baldwin Piano, and S&H Green Stamps formed one-bank holding companies. "In the step which probably catalyzed official responses, Leasco Data Processing Equipment Corp.—one of the attention-stirring emerging conglomerates of those years—tried unsuccessfully to take over Chemical Bank New York Trust Company."[6] Whereas in 1966, one-bank holding companies controlled 4% of deposits, in 1970 they controlled 38 % of commercial bank deposits.

These developments led in 1970 to passage of Amendments to the Bank Holding Act, which placed the one-bank holding company under the jurisdiction of the Federal Reserve System. While the amendments restricted the previously unregulated ability of one-bank holding companies to engage in nonbank activities, they expanded the opportunity for multi-bank holding companies to engage in nonbanking activities. The Federal Reserve Board was given the responsibility for determining permissible nonbanking activities. These activities must be "closely related to banking" and must pass a "net public benefits" test. Possible benefits to the public, which may include greater convenience, increased competition, or efficiency gains, must outweigh possible adverse effects such as increased concentration, decreased competition, or unsound banking practices.[7] The Federal Reserve Board must consider competitive and other factors when assessing individual acquisition applications.

After 1970 bank holding companies expanded aggressively into nonbanking areas. The most attractive activities were consumer and commercial finance, mortgage banking, and insurance agencies as can be seen in table 11-2. "Despite the large amount of non-bank activity, and the high significance of bank-related firms in many of the non-banking fields, total non-bank assets account for only 3 to 5 percent of total BHC assets."[8]

The passage of the 1970 amendments also removed a major impediment for bank expansion through acquisition of banks by holding companies. Prior to 1970 any one-bank holding company that acquired an additional bank would place itself under Federal Reserve regulation and would also limit its ability to engage in significant nonbanking activities. Passage of the amendments eliminated both of these advantages to remaining one-bank holding companies. Whereas in 1960 12% of all bank consolidations approved by the banking authorities were bank holding company acquisitions, in 1970 the proportion was 50% and in 1973, 74%.[9] In 1970, 146 bank company acquisitions of banks were approved compared to 341 in 1973.

The rate of holding company acquisitions slowed down noticeably in 1974 due to depressed stock prices and to a change in the attitude of the Federal Reserve Board. The failure of several large banks made the Board more cautious in approving acquisitions and in extending the list of permissible nonbanking activities. While the number of applications fell from 1973 to 1974, the Board's denial rate for mergers, acquisitions, and formations increased.[10] In addition,

Table 11-2
Volume of Bank Holding Company 4(c)(8) Activity
1 January 1971-26 March 1977

	De Novo Notifications Received	*Proposed Acquisitions Processed by Board*		
		Total Received	*Approved*	*Denied*
Fiduciary and trust	49	12	10	–
Mortgage banking	395	101	77	10
Leasing	364	28	17	3
Investment, financial and economic advisory services	185	14	9	3
Insurance agency or broker	785	169	123	15
Insurance underwriting credit life, accident, and health	66	58	49	–
Finance company				
General	266	3	2	–
Commercial	78	16	12	–
Consumer	413	119	92	9
Insurance premium	5	5	4	–
Mobile homes	–	5	2	2
Agricultural	4	4	3	1
Data processing	114	28	17	1
Factoring	43	11	8	1
Community development	20	3	–	2
Industrial banking	48	19	15	3
Management consulting for banks	–	11	10	–
Savings and loan associations	–	5	2	3
Other	11	19	10	–
Total	2,846	630	462	53

Source: Carter Golembe, *Bank Expansion Quarterly,* p. II-7.
Note: These tabulations are unofficial estimates of the volume of activity.

many applications were undoubtedly withdrawn as it became evident that the Board would deny certain applications. The Board took a harder line on capital adequacy in order to protect the financial stability of the banks. The Board also invoked the issue of potential competition more frequently. Consequently, though bank holding company acquisition activity has slowed from the frantic pace of the early 1970s, the level of activity and its possible economic consequences make a clear understanding of competitive impact a necessity for intelligent public policy formulation.

Acquisitions of Banks

Hypotheses Tested

It has generally been assumed in the analysis of holding company bank acquisitions that the market shares of the acquired banks will increase. Much of this feeling is based on presumed economies of scale in banking and cost advantages of bank holding company affiliation. Acquisition by a larger organization could permit the smaller bank to offer some extra services and thus enable it to attract more customers. The holding company may have a lower cost of capital; thus the acquired bank could expand at lower cost. The holding company may have better and more sophisticated management. Indivisibilities of management may make it difficult for small banks to attract this type of management, and only through affiliation with a larger organization would a small bank be able to use this type of management talent. Finally, the holding companies that are acquiring banks are presumably growth-oriented organizations that will attempt to improve the market position of their acquired banks.

Many studies have implicitly attempted to verify these presumed advantages to holding company affiliation, but the evidence with respect to the relationship among bank operating efficiencies, holding company affiliation and economies of scale remains inconclusive.[11] A recent effort by Benston and Hanweck (1977) using improved techniques, however, has found "that there is a slight difference between affiliates and independents with regard to scale economies, with affiliates showing lesser scale economies or greater diseconomies. Additionally, our results support the conclusion that through affiliation independent banks may reduce average costs in several important banking functions (demand deposits, real estate lending, and administrative services)."[12]

In policy discussions of bank acquisitions, two types of acquisitions have been singled out for special attention: those in which the leading banks in a market are acquired and those in which the smallest banks in a market are acquired. The strengthening of the market position of a leading bank in a market by holding company acquisition has been called "entrenchment." Holding company acquisition of a small bank in a market has been called "foothold" acquisition.

Concern with entrenchment has frequently been expressed by government officials, as evidenced by the following statement by the Justice Department's former director of policy planning for its Antitrust Division: "The Supreme Court has been concerned with . . . the threat that the acquisition of an already dominant firm by a much larger outside firm will in fact entrench the dominance of the acquired firm and perhaps eliminate all competition in the market."[13] Though rarely explicitly presented, the term *entrenchment* is usually used when an organization acquiring a leading bank is accused of either improving the market position of the acquired bank or slowing its loss of market share. Unfortunately, the inexact specification of entrenchment has led to confusion with the concept of potential competition. Entry through acquisition by a banking organization not currently in a market will eliminate one potential competitor and reduce the probability of deconcentration in the future, but the entrenchment doctrine, as defined here, concerns the direct effect of the acquisition on the market position of the acquired bank. If the entrenchment effect actually does occur, the regulatory authorities should use this as an argument for denying the acquisition of banks with substantial market power. Some of the acquisitions would presumably lead to increased market power while others, where the acquired bank was losing its market share, would lessen deconcentration.

Foothold entry has the opposite competitive implication. If bank holding company acquisitions do improve market position, then the acquisition of nonleading banks would make them more effective competitors, and these acquisitions should be encouraged for competitive reasons. Since foothold acquisitions involve banks with smaller market shares (and usually smaller absolute sizes) than entrenchment acquisitions, most of the arguments presented above with respect to the advantages to be gained by holding company acquisitions may be even more compelling here. The Justice Department as well as other regulatory authorities encourages these types of acquisitions:

> A different competitive picture results if the big banking organizations are forced to come into local markets as challengers to the status quo rather than inheritors of it. This occurs where they enter *de novo* or enter by "foothold" acquisition of one of the smaller or weaker banks in the market. Coming in this manner, the new entrant has every incentive to increase its market position—to do this with strong competitive efforts covering new services, lower prices, longer hours and all the rest. This is particularly important in the retail field. The local leaders who have been living quietly have to respond, and thus one ends up with more competitors and harder competition than traditionally existed. This is highly desirable.[14]

The Justice Department analysis equates the competitive effects of de novo entry and foothold entry. Clearly, the formation of a new bank must reduce the market shares of some of the existing banks, but this is not necessarily true for foothold entry. Any procompetitive effect of foothold entry depends on the acquired bank increasing its market share and thus reducing the market shares of other banks.   Current legislative proposals to restructure regulation of holding company acquisitions have used market share criteria that implicitly accept both the entrenchment and foothold entry concepts. Therefore the empirical analysis below tests these two concepts in addition to the general effect on acquired bank market shares and also attempts to identify the conditions most conducive to improved market shares of acquired firms.

Data and Methodology

Data have been collected from the FDIC's semiannual *Report of Condition*[15] for a sample of banks acquired by holding companies between 1965 and 1970 in unit banking states. When a bank is acquired by a holding company, the holding company must keep and report separate records for the acquired bank. However, if a bank is merged into another bank, the acquiring bank need not report the separate status of the merged bank since it becomes a branch of the organization. Branch data can be obtained from the FDIC biennial *Summary of Accounts and Deposits,* but the infrequency of reporting, the unavailability of data for many branches, and the fact that these data go back only to 1966 (and the 1966 data are not totally reliable) limit feasible analysis only to acquisitions.

Most holding company acquisitions of banks have occurred in those states that do not permit branching, the unit banking states. However, there have been a number of acquisitions in branching states, especially those states that have only limited branching laws. In some of these states, the market shares of other banks in a market can be obscured when the bank has offices in more than one market since the *Report of Condition* allocates all deposits to the bank's head office. It may be possible to expand the sample to include acquired banks in some branching states, but in this study these states have been excluded from consideration.

At least three years of postacquisition performance data was required for each bank in the sample. This necessitated choosing banks that were acquired in 1970 or earlier since the latest data used were for December 1972. Since most bank holding company acquisition activity increased rapidly during this period, the sample consists mostly of acquisitions occurring in 1969 and 1970. The sample could be extended to cover more recent acquisitions, but this is not an inconsequential task.

Two years of performance data prior to acquisition were required of every bank in the sample. Thus all new banks sponsored by holding companies as independent banks and then immediately acquired by them have been excluded. The appropriate data go back only to 1960, so all bank acquisitions prior to 1963 have been excluded. Since there were no acquisitions in 1963 or 1964 that were acceptable for inclusion in the sample, the earliest bank acquisition in the sample occurred in 1965.

The 71 banks comprise all banks in the unit banking states acquired through 1970 by holding companies for which the required data were available. Information was gathered for each of these banks and for each of their banking markets, which were considered to be either an SMSA or a county if the banks were not located within an SMSA. Since most of the early holding company acquisition activity occurred in Florida, the sample is heavily weighted with Florida banks. This should not distort the results since the features associated with Florida, such as rapid growth, are taken into account in the analysis. Of the 71 banks, 45 are in Florida, 11 in Missouri, 6 in Colorado, 5 in Iowa, 3 in Montana, and 1 in Minnesota. At the time of acquisition, the average acquired bank had total deposits of $23 million, with the largest of the 71 banks having deposits of $173 million and the smallest $3 million. Thus this study provides no evidence on the consequences of the acquisitions of very large banks. The average bank market share was 12% with a range from 0.2% to 55%. The average number of years the acquired banks were under holding company control was 3.9 years.

The primary focus here is the average market share change of acquired banks and the determination of whether this change is statistically different from zero. In order to do this, several measures of market share change have been developed. The first measure of market share change, X_1, can be calculated by subtracting the acquired banks' market share in the year prior to the acquisition from the market share in the final year (1972) and dividing by the number of years the bank has been under holding-company control. Another measure of market share changed used, X_2, is the compound growth rate of the market share of the acquired bank. Banks with larger initial market shares are weighted more heavily in X_1, and those with smaller market shares in X_2. For example, if an acquired bank with a 10% market share increases its share to 11% in one year, X_1 would equal 1% and X_2 would be 10%. In contrast, an acquired bank that increased its market share from 1% to 2% in one year would have an X_1 of 1% and X_2 of 100%.

If prior to an acquisition, a bank were growing relatively slowly and losing market share, we would still expect the bank to grow slowly subsequent to the acquisition. In order to reverse the previous tendency and increase the bank's market share, a large stimulus by the holding company would be required. For this reason, X_1 and X_2 may be biased measures of the effects of holding company acquisitions. To counteract any possible bias, X_1 and X_2 have been adjusted by the past growth of the market share per year P_1 and the rate of market share growth per year P_2, respectively. The two new measures created, $X_1 - P_1$ and $X_2 - P_2$, are more relevant to the testing of the effects of holding company acquisitions and have been given the central position in the empirical analysis. The terms X_1 and $X_1 - P_1$ are better measures than X_2 and $X_2 - P_2$ of the effect of a market share change of an acquired bank on the level of competition in a market as measured by the concentration ratio.

To test the null hypothesis that the average change in market share is equal to zero against the alternative hypothesis that it is not equal to zero, it is assumed that the sample is drawn from a normally distributed population. The statistic $z = x/s/\sqrt{n}$ is calculated where x is the mean of the sample, s is the standard deviation of the sample, and n is the sample size. When n is greater than 30, the Central Limit Theorem can be applied, and using a two-tailed test, if $z > |1.96|$, the null hypothesis is rejected at the 5% level. When the sample is subdivided, there are occasionally fewer than 30 items. In those cases the t-distribution is applied.

Empirical Findings

Though the possible biases involved in using X_1 and X_2 make $X_1 - P_1$ and $X_2 - P_2$ superior measures of the impact of holding company acquisitions, it is still important to evaluate the unadjusted growth measures. In tables 11-3 and

Table 11-3
Change in Market Share per Year, X_1

Group of Banks	$\bar{x}$	s	n	z
All	0.00012	0.00679	71	0.15
ms > 0.20	−0.00335	0.01131	15	−1.15
ms > 0.15	−0.00110	0.01068	22	−0.48
ms > 0.10	−0.00096	0.00983	29	−0.53
ms > 0.05	−0.00015	0.00909	39	−0.10
ms < 0.05	0.00044	0.00164	32	1.52

ms = market share
$\bar{x}$ = mean of sample
s = standard deviation of sample
n = number of banks in the sample
z = $\dfrac{\bar{x}}{s/\sqrt{n}}$

Table 11-4
Change in Market Share Growth Rate, X_2

Group of Banks	$\bar{x}$	s	n	z
All	0.00835	0.06287	71	1.12
ms > 0.20	−0.00891	0.03366	15	−1.02
ms > 0.15	0.00004	0.03894	22	0
ms > 0.10	−0.00267	0.04730	29	−0.30
ms > 0.05	0.00305	0.05488	39	0.35
ms < 0.05	0.01480	0.07180	32	1.17

11-4, the means of X_1 and X_2 for the full sample and for the various subdivisions of the sample are presented and tested as to whether they are significantly different from zero. As can be seen, since none of the absolute values of z are greater than 1.96, the null hypothesis that the mean of the distribution is equal to zero must be accepted in every case. Consequently, it is concluded that banks acquired by holding companies do not significantly change their market shares subsequent to acquisition. It is useful, though, to examine these results carefully.

The value of z for X_2 is greater than for X_1 when the full sample is considered. Though no statistical significance can be credited to this difference, it nevertheless suggests that the smaller acquired banks grow more rapidly than the larger ones since X_2 is more heavily influenced by smaller acquired banks. The regression results presented later confirm this.

In order to test both the entrenchment and foothold doctrines, the sample of banks has been divided by market shares of the acquired banks.[16] As can be seen in tables 11-3 and 11-4, neither the banks with larger market shares (specified in several ways) nor the banks with market shares less than 5% changed market shares significantly. In fact, those banks with market shares greater than a particular share of the market exhibited decreases in absolute market shares, though these were not significantly different from zero. The relative share changes, X_2, exhibited a pattern similar to X_1.

In table 11-5 the means of the two past growth measures are presented for the full sample, for those banks with market shares greater than 20% and for those banks with market shares less than 5%. For the full sample the measure most sensitive to the growth of the larger banks, P_1, is negative and significant whereas the measure most sensitive to the smaller banks, P_2, is positive. This result is confirmed in the past growth rates of the subsamples. The acquired banks with market shares greater than 20% have experienced decreases in market share for the two years prior to acquisition while the acquired banks with market shares less than 5% have exhibited increases in market share (significant in the case of P_2) in this period. Because of statistical reasons (the regression fallacy), we would expect larger banks to decrease their market shares and smaller banks to increase them. In addition, most larger banks are located in central cities, which typically have been growing more slowly than the suburbs where one is more likely to find the smaller banks. Two conclusions that can be reached are that holding companies, whether by design or by availability of certain types of banks, acquired leading banks that were losing their market positions and foothold entry banks that exhibited positive rates of increase in their market shares prior to acquisition.

By subtracting past growth variables from growth variables subsequent to acquisition, the change in growth induced by the holding company can be found. From table 11-6 it can be seen that neither $X_1 - P_1$ nor $X_2 - P_2$ is statistically significant at the 5% level for either the full sample or for the two primary subsamples, one of which directly tests the entrenchment doctrine and

Table 11-5
Past Market Share Growth per Year, P_1

Group of Banks	$\overline{x}$	s	n	z
All	−0.00185	0.00785	71	−1.99[a]
ms > 0.20	−0.00704	0.00760	15	−3.58[a]
ms < 0.05	0.00025	0.00169	32	0.84

Past Growth Rate, P_2

All	0.01782	0.10737	71	1.40
ms > 0.20	−0.01858	0.01901	15	−3.78[a]
ms < 0.05	0.03921	0.10506	32	2.11[a]

[a]Significant at 5% level.

Table 11-6
Adjusted Change in Market Share per Year, $X_1 - P_1$

Group of Banks	$\bar{x}$	s	n	z
All	0.00196	0.00964	71	1.71
ms > 0.20	0.00370	0.00954	15	1.50
ms < 0.05	0.00019	0.00243	32	0.44

Adjusted Change in Market Share Growth Rate, $X_2 - P_2$

All	−0.00947	0.11857	71	−0.67
ms > 0.20	0.00967	0.03319	15	1.13
ms < 0.05	−0.02442	0.11477	32	−1.20

the other of which tests the foothold entry concept. These results provide the major conclusions of this section. Holding company acquisitions do not have a statistically significant effect on the market shares of acquired banks. In addition, both the entrenchment and foothold arguments have little basis in fact.

Nevertheless, the positive means for the adjusted growth of the leading banks may indicate that certain types of acquired leading banks do have their market positions improved. The sample has been subdivided by absolute size of the acquired bank. Since both the entrenchment and foothold entry doctrines are framed in terms of relative size of the acquired bank, not much emphasis is placed on the absolute subdivisions. However, from table 11-7, it can be seen that the larger banks lost market shares, and the smaller banks increased market shares subsequent to acquisition, but when their growth is adjusted by past growth, no size group exhibits a statistically significant change in market share.

To assess the competitive impact of holding company acquisitions, it must not only be determined whether acquired banks experience significant changes in market share but also how great an impact the change, if any, in market share will have on competition as measured by concentration ratios. Looking at table 11-3, we see that for the full sample the average bank increased its market share by only 0.012% of market deposits per year. Thus if it is assumed that this is the typical market share change per year for an acquired bank, it would take more than 83 years for the acquired bank to increase its market share by 1%. The banks with market shares greater than 20% exhibited decreases in market share of 0.335% per year. The acquisition of banks with market shares less than 5% would typically increase their market shares by 0.044%. This magnitude of change is not likely to have a substantial procompetitive effect for many years, even if it is assumed that the full impact of this increase in market share is felt by the leading banks that would exhibit a corresponding decrease in market share.

Table 11-6 presents the average adjusted change in market share per year for the full sample and the two subsamples. The full sample increases less than 0.2%

Table 11-7
Banks Divided by Absolute Deposit Size

Deposits Greater than $25 Million

Variable	$\bar{x}$	s	n	z
X_1	−0.00268	0.00560	20	−2.14[a]
X_2	−0.02291	0.05247	20	−1.95
$X_1 - P_1$	−0.00030	0.00623	20	−0.22
$X_2 - P_2$	−0.01685	0.08969	20	−0.84

Deposits Less than $25 Million

X_1	0.00121	0.00695	51	1.24
X_2	0.02061	0.06279	51	2.34[a]
$X_1 - P_1$	0.00285	0.01060	51	1.92
$X_2 - P_2$	−0.00658	0.12882	51	−0.36

Deposits Less than $10 Million

X_1	0.00374	0.00575	24	3.19[a]
X_2	0.05222	0.05933	24	4.13[a]
$X_1 - P_1$	0.00409	0.01222	24	1.64
$X_2 - P_2$	0.00699	0.14844	24	0.23

[a]Significant at 5% level.

per year. The change in the growth of market share per year of the smaller banks with less than 5% market share is 0.019%, an increase not likely to have much competitive impact. Only in the case of the banks with market shares greater than 20% of deposits in their markets do we find any possible alteration in the future patterns of competition that may be noticeable. Even in this case it would take a number of years before the reduction in market share loss of leading banks would have a major impact on concentration and the level of competition in the affected markets.

These results do not imply that there may not be cases where a bank acquired by a holding company dramatically improves its market position. They only reveal that on the average, not much change can be expected. To find characteristics that are likely to signal possible dramatic market share increases, a series of multiple regressions have been performed relating market share change to several variables. Some variables have been included in the regressions to check whether the previous results were biased.

Each of the four main measures of market share change has been used as a dependent variable in a regression equation. The regressions were run for all subsamples as well as for the full sample of 71 acquired banks. Since the subsample regressions add no new conclusions, only the equations using the full sample are reported here. The four equations are specified as follows:

$$X_1 \quad = f_1(P_1, MS_a, M, C_3, \Delta B, \Delta M_1, \frac{HC}{D}, \frac{L}{A}) \tag{11.1}$$

$$X_2 \quad = f_2(P_2, MS_a, M, C_3. \Delta B, \Delta M_2, \frac{HC}{D}, \frac{L}{A}) \tag{11.2}$$

$$X_1 - P_1 = f_3(MS_a, M, C_3, \Delta B, \Delta M_1, \frac{HC}{D}, \frac{L}{A}) \tag{11.3}$$

$$X_2 - P_2 = f_4(MS_a, M, C_3, \Delta B, \Delta M_2, \frac{HC}{D}, \frac{L}{A}) \tag{11.4}$$

where

X_1 = change in market share per year
X_2 = change in market share growth rate
P_1 = past market share growth per year
P_2 = past growth rate
MS_a = average market share of acquired bank
M = total deposits in market ($000)
C_3 = three-firm concentration ratio in market prior to acquisition
ΔB = change in number of banks in market subsequent to acquisition
ΔM_1 = absolute deposit growth of market per year ($000)
ΔM_2 = rate of deposit growth of market
HC/D = total deposits of acquiring holding company/total deposits of acquired bank prior to acquisition.
L/A = total loans of acquired bank/total assets of acquired bank prior to acquisition

In the first two regressions, where X_1 and X_2 are the dependent variables, the appropriate measure of past growth, P_1 or P_2, is included as an independent variable. A positive coefficient for the past growth variable would be expected since past growth should be related to subsequent growth.

To eliminate the effect of the regression fallacy, the average market share of the bank before acquisition and in 1972 has been employed. If holding companies have a greater potential to improve the market position of banks with small market shares, this variable would have a negative coefficient.

Rapidly growing markets and those in which there is much entry of new banks may be associated with declining shares for existing firms. Negative coefficients for either the growth of the market or the increase in the number of banks would mean that these factors should be corrected for in the previous analysis. Lack of significant coefficients for these variables would indicate that they have not introduced any significant biases into the analysis of this sample of banks and that they can be ignored.

It is often alleged that the larger holding companies will have a greater effect on the market shares of acquired banks. To test this hypothesis, the ratio of the total deposits of the acquiring holding company to the deposits of the acquired banks has been included as an independent variable. A positive coefficient would confirm the hypothesis. In regressions not reported here, the deposit size of the holding company was used as an independent variable. The results indicated that it mattered little which variable was used.

More aggressive banks may be able to increase their market shares more readily after acquisition. On the other hand, the less aggressive bank may be more susceptible to a possible stimulus by an acquiring holding company. The measure of aggressiveness that is used is the ratio of loans to assets of the acquired bank prior to acquisition. Each of the two hypotheses implies a different sign for the coefficient of this variable, so the results will show which tendency, if either, is more important.

Finally, two variables that are descriptive of the market, total market deposits and three-firm concentration, have been included. These variables not only control for certain market characteristics but also may indicate the types of markets in which changes in market shares of acquired banks are likely to occur.

Table 11-8 presents the results of the linear regressions. The most notable aspects of these results are the lack of significant coefficients (only two are significant at the 5% level) and the low R^2s. This indicates that the variables used here do not explain much of the variation in growth rates from acquired bank to acquired bank. In fact, in the two equations using adjusted growth as dependent variables, none of the coefficients even come close to being significant at the 5% level.

In the first two equations, the coefficients of the past growth variables are not significantly different from zero. The nonsignificance of these variables indicates either than too short a period of past growth has been used or that the market share changes of banks are too erratic to be predicted by past behavior. Even if the first explanation is correct, the validity of using past growth of only two years for the calculation of mean growth earlier is not upset because a large number of banks have been averaged. Any erratic behavior induced by an insufficient length of time will have a more serious effect on the regression results than on the testing of means.

The significantly negative coefficient of the average market share in the first regression and near significant coefficient in the second confirm the earlier findings of greater increases in market share for smaller banks. However, after market share changes are adjusted for past share changes, the coefficients of market share are no longer significant, indicating that bank acquisitions do not significantly stimulate growth performance of smaller banks. The mostly nonsignificant coefficient for the other variables warrant the rejection of several hypotheses. The larger holding companies do not have a greater effect on market share changes than smaller holding companies.[1][7] The means analyzed previously are not significantly biased due to market growth and bank entry. If the time

Table 11-8
Market Share Change Regressions

Dependent Variable	P_1	P_2	MS_a	M	C_3	ΔB	ΔM_1	ΔM_2	HC/D	L/A	R^2
1. X_1	0.085 (0.717)		-0.020 (-2.022)[a]	0.258 E-9 (0.263)	0.871 E-2 (1.436)	0.939 E-4 (0.363)	-0.733 E-8 (-0.657)		0.618 E-2 (0.319)	0.495 E-2 (0.616)	0.1371
2. X_2		0.066 (0.982)	-1.42 (-1.74)	-0.181 E-8 (-0.265)	0.101 (1.966)[a]	0.111 E-2 (0.478)		-0.018 (-0.666)	0.286 (1.714)	0.060 (0.846)	0.2279
3. $X_1 - P_1$			0.011 (0.832)	0.604 E-9 (0.444)	0.923 E-2 (1.100)	0.226 E-3 (0.631)	0.126 E-8 (0.082)		0.039 (1.488)	0.016 (1.437)	0.1656
4. $X_2 - P_2$			0.679 E-2 (0.042)	-0.244 E-8 (-0.178)	0.115 (1.121)	0.184 E-2 (0.396)		0.435 E-2 (0.082)	0.380 (1.138)	0.027 (0.190)	0.1123

t-values are in parentheses beneath coefficient.
The number following "E" is the appropriate exponent of 10; for example, y E-2 = .00y.
[a] Significant at 5% level.

period under holding company control had been longer, this bias might have become a matter of concern. Bank aggressiveness and market size are also unrelated to market share changes. However, the significant positive coefficient of concentration in equation 11.1 and the positive values in the other equations suggest that perhaps market share increases more as a result of holding company acquisition in more concentrated markets.

Implications

The major finding of this section is that the market shares of banks acquired by holding companies do not change significantly as a result of the acquisitions. Since regulatory authorities apparently have been operating under the assumption that bank acquisitions will improve the market positions of the acquired banks, this finding has important policy implications, especially when applied to the acquisitions of leading banks and to the acquisition of banks with very low market shares.

The results here indicate that entrenchment should probably be dropped as an argument for denying acquisition of a leading bank where no direct competition is eliminated. It would still be possible to deny an acquisition of this sort on potential competition grounds if it could be shown that the elimination of the holding company as a potential entrant into the market would seriously restrict the number of firms that could start new banks. The finding that acquisitions of banks with small market shares by holding companies do not improve their market positions casts serious doubt on the regulatory encouragement of foothold entry. If holding company acquisitions do not improve the market positions of banks with small market shares, then an acquisition of this type probably would not be procompetitive. Thus clearly foothold entry should not be considered in the same class as de novo entry. To stimulate competition, the type of entry that should be encouraged is de novo entry, and this would primarily involve relaxing restrictions on bank charters.

Acquisition of Nonbanking Firms

Though considerably less research has been done on the competitive impact of the bank holding company in the nonbanking areas as compared to banking, there are several studies that do provide some relevant evidence. The main problem in doing research in the nonbanking areas is the lack of data. The bank regulatory agencies have been collecting extensive data on banks for years. The nonbanking industries entered by bank holding companies generally do not have government agencies collecting and collating information on all industry members. Data limitations have especially hindered efforts to assess the competitive impact of bank holding companies in these nonbanking areas.

Since 1970 many bank holding companies have aggressively entered a number of nonbanking industries. The most significant entry has occurred in consumer finance and mortgage banking. Some of the entry has been de novo, but most has been through acquisition of existing companies. "In consumer finance, BHCs usually have acquired relatively small or medium sized firms. In mortgage banking, however, BHCs have often acquired companies that were among the largest in the industry in the industry."[18]

Talley (1976), using reports that bank holding companies have been required to file with the Federal Reserve on financial information concerning individual nonbank affiliates, has reviewed the performance of samples of bank holding company affiliated mortgage banking firms and consumer finance firms. He concludes that "bank holding company entry into mortgage banking and consumer finance has not been particularly successful so far. The rate of return earned by BHCs in the two industries has been far below the return traditionally earned in commercial banking, and BHCs have not performed up to industry profitability standards in either activity, even though BHCs generally have a lower cost of funds than their independent rivals. Moreover, in both mortgage banking and consumer finance, BHC affiliates are taking greater risks by leveraging beyond industry standards."[19] He points out, however, that banks may be willing to pay with poor profit performances for longer-run benefits such as "gaining broad geographic coverage in anticipation of further developments in EFTS and possible liberalization of branching laws."[20] Unfortunately, the study does not examine growth.

A study done by this author (Goldberg 1973) examining the competitive impact of conglomerate mergers provides some guidance as to the expected competitive impact of bank holding company acquisitions of nonbanking firms. In both cases the acquiring firm is assuming control over a firm in another industry. Just as bank holding companies have been acquiring firms in related industries, many of the conglomerate mergers involved entry into industries related in one way or another to that of the acquiring company. The conglomerate merger study found that the market shares of acquired firms on the average do not change significantly and that the changes in market share have minimal effects on concentration ratios. The study concluded "that conglomerate mergers should not be prohibited as a general policy based on supposed harmful competitive effects."[21] These results lead us to suspect that bank holding company acquisitions of nonbanking firms will not increase the market shares of the acquired firms and thus will have little direct competitive impact.

Two studies have attempted to assess the competitive effect of bank holding company acquisitions of nonbanking firms. One study deals with mortgage banking and the other with consumer finance. Rhoades (1975) compared the growth rates of servicing portfolios of 16 mortgage banking firms affiliated with bank holding companies and 16 independent firms between 1968 and 1972. He obtains the following regression results:

$$G = 1.803 - 0.052\,AN - 0.000\,S \quad \bar{R}^2 = -0.04$$

The T-values are in parentheses.

where G = growth in mortgages serviced (1969-1972)

AR = 1 if the mortgage banker is affiliated with a bank holding company

0 if it is not affiliated

S = size of the servicing portfolio at the beginning of 1969.[22]

Rhoades concludes that "the results show that neither the affiliation status (AN) dummy variable nor the size (S) control variable are even nearly statistically significant. Moreover, both variables carry an unexpected negative sign. These results indicate that, contrary to the initial hypothesis, mortgage banking firms affiliated with bank holding companies do not grow any faster than non-affiliated mortgage bankers."[23] In further statistical tests, he finds that "commercial banks did not increase or decrease their mortgage lending relative to total lending subsequent to affiliation with a mortgage banker."[24]

As compared to the previously discussed study of bank acquisitions, the study of mortgage banking acquisitions has serious shortcomings. Many of these limitations are recognized by the author and were beyond his control because of lack of data. This study does not focus on the relevant local geographic markets but instead implicitly assumes a national market. No adjustment is made for the growth of the mortgage banking companies prior to affiliation with bank holding companies. The most relevant issue is the effect bank holding company affiliation has had on the growth of acquired mortgage bankers. The measure used in this study provides some evidence, but perhaps not the best evidence.

Rhoades and Boczar (1977) attempt to determine whether there are significant performance differences between bank holding company affiliated and independent consumer finance companies. They compare various performance characteristics of 14 consumer finance companies that became affiliated with bank holding companies by 31 December 1974 to characteristics of 23 nonaffiliated companies. Various performance variables are related to an affiliation dummy variable, company size, and average loan size in a multiple regression format. They found "that prior to their affiliation, the affiliated companies performed no differently than the independent companies in terms of performance and financial soundness. After affiliation, however, tests reveal that the affiliated companies have higher interest and debt expense, lower profits, greater leverage and higher growth than the independent companies. Moreover, results indicate that affiliated companies subsequent to affiliation did not have lower losses, did not open more offices, and did not have lower operating expenses than independent companies."[25]

The most important finding of Rhoades and Boczar in terms of our major concerns here is the finding that bank holding company affiliated consumer finance firms have grown faster than independent firms. Closer examination of this result, however, reveals that it perhaps has been overstated by the authors. The regression equation from which the conclusion is derived is as follows:

$$G = 1.06 + 10.3300BHC + 0.0059AS \qquad \bar{R}^2 = 0.02$$
$$(1.5108)(0.9113)$$

where

G = growth in total consolidated assets from 31 December, 1973 to 31 December, 1974

BHC = 1 if affiliated with bank holding company

 = 0 if independent firm

AS = asset size[26]

The coefficient of BHC is significant at the 10% level if a one-tailed test is used. Employing the standards of statistical significance used in the discussion of bank acquisitions discussed previously, this result would not reject the null hypothesis that there is no difference in growth depending on holding company affiliation. Given the other problems with this analysis, which we will discuss, there are further reasons for requiring higher statistical significance levels to reject the null hypothesis.

This study suffers some of the same faults as the study of mortgage banking. A national market is assumed for lack of the appropriate geographic data. Growth behavior prior to acquisition is not taken into account. In addition, only one year of post acquisition behavior is used. Consequently, we must conclude that there is no convincing evidence that bank holding company affiliated consumer finance companies have grown more rapidly than independent finance companies.

The evidence with respect to nonbank acquisitions is inconclusive. The study of conglomerate mergers suggests that bank holding affiliation will not affect acquired firm growth. The study of mortgage banking acquisitions confirms this suggestion, but the study has methodological faults. The methodological faults of the consumer finance study are even more serious so that its conclusion that bank holding company affiliation stimulates growth can not be accepted. More research is needed in this area, but more research requires ingenious data-gathering efforts.

Public-policy Implications

In this paper we have examined one aspect of banking, bank holding companies, where regulatory rules have been significantly altered. One important possible impact of these changes is in the competitive area. Through original research and through surveying and evaluating other studies, we have analyzed the likely effect of bank holding company acquisitions on competition in the markets of the acquired firms. The evidence indicates that acquired banks do not increase their market shares and that bank holding company acquisitions of banks in other markets generally will not adversely affect competition. The evidence on nonbank acquisitions is not as strong but still suggests a similar conclusion.

The arguments presented here have concentrated on the competitive impact in individual markets. Many critics have asserted, however, that bank holding company acquisitions by increasing aggregate concentration will have harmful economic consequences. Since the theoretical economic base for these types of arguments is usually fairly flimsy, the most convincing type of argument is based on increased political power. The recent evidence, however, indicates that increased aggregate concentration on both the national and state levels due to bank holding company expansion is not a serious problem.

In sum, BHC acquisitions of banks in recent years have only slowed down a decline in nationwide concentration resulting from the slower-than-average internal domestic growth of the nation's largest banking organizations. On a statewide basis, holding company acquisitions of banks have increased concentration sharply in only about a half-dozen states. None of these states, however, is now in the group that is considered to have high levels of concentration. . . . [The] strong movement into certain nonbanking activities . . . has not resulted in a significant increase in the amount of financial assets under BHC control. One reason is that the aggregate total assets in most of the nonbanking industries into which BHC's have moved are small.[27]

The results of this paper have important public-policy implications on two levels, approval of individual acquisitions and new regulatory legislation. When a bank holding company submits an application to the Federal Reserve System to acquire either a bank or nonbanking firm that does not compete in the same geographic and product markets with any of the subsidiaries of the holding company, the regulatory authority should not assume that the market share of the acquired firm will increase, in the absence of any other substantial evidence that this will occur. Acquisition of leading firms will not necessarily reduce competition, and foothold acquisitions will not necessarily increase competition.

The evidence provided here is also relevant to proposed legislation to set proscribed limits to the types of firms large banking organizations will be permitted to acquire. Prohibiting acquisition of leading firms will prevent many competitively harmless acquisitions but at the same time limit the freedom of action for holding companies and thus impede the efficient allocation of resources. There are instances where acquisition of a noncompeting leading firm by a holding company where no direct competition is eliminated should be stopped, such as when a strong potential competition argument can be made, but the decisions should be made on an individual basis.

Notes

1. See, for example, the Hunt Commission Report (*The Report of the President's Commission on Financial Structure and Regulation* 1971) and U.S. Congress, *FINE-Financial Institutions and the Nation's Economy: Discussion Principles* 1975.

2. Talley (1972), p. 13.

3. A standard methodology has been developed to deal with horizontal mergers, though some economists do not fully accept it. It has a theoretical rationale, namely, that greater concentration leads to greater probability of collusive behavior and that this will result in supercompetitive prices and profits. See Rhoades (1977) for a review of the literature testing the structure performance relationship in banking.

4. "One-bank Holding Companies Before the 1970 Amendments," 1972, p. 1001.

5. See Schotland (1976), pp. 236-246, for a discussion of actions of the largest banks prior to the 1970 amendments and after the passage of the amendments.

6. Ibid., pp. 236-237.

7. See Drum (1977), p. 14, for a cataloging of the status of nonbanking activities as of March 1977.

8. Schotland (1976), p. 242.

9. Rhoades (1976), p. 66.

10. See Rosenblum (1975), p. 7 for detailed data.

11. See Lawrence and Talley (1976) for a review of the evidence.

12. Benston and Hanweck (1977), p. 166.

13. Baker (1973), p. 10.

14. Baker (1973), pp. 4-5.

15. Some of the results using this sample have previously been reported in Goldberg (1976).

16. The sample was also divided by the rank of the acquired bank with no significant changes in the results.

17. In other regressions the coefficients of the size of the holding company were more negative than the coefficient of HC/D here. In fact, in one regression it was negative and significant.

18. Talley (1976), p. 42.

19. Talley (1976), p. 44.

20. Talley (1976), p. 44.

21. Goldberg (1973), p. 158.

22. Rhoades (1975), p. 346.

23. Rhoades (1975), p. 347.

24. Rhoades (1975), p. 347.
25. Rhoades and Boczar (1977), pp. 18-19.
26. Rhoades and Boczar (1977), p. 16.
27. Lawrence and Talley (1976), p. 20.

References

Baker, Donald I. "Potential Competition in Banking: After Greeley, What?" Speech delivered at Columbia University, Graduate School of Business, 19 March, 1973.

Benston, George J., and Hanweck, Gerald A. "A Summary Report on Bank Holding Company Affiliation and Economies of Scale." In Federal Reserve Bank of Chicago, *Bank Structure and Competition,* 1977.

Drum, Dale S. "Nonbanking Activities of Bank Holding Companies." Federal Reserve Bank of Chicago, March/April 1977.

Goldberg, Lawrence G. "Bank Holding Company Acquisitions and Their Impact on Market Shares." *Journal of Money, Credit and Banking,* February 1976.

_____. "The Effect on Conglomerate Mergers on Competition." *Journal of Law and Economics,* April 1973.

Lawrence, Robert J. *The Performance of Bank Holding Companies.* Washington, D.C.: Board of Governors of the Federal Reserve System, June 1967.

Lawrence, Robert J., and Talley, Samuel H. "An Assessment of Bank Holding Companies." *Federal Reserve Bulletin,* January 1976.

"One-bank Holding Companies Before the 1970 Amendments." *Federal Reserve Bulletin,* December 1972.

The Report of the President's Commission on Financial Structure and Regulation. Washington, D.C.: U.S. Government Printing Office, 1971.

Rhoades, Stephen A. *Structure-Performance Studies in Banking: A Summary and Evaluation.* Washington, D.C.: Board of Governors of the Federal Reserve System, Staff Economic Study (92), 1977.

_____. "Changes in the Structure of Bank Holding Companies Since 1970." *Bank Administration,* October 1976.

_____. "The Effect of Bank Holding Company Acquisitions of Mortgage Bankers on Mortgage Lending Activity." *Journal of Business,* July 1975.

Rhoades, Stephen A., and Boczar, Gregory E. *The Performance of Bank Holding Company-Affiliated Finance Companies.* Washington, D.C.: Board of Governors of the Federal Reserve System, Staff and Economic Study (90), 1977.

Rosenblum, Harvey. "Bank Holding Company Review 1973/74—Part I." *Business Conditions.* Federal Reserve Bank of Chicago, February 1975.

Schotland, Roy A. "Bank Holding Companies and Public Policy Today." In U.S.

Congress, House Committee on Banking, Currency, and Housing. *FINE– Financial Institutions and the Nation's Economy,* Book I, pp. 233-283. Committee Print. 94th Cong., 2d sess., 1976.

Talley, Samuel H. *The Effect of Holding Company Acquisitions on Bank Performance.* Washington, D.C.: Board of Governors of the Federal Reserve System, Staff Economic Study (69), 1972.

_____. "Bank Holding Company Performance in Consumer Finance and Mortgage Banking."*Bank Administration,* July 1976.

U.S. Congress. House Committee on Bank, Currency and Housing. *FINE- Financial Institutions and the Nation's Economy, Discussion Principles.* 94th Cong., 1st sess., 1975.

12

Bank Capital: The Regulator Versus the Market

Benjamin Wolkowitz

Capital positioning, an important issue for any type of firm, is particularly significant in the context of banking because beyond the traditional functions of capital, bank capital is a source of soundness. Since in practice it is a fund against which the bank can charge off unanticipated losses that exceed current income, bank capital can appropriately be viewed as an offset against portfolio risk. Consequently, both bank regulators and investors have good reason for focusing on capital when reviewing individual banks and also for attempting to influence management's capital decision.

Ideally, public-and private-sector concerns with the same issues should result in a cooperative venture. This unfortunately is not the case with bank capital. Regulatory efforts aimed at bank capital adequacy have been criticized by various members of the private sector for being overly constraining and inconsistent with the concerns and objectives of the banking industry and the market.[1] Much of this criticism is self-serving, but it is not entirely without substance. Alternatively, relegating complete responsibility for the soundness of the banking industry, which in the current context requires designing and enforcing capital standards, to the private sector seems unwarranted. Evidence on the effectiveness of market regulation is mixed, and the historical record, especially including the period of the Depression, is not impressive. Further, the private sector's objectives with regard to capital positioning are not precisely the same as those of the public sector. Thus even if market regulation were effective, it might not result in adequate capital positions from a social viewpoint.

Yet the current situation of having one source of regulation—the public regulator—completely dominate another presumably willing source of influence, the market, presents a possible candidate for reform. There has certainly been no lack of suggestions. Prominent among them are substituting deposit insurance for capital standards, instituting variable rate premiums for deposit insurance, resolving bank failures in a number of different ways, and revamping the regulator's method of determining how much capital is adequate. The fundamental problems with most considerations of such reforms is that they are too partial in nature. A proper reform of capital adequacy regulation will have to depend on several components, not just one modification addressed to one portion of this whole area.

The views expressed in this paper are those of the author and not necessarily those of the Board of Governors or its staff. I would like to acknowledge the assistance provided by Robert Eisenbeis, Peter Lloyd-Davies, and John Mingo in clarifying my thoughts on this subject. Carol Keyt supplied excellent computational assistance.

243

This paper describes several sets of possible reforms of capital regulation. Polar cases in terms of impact are discussed, but the more attractive alternative is a middle ground. Prior to a description of these regulatory scenario is a consideration of what have been the historical and recent trends in bank capital positioning. Also a short review of the literature examining the effectiveness of formal regulation and market regulation is provided.

Empirical Evidence[2]

The emphasis in this paper is on recent trends in bank capital, but it is interesting and informative to take a casual look at bank capital experience throughout the history of American banking. Figure 12-1 provides some basic insights into the long-term trend in capital, indicating an almost continuous decline from 1800 to the present, which has been interrupted by only several minor upswings. Disaggregating this long trend into shorter periods indicates that

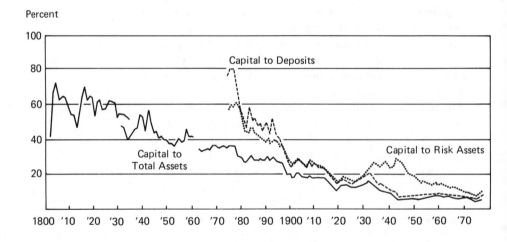

Source: Adapted from Wesley Lindow, "Bank Capital and Risk Assets," *The National Banking Review*, September 1963, p. 2; updated from 1963-1976. Derived from data (as of June 30): 1803-1835 for Massachusetts banks—1876 *Report of the Comptroller of the Currency*, p. 98. 1834-1862 for all banks in the United States—*Historical Statistics of the United States*, 1949, p. 263. 1865-1962 for all commercial banks in the United States—*Annual Reports of the Comptroller of the Currency*, 1865-1874; *Journal of Political Economy*, December 1947, p. 559; *Historical Statistics of the United States*, 1957, pp. 631-62; *Banking and Monetary Statistics*, Board of Governors of Federal Reserve System, 1962 Supplement, p. 28; *Federal Reserve Bulletin*, March 1962, p. 346. 1963-1970 *Banking and Monetary Statistics* 1941-1970, Board of Governors of the Federal Reserve System, pp. 29-31. 1971-1975 *Annual Statistical Digest*, Board of Governors of the Federal Reserve System, p. 61. 1976 FDIC *Annual Report* Table 106.

Figure 12-1. Bank Capital as a Percentage of Assets and Deposits 1803-1976

the various capital ratios are related to periods of loan expansion and contraction. For example, at the close of the nineteenth century, the ratio of total capital to risk assets[3] reached a high of 60%, declining to approximately 25% after the turn of the century. While the period from World War I through the 1920s was one of prolonged loan expansion associated with a decline in this ratio, the Depression saw a major contraction in loans that was associated with an increase in the capital to risk assets ratio that was sustained until the end of World War II. The postwar period loan expansion was accompanied by a decline in the ratio of total capital to risk assets, which continued to the early 1970s. However, with the slowdown in economic growth and the general economic contraction of the mid-1970s, the capital ratios again moved slightly upward. Most recently the long-term downward trend seems to be reappearing as the economy improves, and there is an attendant increase in loan demand.

An intensive overview of recent bank capital behavior is provided by table 12-1 which contains values for four popular capital ratios for all insured commercial banks from 1969 to 1977. All four measures move together and in apparent relationship to the general state of the economy. In particular, for a few years prior to 1969 until 1974, the economy was robust. This same period is

Table 12-1
Selected Capital Ratios for All Insured Commercial Banks
(in percent)

Yearend	Equity Capital/ Total Assets	Equity Capital/ Risk Assets	Total Capital/ Total Assets	Total Capital/ Risk Assets
1969	7.90	11.21	8.27	11.73
1970	7.62	10.86	7.96	11.35
1971	7.25	10.26	7.68	10.87
1972	6.79	9.55	7.29	10.26
1973	6.49	8.93	6.93	9.53
1974	6.45	8.64	6.86	9.18
1975	6.71	9.28	7.11	9.83
1976	6.71	9.35	7.15	9.96
1977	6.50	9.00	6.93	9.60

Source: Consolidated foreign and domestic *Report of Condition.*
Note: Equity capital is defined to include the reserve for losses on loans and securities.

Total capital equals equity capital as defined above, plus subordinated notes and debentures.

Total assets includes consolidated foreign and domestic assets.

Risk assets equals total assets less cash and due from banks, less U.S. Treasury and government agency securities.

Ratios are based on aggregate data for all insured commercial banks.

Because of certain accounting changes introduced in 1976, adjustments were made in calculating total assets after 1976 in order to obtain a consistent series. Beginning in 1976, loans are reported net of the reserve for loan losses (the valuation portion). This valuation portion has been added back into total loans, and therefore total assets, so that the treatment is consistent throughout the time period.

characterized by declining capital ratios and expanding bank assets. (Throughout this period total assets in the banking industry grew by at least 10% per year and in some years by as much as almost 17% per year). With the substantial economic slowdown in 1974-1975, bank capital ratios rose (and bank assets grew by only 4.74%). This turnaround in the long-term trend was short-lived, however, and the recent improvement in the economy has seen a reassertion of the downward trend.

In general, regardless of size class, banks have demonstrated in their capital positioning some sensitivity to the state of the economy. But as can be seen from table 12-2 it is the largest banks that are more leveraged and whose capital ratios fluctuate more with the state of the economy. Adjusting for size, total assets varied almost three times more than total capital,[4] but clearly larger banks accounted for most of this variation. Thus it is the larger banks whose capital ratios demonstrate more fluctuation, and this fluctuation is probably due more to variation in asset composition than actual changes in capitalization.

This type of casual comparison suggests that if capital positioning is effectively regulated at all, regardless of the source, it is only constrained within a rather broad range of values. Furthermore, the market appears to have a tolerance for declining capital ratios that occur as a consequence of extensive growth. Of course, a more analytical approach is needed to verify such conclusions and inferences concerning the efficiency of the two potentially major influences on bank capital positioning.

Table 12-2
Capital Ratios[a] by Asset Size for All Insured Commercial Banks
(in percent)

	Asset Size Class ($ millions)							
Date	0-10	10-50	50-100	100-500	500-1,000	1,000-5,000	5,000 & Over	All Banks
Dec. 1969	9.51	8.51	8.46	8.69	8.80	8.31	7.25	8.27
Dec. 1970	9.62	8.44	8.38	8.46	8.60	7.79	6.84	7.96
Dec. 1971	9.49	8.21	8.08	8.18	8.28	7.54	6.64	7.68
Dec. 1972	9.26	8.08	7.87	7.90	7.97	7.18	6.12	7.29
Dec. 1973	9.57	8.25	8.00	7.91	7.86	6.87	5.30	6.93
Dec. 1974	10.29	8.53	8.27	8.15	7.74	7.16	4.92	6.86
Dec. 1975	10.25	8.53	8.36	8.13	8.00	7.41	5.27	7.11
Dec. 1976	10.25	8.65	8.45	8.19	7.90	7.44	5.48	7.15
Dec. 1977	10.17	8.61	8.33	8.05	7.62	7.30	5.22	6.93

Source: Consolidated foreign and domestic *Report of Condition.*
Note: Total assets are gross of reserve for loan losses beginning in 1976.

[a]Consolidated foreign and domestic capital ratio equals total capital (equity + reserves + capital notes and debentures) divided by consolidated foreign and domestic total assets. Ratios are weighted averages.

Regulatory Influence on Bank Capital

Three empirical studies addressed primarily to determining the effectiveness of regulation on bank capital investment have produced somewhat conflicting results. Sam Peltzman (1970) evaluated the impact regulators have on the capital decision by attempting to explain empirically the annual change in bank capital (using 1963-1965 data) in the context of a fairly complete model of capital investment.[5] Although there are justified reservations with Peltzman's method, his conclusions are interesting and worth reporting. Variables he found to be significant in explaining bank capital investment include: the expected rate of return, the ratio of U.S. government securities to total deposits, and the percentage of deposits insured by the FDIC. These results imply that bankers emphasize their overall soundness level in determining capital investment so that a relatively less risky portfolio and deposit insurance substitute for capital investment. Furthermore, bankers appear to have some notion of a desired level of capital; the higher their actual capital position, the lower their capital investment. And finally, capital investment is related to income; the higher the return on capital, the greater is capital investment. However, Peltzman did not find to be significant any variables reflective of portfolio regulation, that is, capital adequacy requirements.

The shortcomings of the Peltzman study led John Mingo (1975) to reconsider the issue of bank capital investment. Besides using a different sample, Mingo respecified the regulatory variable to reflect the hypothesis that banks deficient in capital will be pressured to improve while those banks holding capital in excess of regulatory minimum will be ignored. The results of this empirical work are the opposite of Peltzman's in that Mingo found regulators do have an influence on bank capital positions. Also in contrast to Peltzman, few factors besides regulation were shown to influence capital investment; however, Mingo did find evidence that bankers behave as if they have at least a general notion of a desired level of capital investment.

Lucille Mayne (1972) considered the same general issue from a somewhat different perspective; her first priority was to determine if different regulatory agencies have a differential impact on bank capital. By comparing a sample of national banks, state Federal Reserve members, and nonmembers, Mayne concluded that there was not a significant difference among capital positions even though there are marked differences in the capital adequacy guidelines among the state and various federal bank regulatory agencies. These results were augmented by a survey directed at determining differences in compliance with regulatory requests for additional capital. Interestingly, the greatest degree of resistance was found among those bankers under the greatest amount of pressure to increase capital.

These three studies taken as a group lead to the guarded conclusion that regulators appear to influence bank capital, but their influence is generally minor. Furthermore, bankers appear to have a notion of a desired capital level, but it is nonspecific and highly variable.

Market Influence on Bank Capital

Evidence on the influence of the market on capital positioning, as with the studies on regulatory influence, is more suggestive than conclusive. Most studies of the market's influence examine the relationship between the cost of equity, typically measured by the price-earnings ratio, and the degree of bank leverage, typically measured by the debt-equity ratio. Generally, the conclusion of these studies is that there is very little overall support for the hypothesis that the marketplace actively evaluates the riskiness of a bank on the basis of its leverage position.[6] That is, in the majority of cases, leverage is not statistically significant in explaining the observed variation in the cost of capital funds. What appear significant in explaining the price of equity are variables reflective of earnings, income to the investor, and growth. Thus rather than curtailing growth, limiting loan expansion, and discouraging risk, the market "rewards" the aggressive banking firms with a lower cost of equity.

These conclusions are not unequivocally supported in the literature. Jacobs, Beighley, and Boyd (1975), and Gendreau and Humphrey (1978) find some evidence that the market responds to leverage by requiring a higher return on investment, which results in a higher cost of capital for the more levered firm. The Jacobs-Beighley-Boyd study found such market sensitivity evident for a sample of bank holding companies in 1972 and 1973. Using a somewhat more sophisticated approach, Gendreau and Humphrey found that from 1970 to 1975 the market generally "regulated" larger banks. Another study by Weaver and Herzig-Marx (1978) examining the relationship between leverage and the cost of debt adds support for the argument that the market responds to extremes in leverage. Thus these studies suggest that the market probably responds to extreme cases of leverage, but it does not necessarily monitor the capital positions of individual banks in a way that is expected of bank regulators.

The Market and the Regulator: A Case of Overcrowding

The inconclusiveness of the statistical studies described in the two preceding sections may be due in part to the competing efforts of regulators and the market in attempting to influence bank capital positioning. From a purely technical perspective, these statistical models may be subject to a problem of identifiability. That is, if a certain quantity is being influenced in much the same way by several factors, it may be impossible to separate the quantitative impact of the competing factors. In this particular case, the market, the regulators, and, of course, bank management presumably wish to avert failure; however, it may be impossible to identify to what extent each is affecting a particular capital decision as a means of insuring against failure.

This line of reasoning is consistent with the finding that both the market and the regulator respond only to the extreme cases of leveraging. If as a result of a combination of influences, bank capital standards are generally at a reasonable level, it could be difficult to untangle precisely which source influenced any particular bank. However, in cases of extreme leveraging that elicits a marked response from either the regulator or the market, it should be easier to assign attribution to the appropriate source of "regulation."

Furthermore, it could be argued that observed capital positions are the result of effective regulation regardless of the source of such regulation, even though the long-term trend in capital positioning underscores a continuing decline. It has been alleged (with some justification) that since the riskiness of banking operations has declined as a consequence of the increased sophistication of management and managerial techniques, capital positions should decline. Therefore what is observed, rather than being attributable to ineffective regulation, is actually the product of sensitive and sophisticated regulation.

An alternative but less favorable explanation for the empirical results on capital positioning is that factors external to the bank attempting to influence its capital are for the most part ineffective. According to this scenario, regulators with limited punitive powers can do little more than try to convince undercapitalized banks to adhere to regulatory standards. Meanwhile the presence of regulators, responsible for enforcing a number of regulations concerned with bank soundness and generally supposed to be preventing bank failures, precludes the necessity for effective market regulation. Potential investors in bank debt or equity probably spend less time analyzing banks because they are regulated than they do analyzing alternative investments in less regulated industries. Further, insured depositors, who are the largest class of bank liability holders and probably the most secure as a result of regulation, appear to exert little influence on bank management. Consequently, analyses of market regulation in banking typically ignore depositors as a possible source of influence.

These conflicting explanations share a common ground concerning the market—the implicit presumption that the market could provide more discipline than it currently does. And the current status of the market (and, in fact, of all liability holders) is largely attributable to the presence of regulation. Further, to the extent that an expanded market role is considered socially desirable, an evaluation of current procedures in bank capital regulation is probably necessary. However, such an evaluation should not ignore the possible differences in objectives between regulators and the market.

An investor considering the purchase of a particular liability is certainly concerned with the trade-off between risk and return vis-à-vis other investments.

This would presumably be true of most bank liability holders in an unregulated environment. Thus potential investors would more carefully compare the risk-return trade-off available in banking with those available elsewhere. The worst case that such an investor would have to consider is the bankruptcy of the firm and the loss of the value of the investment. Thus the worst possible loss for the investor is the loss of some portion of the investor's own net worth.

Regulatory concerns are presumably somewhat more global, being motivated by social rather than private concerns. These include the stability of the money supply, the soundness of the banking system, and the protection of the small depositor. It is the first that motivates the regulator to be concerned not only with failure but also with the ramifications of failure. The Great Depression provides an example of the worst case. But presumably deposit insurance and the orderly resolution of failure have ended the possibility of a replay of such a crisis. Even so, regulators have to be cautious since there is no rate of return that can compensate the regulator for added risk exposure. As a result, market discipline unencumbered by the presence of regulation is likely to result in more leveraging and more risk taking than the regulators would prefer.

The objectives of responsible reform should account for the limitations inherent in relying entirely on the market. Yet there should still be some way of allowing for a more significant market presence while not sacrificing the objectives of the regulators. Several analysts have offered solutions, but most have fallen short of satisfying these constraints. Either they have sought to serve an interest group while attempting to give the appearance of responsible reform, or they have been partial in approach, ignoring the interactions inherent in various aspects of regulation and market behavior. However, by liberally adjusting and incorporating several suggested reforms, it is possible to devise procedures that would reconcile the objectives of the regulator with the operations of the market.

All the reform plans about to be discussed explicitly recognize that bank capital is a form of insurance. It is self-insurance against failure. As viewed by regulators, capital adequacy requirements prevent an occurrence of the externalities associated with bank failure. Insofar as the latter function is concerned—the avoidance of the externalities of failure—the deposit insurance provided by the FDIC could effectively substitute for capital requirements. To varying degrees, it may be possible to rely on expanded deposit coverage to offset decreased capital positions. However, the extent and manner of such trade-offs have important implications.

Regulatory Reform

There is a continuum of regulatory reforms that would allow for increased market influence with increased risk taking while still achieving to some degree the objectives of bank regulators. Rather than present such a listing of regulatory scenarios, it is instructive to examine two polar cases and the characteristics associated with a middle ground.

Increased Liability Insurance

The basis of this approach is the substitutability of deposit insurance for capital adequacy requirements in the maintenance of public confidence in the banking industry.[7] How much confidence is presumably related to how much of a bank's liabilities are insured. The greater is the proportion of insured liabilities, the less likelihood there is of a run generated by a failure. At the least, for this proposal to be effective, 100% of all deposits would have to be insured. Variants of this proposal call for insuring all liabilities.

How important is insuring all or a portion of all liabilities depends in part on how failures will be resolved. Currently the FDIC favors assumptions over payoffs. That is, rather than liquidate a failed bank's remaining assets so as to pay off the liability and equity holders, failed banks' assets and obligations are largely assumed by financially sound and willing banks. Assumptions, in contrast to payoffs, result in a minimum of losses to the holders of obligations of the failed bank. In practice, only the equity holders incur any losses. Therefore resolving failures by assumption is de facto equivalent to expanded insurance.

Expanded insurance used in place of capital adequacy requirements may on balance result in more bank failures. Banks probably will become more leveraged in the absence of capital regulation, banks will assume more portfolio risk, and failures will result in part from a lack of capital. Although expanded insurance and failure resolution by assumption will guarantee that most regulatory objectives will continue to be met, some analysts are nonetheless concerned about the probably higher incidence of failure under such a proposal.

The most appealing way of avoiding the possibility of a higher incidence of failure is to adopt a mechanism that would, like capital adequacy requirements, constrain risk taking. A natural complement to increased insurance which could, if properly designed, constrain risk taking is variable rate premiums. There is an appealing equity aspect to the notion that premiums for FDIC insurance, as with private liability insurance, should reflect the risk the insured party places on the insurance fund. Furthermore, if premiums are set so that the charge for taking on risk in excess of what regulators find desirable exceeds the expected return from the additional risk, the variable rate premiums can be an effective policy substitute for capital adequacy standards.

The variable rate premiums proposal has attracted a number of advocates because of its logical appeal and similarity to private sector practices. However, it does suffer from a fundamental problem. Setting an appropriate rate structure for premiums is an extremely difficult task rivaling the current regulatory problems of determining how much capital is adequate for a given bank. Interrelationships within a portfolio make a determination of risk an individual bank matter, and broadbased rules of thumb for setting premiums could prove inadequate and inconsistent with regulatory objectives. Thus rather than streamline regulation, variable rate premiums will provide an all too perfect substitute for the setting of current capital adequacy requirements.

On balance, this proposal offers little change over current practices except that banks would probably hold less capital. There would be no reason, however, for market discipline to increase since fewer bank liability holders would be subject to risk of financial loss than is currently the case. Clearly, the fault of this proposal is that it provides too much insulation against investor's loss so that the market's likely concern for risk taking is justifiably slight.

Radical Approach

This approach is at the opposite end of the spectrum from the previous approach, although the starting point is the same: the substitution of deposit insurance for capital adequacy requirements.[8] Exactly by how much deposit insurance coverage should be expanded is open to discussion. At an extreme, deposit insurance could be kept at its current level since that has proven adequate to avert lapses in public confidence in the banking industry. However, since other aspects of this proposal would probably encourage an increase in the riskiness of banking activities, some expansion of insurance coverage is prudent. Given the social objectives associatedwith insuring bank liabilities, probably insuring a limited definition of the money supply (for example, M2) is justified in the context of this entire proposal. At any rate, regardless of the amount of coverage, deposit insurance would replace capital adequacy requirements under this approach.

Another important component of the radical approach is that failures will no longer be resolved by assumption, only by payoffs. This is a critical element of the proposal since it removes a unique characteristic of bank failure—the usual absence of significant losses. Under this scenario, losses among uninsured liability and equity holders of failed banks will become more commonplace. As a consequence, the market (all uninsured investors) will be motivated to scrutinize more carefully a bank before placing funds. In effect, market discipline will be given an unconstrained opportunity to demonstrate its effectiveness.

Further, premium schedules for deposit insurance will not be changed to variable rates. A primary objective of this proposal is the removal of regulatory influence over individual bank decisionmaking. Variable rate premiums run counter to this basic objective.

The significant costs of information hamper the operation of markets. Banking, an industry never known for candor, could defeat the efforts of well-intentioned markets by being less than forthcoming about individual operations. Regulators will, even in the absence of capital requirements, continue examinations of banks as part of the enforcement of a variety of regulations. Such examinations will probably result in banks' being assigned to one of several categories reflecting relative riskiness. Such classifications could be put into the public record by the regulators, thereby adding to available information for the investor.

Such a proposal will probably result in an increase in failures as a consequence of investors' tolerance for risk taking. However, properly expanded deposit insurance will promote the attainment of objectives regulators currently achieve through a combination of capital adequacy requirements and limited deposit insurance in spite of a higher incidence of failure. What makes this proposal radical, besides the significant number of changes in current regulatory practices, is the possibility that it will foster an unsettled period. Market discipline may take some time to become effective, and at best it may still demonstrate a socially undesirable tolerance for failure. As a consequence, failures may become more common, putting pressure on public authorities both to avert any negative ramifications of such failures and also to continue to pay off insured depositors without jeopardizing the integrity of the insurance fund. The possibility that failures will so abound as to defeat the best efforts of public authorities makes this a very radical proposal.

Middle Grounds

Rather than provide a single middle ground approach, it is useful to consider the types of reforms that would characterize such an approach. Generally, the reforms associated with a middle ground approach would allow some opportunity for market discipline while not jeopardizing the stability of the banking industry. Although more limited than the radical approach, the middle ground still incorporates a number of significant reforms.

In common with the other two proposals, middle ground scenarios replace current capital adequacy regulation.[9] Ending the setting of capital standards is necessary if the market is to be allowed the opportunity to discipline risk behavior effectively. As discussed in the other reforms, the logical substitute for capital adequacy standards insofar as regulatory objectives are concerned is deposit insurance. Under this approach it is probably not essential that insurance coverage be expanded given the other components of this reform; however, it would be prudent to expand insurance consistent with regulatory objectives. Therefore, insuring the money supply is probably desirable.

Failure resolution through assumption must definitely continue. Because increased risk taking by banks will probably result from this approach and as a consequence, the likelihood of failure will increase, it is important that such failures be resolved with a minimum of negative ramifications. However, as previously mentioned, resolution of failure by assumption reduces the effectiveness of market regulation since the losses associated with failure are limited. It is this insistence on failure resolution by assumption that underscores the bias of this approach. Resolution of the inherent conflict between market regulation and the regulators favors the regulator. That is, although some added risk taking is tolerable, achievement of regulatory, that is, social objectives, is considered essential.

As previously mentioned under the "radical approach," information costs could pose a barrier to effective regulation by the market. Both banks and regulators could assist by making more information easily accessible. A balance would have to be reached between supplying information that would truly assist the market and withholding information that could be misleading. However, the difficulty in achieving such a balance should not be used to justify a lack of change from the current situation.[10]

These middle ground proposals, although they may err in favor of regulatory objectives, do not attempt a near-perfect replacement for capital requirements. Therefore, variable rate premiums are not a part of these middle ground approaches. The presumption is that retaining the current inequity in the FDIC insurance premium structure is justified by the increased market discipline that should result. Such market discipline would satisfy one of the other objectives of variable rate premiums, introducing the pricing mechanism so as to allow each institution to decide on its desired trade-off between safety and profitability in light of the true costs of each. In these middle grounds, the market rather than the premium structure will enable the bank to evaluate its risk-return trade-off.[11]

On balance, these middle ground approaches do not induce the market to discipline banks as much as is theoretically possible. However, the market does receive an added incentive to scrutinize banks more closely while a high priority is still put on attaining regulatory objectives. In fact, a judicious mix of deposit insurance coverage and increased availability of information could conceivably result in an environment that from a social perspective is superior to current practices.

Notes

1. A precise definition of the market as used in this context has not been established. Typically, "the market" refers to the equity and sometimes to the debt markets. Theoretically, it should include the market for all bank liabilities and equity.

2. The material in this section is in large part taken from Orgler and Wolkowitz (1976).

3. Total capital will in general be defined to include total equity, reserves for losses on loans and securities, and subordinated notes and debentures. Risk assets are defined as total assets less cash less government securities issued by the U.S. Treasury Department.

4. The coefficient of variation for the growth in total assets (1969-1977) was 4.0 while it was 1.35 for the growth in total capital.

5. Among his explanatory variables were several regulatory measures of capital adequacy including: the New York Federal Reserve Formula and its closely related Analysis of Bank Capital Formula (as had been used by the Federal Reserve), and a risk-assets ratio adjusted in a manner similar to the FDIC procedure.

6. For example, see studies by David Durand (1957), James Van Horne and Raymond C. Helwig (1966), S.D. Magen (1971), and David B. Humphrey and Samuel B. Talley (1977).

7. Dropping capital standards completely is not essential to this proposal. Establishing minimum standards below current adequacy requirements is consistent with the spirit of this reform.

8. At the most radical extreme, capital requirements of any kind could be suspended, although the capital standards associated with new charters would probably continue.

9. However, in the true spirit of compromise solutions, some minimum capital requirements should probably be retained.

10. Appropriate disclosure requirements is an issue beyond the scope of this paper, but it will have to be resolved before the market can be relied on to even partially substitute for formal regulators.

11. Another objective of variable rate premiums is protection of the insurance fund. Such protection is largely provided for by the assumption procedure of failure resolution.

References

Durand, David. *Bank Stock Prices and the Bank Capital Problem.* New York: National Bureau of Economic Research, Inc., 1957.

Gendreau, Brian C., and Humphrey, David B. "Feedback Effects in the Market Regulation of Bank Leverage: A Time-series and Cross-section Analysis." Unpublished manuscript, Board of Governors, Federal Reserve System, April 1978.

Humphrey, David B. "100% Deposit Insurance: What Would It Cost?" *Journal of Bank Research* 7 (Autumn 1976):192-98.

Humphrey, David B., and Talley, Samuel H. "Market Regulation of Bank Leverage." Unpublished Research Paper in Banking and Financial Economics, Board of Governors, Federal Reserve System, January 1977.

Jacobs, Donald P.; Beighley, H. Prescott; and Boyd, John H. *The Financial Structure of Bank Holding Companies.* A study prepared for the trustees of the Banking Research Fund, Association of Reserve City Banks, Chicago, Illinois, 1975.

Magen, S.D. *The Cost of Funds to Commercial Banks.* New York: Dunellen, 1971.

Mayne, Lucille S. *Impact of Federal Bank Supervisors on Bank Capital.* New York: New York University, Graduate School of Business Administration, 1972.

Mingo, John J. "Regulatory Influence on Bank Capital Investment." *Journal of Finance,* September 1975, pp. 1111-1121.

Orgler, Yair E., and Wolkowitz, Benjamin. *Bank Capital.* New York: Van Nostrand Reinhold, 1976.

Peltzman, Sam. "Capital Investment in Commercial Banking and Its Relation to Portfolio Regulation." *Journal of Political Economy,* January/February 1970, pp. 1-26.

Van Horne, James C., and Helwig, Raymond C. *The Valuation of Small Bank Stocks.* East Lansing, Michigan: Michigan State University, Graduate School of Business Administration, 1966.

Weaver, Anne S., and Herzig-Marx, Chayim. "A Comparative Study of the Effect of Leverage on Risk Premiums for Debt Issues of Banks and Bank Holding Companies." Research Paper No. 78-1. Federal Reserve Bank of Chicago, 1978.

Comment

Neal M. Soss

Our chairman, Professor Altman, has given the discussants a great deal of freedom to comment on the papers presented this morning or to take off on topics that were perhaps not treated as adequately as we would like. Since the theme of our conference is deregulation, I am going to take him at his word and exploit the freedom he has permitted.

I would like to begin by offering a general definition of *regulation,* which will lead into the first point I would like to offer for consideration. *Regulation* is the body of general industry ground rules that defines the ways in which firms within the industry may compete with one another and with firms in other industries. Regulation is, therefore, a set of constraints on privately motivated, profit-maximizing behavior.

Viewed this way, it is no wonder that a normative, if not evangelistic, tone has predominated our deliberations. Indeed, only Professor Goldberg's paper offered extensive empirical research of a descriptive nature, and even he could not resist the temptation to include public policy considerations in the title. Schooled in Paretian welfare economics, it is natural for us to view the constraints that natural scarcity and the limits of our technological capabilities impose on us as bad enough, without our imposing additional constraints of our own. Starting from a Pareto-optimal state of the world, modern welfare economics teaches that the imposition of an additional binding constraint must reduce the level of welfare that can be achieved. To say that regulation imposes binding constraints is, from this perspective, tantamount to saying that deregulation is a good thing.

But modern welfare economics is a more sophisticated body of thought than this. One of the most important, albeit least comforting, insights of modern welfare economics is the theorem of the second best. Consider an economy operating with certain distortions so that it has not attained a Pareto-optimal state. Consider further that the general equilibrium characteristics of the economy are not fully known to policy makers. Stated very loosely, the theorem of the second best asserts that under these circumstances it is not possible to know for sure whether removal of an additional constraint will result in an improved state of the world or whether imposition of an additional constraint will result in a worse state. Local and global optima may not coincide.

I submit that even leaving aside the structure of bank regulation, we do not confront an economy in a Pareto-optimal state. Furthermore, we have not yet attained a comprehensive empirical fix on the way our economy functions. The

The views and opinions expressed here are the author's and do not necessarily reflect the official policy of any institution with which he is associated.

257

theorem of the second best therefore applies to our policy deliberations. But the scientific agnosticism of the theorem of the second best simply will not do for those who are charged with managing the regulatory apparatus. We cannot in good conscience make decisions by the toss of a coin simply because we may not have complete knowledge of the effects of any decision. We must gather as much knowledge as we can and apply as much good judgment as we possess.

This brings me to the first general point I want to make. Policy changes by way of deregulation, which by themselves seem desirable, must nonetheless be considered in the context of all those other constraints that will remain after the one is removed.

I would cite, for example, the recent decision by federal bank regulatory authorities to permit automatic transfers from interest-bearing savings accounts to non-interest-bearing checking accounts. I am sure that every economist on this panel or in this audience believes that the current prohibition on the paying of interest on demand balances makes no sense in and of itself. Indeed, I am sure that we would all agree that it leads to inefficient non-price competition for demand balances on the part of banks and in turn to inefficient overconsumption of checking account services. Michael Laub's paper covers this ground very well. Therefore, the creation of a mechanism that tends to rationalize this situation should be applauded by us all.

There are, however, at least two side-effects of this policy initiative that deserve consideration. The first is that the consumer of checking account services is likely to be given a strong incentive to reduce checking account balances and substitute transferable savings balances instead. This has the effect of freeing reserves—since savings deposit reserve requirements are lower than those on demand deposits—and permitting greater growth of bank lending than would otherwise have been possible at any given level of free reserves. Moreover, the traditional conduct of monetary policy based on M1 will have to be modified to account for this new reality. This is not to say that automatic transfers should not be permitted nor that any attendant problems cannot be resolved, only that attention to the transition to the new equilibrium will be required.

A second effect of automatic transfers is on the competitive equilibrium between commercial banks and savings and loan associations, particularly in those parts of the country where thrifts do not have third party payment powers. Despite the differential permitting higher interest payments by thrifts, the new automatic transfer service will induce some shift of deposits and deposit growth from thrifts to commercial banks, thereby reducing the competitive position of the thrifts. In states like New York where thrifts generally have third party payment powers, the maintenance of the Regulation Q differential for automatic transfer accounts will likely have the opposite effect.

Now there is nothing sacred about existing patterns of interindustry competition, and regulation should not be used to preserve them indefinitely.

Nor indeed is the protection of inefficient firms within an industry a valid purpose of regulation. But I think that the maintenance of consumer and investor confidence in the financial intermediary system is sufficiently important—and the history of banking panics in this and other countries bears this out—as to argue for a moderate and balanced pace of change in the basic ground rules of inter- and intraindustry competition. There is, in other words, a social benefit in an orderly transition from one equilibrium to another.

Comparative statics analysis has important lessons, but dynamic analysis of the path from the status quo to a new equilibrium is at least equally important, for we live in real time and experience the transition paths at least as much as the equilibrium states. This need not stop us entirely from removing any given constraint(s). But it does impose the need to consider the path of the transition from the status quo to a new, better state of the world.

Still another illustration of this general point, of more parochial interest, concerns the newly authorized eight-year maturity consumer savings instrument. Thrift institutions are permitted to pay up to 8% interest on such time deposits, which compounds to an effective annual yield of approximately 8.45%. New York currently (late May 1978) has a usury statute that limits certain classes of loans, including especially residential mortgages, to 8.5%. It is not very likely that New York thrifts will be able to fund in-state mortgages at 8.5% with money that costs them 8.45%. This is not to say that savers should continue to be prohibited from receiving this rate of return on their savings. But it does illustrate the point that removing one constraint (on savers) in a context where other constraints remain (the usury statute) may have unintended disadvantageous results on others (for example, potential sellers and buyers of homes, realtors, and builders).

Having offered this cautionary observation on the need for care in removing regulatory constraints piecemeal, I would like to touch briefly on a current effort at deregulation being spearheaded here in New York.

It is now widely recognized that a major motivation for the explosion of U.S. bank presence abroad—to the point where U.S. bank liabilities overseas, at $250 billion, now constitute one fifth of the total liabilities of the U.S. commercial banking system—was the imposition of balance of payments related regulatory restraints at home and the relatively unregulated environment abroad. Currently three main regulatory distinctions remain: (1) reserve requirements are imposed on dollar deposits held in the United States but not abroad, (2) interest may not be paid on deposits with maturities under 30 days within the United States but may be paid on such deposits abroad, and (3) in some states, notably New York, relatively heavy state and local taxes are imposed on bank income earned at home whereas income earned abroad is tax exempt.

Whatever the policy goals that led to the creation of this set of constraints, it is clear that their primary current result is to alter the geographic locus of international banking activity by U.S. banks. If the intent was to prevent U.S.

banks from engaging in this business, the constraint does not bind. In particular, the same, larger U.S. banks that would otherwise engage in international finance continue to do so, but from offshore locations rather than from their home offices.

A proposal has been developed by the New York banking community to permit the conduct of international business, carefully defined, within this country on a regulatory footing competitive with what exists abroad. One advantage of adopting such a proposal is the repatriation of employment opportunities currently located offshore.

One of the requirements of this proposal is creation of equal state and local tax-exempt status for international business whether conducted here or abroad. And, in an election year, the New York State Legislature has passed almost unanimously what might well be perceived as a tax preference for banks. The reason for this, I think, is very simple, and it illustrates the second general point I want to make. The pace of efforts at deregulation will be quicker, I think, in those areas where regulatory constraints bind only as to form rather than to substance.

The third point I want to make concerns the distinction between regulation and supervision. Regulation, as noted earlier, is the body of general industry ground rules; *supervision* is the process by which regulation is enforced in specific instances. It is, in particular, the medium through which most banks in fact experience regulation in the most intimate way. Reforms in supervisory procedures can in some instances substitute for deregulation, at least in the sense that Ben Wolkowitz was using the term in his paper. This is, I submit, a fruitful area for further research.

A generation ago, for example, bank examinations routinely included hordes of examiners counting vault cash, verifying the existence of securities in the investment and trading accounts, confirming correspondent bank balances, and so forth. With the advent of more extensive branch networks—Marine Midland has the largest branch network (320) among New York State chartered banks—and electronic data-processing systems, which reduce the scope of error in such matters, bank examination has by and large shifted focus. Such verification matters are now generally left to internal and external auditors at the banks while examination focuses on evaluating the adequacy of such audit procedures. Bank examination, the front line of the supervisory process, is now more akin to management consulting in this regard.

Similarly, as Ben Wolkowitz observed, bank supervision is increasingly looking at a bank's condition the way the market does. The developing early-warning systems, for example, use publicly available balance sheet and income statement data in an attempt to glean from them an assessment of a bank's condition. While this has not supplanted the traditional on-site, labor-intensive, bank supervision process, it is increasingly being used as an aid to the scheduling of on-site examinations and to provide focus and direction to on-site examinations.

This is in part explainable as a substitution of capital for labor in the production of bank supervision, but it also reflects a change in attitude toward more market-oriented tests of bank condition and performance. This change in attitude is, I think, closely related to the deregulation attitude we have explored at this conference.

Comment

Barbara Goody Katz

Michael Laub noted in closing that "the right combination of market pressures, technological innovation, and regulatory piecemealing needed to induce sensible financial reform has not occurred." In the paper he has just presented, he focuses on three areas in which regulatory change was attempted: deposit interest rate ceilings and the powers of thrift institutions, redlining, and credit allocation. Although he asserts that bankers, and other wise people, would agree that regulation is a second-best solution and therefore would be pleased to jump on the deregulation bandwagon, he carefully points out that banking is, in fact, looked at differently than, for examples, the airlines, motor carriers, natural gas, and electric power industries, despite the fact that inferior resource allocations also occur in banking as a result of what he calls "unwarranted regulation."

I believe I am not quibbling when I call your attention to the phrase "unwarranted regulation." Underlying Laub's paper is an approach that suggests that regulation that impairs bank profitability or increases bank risk even temporarily is unwarranted, while regulation that confers on banks varying degrees of market power through the control of entry is not only desirable but necessary for the safety of the banking system. In short, it is warranted regulation with which we should not tamper for any reason, including a social reason. The fact that a social reason prompted all regulations concerning banking safety is completely ignored. That social reason is, of course, the presumption that bank failures impose social costs on communities that are in excess of the costs to the failed banks themselves. The problem seems to be that regulation attempting to limit the risk and thereby the social costs of bank failure limits entry and creates market power, whereas the regulation attempting to deal with the existing prisoner's dilemma, which underscores the failure in the urban mortgage market, and its social costs, is perceived to increase bank risk and reduce bank profits. The thrust of Laub's position is that the banking sector should not be regulated to meet societal needs unless such regulation also enhances bank profits. Thus he sees the Home Mortgage Disclosure Act and the Community Reinvestment Act (assuming the regulations get written) as unwarranted regulation. Or, specifically in the latter case, new regulation of charter granting interfering with still other existing regulation on charter granting.

Although this theme is expressed most strongly in the discussion on redlining, it also is contained in the other sections of the paper, and in particular in the section on interest rate ceilings and the powers of thrift institutions. There Mr. Laub seems less than eager to support the Hunt Commission proposals that would accord liberal conversion powers within the finance business and end rate ceiling differentials on time and savings deposits: He claims that by retaining the

263

interest prohibition on demand deposits and dispensing with rate ceiling differentials on time and savings accounts, thrifts would be put on a par with banks (even if they did not choose to convert directly to commercial banks), yet the thrifts would be lacking the years of experience at handling, as he calls it, "the heavier lobby traffic and more burdensome transfer problems associated with checking accounts." I suspect that this empathy for the inexperienced thrift institutions is, in fact, something else: fear of entry, replete with its consequences of increased competition and potentially lower profits. Without entry, or the equivalent power restrictions, thrifts could determine whether the extra revenues generated by additional services or actual conversion would be equal to or greater than the extra costs incurred and make reasoned economic decisions, something they are prevented from doing in most states today. To his credit, Laub does not claim it would be against the interests of public safety to allow thrifts to enter the banking business, only that it would be hard for them to get accustomed to the rigors of banking. I believe Laub presents a position against regulation when it hampers bank profitability and for regulation when it sustains market power.

While, as I noted earlier, this approach also underlies the redlining discussion there are other aspects of that discussion on which I want to comment. First, Laub infers from the existence of blockbusting that there is no shortage of credit available to purchase homes. I think such an inference is mistaken. Mortgage companies, acting as conduits for unscrupulous real estate brokers engaging in blockbusting tactics, stand to gain considerably from panicked selling: That mortgage companies would grant a mortgage in a block targeted by real estate agents for heavy solicitation suggests not an ample availability of credit but rather forecasts the almost certain decline of available mortgage money from both thrift institutions and commercial banks. That neighborhoods undergoing rapid change are outside the pale of the usual mortgage arrangements is well documented in the report written by Lindsay, Tobier and others for the New York State Banking Department entitled *Mortgage Financing and Housing Markets in New York State: A Preliminary Report.*

Second, Laub claims, following Allan Meltzer, that since our economy has a surfeit of mortgage credit, urban problems cannot be traced to the lack of available credit. Clearly, whether or not there is an overall glut of mortgage money says nothing about its distribution, yet the distribution is crucial to determining whether or not redlining, or geographic stereotyping, is taking place. I refer again to the Lindsay-Tobier report, which contains a valuable case study of redlining in Brooklyn. In the one-year period from 1 June, 1975 to 31 May, 1976, 91% of the value of the residential mortgages granted in Brooklyn were in areas with less than 10% nonwhite populations. And Brooklyn is a very racially segregated area with only 4% of its nonwhites' living in census tracts that are 10% or less nonwhite. This mortgage flow measure of 91% is an accentuation of the stock measure in which 85% of the value of the residential mortgages held by the savings banks studied were in census tracts with less than 10% nonwhites, although these areas only have 55% of Brooklyn's population and below 70% of its residential structures. Several measures, all discussed in the Lindsay-Tobier report, indicate very limited mortgage lending in areas over 10% nonwhite: in 1970 only about 1% of the stock value of residential mortgages was in census tracts 80% or more nonwhite.[1]

A further and very specific example of geographic stereotyping is found in the central portion of Brooklyn, including all of Bedford-Stuyvesant and parts of Brownsville and northern Crown Heights. According to the Lindsay-Tobier report, this virtually all-black area in 1976 had 2,000 completely vacant residential structures. However, these vacant buildings were not uniformly distributed over this area: Approximately 80 blocks, or 12% of the blocks in the area, contained 860 vacant buildings, more than 40% of the total vacant buildings, while one quarter of the blocks had no vacant buildings, and another 47% of the blocks had from 1 to 4 vacant buildings, with an average of 2 per block. Mortgage lending in the entire 650-square-block area studied, however, is negligible, despite the fact that there are census tracts, particularly in the Stuyvesant Heights Historic District, with stable populations and no foreclosures in the five-year study period 1970-1975. Of the 81 sales in 1976 in this area, with a total value of $1.4 million, only 4 received mortgages from the banks in the study, and the total value of the mortgages was $70,000. The stock coverage figure, that is, the total number of mortgages as a percent of the total number of buildings for this historic area of 45 square blocks, is 2%, which is even less than 3.2% average for census tracts 80% and over that are nonwhite. (The stock coverage in Brooklyn census tracts less than 10% nonwhite is 17.7%.) While these figures clearly document geographic stereotyping, perhaps in the future some banks will follow the lead of the Philadelphia banks that no longer refuse mortgages simply because other nearby blocks have high vacancy rates but instead focus more narrowly on the exact block location of the house for which the mortgage is sought. In fact, just recently the Federal Home Loan Bank Board adopted a set of regulations prohibiting the member S&L's from automatically refusing to lend because of the age or location of a house.

Since redlining is also used to describe the acceptance of deposits from areas in which there is limited, if any, mortgage activity on the part of the deposit-accepting institutions, let's look at a few facts relating to this issue. Again I refer to the Lindsay-Tobier report. The stock ratios of mortgage holdings in 1976 as a percentage of time deposits show the New York metropolitan area at the low end of the range with a ratio of 15%, compared with the Nassau-Suffolk metropolitan area at the top of the range with a 62% ratio. Within the New York area the ratios were 8% in New York City, 11% in Brooklyn, and 48% in Richmond, for examples. On the basis of the information I have just presented, I disagree with Laub's statement, and I quote, "The unproved claim of the antiredliners is that banks are gathering deposits from local areas and not lending them back into these areas." He seems to believe redlining does not exist: I wish it were so.

The Community Reinvestment Act is an attempt to induce banks to be more responsive to the credit needs of the community in which they operate. Obviously there are definitional problems, but they are not new: These same definitional problems appear, for example, in the Banking Act of 1935, which required federal banking authorities to consider, among other things, "The convenience and needs of the community to be served by the bank" before a newly organized commercial bank could be covered by deposit insurance. As long as the phrase "the convenience and needs of the community" was exclusively interpreted to mean protecting the public from the alleged harm of bank failures through "overbanking" and therefore used to restrict entry, bankers seemed to have no trouble with the phrase. However, as soon as the same phrase appears in a context where it is interpreted to mean protecting the public from the consequences of urban mortgage market failure rather than protecting existing banks from increased competition, the phrase becomes difficult to define and an undue interference.

In a perfect, nondiscriminatory world, markets would be perfect, and such a regulation as the Community Reinvestment Act would not be needed. Unfortunately, this is not the case. I believe it is with misplaced priorities that some consider the *risk* of bank failure, and its potential costs, worthy of market interfering, entry restricting regulation, while at the same time dismissing the *existence* of failure in the urban mortgage market and its consequent social costs as somebody else's problem, and certainly not an area in which to accept some inefficiency as a by-product of ameliorative regulation.

Note

1. Lindsay, Tobier et al. (1977), part IV-D13.

References

Lindsay, Robert, and Tobier, Emanuel, et al. *Mortgage Financing and Housing Markets in New York State: A Preliminary Report.* Presented by the New York State Banking Department to the New York State Legislature, 10 May 1977.

Studies in Banking Competition and the Banking Structure. U.S. Treasury. Washington: Office of the Comptroller of the Currency, 1966.

Comment

A. Gilbert Heebner

My comments are directed to the papers of Lawrence Goldberg and Benjamin Wolkowitz. In a word, I feel that both papers are of good professional quality, address themselves to significant questions, and make a number of analytical contributions. The points that I mention here are not intended to detract from that overall conclusion but to carry out the discussant's role of raising questions and criticisms of the more vulnerable aspects of the papers.

Early in the paper Goldberg says that "change in market share, given data limitations, is still the best way to measure competitive impact." It may in fact be that data limitations prevent other approaches, but it should be recognized that change in market share may sometimes tell little about competitive conditions in the market. For example, when an outside institution gains what Goldberg calls "foothold entry," it is quite possible that the other banks in the market may compete more vigorously and that the acquired bank may therefore not increase its market share. Still, there would have been a procompetitive effect of the acquisition.

Moreover, even if change in market share is employed to measure competitive impact, deposit share may not be the most relevant observation. In some cases, loan share may reveal more about competitive behavior. An acquired bank, for example, may have been a sleepy little organization sitting on relatively large holdings of Treasury securities and selling federal funds rather than making loans. After acquisition, such a bank may not increase its deposit share, but if it increases its share of the loan market by reducing its investments and sales of federal funds, the loan market may have become more competitive.

One of Goldberg's major conclusions is that "holding company acquisitions do not have a statistically significant effect upon the market shares of acquired banks." The trends observed in support of this conclusion, however, are based on data for only two years before the mergers and at least, but not much longer than, three years after the mergers. Goldberg argues that "the validity of using past growth of only two years for the calculation of mean growth earlier is not upset because a large number of banks have been averaged." That may be so, but I am still bothered by the short span of time employed. My concern also applies to the postmerger period. Quite a few years may elapse after a merger before it really begins to take effect on the performance of the acquired banks. The acquiring bank may tread lightly for a while in changing policies and personnel, preferring first to evaluate the situation and to gain acceptance in the community. That "digestion" could easily encompass the three years that Goldberg has employed in his analysis.

The slowdown in the rate of holding company acquisitions in 1974 is attributed by Goldberg to "depressed stock prices and to a change in the attitude of the Federal Reserve Board." Another reason was probably that the holding companies perceived the need to consolidate the acquisitions that had occurred in previous years and to concentrate on managing them to achieve desired results. Also some of the holding companies may have been less than satisfied with their early experience with their nonbank acquisitions.

Turning to the Wolkowitz paper, the thrust of the examination—reform of capital regulation by allowing the market to have a greater influence—is indeed commendable. The present system under which the public regulators dominate in the setting of capital adequacy standards leaves much to be desired. Not only is it probable that this system suffers from the limitations of the wisdom of the regulators, but much confusion is introduced. To the banker, it appears that the regulator is saying that capital adequacy is revealed to a considerable extent by various ratios, but it is not always clear which ratios the regulators are principally watching and how much weight is being attached to one or the other. The usual answer that the banker hears is that it is necessary to look at all the ratios as a guideline, but this is not very helpful as an objective discipline. Interestingly, the four key ratios that are shown in table 12-1 do not include one that I have thought the regulators consider important, namely, earning assets to capital. My point is not that I would like to see the regulators set forth more explicit and arbitrary ratio standards, but that in keeping with the Wolkowitz paper, reform should take the direction of allowing the market to have greater influence than it now does in establishing capital adequacy standards.

Of the three general avenues of regulatory reform Wolkowitz discussed, the middle-ground approach appears to be the most reasonable. He is not endeavoring to present a detailed blueprint of what this approach would entail, but the reader is left wanting to hear more about the middle ground. In the author's words, it seems to amount to a "judicious mix of deposit insurance and increased availability of information." The paper could be strengthened by an expanded discussion of this "judicious mix," or such discussion could be the basis of a subsequent paper.

Wolkowitz did say that under the middle-ground approach, insuring the money supply (M_2) is probably desirable. Admittedly it is a matter of judgment, but I wonder whether that would not be coming too close to total insurance. To be sure, insuring M_2 would leave out large negotiable certificates of deposit, but it would include all demand deposits, and even with the advent of active cash management, business demand deposits are still in substantial magnitudes in many cases. My preference would be to limit the magnitude of deposit insurance to less than full coverage of the money supply.

In the discussion of the influence of the degree of bank leverage on the market's evaluation of risk, I feel that the significance of leverage is dismissed too lightly. The market appears to accept higher leverage in larger banks, but within a size class, there does seem to be a premium on the lower levered bank.

Market attitudes toward leverage change over time; for example, after the difficulties in 1974, market sensitivity to leverage appeared to increase. Wolkowitz does, however, qualify his conclusions by pointing to certain studies that give some evidence that the market requires a higher return on investment from the more highly levered firm.

Part IV
The Intersection of the
Two Industries and
Glass-Steagall

13 Banks and Securities Activities: Legal and Economic Perspectives on the Glass-Steagall Act

Franklin R. Edwards

Introduction

Since 1933 a fundamental tenet underlying our banking system has been the mandated separation of commercial banking from the "securities business." Four sections of the Banking Act of 1933, Sections 16, 20, 21, and 32, which are commonly known as the Glass-Steagall Act, make this separation clear. Section 21 contains the basic restrictions, making it unlawful for

> Any person, firm, corporation, association, business trust, or other similar organization engaged in the business of issuing, underwriting, selling, or distributing, at wholesale or retail or through syndicate participation, stocks, bonds, debentures, notes, or other securities, to engage at the same time to any extent whatever in the business of receiving deposits subject to check or to repayment upon presentation of a passbook, certificate of deposit, or other evidence of debt, or upon request of the depositor . . . .

The three other sections clarify the above prohibition. Section 20 prevents circumvention of the prohibition through the use of affiliates. Section 32 makes it clear that where "affiliation" would not amount to a control situation, any interlocks—through common officers, directors, employees, or partners— between investment banking firms and commercial banks are similarly prohibited. Last, Section 16 further modifies the basic prohibition in two ways: It allows banks to deal in or underwrite both the obligations of the United States and the general obligations of any state or any political subdivision, and it provides that the "business of dealing in securities and stock (by a national bank) shall be limited to purchasing and selling such securities and stock without recourse, solely upon the order, and for the account of, customers, and in no case for its own account . . . ."

While the Act makes it clear that commercial banks cannot underwrite or distribute corporate securities, the latter section seemingly does not foreclose to

---

The author wishes to thank the Center for Law and Economic Studies of Columbia University for providing support for this project.

banks all activities that are currently undertaken by securities firms. It is not surprising then that the meaning of the Glass-Steagall Act is a subject of constant debate, especially between the banking and securities industries.

In recent years both banks and securities firms have engaged in activities which test the limits of the Glass-Steagall prohibitions. During the 1960s major banks began to offer various investment services such as collectively managed agency accounts (or common trust funds for agency accounts), automatic investment services, dividend reinvestment plans, individual portfolio management services, and advisory services to investment companies. In addition, they have increasingly extended both the volume and the length of their term lending and have begun to a limited extent to arrange private placements for customers.

The Glass-Steagall prohibitions have also been eroded by the spread of multinational banking. Many large U.S. banks either own or are closely affiliated with foreign investment banking firms and thereby engage in such traditionally prohibited activities as the underwriting and dealing in corporate bonds and stock. Further, it is not uncommon for the London-based subsidiaries of U.S. banks to act as the managing or "lead" bank in initiating and syndicating huge long-term Eurodollar loans to corporate borrowers (in some cases taking a significant portion of these loans into their own portfolios). The distinction between this activity and the underwriting of corporate bonds is not great. Finally, because of the patchwork regulatory structure that applies to the activities of foreign banks in this country, foreign banks engage simultaneously in both a commercial banking and an investment banking business in New York City and other major U.S. financial centers.[1]

Security firms, buffeted by recent structural changes in the securities industry, are also eyeing the banking business as a potential earnings haven. It is not unusual for firms in a declining industry to seek survival through diversification, and banking is a clear attraction to securities firms. A fairly obvious future scenario for the securities industry is for mergers among smaller firms to continue to the point where the remaining firms become large, diversified financial conglomerates.

Merrill Lynch probably provides the best picture of the future. Of particular interest is Merrill Lynch's recently offered CMA money trust plan. This plan enables customers who hold conventional securities margin accounts to use these accounts much as they would a traditional bank checking account while at the same time keeping these balances fully invested in an earning asset. It accomplishes this by granting customers with margin accounts the right to use a VISA transaction card to access these funds for transaction purposes, and by automatically investing customers' free credit balances in a no-load, diversified, open-end investment company. These "deposit" accounts are more attractive than any a bank can now offer, at least for larger customers. (The legality of this plan is being contested.) Several other securities firms are also currently sponsoring money market funds with check writing privileges.

Abroad, U.S. securities firms have been more direct. In 1976 Merrill Lynch established a full-service Panamanian banking corporation with $76 million of capital, and this corporation in turn owns another bank in London. These banks accept deposits and make commercial loans, just like other banks. Other large securities firms have been less venturesome but are on the same track. For example, White Weld has entered into a highly successful joint venture with Credit Suisse, one of Switzerland's largest banks.

Thus recent developments point to a growing intersection of the banking and securities businesses—both the number of firms and the range of services involved is expanding. Banks and at least some major securities firms are clearly anxious to enlarge the boundaries that have historically (at least since 1933) defined their industries. We can therefore expect continued confrontation and litigation over the Glass-Steagall Act, both as to its statutory meaning and the congressional intentions that underly it.

In this paper I will not engage in a polemical discussion of either the statutory interpretation of this law or its legislative history. I also ignore the controversy over whether the banking laws are presently more or less onerous than the securities laws, or the question of whether banks enjoy a competitive advantage.[2] While this last issue is important to the industries involved, I assume that if and when it is decided that banks can do a securities business, and vice versa, it should not be difficult in principle to place both institutions under essentially similar laws.

The perspective taken in this paper is that of a social architect and economist. I attempt to identify the major social issues raised by the inter-mingling of banking and securities activities and to analyze and assess the possible dangers inherent in this development. To identify these dangers, I draw primarily on two sources: scholarly analysis of banking experience prior to the Glass-Steagall Act, when banks were major underwriters of corporate stocks and bonds, and court decisions dealing with the recent securities activities of banks. Together these sources, I believe, articulate the various public policy issues surrounding the Glass-Steagall Act. After identifying these issues, I attempt to analyze the logic that underlies them and to assess its validity. Finally alternative regulatory responses to these dangers are discussed. Much of the debate currently surrounding the Glass-Steagall Act is understandably motivated by the desire of vested interest groups to protect their own interests. A major objective of this paper is to cut through this debate to expose the public policy concerns which lie at the heart of the Glass-Steagall Act.

Securities Activities of Banks Before 1933

From 1916 to 1929 there was continuous growth in the securities activities of banks. Conservative banks commonly rendered investment advice, executed orders for customers, and distributed government and municipal bonds, while the more progressive banks did a large business in originating, underwriting, and distributing investment securities (both corporate bonds and stocks). These activities were concentrated in the larger commercial banking institutions, and were carried out initially through the bank's bond department and then subsequently through the establishment of full-service security affiliates. Table 13-1 shows, for each year from 1922 to 1933, both the number of banks directly engaged in the distribution of securities or dealing in securities through their bond departments, and the number of banks operating security affiliates.

Prior to 1933, national banks were not prohibited from engaging in the business of buying and selling investment securities or from organizing affiliates to conduct this business. Until 1927 they carried on this business under their "incidental powers," but in 1927 the McFadden Act explicitly granted to national banks the power to buy and sell, without recourse, marketable obligations evidencing indebtedness of any person, copartnership, firm, association, or corporation in the form of bonds, notes, or debentures (but not stocks). It is generally acknowledged that the intention of the framers of this act was to give banks the right to distribute securities to their customers.[3]

As to bank security affiliates, Congress and bank regulators did not interfere with their development until 1933. Further, by enacting the McFadden Act. Congress undoubtedly encouraged the trend toward banks' entering the securities business. It was not until we were in the throes of the Great Depression and

Table 13-1
The Number of National Banks, State Banks, and the Affiliates of
National and State Banks Engaged in the Securities Business,
1922-1933

	National Banks		State Banks		
Year	Directly Engaged in Securities Business	Operating Security Affiliates	Directly Engaged in Securities Business	Operating Security Affiliates	Total
1922	62	10	197	8	277
1923	78	17	210	9	314
1924	97	26	236	13	372
1925	112	33	254	14	413
1926	128	45	274	17	464
1927	121	60	290	22	493
1928	150	69	310	32	561
1929	151	84	308	48	591
1930	126	105	260	75	566
1931	123	114	230	58	525
1932	109	104	209	53	475
1933	102	76	169	32	379

Source: Peach (1975), p. 83.

until after the failure of the Bank of the United States in New York City in 1930, with its 59 affiliates, that Congress reversed itself and enacted the Banking Act of 1933, which severed commercial banks from their securities affiliates.

A thorough analysis of the alleged abuses and defects that led to this legislation was completed in 1939 by Nelson Peach.[4] Peach's analysis suggests four classes of abuses.

> First, there were abuses which were common to the conduct of the investment banking business generally during the decade of the twenties. Examples of such abuses were the issuance of unsound and speculative securities, untruthful and misleading information contained in prospectuses accompanying new issues, and pool operations.
>
> Second, there were pool operations in the stock of parent banks by affiliates.
>
> Third, there were abuses which may be attributed to the use of affiliates for the personal profit of officers of banks and affiliates.
>
> The fourth class of abuses had to do with the mixing of commercial and investment banking functions. On the one hand frozen bank loans might be converted into security issues and sold to the public by affiliates, or affiliates might be used as receptacles for bad loans. On the other hand, banks might be used as receptacles for unsuccessful issues of securities brought out by their affiliates, or banks might make undesirable loans in order to protect securities brought out by their affiliates.[5]

After investigating these abuses, Peach concluded that "the first three abuses ... were of such a nature as might be remedied by legislation ..." and that such legislation need not "hamper the legitimate transactions involved in the flotation of long-term securities."[6] However, he concluded that "it does not seem possible ... to prevent by legislation certain abuses which grew out of the mixing of the commercial and investment phases of the banking business."[7]

Peach's major concern was the temptation that banks would have to aid their (unsound) affiliates and to protect the securities brought out by their affiliates, even if doing so threatened the bank's own solvency.

> Since, when the securities were sold, the public had been persuaded that the bank and affiliate were parts of the same organization, the bank could not escape responsibility for the activities of its affiliate when the securities began to decline in value after the stock market crisis of 1929. It became necessary for banks to assist their affiliates because they were aware that any diminution in the good will of their affiliates would bring with it a corresponding diminution in their own. This is the chief difficulty in the affiliate system. ...[8]

Further, he argued that these temptations could not be removed by legislation without destroying the benefits that derive from combining commercial and investment banking.[9]

Thus Peach's analysis of banking experience prior to 1933 led him to the conclusion that the most serious concern in permitting banks to engage in investment banking is the possibility that such activities will undermine the soundness of the banking system. This danger, moreover, he believed to be independent of the precise corporate structure used by banks to engage in investment banking—either directly through their bond departments or indirectly through separate affiliates.

Recent Court Decisions

Issues similar to those Peach studied have been raised again in litigation over the recent securities activities of banks. In the leading case, *Investment Co. Institute v. Camp*,[10] the Supreme Court held that operation by a national bank of a commingled investment fund for large investors violated Sections 16 and 21 of the Glass-Steagall Act.

A central feature of this case, and all Section 16 and 21 cases, is the determination of whether the activity in question constitutes a purchase of securities or stock by the bank for its own account (in violation of Section 16) or whether it involves the issuing, underwriting, selling, or distributing of securities or stocks (in violation of Section 21). However, since there is always considerable leeway in defining the "security," or in determining what activities constitute the issuing, underwriting, selling, or distributing of a security, the courts have examined the congressional purpose in enacting Section 16 and 21 and used this analysis to formulate their decisions.

In the *Camp* case the Supreme Court did this and concluded that the potential hazards and abuses that arise from a bank's operation of a commingled investment fund are similar to those that would arise from a bank's operation of a security affiliate. Consequently, they are the very same hazards and abuses that Congress sought to prohibit by the Glass-Steagall Act.[11] (The potential hazards identified by the Court are also those noted by Peach.) Moreover, the Court took explicit cognizance of the argument that the "Glass-Steagall Act reflected a determination that policies of competition, convenience, or expertise which might otherwise support the entry of commercial banks into the investment banking business were outweighed by the 'hazards' and 'financial dangers' that arise when commercial banks engage in the activities prescribed by the Act."[12]

At the top of the list of hazards noted by the Court is the threat that securities activities pose to bank soundness. It notes that engaging in investment banking

places new promotional and other pressures on the bank which in turn create new temptations. For example, pressures are created because the bank and the affiliate are closely associated in the public mind, and should the affiliate fare badly, public confidence in the bank might be impaired. And since public confidence is essential to the solvency of a bank, there might exist a natural temptation to shore up the affiliate through unsound loans or other aid. Moreover, the pressure to sell a particular investment and to make the affiliate successful might create a risk that the bank would make its credit facilities more freely available to those companies in which stock or securities the affiliate has invested or become otherwise involved. Congress feared that banks might even go so far as to make unsound loans to such companies. . . .

[Banks might also] be tempted to make loans to customers . . . to facilitate the purchase of stocks and securities.[13]

Next the Court cites certain potential conflicts of interest, and in particular, "the plain conflict between the promotional interest of the investment banker and the obligation of the commercial bankers to render disinterested investment advice."[14] Also "security affiliates might be driven to unload excessive holdings through the trust department of the sponsor bank."[15]

In arguing that these concerns apply with equal force to the operation of a commingled investment fund the Court said:

The bank's stake in the investment fund might distort its credit decisions or lead to unsound loans to the companies in which the fund had invested. The bank might exploit its confidential relationship with its commercial and industrial creditors for the benefit of the fund. The bank might undertake, directly or indirectly, to make its credit facilities available to the fund or to render other aid to the fund inconsistent with the best interests of the bank's depositors. The bank might make loans to facilitate the purchase of interests in the fund. The bank might divert talent and resources from its commercial banking operations to the promotion of the fund.[16]

The Court's major arguments against permitting banks to engage in the traditional activities of securities firms, therefore, appear to fall into two general types of hazards: the danger that such activities will undermine bank solvency and the potential conflicts that bank managers will confront in having to balance the interests of its borrowers versus its investment fund clients, of its depositors versus its fund clients, and of its stockholders versus its fund clients. In other words, the multiple relationships created by the tie between commercial banks and securities activities may result in multiple conflicts of interest. Further, these hazards are thought to be independent of the specific corporate structure under which such activities are carried out: No distinction is made between doing these activities indirectly through separate bank affiliates or directly through a department of the bank itself. Consequently, in the next section, which probes the economic rationales that underlie these fears, we assume for purposes of clarifying the various arguments that banks engage in securities activities directly (or that such activities are only done as an integral part of the commercial banking entity). This assumption is later relaxed, and the implications of spinning off these activities into separate affiliates is explored. By ruling out the use of affiliates, we simplify the problem by assuring that all the bank's activities have common (or identical) stockholders and creditors; when separate affiliates are permitted, this may not be true.

Analysis of Recognized Dangers

Bank Soundness

The regulatory and social objective of maintaining bank soundness stems partly from the belief that there are "negative externalities" associated with bank failures.[17] In particular, it is feared that bank failures will undermine public confidence in the banking system and precipitate a "bank run," which may result in uncontrollable instability in the money supply. In addition, some proponents of bank soundness policies argue that it is necessary to protect depositors because they lack both the necessary information and requisite financial sophistication to protect themselves. In response to these social objectives, we have adopted regulation to foster a safer banking system than would exist in the absence of regulation.

The chief dimensions of our regulatory approach to maintaining bank soundness are deposit insurance and the various detailed solvency regulations, of which activity restrictions (such as the prohibitions against securities activities) are one.[18] The role of deposit insurance is clear; that of activity restrictions less clear. Presumably, these restrictions are directed at keeping banks out of high-risk business activities, and thereby reducing the likelihood that any particular bank will become insolvent. Alternatively, they can be viewed as a supplement to the present system of a "level-premium" deposit insurance. Specifically, under this insurance system premiums do not reflect individual bank riskiness, so that banks have an incentive to undertake more risk than they might otherwise. Thus detailed solvency regulations such as activity restrictions are intended to counter this moral hazard problem. In either case, by keeping banks out of high-risk ventures, activity restrictions seek to limit the number of bank failures.

What are the risks associated with permitting banks to engage in investment banking, or to offer commingled investment funds? Traditional investment banking is undoubtedly a highly cyclical business. Earnings tend to oscillate widely over time: The volume of security underwriting varies substantially with swings in business activity, and there are significant risks associated with holding inventories of stocks and bonds. But are these risks qualitatively any different than those that banks already assume? And, is it the simple variability in the earning stream of an activity that is the relevant dimension of risk?

Clearly not. The riskiness of a particular activity is not the absolute earnings variability associated with an activity but its relative variability: It is the contribution that a particular activity makes to the earnings variability of the bank's total portfolio. An activity with a high-earnings variability may, when added to the bank's other business activities, increase its total earnings variability, but it need not. Whether it does or does not will depend critically on the covariance of that activity's earnings stream with the earnings of the other assets in the bank's portfolio. If it has a negative correlation coefficient, or one that is considerably less than positive one, it is likely to decrease, not increase, the variability of total earnings. Thus whether allowing a bank to engage in a certain "high-risk" activity will increase or decrease the bank's overall riskiness (or earnings variability) depends importantly on what other assets the bank holds in its portfolio, or on its other business activities. A priori, it is impossible to generalize.

The risks associated with investment banking do not seem to be much different than those to which banks are already exposed. Banks presently engage in many activities having highly variable earnings patterns. In addition, they underwrite and hold municipal bonds as well as some types of revenue bonds. Also in making long-term loans, banks are exposed to the same kind of bankruptcy risks involved in holding corporate bonds, and these risks are certainly greater than would be involved in most underwriting situations where the securities are held only for short periods of time (if at all). Further, the underwriting of stocks may even reduce bank riskiness. Over the standard business cycle the values of bonds and stocks customarily exhibit an inverse relationship, which should stabilize a bank's cash flow. Similarly, the operation of a commingled investment fund would be unlikely to increase the instability of a bank's earnings.

Finally, if after thorough analysis it is concluded that securities activities would result in a significant rise in bank riskiness, an appropriate regulatory response might be to increase the deposit insurance premium on banks that engage in these activities. This policy would both counter the perverse managerial incentives fostered under the current level premium insurance system and alleviate the need to rely on such drastic remedies as complete prohibition of an activity. I recognize, of course, that this insurance scheme would be a significant departure from present thinking, but it seems worth considering.

In my opinion, the fear that permitting banks to engage in securities activities will undermine bank soundness stems from the belief that these activities will pervert bank managers by creating conflicts of interest, rather than from the conviction that there are large intrinsic business risks associated with such activities. In the absence of distorting managerial effects, the securities business does not appear to be so risky for banks as to warrant its prohibition. Moreover, I argue later in the paper that the feared perverse effects on managers' incentives spring not from the basic nature of the securities activities but from the use of separate affiliates by banks through which to conduct these activities.

Conflicts of Interest

It seems appropriate to begin a discussion of the conflicts of interest that arise out of a commercial banking-securities business nexus by making the general point that conflicts of interest are everywhere. All of us, at one time or another, are in a position of wearing two hats. As a professor, I have a conflict over which book to require my students to buy: mine or someone else's.[19] The critical question is whether these conflicts are serious enough to require regulation.

The chief social concern that seems to underlie the conflict-of-interest question is "fairness." A conflict of interest exists whenever one is serving two or more interests and can put one person in a better position at the expense of another. If all parties were perfectly informed and equally capable of taking care of themselves, however, it is difficult to see why abusive conflicts would ever arise. A firm's mistreatment of certain parties would quickly become known to the market and would result in a diminishment of future business and profits for the firm. At heart, our concern over conflicts of interest derives from the (quite plausible) belief that some people are better informed than others and are better able to protect their own interests. The focus of regulation, therefore, is to safeguard the interests of those who are incapable of protecting their own interests, either by completely eliminating the potential for abusive conflicts or by constraining the behavior of those who occupy privileged positions (for example, bank managers). (For example, restrictions on "insider trading" might be viewed as a regulatory response to a conflict of interest problem.)

Are the conflicts of interest that arise out of a banking-securities business tie serious enough to require regulation or to warrant the present mandatory separation of these businesses? I will attempt to respond to this question only in a relative way, by asking whether these conflicts are of any more concern than those that already exist within commercial banks and securities firms. If the potential hazards are no greater, the appropriate regulatory response would seem to be to adopt similar regulations to those that we now use to check other already existing conflicts of interest (rather than a policy of outright separation). While this approach is obviously piecemeal in that it takes as given the present scope of commercial banking rather than addressing the fundamental issue of what the proper boundaries of banking should be, it does have the virtue of emphasizing regulatory consistency in the treatment of the various banking activities.

A source of the confusion that surrounds the conflicts issue is a misunderstanding as to why conflicts of interest exist within a bank in the first place. If all activities were done within the bank itself (or out of different departments in the bank), from a stockholder perspective, there is clearly no incentive for managers to favor one line of activity over another. To make one line of business more profitable at the expense of another is simply to take money out of one stockholder pocket and put it in another (such a transfer may even reduce overall stockholder wealth). Of course, to the extent that managers act independently of stockholders' interests, a characteristic commonly associated with large firms, a conflict between managers' and stockholders' interests may still exist. But such conflicts are not unique to securities activities; they are common to all activities of such firms. Consequently, this cannot be the kind of conflict that distinguishes securities activities from other bank activities.

Conflicts may also arise between customers. For example, in *Camp* the Court argues that "the bank might undertake, directly or indirectly, to make its credit facilities available to the fund or to render other aid to the fund inconsistent with the best interests of the bank's depositors."[20] Or, bank trust accounts might be used as receptacles for unsuccessful issues that the bank underwrites.[21] In the first case fund holders are benefited at the expense of depositors; in the second underwriting clients gain at the expense of trust beneficiaries.

The implicit assumption that underlies this concern over "customer conflicts" is that all customers are not equal with respect to being able to look after their interests. Or, alternatively, some customers simply do not adequately monitor their banks. There are at least three reasons why this might occur. First, certain existing regulations act to remove some customers' incentives to safeguard their interests. For example, deposit insurance clearly perverts depositors' incentives to look after their own interests as they would if left uninsured. More generally, pervasive regulation of banks may lull bank customers into a complacent attitude toward protecting themselves. Second, some customers may be better informed than others, probably because they have a greater economic incentive to keep informed. Large customers, for example, can be expected to purchase more information than small customers: They have more to lose and information costs are clearly subject to economies of scale. Last, even if all customers were equally informed, some might be more literate with respect to financial institutions and markets than others. Thus there are reasonable grounds on which to base a concern about "customer conflicts."

Conflicts may also arise because bank managers have access to "inside information." In *Camp* the Court argued that a "bank might exploit its confidential relationship with its commercial and industrial creditors for the benefit of the (investment) fund."[22] In this case the bank would benefit both its fund holders and its stockholders (since its better performance will attract more fund clients) at the expense of unknown third parties (outsiders), who are buying or selling securities without having the benefit of the same information. This is, of course, the usual "insider" problem that has bedeviled the SEC and the courts for decades.

Are these hazards—"customer conflicts" and the possession of "inside information"—unique to securities activities? Or does the mixing of these activities with banking result in a particularly odious situation, where the potential abuses are especially severe or widespread and where regulatory control is particularly difficult? It seems obvious that these conflicts are not special to the prohibited securities activities. In a thorough study of banks' trust operations, Lawrence Jones observed that:

> The multiple relationship engendered by the commercial banking-trust department does in turn create multiple conflicts of interest. A bank's choice of securities to purchase for trust accounts may inevitably be influenced by commercial relationships; a sale of equity shares in the interest of trust beneficiaries may adversely affect a creditor relationship or enforcement of indenture provisions in a loan agreement may be wise from a creditor's perspective but impair the position of trust account shareholders. There may be inherent conflicts in allocation of attractive investments between the commercial bank portfolio and trust portfolios and in joint participations between trust department accounts and the bank's own loan or investment account. The dual creditor-shareholder relationship also raises questions about privileged access to information through exercise of creditor prerogatives whether or not the information obtained is legally construed to be "inside information." All of the conflicts which arise out of the joint creditor-shareholder roles exist, of course, for the major life insurers and perhaps some investment advisors as well.[23]

Clearly, the potential conflicts-of-interest abuses that arise out of banks' doing a securities business are quite similar to those that exist already as a result of banks' engaging in multiple traditional banking activities. About the only thing that can be said is that by allowing banks to engage in even more activities, we may increase the potential for abuse. Even so, it is by no means obvious that these potential abuses cannot be adequately controlled by regulatory sanction. Indeed, current SEC laws against insider trading, The Investment Advisers Act of 1940, the Employee Retirement Income Security Act of 1974, as well as existing banking law would already seem to cover most of them.[24]

In conclusion, the kinds of conflicts of interest that arise from commercial banking-securities business ties are quite similar to those that already exist, and therefore would be amenable to the same types of regulatory control. Thus a policy of complete prohibition of securities activities seems neither required nor consistent with our other regulatory postures. If, of course, the conflicts of interest that presently exist within banks are already considered unacceptable, then those that arise out of banking-securities activities ties would be unacceptable as well. Such a stance, however, logically requires a complete redefinition of what banking should be (which is, fortunately, well beyond the purview of this paper).

Before completing this discussion, it should be noted that my conclusion is not in harmony with the majority opinion in *Investment Co. Institute* v. *Camp*. There the Court said, of the hazards just discussed above

These are all hazards that are not present when a bank undertakes to purchase stock for the account of its individual customers or to commingle assets which it has received for a true fiduciary purpose rather than for investment. These activities, unlike the operation of an investment fund, do not give rise to a promotional or salesman's stake in a particular investment; they do not involve an enterprise in direct competition with aggressively promoted funds offered by other investment companies; they do not entail a threat to public confidence in the bank itself; and they do not impair the bank's ability to give disinterested service as a fiduciary or managing agent. In short, there is a plain difference between the sale of fiduciary services and the sale of investments.[25]

However, Justice Blackmun in his dissenting statement said:

There is ... an element of illogic in the ready admission by all concerned, on the one hand, that a national bank has the power to manage, by way of a common trust arrangement, those funds that it holds as fiduciary in the technical sense, and to administer separate agency accounts, and in the rejection, on the other hand, of the propriety of the bank's placing agency assets into a mutual investment fund. The Court draws its decisional line between the two. I find it impossible to locate any statutory root for that line drawing. To use the Glass-Steagall Act as a tool for that distinction is, I think, a fundamental misconception of the statute.[26]

Needless to say, I agree with Justice Blackmun. If there is a distinction between the sale of fiduciary services and investment services, it is not obvious on its face. Banks benefit from providing fiduciary services, just as they do any other service. The more thay sell, the greater their profits. The basic promotional incentives are the same.

Use of Affiliates

The use of separate affiliates by banks to conduct a securities (or other "nonbanking") activity adds another dimension to the problem: It is likely to exacerbate rather than diminish most of the dangers discussed previously. Use of affiliates can easily result in managerial incentives and temptations that jeopardize the solvency of a bank. Further, it may create additional conflicts of interest. This section analyzes how the use of affiliates changes the situation discussed where I assumed that banks conducted their securities business directly through a department of the bank.

The major reason banks formed security affiliates in the 1920s was to evade the legal restrictions imposed on the bank itself. In his analysis, Peach observed that "the business that the affiliates were ostensibly organized to conduct was to consist mainly in providing customers of the banks with financial facilities not permitted under the national banking laws."[27] This motive, of course, is the same one that gave rise to the one-bank holding company movement in the late 1960s and which in turn led to legislation in 1970 loosening the restrictions on bank holding companies.[28] Today just as in the 1920s, we are spawning a broad-based affiliate system as the basic corporate structure for doing a banking business. (Affiliate systems are also becoming common features of other financial industries as well—securities firms, insurance companies, and so on.)

Use of affiliates can cause additional dangers because affiliates may have different capital and ownership structures than the parent bank. Specifically, the stock of the affiliate may not be owned ratably by the stockholders who own the parent bank, and the leverage structure (the debt-to-equity ratio) may be different for the affiliate than for the bank. Either of these can foster undesirable managerial incentives.

If the stock of the bank and affiliate are not owned ratably by the same stockholders, an obvious conflict arises between the interests of the stockholders of the bank and those of the affiliate. Managers face still another conflict of interest: They may take an action that benefits one set of stockholders at the expense of another. The worst situation is undoubtedly where the officers and directors of the bank own all or most of the stock of the affiliate but little or none of the stock of the bank.[29]

Given such a corporate structure, it is not hard to see why bank managers might make imprudent or unsound loans to the affiliate or do other things that jeopardize the solvency of the bank itself. Nor is it difficult to understand why in 1933 Congress was so concerned about this danger. An important reason for the historical view that securities activities represent a danger to bank soundness stems from the widespread practice of banks in the 1920s of doing this business through separate affiliates having different ownership and capital structures. Indeed, if one were to have the affiliate system in mind, the reservations expressed by the Court in *Camp* would be more understandable.[30]

In the absence of an affiliate system, however, there is no reason to think that sound managerial incentives would not continue to exist. Whatever threat there is to bank soundness from doing a securities business under these circumstances would flow from the intrinsic riskiness of this business, and our previous analysis suggests that this risk is not likely to be great.

It is ironic to note that a popular belief is that it is *safer* for banks to conduct their riskier "nonbanking" activities through separate affiliates since in the event of bankruptcy of the affiliate, the bank's assets are unreachable by the affiliate's creditors. Although this view has been questioned (on the grounds that banks will, in fact, stand by their unlucky affiliates despite the protections afforded by the law), it has not been widely recognized that the operation of an affiliate system may actually *increase* the risk of bank insolvency as well as exacerbate the conflict-of-interest problem. An important regulatory issue for the future is whether banks should be permitted to operate affiliates at all, and if they are, what limitations should be placed on the ownership and capital structures of these affiliates. This issue goes beyond the question of whether banks should be permitted to engage in securities activities; it encompasses the entire holding company movement in financial markets.

Finally, even if the stock of the bank and affiliate are owned ratably by the same stockholders, a problem may still arise if the capital structures of the two institutions are different. If one of the institutions is more leveraged than the other, it may be in the interests of stockholders to transfer "bad assets" into the most leveraged entity since this procedure could minimize stockholders' losses in the event of bankruptcy of these assets. Whether this incentive operates to make the banking entity more or less risky depends on the bank's capital structure relative to that of its affiliates. Here the managerial conflict of interest arises because there are two sets of creditors, those for the bank and those for the affiliate; and, once again, this is a conflict that does not arise when all the bank's activities are carried out under one roof.

In sum, the question of whether banks should be permitted to engage in securities activities, and vice versa, has been continuously confounded with the larger issue of the potential abuses arising from the conflicts of interest inherent in the affiliate system. These are distinct issues. Further, when the mixing of the banking and securities businesses is viewed separately from the affiliate system problem, it is not evident that this interface creates either a significant threat to bank soundness or an exceptional conflict of interest problem.

Some Additional Concerns: Competition and Bigness

Other concerns that are voiced in response to the spectre of commercial banks' invading the securities industry are that its ultimate effect will be to diminish competition and to establish financial conglomerates having enormous economic and political power. These fears, however realistic, are again not unique to the securities business but are common to the entire bank holding company movement.

With respect to the concern over competition, for every nonbank acquisition by a bank holding company, the Federal Reserve Board must apply the "public benefits" test,[31] of which the most important element is the determination of whether the acquisition increases or decreases competition. Common arguments are that banks will have a competitive advantage because of their lower cost of funds, that they will engage in injurious tie-in sales, and that they will have access to confidential information about competitors. Ultimately, so the argument goes, banks will drive out competitors and monopolize the market.[32] Needless to say, these arguments are no more or less applicable to securities activities than to any other line of commerce so that there seems little reason to treat securities activities any differently than we treat the other nonbanking activities. These competitive fears therefore also do not support a policy of total prohibition.

Nor does the concern that banks (or the future Merrill Lynches of the securities industry) might become huge financial colossuses capable of wielding immense economic and political power support such a policy. This concern is not special to the securities business but relates to all the activities in which banks engage. The argument pertains to the "bigness" of firms (not only banks), and should be dealt with as such—by policies that are specifically directed at firm size. The separation of banks from securities firms is only indirectly related to this social issue.

Summary and Conclusions

This paper has examined the arguments that support our present policy of completely separating banks from the securities business. Two general rationales are commonly cited: that permitting banks to engage in securities activities will undermine bank soundness and that such a relationship will result in severe conflict-of-interest problems that cannot be adequately controlled by direct regulation.

Leaving aside the hazards inherent in the affiliate system and assuming that banks were to engage in securities activities directly (through a department of the bank), the analysis in this paper suggests two conclusions. First, the threat to bank solvency associated with banks' doing a securities business does not seem to be qualitatively any different from that associated with many other bank activities. Further, whatever risks do exist are susceptible to regulatory control, using traditional regulatory tools. Second, although mixing banking with securities activities undoubtedly does create conflicts of interest, these conflicts are not unlike those that already exist in banking, in response to which we have adopted specific regulations directed at the potential conflict in question.[33] Thus the social hazards associated with banks' doing a securities business are neither unique nor qualitatively more threatening than those associated with many other bank activities.

The policy implications of these conclusions, however, are not unambiguous. They may suggest that what we need is radical surgery on banks: a complete redefinition of the "banking business." Perhaps banks should be forced to divest themselves of their trust operations, REITs, and so on. The feasibility and wisdom of such surgery is obviously beyond the scope of this paper. However, absent such radical surgery, the policy implication of this paper is clear: Banks should be allowed to enter the securities business and vice versa, given the proper regulatory safeguards. Logic and consistency require it. Further, this policy will enhance competition, which is desirable for several reasons, not the least of which is that greater competition (accompanied by a regulatory policy of requiring greater disclosure) will act to mitigate or control potential conflict-of-interest problems.

The conclusion of this paper with respect to the use of affiliates—whether used to engage in securities activities or other "nonbanking" activities—is much less sanguine. An affiliate system can generate managerial incentives and temptations that both exacerbate the conflict-of-interest problem and endanger the solvency of banks. A major reason for the present use of affiliates, of course, is that they allow banks to evade geographical restrictions on their activities, restrictions that are themselves probably not in the public interest. Nevertheless, this paper suggests that regulatory authorities should take a hard look at the risks inherent in the widespread use of affiliates. They may wish to place restrictions on both the ownership and capital structures employed by the affiliates; and in the event that we someday arrive at a state where national branching is permitted, they may wish to give serious consideration to abolishing the affiliate system altogether.

Finally, if banks are permitted to enter the securities business and vice versa, it goes without saying that this policy should be accompanied by a tough pro-competitive (or antitrust) policy as well as by disclosure requirements similar to those the SEC now requires for non-financial firms.

Notes

1. See Edwards (1974).
2. Commercial banks are largely exempt from the Securities Exchange Act of 1934 and the Federal Securities Act of 1933.
3. See Willis (1934), p. 104.
4. Peach (1975).
5. Peach (1975), pp. 113-114.
6. Peach (1975), p. 141.
7. Peach (1975).
8. Peach (1975), p. 142.
9. Peach (1975).
10. 401 U.S. 617, 91 S. Ct. 1091 (1971).
11. 401 U.S. 617, 91 S. Ct. 1091 (1971), pp. 636-637.
12. 401 U.S. 617, 91 S. Ct. 1091 (1971), p. 630.
13. 401 U.S. 617, 91 S. Ct. 1091 (1971), pp. 630-632.
14. 401 U.S. 617, 91 S. Ct. 1091 (1971), p. 633.
15. 401 U.S. 617, 91 S. Ct. 1091 (1971).
16. 401 U.S. 617, 91 S. Ct. 1091 (1971), pp. 637-638.
17. For a discussion of the various rationales that underlie bank-solvency regulation, see Edwards and Scott (1978).

18. Edwards and Scott (1978).

19. See Schotland (1978) and Peltzman (1978).

20. 401 U.S. 617, 91 S. Ct. 1091 (1971), note 16.

21. 401 U.S. 617, 91 S. Ct. 1091 (1971), note 5.

22. 401 U.S. 617, 91 S. Ct. 1091 (1971), note 16.

23. Jones, (1969), p. 22.

24. See appendix 12A.

25. 401 U.S. 617, 91 S. Ct. 1091 (1971), p. 638.

26. 401 U.S. 617, 91 S. Ct. 1091 (1971), pp. 643-644.

27. pp. 52, 61-62, note 89, and 63-64, note 96.

28. See Edwards (1969).

29. These occurrences were common in the 1920s. See Peach (1975), pp. 130-131, note 77.

30. 401 U.S. 617, 91 S. Ct. 1091 (1971), pp. 630-632. In this case, however, the investment fund in question was not operated as a separate affiliate but through a department in the bank.

31. See Section (4)(c)(8) of the Bank Holding Company Act, 12 U.S.C. 1848 (1970).

32. See the recent decision by the Federal Reserve Board authorizing banks to engage in automobile leasing. *Federal Reserve Bulletin* (1975).

33. For example, in issuing its rules that apply to bank holding companies' acting as investment advisers, the Federal Reserve Board recognized certain potential conflicts of interest and responded with the following rules: "A bank holding company and its bank and nonbank subsidiaries should not (1) purchase for their own account securities of any investment company for which the bank holding company acts as investment adviser; (2) purchase in their sole discretion, any such securities in a fiduciary capacity (including managing agent); (3) extend credit to any such investment company; or (4) accept the securities of any such investment company as collateral for a loan which is for the purpose of purchasing securities of the investment company." 12 C.F.R. 225.125 (g) (1977). See also appendix 13A.

References

Edwards, F. *Issues in Financial Regulation.* New York: McGraw Hill, 1979.

_____ . "Regulation of Foreign Banking in the United States: International Reciprocity and Federal-State Conflicts." 13 *Columbia Journal of Transnational Law* 2 (1974):239-268.

_____ . "The One-Bank Holding Company Conglomerate: Analysis and Evaluation," 22 *Vanderbilt Law Review* 1275 (1969):1275-1309.

Edwards, F., and Scott, J. "Regulating the Solvency of Depository Institutions: A Perspective for Deregulation." In *Issues in Financial Regulation*, edited by F. Edwards. New York: McGraw Hill, 1979.

Federal Reserve Board. *Federal Reserve Bulletin,* November 1975, pp. 930-940.

_____. *Investment Co.* v. *Camp.* 401 U.S. 617, 91 S. Ct. 1091 (1971).

Jones, L. "Bank Trust Activity and the Public Interest." Paper prepared for the President's Commission on Financial Structure and Regulation (1969).

Peach, W. Nelson. *The Security Affiliates of National Banks.* Baltimore: John Hopkins Press, 1941; New York: Arno Press, 1975.

Peltzman, S. "Comment on 'Conflicts of Interest Within the Financial Firm: Regulatory Implications.' " In *Issues in Financial Regulation,* edited by F. Edwards. New York: McGraw Hill, 1979.

Schotland, R. "Conflicts of Interest Within the Financial Firm: Regulatory Implications." In *Issues in Financial Regulation,* edited by F. Edwards. New York: McGraw Hill, 1979.

Willis, H. Parker. "The Banking Act of 1933—An Appraisal." *American Economic Review Supplement* XXIV (March 1934).

Appendix 13A
FDIC, Unsafe and
Unsound Banking
Practices

12 C.F.R. §337.3 (1977) (footnotes omitted)

§337.3 Insider Transactions

(a) *Definitions* (1). The term "bank" means an insured State nonmember commercial or mutual savings bank, and any majority-owned subsidiary of such bank.

(2) *Person.* The term "person" means a corporation, partnership, association, or other business entity; any trust; or any natural person.

(3) *Control.* The term "control" (including the terms "controlling," "controlled by," and "under common control with") means the possession, directly or indirectly, of the power to direct or cause the direction of management and policies of a person, whether through the ownership of voting securities, by contract, or otherwise.

(4) *Insider.* The term "insider" means any officer or employee who participates or has authority to participate in major policy-making functions of a bank, any director or trustee of a bank, or any other person who has direct or indirect control over the voting rights of ten percent of the shares of any class of voting stock of a bank or otherwise controls the management or policies of a bank.

(5) *Person related to an insider.* The term "person related to an insider" means any person controlling, controlled by or under common control with an insider, and also, in the case of a natural person, means:

   (i) An insider's spouse;

   (ii) An insider's parent or stepparent, or child or stepchild; or

   (iii) Any other relative who lives in an insider's home.

(6) *Insider transaction.* The term "insider transaction" means any business transaction or series of related business transactions between a bank and:

   (i) An insider of the bank;

   (ii) A person related to an insider of the bank;

   (iii) Any other person where the transaction is made in contemplation of such person becoming an insider of the bank; or

   (iv) Any other person where the transaction inures to the tangible economic benefit of an insider or a person related to an insider.

(7) *Business transaction.* The term "business transaction" includes, but is not limited to, the following types of transactions:

   (i) Loans or other extensions of credit;

    (ii) Purchases of assets or services from the bank;

    (iii) Sale of assets or services to the bank;

    (iv) Use of the bank's facilities, its real or personal property, or its personnel;

    (v) Lease of property to or from the bank;

    (vi) Payment by the bank of commissions and fees, including brokerage commissions and management, consultant, architectural and legal fees; and

    (vii) Payment by the bank of interest on time deposits which are in amounts of $100,000 or more.

For the purpose of this regulation, the term does not include deposit account activities other than those specified in paragraph (a)(7)(g) of this section, safekeeping transactions, credit card transactions, trust activities, and activities undertaken in the capacity of securities transfer agent or municipal securities dealer.

    (b) *Approval and Disclosure of Insider Transactions.* An insider transaction, either alone or when aggregated in accordance with paragraph (c) of this section, involving assets or services having a fair market value amounting to more than:

    (1) $20,000 if the bank has not more than $100,000,000 in total assets;

    (2) $50,000 if the bank has more than $100,000,000 and not more than $500,000,000 in total assets; or

    (3) $100,000 if the bank has more than $500,000,000 in total assets

shall be specifically reviewed and approved by the bank's board of directors or board of trustees, provided, however, that, when an insider transaction is part of a series of related business transactions involving the same insider, approval of each separate transaction is not required so long as the bank's board of directors or board of trustees has reviewed and approved the entire series of related transactions and the terms and conditions under which such transactions may take place. The minutes of the meeting at which approval is given shall indicate the nature of the transaction or transactions, the parties to the transaction or transactions, that such review was undertaken and approval given, and the names of individual directors or trustees who voted to approve or disapprove the transaction or transactions. In the case of negative votes, a brief statement of each dissenting director's or trustee's reason for voting to disapprove the proposed insider transaction or transactions shall be included in the minutes if its inclusion is requested by the dissenting director or trustee.

14

The Intersection of the Banking and Securities Industries and Future Deregulation

James W. Stevens

Perhaps you all should beware of an old NYU grad bringing wisdom and truth to today's discussion of the intersection of the securities and banking businesses, given my present employment. It may be that my real claim to some objectivity is represented by the fact that I have labored on both sides of the Street, having been a commercial banker, an investment banker, and a merchant banker in the first twenty years of my working life. I see this intersection driven by economic issues and doubt that we will see a great deal of deregulation in the financial markets; however, it is likely that we will see significant changes in regulation and business opportunity for financial service organizations.

My main thesis today is that this intersection is not just a wrangle over turf between the New York investment and commercial banks, but part of a much more comprehensive evolution in the financial service business. To think about it clearly, it is my conviction that you must consider the broader competitive environment and the impact that it is having on the thinking of the men and women in these organizations as they plan and build for the future. Broad evolution is the accumulation of lesser trends, so let me break them down.

Let me start with the commercial banking business. My view is that the lending business is going through an inevitable adjustment process from having demand deposits as an important base for providing services and lending to becoming an interest differential business—one where we buy money, lend it out at the best spread over cost that we can get. In short, a commodity-type business. The value of money in an inflationary world has risen in gross terms to all who have it in excess. The efforts to speed collection and invest excess funds are well known.

The world has also gotten much more competitive for commercial bankers, with enormous pressure from the likes of the commercial paper market, foreign banks lending in the United States and around the world, and nonbank competitors in the financial services market. For example, in 1977 commercial paper debt outstanding to nonfinancial corporations increased by almost $2 billion, a 16% increase,[1] while commercial and industrial (C&I) loans of large weekly reporting commercial banks in New York City increased only by $1.4 billion or 4%, and all large weekly reporting banks experienced an increase of 10% in C&I loans.[2]

The growth of foreign banks' presence in the U.S. market as the global economy becomes increasingly interdependent is rapid. According to an unpublished paper by two Federal Reserve Board economists, C&I loans of foreign banks in the major U.S. money centers have grown from $9 billion in November 1972 to $21 billion in May 1977, an increase in the foreign bank market share of the weekly reporting banks from 10% to 18%. Between November 1974 and May 1977, when C&I loans of the weekly reporting banks actually declined by $13.7 billion, C&I loans of the U.S. offices of foreign banks increased by $2.9 billion. Moreover, $1.6 billion of this increase represented C&I loans to domestic borrowers. The authors went on to say: "the expected long-run results of this increased competition should be smaller net interest rate spreads on domestic U.S. lending and a closer convergence between domestic and Euro-currency lending rates."[3]

Nonbank competitors are also lending money to nonfinancial businesses at an increasing rate. From 1970 to 1977, finance company loans to nonfinancial corporate business increased at an average annual compound growth rate of 18.4% while nonmortgage bank loans increased at a rate of 9.1%. Over this time period, finance company loans increased from $14 billion to $46 billion or from 14% to 24% of bank loans outstanding to nonfinancial corporate business.[4]

As a result of these competitive pressures, spreads have narrowed, and more money must be loaned with attendant requirements for capital. That has caused commercial banks to change their attitudes toward fee-producing activities. They are fundamentally more attractive to us as these basic trends continue. To look at it another way, banks are now seeking payment in fees for services that once were supplied in exchange for the use of interest-free demand deposits.

From the securities industry side, economic forces combined with legislative and regulatory actions have caused fundamental structural changes in the industry. When I came to New York in 1958, the securities industry operated on the basis of a fixed commission schedule and had a variable cost structure. That condition has now entirely reversed itself, with commissions becoming variable and under constant downward pressure in the institutional sector and with fixed costs of people, space and computers rising. No longer can a brokerage firm keep top talent with a very modest monthly draw against production paid semiannually or annually. People are not willing to live that way any longer.

The bull markets of the 1960s brought tremendous operational and cost pressures to the securities industry as it struggled to keep up with the paperwork necessitated by the huge trading volumes. The subsequent bear market of 1969-1970 applied to further pressure of a precipitous revenue decline. Almost 200 New York Stock Exchange firms left the industry through merger or liquidation in the early 1970s.[5] On 1 May, 1975 the industry's fixed commission schedule terminated. The Securities Act Amendments of 1975 mandated further far-reaching changes in the structure of the securities industry, including a National Market System, a national clearance and settlement system, and a more open and competitive securities trading environment. The securities industry has demonstrated a great resilience but continues to be buffeted by volatile earnings swings. In 1976 industry profits exceeded the peak level of 1968 as large trading volumes and bond trading profits offset the commission losses caused by negotiated rates. However, 1977 was a disappointing year for the industry, owing to a decline in underwritings and adverse trading markets for stocks and bonds. The wave of securities industry mergers, acquisitions, and consolidations of the 1970s reduced the number of firms but strengthened the capital position of individual companies and broadened their revenue sources. Retail firms merged with investment banks. Domestic firms reached out to link up with European firms or expanded into the international arena on their own. Even Morgan Stanley, once the pure investment bank, has entered the institutional equities business, acquired a retail brokerage firm on the West Coast, and moved into the bond-trading business in a major way, just since 1972.[6]

This brief history, though oversimplified, helps to explain the expansion of fee-based business by banks and the reaction we are getting from our friends on Wall Street. It may also help to explain why some securities firms are increasingly interested in lending money, acquiring trust powers, and being in the insurance business in the quest for less volatile income streams. In its 1977 annual report, Merrill Lynch states: "For the future, we are dedicated to expand further the range of services we offer, to meet the needs of our customers through profitable innovation and, ultimately, to smooth the cycles which characterize the operations in the securities industry." My basic point is that both industries are driven by economic changes and a quest for orderly stable growth in revenues and profits.

What is it the banks want to do and do not want to do?

Banks want to assist their clients with financial advisory, consulting, and fund raising services as appropriate within the context of the Glass-Steagall Act. We want to help develop financial plans and assist in their execution—including advice on private placements, acquisitions, divestitures, overseas fund raising and currency transactions designed to mitigate the financial statement impact of foreign exchange fluctuations.

The corporate finance activities of banks are not new, as many would have you believe. Citibank, for example, has had officers working on financial planning, advising on private placements, and consulting on acquisitions and divestitures for nearly twenty years. We have, however, placed more emphasis here in the last five years, are running the business as a profit center, and are doing some good business. This stepped-up activity has been the lightning rod for the securities industry. It has also drawn extensive scrutiny from the SEC, the Federal Reserve, the Comptroller of the Currency, and Congress. Currently, 80 banks are being surveyed by their regulators on 1977 activities in the private placement area. They include the 40 largest banks in the country and 40 regional banks chosen at random. I would estimate that no more than 25 to 30 of these banks are in the business. Most of them have just a few people providing some kind of advisory services in corporate finance. Morgan Guaranty and Citibank are probably the most active, with Bank of America and Chase evidencing greater interest in the corporate finance types of services.

We consider our activities to be legal and in the public interest, and we are prepared to work hard to protect our right to serve our clients. For a bank like Citibank, these services are designed to produce earnings for our shareholders and to enhance our strategic worth to our clients—to differentiate the color of our money or the relationship with our bank. We do not control our competitive environment any more than our friends in the securities business control theirs. Our increased activities, like theirs, should be viewed as realistic responses to perceived opportunities for growth within a continuously changing competitive environment.

Our whole economic system is built on a vital and viable securities industry. We need to have public underwriting markets for corporate debt and equity securities. I do not know a single bank in the United States that has any interest in amending Glass-Steagall to allow banks to underwrite corporate debt or equity securities. Nor do I know of any bank currently interested in providing a general brokerage service to the public. For Citibank's part, we have gone on record to this effect, in a letter from Walter B. Wriston to Roderick M. Hills, former chairman of the SEC:

> Based upon the current structure and functioning of the U.S. securities markets, Citibank does not desire to enter into the public brokerage business or the business of underwriting, or dealing in, securities of other corporations in general competition with the investment banking industry. Accordingly, we do not feel that any substantive changes in the Glass-Steagall Act are necessary or desirable.
>
> Citibank does, however, feel that the commercial banking industry can contribute to the efficiency of the capital formation process in the U.S. in a manner which is consistent with purposes of the Glass-Steagall Act and complementary to the function performed by the investment banking community. Specifically, we feel that commercial banks can, without undue risk to their financial integrity or undue exposure to conflicts of interest, provide advisory services to clients seeking capital as well as provide channels to capital markets for customers seeking investment opportunities. These activities, we feel, can benefit the public by enhancing the capital formation process—in some cases, by having commercial banks compete with investment banks and, in other cases, by having commercial banks acting as complements to investment banks.[7]

It seems to me that this position is abundantly clear.

At this point I must add that most bankers do not believe that the Glass-Steagall Act was designed to provide a blanket of protection from competition for the securities industry. We are of the opinion that it was enacted to protect bank depositors from the perceived risks of underwriting corporate debt and equity securities. Though one may debate the true merits of this separation, the nation's commercial banking industry will continue to respect it. It is only outside the United States—in response to competitive pressures from European commercial banks and nonbank financial competitors such as American Express—that U.S. commercial banks seek to build a more broadly based merchant banking business.

Within the United States, a legislative change we seek is the authority to underwrite municipal revenue bonds. The fundamental point made by commercial bankers here is that we can add depth to competitive-bidding syndicates at a cost saving to issuers in what is now a generally negotiated market. About 60% of revenue bond issues are presently sold on a negotiated basis. This compares with less than 20% of general obligation bond issues.[8] Professor Phillip Cagan of Columbia University has estimated that issuers of bank ineligible revenue bonds would have saved more than $400 million in interest cost and reduced dealer spreads in 1977 if banks had been permitted to underwrite the issues.[9]

The Glass-Steagall Act exempted general obligation bonds of states and their subdivisions. It is our opinion that Congress would have exempted municipal revenue bonds had they been around at the time. It must be said that revenue bond financing is a very big and profitable business today.

I suspect that there is one other area where commercial banks and securities firms will continue to compete, and that is in seeking ways to offer profitable investment advisory services to the small investor. This area has been the subject of extensive litigation and years of debate.

The banking industry lost its ability to offer a commingled investment fund in the well-known Supreme Court decision on the *ICI* vs. *Camp* case in 1971. You may recall that the Supreme Court decision was not unanimous with two Justices dissenting on the majority opinion.

The banking industry has a natural, marketplace-driven interest in providing investment services to the smaller investor. I noted in a recent trade publication that the American Bankers Association would like to get the commingled investment trust back on the agenda for debate in future Senate hearings. I consider this further evidence that a broad representation of banks around the country feel the need to offer investment products to their customers that are structured in such a way that the banks can make some money.

Now let's turn to the subject of the securities industry's interest in the banking field. I'm sure that a number of you may be watching what Merrill Lynch is doing these days with its Cash Management Account program. I remind you that they have 248 retail branches in 45 states and have announced the intention to open 31 new offices in 1978. Depending on the success of its CMA introductions, Merrill Lynch could end up with the broadest product line offered by a nationwide financial service organization without any geographic constraints on the provision of banking-like services. Demonstrated success could encourage other large brokerage firms such as E.F. Hutton & Co. and Bache, Halsey Stuart to introduce a similar product.[10] While major money center banks may feel that they can meet this competition, local banks such as those in Colorado consider this trend with alarm and have requested the Colorado Banking Board to conduct hearings to determine if Merrill Lynch and City National are conducting banking operations across state lines in violation of state law.

Another important trend is the interest shown by the major brokerage firms in the insurance fields. Merrill Lynch, E.F. Hutton, Bache, and Smith Barney all either have registered insurance agents in their offices or own insurance-related companies. E.F. Hutton reported in its 1977 annual report:

> Since 1972, when the New York Stock Exchange first allowed its member firms to sell insurance, Hutton has emerged as one of the largest independent life insurance agencies in the United States. The acquisition of Life Insurance Company of California [effective December 31, 1977] will allow us to retain underwriting profits currently accruing to the benefit of the issuers of the insurance products which we sell. The retention of these significant profits, together with the underlying profitability of Life Insurance Company of California, add important new sources of net income to E.F. Hutton.

I expect to see more such activity. Unlike the securities firms, the banks clearly have been ruled out of the insurance business except in very limited respects. I think this trend will bear some watching for those who like to follow where things are going.

In the international arena, Merrill Lynch, for one, is building a London-style merchant bank à la Morgan Grenfell, which combines commercial lending, money management, and investment banking. To quote from its 1977 annual report:

> Through its subsidiaries, Merrill Lynch International Bank Inc. of Panama and Merrill Lynch International Bank Ltd. a London based merchant bank, MLI has expanded its foreign activities to encompass those engaged in by commercial banks, including acceptance of deposits, short-term lending and the syndication and granting of term loans.

Having considered why the intersections are taking place today and the continuing aspirations of both sides, I would like to review and comment on the objections most frequently raised against bank expansion in merchant banking in the United States.

Objection 1

The capital-formation process is being damaged by this step-up in bank activity. This argument presupposes that banks have unrestrained financial muscle and overwhelming competitive advantages and will squeeze the securities industry out of the financial intermediation process, thereby reducing the availability of capital to American corporations. The reality is that banks are not interested in the equity and debt underwriting business. In the private placement area, they are doing only 6 to 7% of the business volume.[11] In the acquisition field, banks do less than 1% of the transactions.[12] Even in an area where commercial banks have been competing vigorously with the securities industry all along—the underwriting of general obligation municipal bonds—commercial banks in 1975 accounted for only 25% of the revenue from this activity,[13] hardly market dominance.

Objection 2

Banks cannot contribute to the capital-formation process because the long-term money is there in the insurance companies, pension funds, and savings banks, and the banks do not add anything to it. This idea can be turned around to say that our friends in the securities industry do not create this capital either. But in any case, I think this objection misses the point. What many banks are doing is serving entities that need assistance but are not necessarily customers of Wall Street. Examples include farm cooperatives, foreign airlines, and smaller businesses, those not large enough to be underwriting candidates. In addition, we at Citibank tend to get involved in complicated, long-lead-time, project-related business. In any case, the private placement market could benefit from increased competition. According to the 1977 New York Clearing House Association paper, *Commercial Bank Private Placement Advisory Services:*

> During the last two years [1975 and 1976], the leading five investment banking firms acted as advisors in approximately 44% of all private placements involving financial advisors. In each of the last five years [1972-1976], the top five positions in the private placement market have been held, with only two exceptions, by only six investment banking firms.[14]

I submit that there is value added to bank involvement in this activity, and my best evidence is that our customers are receptive to our desire to help.

Objection 3

Banks' activities will threaten the solvency of the banks. Of all the securities-related services offered by banks, only the U.S. government dealer and municipal operations include money or capital risk taking, and banks have been in those businesses for decades. They have shown the ability to manage this risk. The advisory businesses have a relatively minor risk limited to salaries, space, and legal expenses. Bankers are not likely to expand these efforts without some sign of payoff from small initiatives first.

Objection 4

Banks have competitive advantages because they can lend money also. My experience tells me that the lending relationship is strongly balanced competitively by the investment banker's ability to underwrite and make markets in bonds and stocks. The February 1978 issue of *Institutional Investor* magazine quoted one corporate treasurer on the matter. His comment was much closer to the realities of competitive banking as I know it on a day-to-day basis. He said, "If any of my commercial bankers told me I ought to give them my private placement business just because I've got some loans out from them, I'd laugh in his face." As I was quoted in the same article: We have no special shot at a piece of business simply because we have our Citibank sweatshirt on. Because we're from Citibank, we may get entree and a chance to tell our story, But it's a highly competitive game, and unless you provide highly professional advice, you don't get the business.

Objection 5

Banks have conflicts of interest in being in private placements. My answers to that are:

1. Banks do not do business with their trust departments because of regulatory constraints and the inability to charge clients fees for private placement advisory services under the Employee Retirement Income Security Act of 1974.
2. The private placement investors do their homework, are sophisticated, and do not represent a home for troubled bank loans.
3. Full disclosure of a bank's credit involvement is made in the private placement memorandum.
4. We have professional people conducting the business who have their reputations on the line at all times.
5. Banks have no more of a potential conflict of interest in separating private placement activity from investment or lending activities than securities firms do in isolating it from their investment or underwriting function. Both industries are equally capable of managing the element of risk in these potential conflicts.

Objection 6

Bank's participation in these activities would result in undue concentration of financial power by the large money center banks and could involve control of the allocation of capital in our economy. Where is the evidence of this unhealthy control? What are the facts? I maintain that the large money center banks are less vulnerable to this charge today than at any time since the 1920s. Consider the increasing competition within the banking industry both domestically and internationally. Consider the emergence of nonbank competitors, including the securities industry.

At year end 1975 there were 80 regional banks with deposits over $1 billion competing with the 10 largest money-center banks. By year end 1977 there were 104.[1][5] With more foreign banks active in the U.S. market, the commercial paper market growing, and nonbank financial institutions flourishing throughout the U.S. economy, clearly the financial intermediation process is becoming less concentrated rather than more.

The enormous capital needs for major project development of our nation's resources far exceed the financing capability of even the largest commercial and investment banks. On the other end of the spectrum, the nation's smaller businesses are finding it increasingly difficult to meet their financing needs. The clear message is that more, not fewer, participants are needed in the capital-raising function.

Where does all this controversy lead, and what can we expect in the months and years ahead?

Both industries are serious about their economic interests and health. Both are feeling competitive pressures and are grappling with meaningful new business opportunities. These facts suggest that this controversy will not go away. The regulators and Congress are embarked on a meaningful search for ways to improve the competitive environment of financial institutions within constructive public policy guidelines. It is likely that we will have many more legislative hearings and that we will all be reading and hearing about these subjects for years to come. From our point of view, this competition is healthy, as is the debate accompanying it. We believe that vigorous and innovative financial intermediaries are essential for a sound and growing economy. The commercial banks expect to be a vital part of this evolving business and believe they have a very constructive role to play.

Notes

1. Federal Reserve Board of Governors. Unpublished *Flow of Funds* tapes.

2. Federal Reserve Board of Governors, *Federal Reserve Bulletin* tables A20 and 21, February 1977 and February 1978.

3. Terrell and Key, "U.S. Activities of Foreign Banks," p. 6.

4. Federal Reserve Board of Governors. Unpublished *Flow of Funds* tapes.

5. SRI International, *U.S. Securities Industry,* p. 1.53.

6. Robertson, "Future Shock at Morgan Stanley," pp. 83-84.

7. U.S., Congress, Senate, *Securities Activities Hearings,* p. 753.

8. Public Securities Association, *Municipal Market Developments,* table 5, part 1, 29 March, 1978.

9. Cagan, "New Study," p. 14.

10. Yahn, "Brokerage Firms," p. 1.

11. Securities and Exchange Commission, *Bank Securities Activities,* p. 64.

12. SEC, *Bank Securities Activities,* p. 99.

13. SRI International, *U.S. Securities Industry,* p. 7.8.

14. The New York Clearing House Association, *Commercial Bank Private Placement Advisory Services,* p. 20.

15. *American Banker,* Special Supplement—Compilation of the Largest Banks in the United States, 28 February, 1978.

References

Cagan, Philip. "New Study Indicates $400 Million Saving in '77 if Banks Underwrote Revenue Bonds." *The Weekly Bond Buyer—DBA Supplement,* 20 March, 1978, pp. 3-14.

The New York Clearing House Association. *Commercial Bank Private Placement Advisory Services: An Analysis of the Public Policy and Legal Issues,* April 1977.

Robertson, Wyndham. "Future Shock at Morgan Stanley," *Fortune,* 27 February, 1978, pp. 82-92.

Securities and Exchange Commission. *Final Report on Bank Securities Activities,* 30 June, 1977.

SRI International. *Outlook for the U.S. Securities Industry—1981.* A privately sponsored study of the Securities Industry, June 1977.

Terrell, Henry S., and Key, Sydney J. "The U.S. Activities of Foreign Banks: An Analytic Survey." An unpublished paper presented on 6 October, 1977 at a conference, *Key Issues in International Banking,* sponsored by the Federal Reserve Bank of Boston.

U.S., Congress, Senate, Committee on Banking, Housing and Urban Affairs, *Hearings before the Subcommittee on Securities in furtherance of the Study of the Securities Activities of Commercial Banks,* 94th Cong., 2d sess., 4, 5, and 6 August and 1 September, 1976, p. 753.

Yahn, Steve. "Brokerage Firms Invade Credit Card, Check Fields." *Advertising Age,* 27 June, 1977, p. 1.

15 The Intersection of the Banking and Securities Industries and Future Deregulation

Harvey A. Rowen

Overview of Regulation of the Financial Services Industry

Banks and brokers are major suppliers of financial services to individual and institutional customers. In providing these services, banks and brokers compete against each other and against other such providers. In recent times this business has come to be called the financial services industry. Regulation of the financial services industry is comprehensive and complex. Figure 15-1 shows a simplified scheme of the regulatory pattern in the financial services industry. The figure indicates a wealth of federal, state, and local regulations administered by a large group of regulatory authorities.[1]

Over the last few years questions have been raised as to the desirability of this regulatory pattern. Some have argued that regulation should be reduced and that decisions concerning the supplying and pricing of services should be left more to the forces of the marketplace. Those opposed to increased reliance on the forces of the marketplace generally argue that the elimination of regulation will lead to destructive price competition and concentration in the affected industry, which would in time lead to decreased service and higher prices for consumers of the services being provided.

The present debate concerning deregulation has not prevented new regulation in areas where there is a perceived need. While few argue with the goals underlying regulation, there is considerable debate over the means chosen to achieve these goals. Alternatives suggested include (1) increased reliance on the forces of competition; (2) different forms of regulation or configurations of regulators; and (3) federal preemption in areas now subject to state regulation.

Regulation of the financial services industry grows out of four public policy concerns, as follow.

Prevention of Concentration of Power

Financial services are provided by a highly fragmented industry. This fragmentation has been shaped largely by a legal structure that was motivated by economic doctrine. Economists have generally believed that an unregulated financial sector

305

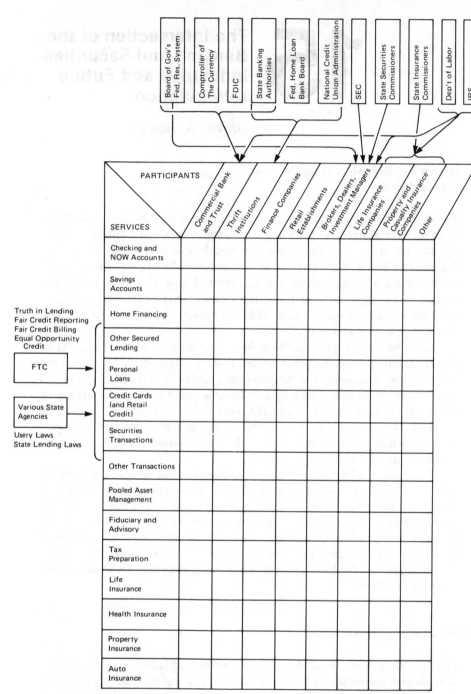

Figure 15-1. Overview of Regulatory Pattern.

would lead to dominance by a few large institutions. Regulatory policy has evolved to keep the economic power of financial institutions relatively dispersed.

Solvency

A financial institution such as a bank holding the assets of a consumer must provide security since its products are fundamentally contacts for contingent claims. This concern has engendered regulation directed to ensuring solvency of such institutions (for example, regulation over form of organization, capital and surplus requirements, reserve requirements, provision for examinations, and regulations concerning investments) and to guaranteeing consumers against loss in case of collapse (for example, the Federal Deposit Insurance Corporation and state laws providing some type of guarantee fund).

Imperfect Information

A feature of some financial services is relative ignorance on the part of the consumer about the service being purchased, for example, the consumer is not clear about the specific terms of the agreement into which he has entered. Regulations adopted to meet this concern include truth in lending and fair credit billing, regulations governing advertising, laws requiring forms to be produced in a language in addition to English, and regulations designed to provide uniform provisions in contracts. Inequality of bargaining position, or complexity of the service being offered, may make it difficult for the consumer to assure that he is treated fairly. A person in dire need of credit, for example, may be in a position to be taken advantage of. The government has determined that it should assure fairness and has adopted such regulations as those controlling rates, terms, and qualifications of the persons selling the service, and prohibiting certain defined practices because they are "unfair."

Social Goals

Numerous regulations that are adopted are designed to achieve social goals, which may provide subsidization of one class of consumer by another class. To attempt to ensure an adequate supply of housing, some lending institutions are allowed to attract funds by paying higher rates of interest than others. To help people buy homes, the government imposes ceilings on the interest rates that may be paid on some kinds of mortgage loans, and guarantees those loans against default. To attempt to ensure adequate flows of funds into areas populated by lower income groups, redlining legislation is passed. And to provide equality in the supplying of credit, laws such as the Equal Credit Opportunity Act have been passed.

Regulation of Brokers and Bankers

Brokers and bankers are a subset of the providers of financial services with which this paper deals. Brokers and bankers are subject to two quite different types of regulation. One type is regulation defining the lines of business in which we may engage. For example, the Glass-Steagall Act provides that a company in the business of underwriting, selling, or distributing securities may not at the same time engage in the business of receiving certain kinds of deposits. Conversely, an organization engaged in the business of receiving deposits may not at the same time be in the business of underwriting, selling, or distributing securities except in certain instances enumerated in the Act.

The second type of regulation is the regulation of those businesses in which brokers and bankers are allowed to engage. This encompasses all the rules and regulations adopted by all the regulatory bodies that have jurisdiction over brokers and bankers. There are a myriad of federal, state and "self" regulatory organizations that act on brokers and bankers.

The thesis of this paper is that the first kind of regulation will diminish as the lines that have separated the providers of financial services begin to blur, while the second kind of regulation will increase as the regulators continue to load rules and regulations on the brokerage and banking communities.

Regulation Separating the Providers of Financial Services

The Changing Public policy Perspective

Financial services are provided by a highly fragmented group of vendors. The regulatory barriers separating those vendors are coming down. While public policy will continue to oppose undue concentration of economic power, it will rely to an increasing extent on disclosure, fiduciary and antitrust laws, and competition, with respect to who may provide what kind of services.

The erosion of these barriers to competition can be traced at least to 1970, when the President's economic report pointed out that the American experience with regulation "has had its disappointing aspects." The report said that "regulation has too often resulted in protection of the status quo. Entry is often blocked, prices are kept from falling, and the industry becomes inflexible and insensitive to new techniques and opportunities for progress." The report concluded that, "there is no clear safeguard against these dangers, but more reliance on economic incentives and market mechanisms in regulated industries would be a step forward. . . ."[2]

The focus on competition was brought to bear on the brokerage community in a 1972 report of the House of Representatives' Subcommittee on Commerce and Finance (now Consumer Protection and Finance). In a report culminating a year-long comprehensive study of the brokerage industry, it was concluded that "in the securities industry undue emphasis has been placed on regulation instead of competition" and concluded that such emphasis had been "unwarranted." The report called for replacing regulation with competition in certain major respects.[3] This theme was sounded in the bank area when President Ford sent his draft of the Financial Institutions Act to Congress in 1975. In a statement accompanying that legislation, the President said that he had "announced a number of initiatives to speed the Nation's return to economic health," and that part of that effort was "a review of government regulations," some of which were "outdated and had outlived their usefulness." He said those regulations "impose a greater cost on the American consumer than they provide in benefits" and that a "key element of reform concerns our financial institutions" (referring primarily to depository institutions). President Ford said that "the regulation of our financial institutions has not been fully responsive to either the changing needs of our economy or to the changes in the scope and function of our financial institutions."[4]

The same theme was adopted by the Senate Banking Committee in reporting the Financial Institutions Act of 1975, when the committee report said that the "purpose is to eliminate unnecessary and outdated regulation that prevents the depository institutions from competing effectively. . . ."[5]

The Carter Administration has continued along the same line. In his message to Congress on regulatory reform of domestic commercial aviation, President Carter said:

> One of my Administration's major goals is to free the American people from the burden of over-regulation. We must look, industry by industry, at what effect regulation has—whether it protects the public interest, or whather it simply blunts the healthy forces of competition, inflates prices, and discourages business innovation. Whenever it seems likely that the free market would better serve the public, we will eliminate government regulation.[6]

These statements all were made with respect to competition within an industry, that is, brokers competing against brokers, banks against banks, and airlines against airlines. It is not unreasonable to believe that this same idea will spill over with respect to competition between providers of financial services, that is, brokers versus banks, banks versus thrift institutions, and so on.

Intersection of Banks and Brokers Today

The intersection of banks and brokers has already taken place to some degree. A number of foreign banks have U.S. broker-dealer subsidiaries that are actively engaged in the securities business. Some foreign banks have ownership interests in established NYSE member firms—for example, Drexel Burnham Lambert and Becker Warburg Paribas. On the other side, Merrill Lynch owns a commercial bank in London where we are engaged in the commercial banking business.

On the domestic front banks and brokers compete today with respect to a number of financial services. Some of this competition is traditional. As the Securities and Exchange Commission pointed out in its *Study of the Securities Activities of Banks,*[7] "Banks have long played a major role in customer purchases and sales of treasury securities, federal agency securities, tax exempt securities and money market instruments."[8] Some of this competition, however, is of more recent vintage and pertains to a different product—corporate securities. Says the SEC: "In the years since 1968, a period of declining individual ownership of corporate securities, more than one million investors began using the services of banks to buy corporate securities."[9]

The banking community's involvement in the purchase and sale of corporate securities can be broken down into three areas: (1) investment management and advisory activities traditionally performed by bank trust departments; (2) various kinds of formal plans involving the purchase and sale of stock, which most participating banks started offering within the last ten years; and (3) corporate finance services, which most participating banks started offering formally within the past five years. An examination of these services is instructive.

Investment Management and Advisory Services. "Banks constitute, in terms of both numbers of the accounts and assets managed, the largest providers of investment management and advisory services in the United States today."[10] Commercial banks in 1975 "managed one and one-quarter million accounts holding nearly $400 billion in assets. Of that amount 73.4 percent was invested in corporate securities."[11] In addition to managing accounts for their customers, a number of banks sell investment research and advice directly to customers in the form of newsletters, subscription services, and even advice by telephone.[12] Moreover, banks render investment management and advice to registered investment companies. The SEC found that "slightly more than $2 billion in investment company assets receive some degree of advice from banks. . . ."[13] Some of this advice was provided by nonbank affiliates of bank holding companies. The SEC surveyed the largest 115 banks and trust companies and found that they have 42 nonbank affiliates that provide investment management and advisory services to others such as investment companies, employee benefit funds, and individuals.[14] These affiliates managed $16.75 billion as of 30 September 1976, an amount equal to 4.8% of the total assets managed by those banks' trust departments.[15]

These statistics make clear that bank investment management and advisory activities are a dominant force. What is disturbing, however, given what Congress thought it was accomplishing when it passed the Banking Act of 1933, is the SEC's conclusion that "with respect to the purchase and sale of securities for their managed accounts, bank trust departments are performing in many respects the same activities as are performed by retail brokerage firms."[16]

Plans Involving the Sale of Stock.

Dividend Reinvestment Plans. Dividend reinvestment plans ("dividend plans") permit participating shareholders of a company to invest dividends and to make cash purchases in securities of the company offering the plan. Although dividend plans were not offered by banks until 1968,[17] banks "dominate"[18] the dividend plan market. As of 30 September 1976, 68 banks administered dividend plans for 727 companies. Those plans had over 1.8 million participants who purchased more than $130 million of stock through the plans during the third quarter of 1976.[19] As of 30 September 1976, banks held stock purchased through those plans having an aggregate fair market value of $1,179.3 million, while plan participants held directly $5,901.2 million of such stock.[20]

Of bank-sponsored dividend plans, 94% permit plan participants to make cash payments into the plan. For the period 1 July 1976 through 30 September 1976, $32.8 million in such cash payments were made to dividend plans.[21]

Although all dividend plans were initially secondary market plans (that is, the dividends were invested in already issued shares of the company traded in the secondary market), some companies began to offer original issue dividend plans in 1973. In 1975, the last year for which complete data were available to the SEC Bank Study, $1.6 billion of stock was registered with the SEC for issuance in connection with original issue dividend plans.[22]

Employee Stock purchase Plans. Employee stock purchase plans (employee plans) allow participating employees to invest in the securities of a company offering the plan, or the affiliates of such a company, through voluntary periodic payroll deductions. In addition, many employee plans permit additional cash contributions by participating employees, and cash dividends on shares purchased may be invested in the plan to purchase additional shares.

As of September 1976, 59 banks offered 105 employee plans, having 165,403 participants and $120.6 million in assets.[23] Of the 105 plans, 7 are original issue plans while the rest make secondary market purchases.[24]

Automatic Customer Purchase Plans. Dividend plans and employee plans are designed for the shareholders and employees of companies choosing to offer the service. Banks also offer automatic customer purchase plans that are aimed at a still larger market—all existing and potential bank customers.

The most well-known automatic customer purchase plan is the Automatic

Investment Service, which provides an opportunity for bank customers to invest in a limited number of common stocks through automatic monthly deductions from their checking accounts. This service is also provided under the name Monthly Investment Service. In addition, one bank allows checking customers to buy that bank's stock through periodic withdrawals from checking accounts.[25]

Automatic Investment Service was first offered in mid-1973. As of 30 September 1976, eighteen banks offered this service with 4,543 accounts. In 1976 slightly more than $4 million was invested through this service, and the aggregate market value of shares held by banks for participants as of 30 September 1976 was approximately $9.4 million.[26]

In October 1976 Chemical Bank instituted a program that took the Automatic Investment Service another step by offering to purchase any security (rather than only the 25 top Standard & Poor stocks allowed by the banks offering Automatic Investment Services), by advertising this service vigorously, by accepting orders by telephone, by offering safe-keeping and portfolio-valuation services, and by changing the normal fee structure somewhat.[27] This service did not attract the business anticipated, and Chemical Bank has discontinued the program.

Customer Transaction Services. Most banks will, if asked, assist their customers in the purchase and sale of corporate stock. This customer transaction service is normally an informal service provided as an accommodation to bank customers. It is rarely marketed to bank customers and often not mentioned in bank literature. However, more banks offer this informal service than all of the formal bank securities services combined,[28] with approximately 4,300 commercial banks providing such a service.[29] For the month of October 1976 these banks received 10,348 purchase and sell orders totaling a little less than $120 million.[30]

Corporate Finance Services. The services described previously being offered by banks mirror to some extent the brokerage services offered by broker-dealer firms. Banks also have begun recently to provide formal services that mirror to some extent services provided by investment banking concerns or the investment banking departments of fully integrated brokerage firms. These corporate financing services encompass "advice and assistance to business on a wide range of corporate and financial matters, including capital structure, debt capacity, corporate and financial planning, the issuance of securities, mergers, acquisitions and divestitures, and similar matters."[31] Two such services surveyed by the SEC in its *Bank Study* were private placement services and mergers, acquisitions, and divestiturers.

Private Placement Service. As the SEC noted, "the private placement services provided by bank corporate financing groups are similar in most respects to those provided by investment banking firms."[32] The offering of these services by banks is a recent phenomenon and a growing trend. Of the 26 banks offering this service on 30 September 1976, 20 have been offering the formalized service only since 1970, and 12 of this 20 only since 1974.[33] The number and dollar volume of private placement transactions handled by banks have increased steadily. The number of bank-assisted private placements (other than in connection with lease financings) rose from 12 in 1972 to 44 for the nine months ended 30 September 1976.[34] For the same period the total dollar amount of placements rose from $128.9 million to $498 million.[35] As a percentage of total nonlease private placements, bank-assisted private placements of debt issues went from 2% in 1972 to 6.6% in 1976. With respect to equity issues, there were no bank-assisted placements in 1972. By 1976 banks participated in 3.1% of all assisted private placements of equity issues not involving lease financing.[36] While these percentages may be small, the trend is evident.

Mergers, Acquisitions, and Divestitures. As with private placement activities, the SEC found that "[b]ank acquisition and divestiture activities are similar in most respects to those provided by investment banking firms. . . ."[37] Again this service is relatively new. Of the 26 banks offering this formal service as of 30 September 1976, more than half initiated the service since 1970.[38] The number of banks offering this service increased from 20 in 1972 to 26 in 1976, and the approximate total dollar value of mergers, acquisitions, and divestitures completed increased from $156.9 million in 1972 to $223.6 million on an annualized basis for 1976.[39]

Future Intersection of Banks and Brokers. The breadth of the securities services now being offered by banks would certainly surprise Senator Glass and Congressman Steagall. But the American Bankers Association has recently disclosed a program for even further involvement of banks in securities-related areas. That program has three prongs: (1) to amend the Glass-Steagall Act to allow banks to underwrite revenue bonds; (2) to amend the Glass-Steagall Act to overrule the Supreme Court's 1971 decision in *Investment Company Institute* v. *Camp,* 401 U.S. 617; and (3) to preserve and expand banks' corporate finance activities.

Revenue Bond Underwriting. As a general proposition, the Glass-Steagall Act allows banks to underwrite general obligation bonds but not revenue bonds.[40] The banking community has been trying for over a decade to have the Glass-Steagall Act amended to allow banks to underwrite revenue bonds.[41] Legislation to accomplish this result passed the Senate in 1967 and 1974 but was not approved by the House. Senator Proxmire, chairman of the Senate Banking Committee, has again introduced legislation[42] to allow banks to underwrite revenue bonds. A companion bill[43] has been introduced in the House by Representative Gladys Spellman, a member of the House Banking Committee.

The banking community argues that passage of this legislation would reduce costs to municipalities issuing revenue bonds. The securities industry disputes the cost-savings argument and points to potential conflicts of interest if banks are allowed to engage in this activity. Securities firms also raise the question of concentration of economic power.

Since 1978 is an election year and Congress most probably will adjourn in October, it is unlikely that legislation on the revenue bond issue will be acted on during the 95th Congress. However, the issue is not likely to go away.

Commingled Managed Agency Accounts. In 1971 the Supreme Court ruled in *Investment Company Institute* v. *Camp,* 401 U.S. 617, that the offering of a commingled managed agency account by a national bank violated the Glass-Steagall Act. The American Bankers Association has determined to seek legislation to reverse that decision.[44] No such legislation had been introduced as of the writing of this paper. Rather, the ABA is drafting a position paper on the matter and is likely to argue that the offering of these accounts will help attract small investors back into the equity marketplace. It is not unreasonable to assume that the Investment Company Institute (the trade association for the mutual fund industry) and the Securities Industry Association will oppose this legislation. Again, it appears that it will not be until the 96th Congress that this issue will be addressed.

Corporate Finance Activities The growing corporate finance activities of the banking community has stirred concern in the securities industry. In response to that concern, Chairman Reuss of the House Banking Committee asked the Board of Governors of the Federal Reserve System to study one aspect of those activities—the private placement aspect. In connection with that study, both the Securities Industry Association and the New York Clearing House Association filed memoranda with the Federal Reserve Board.[45] In June 1977 the Board released a staff study that generally concluded that this activity does not violate the Glass-Steagall Act.[46] Subsequently, the governors themselves adopted the conclusions of this study[47] as did the staff of the Comptroller of the Currency[48] and the Federal Deposit Insurance Corporation.[49]

This has not ended the matter, and Chairman Reuss has requested the federal bank-regulatory agencies to gather data on the private placement activities of banks.[50] The first report on this subject is scheduled to be completed by 1 June, and periodic reports are to follow thereafter.[51] If these reports show that bank activity in the corporate finance area continues to grow as it has over the past five years, it can be expected that there will be considerable movement on the part of the securities industry to have Congress limit the banks in this area.

Public Policy Considerations. The arguments that will be made as Congress considers these issues seem fairly clear. The banking community will argue that allowing it to provide these additional services will mean increased competition and therefore benefits to consumers of these services. The securities industry will point to areas of regulatory inequity, conflict of interest, and concentration of power. While I do not intend to explore these matters at length in this paper, some preliminary thoughts may be useful.

Many of the services now being offered by banks, and proposed to be offered by banks in the future, would make banks subject to the federal securities laws and regulation by the SEC were it not for the fact that the definition of "broker" and "dealer" found in the Securities Exchange Act of 1934 specifically excludes banks. Thus although banks and brokerage firms may offer quite similar services and perform quite similar functions in certain areas, they are subject to quite different regulation. The SEC itself has pointed out the differences:

> the approach of banking regulation is different from that of securities regulation. The bank regulatory authorities . . . have focused their attention principally upon the financial soundness and stability of the bank, rather than on protection of investors. Insofar as banking regulation and supervision does deal with investor protection, it differs from regulation by the Commission in its greater reliance upon general statements of conduct and non-public criticisms in bank examinations rather than upon specific rules.[52]

The difference in regulation makes it virtually impossible to have a fair field of competition between brokers and banks. Regulatory costs are incurred by some competitors, but not by others. Business practices are denied to some competitors, allowed to others. While the SEC has proposed legislation that addresses some of these problems,[53] that legislation perpetuates the division of regulation of securities activities between the SEC and the banking agencies. Given the differences in attitude and manner in which these organizations function, split jurisdiction will not solve the problem.

The concentration-of-power issue is also difficult. As pointed out earlier, financial services now are provided by a wide array of organizations. Among those, commercial banks are clearly the largest and consequently wheel the greatest amount of power. Is it sound public policy to allow these institutions to grow even larger and more powerful? Certainly there are economic systems where banks have been allowed to assume this dominant position. I submit, however, that this country is better served by a financial system where one sector of that system is not disproportionately more advantaged than its competitors. Merrill Lynch is by far the largest broker-dealer in the securities industry. But in terms of total assets at year end 1977, it would be only the twenty-third largest commercial bank in this country. First Boston, Inc., would rank thirty-eighth; Paine Webber Incorporated would rank only ninety-seventh; the Bache Group, Inc., one hundred third; the E.F. Hutton Group, Inc., one hundred fourteenth, and the Dean Witter Organization, Inc., one hundred fifteenth. Shearson Hayden Stone, Inc., would not be among the two hundred largest banks based on total assets.[54]

I believe that there is sufficient competition among those now providing the services the banks are seeking to expand into so that the consumers of these services are being well served. Clearly, we need a strong banking community in this country, and we have such a community. But we need also a strong securities industry to perform the intermediary function in both the primary and secondary capital markets. If banks extend further into the securities business, there could be harmful effects on a good number of providers of these services outside the banking industry. Whether that is good for the United States is a matter that Congress will have to decide. In passing the Securities Acts Amendments of 1975, Congress adopted a standard of balancing competitive impacts against broader public policies. Congress will have to engage in a similar balancing when deciding the issues discussed in this paper.

Regulation of the Services You Are Allowed to Provide

As we have indicated, the regulation that separates the providers of financial services is blurring and may continue to diminish. On the other hand, the regulation of the services being provided by those vendors is increasing and is likely to continue to do so at an alarming rate.

To say that government regulation is increasing is to state the obvious. A few statistics may be illustrative. The regulations of federal departments and agencies must be published in the federal register. In 1967 the federal register contained 21,088 pages of proposed and adopted regulations. In 1972 that number had grown to 28,924 pages. But by 1977 it had reached the staggering total of 65,603 pages. It has been reported that more than 4,400 different federal forms alone must be filled out by the private sector each year, requiring 143 million person-hours. The Federal Paperwork Commission estimated that the total cost of federal paperwork imposed on private industry ranges from $25 billion to $32 billion a year and said that a "substantial portion of this cost is unnecessary." Another study has estimated that the aggregate cost of government regulation will be $102.7 billion in fiscal year 1979, consisting of 4.8 billion of direct expenses by the regulatory agencies and $97.9 billion of compliance on the part of the private sector. This compares to an estimated cost of $79.1 billion in the 1977 fiscal year.[55]

State and local governments have also grown appreciatively in recent years. In 1966 there were 7.3 million state and local government employees; their annual compensation totaled $44.1 billion. By 1976 the number of state and local government employees had grown to 12.2 million, and their annual compensation had risen to $129.2 billion.[56]

As the American people began to groan under the weight of this government intrusion into their daily lives, a limited effort has been made at relief. Early in his administration, President Carter asked his cabinet members to read the regulations put out by their agencies (a request that proved impossible to fulfill) and to have the names of those persons writing the regulations appear on the regulations when they were made public. President Carter has recently promulgated an executive order, "Improving Government Regulations."[57] Some attempts have been made to rationalize regulation. It is on this basis that Senator Proxmire introduced a bill to reorganize and consolidate certain functions of the Office of the Comptroller of the Currency, the Federal Deposit Insurance Corporation, and the Federal Reserve Board.[58] Other people have suggested other consolidations in the financial regulation sector.

None of these proposals goes to the heart of the matter, which is excessive government regulation. What is needed is not to make regulation more understandable or less duplicative—what is needed is to eliminate regulations that are not essential to the protection of the American people. What must be done is for each government department and agency to review its existing regulations and repeal inappropriate regulations, while at the same time adopting a policy and program to hold to the absolute minimum necessary the adoption of new regulations. All new regulations should contain a "sunset" provision, by which the regulation would automatically expire unless renewed.[59] In deciding whether to renew any regulation, the governmental unit involved should be required to undergo the analysis set forth in Section 4 of Executive Order 12044.[60] Those proposing to adopt new regulations should bear the burden of showing that the marketplace cannot regulate the matter on its own. Unfortunately, today the burden seems to be the other way about, with those proposing regulations seeming to require that those advocating the discipline of the marketplace bear the burden of demonstrating that the matter is best left to the private sector.

Unfortunately, such changes in regulatory policy are not likely to occur. Members of Congress run for office on a record of bills authored and measures passed, not bills not written and measures defeated. Federal departments and agencies justify continuously increasing budgets based on the new regulations they have adopted, not on regulations they have eliminated.[61] Indeed, the problem of expanding regulation is only now being recognized by the commentators.[62] I see little hope in the foreseeable future for any reduction in the flood of rules and regulations that is engulfing not only business but all Americans in all facets of their lives. For the financial community this means that while we may be allowed to do more, what we choose to do will be regulated more. A funny kind of "deregulation."

Notes

1. Regulations are administered in a variety of ways. In some situations federal regulation will predominate, as in the case of national banks or in the administration of the truth-in-lending laws. In other situations regulation is administered principally on the state level, as in the insurance industry. A combination of federal and state regulation is found frequently, as with respect to state banks that are members of the Federal Reserve System, or with respect to finance companies. Or patterns of "self-regulation" may exist, as in the securities industry.

2. 1970 Economic Report of the President of the United States, transmitted to the Congress, February 1970, pp. 107, 108.

3. Securities Industry Study, Report of the Subcommittee on Commerce and Finance of the House Committee on Interstate and Foreign Commerce, H. Rept. 92-1519, 92d Cong., 2d sess., 1972.

4. Message from the president of the United States to Congress dated 19 March, 1975, proposing the Financial Institution Act of 1975, Weekly Compilation of Presidential Documents, vol. 11, no. 12 (24 March, 1975) pp. 287-288.

5. Financial Institutions Act of 1975, Report of the Senate Committee on Banking, Housing and Urban Affairs, S. Rept. 94-487, 94th Cong., 1st sess., 1975, p. 2.

6. Message to Congress of 4 March, 1977 on Reduced Federal Regulation of the Domestic Commercial Airline Industry, Presidential Documents, Vol. 13, No. 10 (7 March, 1977), p. 285.

7. The SEC filed three reports with Congress during the course of this study—an Initial Report dated 3 January, 1977 ("Initial Bank Study Report"); a Second Report dated 3 February, 1977; and a Final Report dated 30 June, 1977 ("Final Bank Study Report").

8. Initial Bank Study Report, p. 77.

9. Ibid., p. 1.

10. Final Bank Study Report, p. 123.

11. Ibid., pp. 123-124 (footnote omitted).

12. Ibid., p. 156.

13. Ibid., p. 147.

14. Ibid., p. 158.

15. Ibid., p. 163.

16. Ibid., p. 121.

17. Initial Bank Study Report, p. 15.

18. Ibid., p. 11.

19. Ibid., p. 15.

20. Ibid., p. 25.

21. Ibid., p. 25.

22. Ibid., p. 24.

23. Ibid., p. 37.

24. Ibid., p. 40.

25. For a description of these services, see the Initial Bank Study Report, pp. 54-55.

26. Ibid., pp. 62-63.

27. Ibid., p. 89.

28. Ibid., p. 78.

29. Ibid., p. 81.

30. Ibid., p. 85.

31. Final Bank Study Report, p. 51.

32. Ibid., p. 58. The SEC described the service this way:

If a bank is retained by a company in connection with a private placement, it will advise the client as to the structure of the proposed financing, including matters such as timing, the proposed interest rate, maturity and the terms and conditions that are likely to be required by institutional purchasers. The bank typically will assist the client in the preparation and drafting of a private placement memorandum describing the proposed financing and the client's business. Thereafter, the bank will identify potential purchasers of the securities and, in most instances, will contact those institutions to determine whether they are interested in participating in the transaction. If so, the bank will arrange introductions and meetings between its client and the potential purchasers.

The SEC went on to point out that "[b]anks normally provide advice and assistance to their customers in negotiating the terms and conditions of the private placement" and that "banks frequently play an active role in the negotiations leading to consummation of a transaction" (pp. 58-59).

33. Final Bank Study Report, p. 62.

34. Ibid., p. 64.

35. Ibid.

36. Ibid., p. 69.

37. Ibid., p. 92. The SEC described the service as follows:

In representing selling companies, banks typically will ascertain the marketability of the business to be sold, advise as to the value of the business and reasonable price range, advise as to the most advantageous merger or acquisition structure in terms of price, tax consequences, estate planning (in the case of closely-held businesses) and other factors, and prepare or assist in the preparation of an offering memorandum describing the business. In advising potential acquiring companies, banks generally will assist in developing or reviewing acquisition procedures and acquisition criteria based on return on investment and cost of capital studies, industry studies, and other factors.

Banks will assist in locating and evaluating potential buyers or sellers meeting the requisite criteria, using both internal lists of companies developed by bank personnel as well as publicly-available data. Once potential buyers or sellers have been identified, the bank will make inquiries on behalf of its client, often on an undisclosed basis, and if there is an indication of interest, will arrange a meeting between the principals.

The SEC also noted that "most banks stated that they will participate fully in advising the client during all aspects of negotiations if requested to do so by a client" (pp. 92-93).

38. Ibid., p. 95.

39. Ibid., p. 98.

40. Section 16 of the Glass-Steagall Act, 12 U.S.C. 24, paragraph seven; see also 12 U.S.C. 335.

41. Recently disputes have arisen over whether particular issues were revenue bonds or general obligation bonds. See *Securities Week* edition of 3 April, 1978, p. 8. General obligation bonds are generally defined to mean a bond secured by the pledge of the issuer's full faith, credit, and taxing power. Revenue bonds are bonds payable from revenues secured from a project that pays its way by charging rentals to the users such as toll bridges or toll highways, or from revenues from another source that are used for a public purpose. See *Fundamentals of Municipal Bonds,* Securities Industry Association, 9th ed., 1972 pp. 166-167.

42. S. 2674, 95th Cong., 2d sess., 8 March, 1978.

43. H.R. 7485, 95th Cong., 1st sess., 26 May, 1977.

44. See *The American Banker,* 8 February, 1978 edition, p. 1, cols 3-4. A managed agency account is one in which a bank (normally through its trust department) has an agency relationship with the account but provides investment review and management taking such action as the bank, in its discretion, deems best with respect to investments. The addition of the commingled feature means that the assets of a number of managed agency accounts are pooled and collectively managed, with each account sharing proportionately in expenses, gains, or losses.

45. Private Placement Activities of Commercial Banks, Memorandum to the Federal Reserve Board, Securities Industry Association (May 1977); Commercial Bank Private Placement Advisory Services, An Analysis of the Public Policy and Legal Issues, the New York Clearing House Association (April 1977).

46. *Commercial Banks Private Placement Activities,* Federal Reserve Board Staff Study (June 1977).

47. Letter dated 29 July, 1977 from Honorable Arthur F. Burns, Chairman of the Board of Governors of the Federal Reserve System to the Honorable Henry Reuss, chairman of the House Banking Committee.

48. Letter dated 9 December, 1977 from Honorable John G. Heimann, Comptroller of the Currency, to the Honorable Henry S. Reuss.

49. Letter from Honorable George A. Le Maistre, Chairman, Federal Deposit Insurance Corporation, to Honorable Henry S. Reuss, reported at BNA Washington Financial Reports, Number 43, 7 November, 1977, p. A-6.

50. Letter dated 19 December, 1977 from the Honorable Henry S. Reuss to the Honorable John G. Heimann.

51. Letter dated 23 February, 1978 from Honorable J. Charles Partee, Member of the Board of Governors of the Federal Reserve System to the Honorable Henry S. Reuss.

52. Initial Bank Study Report, p. 6.

53. S. 2131, 95th Cong., 1st sess., 22 September, 1977.

54. These rankings were compiled by comparing the total assets of the organizations named against the list of the 200 largest banks set forth in the 17 April, 1978 edition of *Business Week*. The asset figures are as of 31 December, 1977, except that for Bache they are as of 31 January, 1978 and for Dean Witter they are as of 28 February, 1978. The total assets of these organizations are as follows:

	$ Mil
Merrill Lynch & Co., Inc.	8095
First Boston, Inc.	4224
Paine Webber Incorporated	1827
Bache Group Inc.	1700
E.F. Hutton Group Inc.	1594
Dean Witter Organization Inc.	1576
Shearson Hayden Stone Inc	755

55. "Washington & Business, Complying with Government Regulations," *New York Times,* 13 April, 1978, page D1, cols 2-5.

56. See U.S. Department of Commerce, Bureau of the Census, "Public Employment in 1976," table 2: Employment and Payrolls of State and Local Governments 1953 to 1976; U.S. Department of Commerce, Bureau of Economic Analysis, "The National Product Accounts of the United States, Statistical Tables," table 3.4: State and Local Government Receipts and Expenditures, Annually; updated in "Survey of Current Business," vol. 57, no. 7 (July 1977).

57. Executive Order 12044 (23 March, 1978), Weekly Compilation of Presidential Documents, vol. 14, no. 12 (27 March, 1978) pp. 558-564.

58. S. pp. 2750, 95th Cong., 2d sess., 15 March, 1978.

59. Executive Order 12044 itself contains a sunset provision but refuses to apply this requirement to all government regulations for reasons this writer finds unpersuasive. See Federal Register, vol. 43, no. 58 (24 March, 1978) p. 12669.

60. That section deals with voluntary agency review of existing regulations, and directs agencies to consider (a) the continued need for the regulations; (b) the type and number of complaints or suggestions received; (c) the burdens

imposed on those directly or indirectly affected by the regulations; (d) the need to simplify or clarify language; (e) the need to eliminate overlapping and duplicative regulations; and (f) the length of time since the regulation has been evaluated or the degree to which technology, economic conditions or other factors have changed in the area affected by the regulation.

61. One new arrival to the federal government described this situation as "the output of government officials trying to make a record of their accomplishments in a competitive society which gives prizes for new products." Speech of Robert S. Karmel, Commissioner, Securities and Exchange Commission, to the Compliance and Legal Seminar Sponsored by the Securities Industry Association (20 March, 1978), p. 3.

62. See, for example, Manning, "Too Much Law: Our National Disease," 33 Business Lawyer 435 (November 1977).

16

Deregulation of the Intersection of the Banking and Securities Industries

David L. Ratner

The subject of deregulation of intersections naturally brings to mind thoughts of cars and policemen and traffic lights. While these may seem far removed from the banking and securities field, they are not a completely inapt analogy to the problems under discussion here.

First, both the banking and the securities industries are what I would call "funnel" industries. They do not involve the passage of products from manufacturers to wholesalers to retailers to the public, but rather provide funnels through which funds and financial instruments can move from one set of consumers or investors to others.

A second distinctive aspect of the banking and securities industries is that the firms participating in them, unlike those engaged in manufacturing, cannot operate in disregard of the manner in which their competitors are operating. The nature of each business requires that the firms engaged in it be able to interact and cooperate with one another, even though they are competitors. This requires a certain level of regulation to assure that all firms speak the same language and process transactions in a similar way so that the market for funds or securities can operate in an efficient and orderly manner.

It is also important to remember that in each of these industries we are really dealing with three different product markets: The market for the thing which is being transferred (in this case money or securities), the market for services associated with the transfer process, and the market for the facility through which the transfers are effected. Many of the competitive problems in both securities and banking arise from the fact that the firms that provide the services also own or control the facility and use that ownership or control to insulate themselves from competition in the service market.

As the previous speakers have clearly shown, the deregulation of a single industry involves enormously complex questions, particularly when the industry is as complicated as the banking or securities industry. One question is the types of regulation to be retained or removed. There may be regulation of entry into the business, of the rates that can be charged, of the types of activities that a firm may conduct, or of the conduct of a firm toward its customers or others. Examples of each of these are found in banking and securities.

A second question is the nature of the industry—in certain kinds of industries, restrictions may enhance rather than limit the ability of firms to

323

compete. This is particularly true of "funnel" industries such as banking and securities.

A third question is who is doing the regulating. Regulation may be by an independent government agency, by industry groups, or by some combination thereof. In the banking and securities industries, we have examples of several different kinds of mixture between government regulation and self-regulation and between federal and state regulation.

When we come to the question of deregulation of an intersection between two industries, we have in addition a whole set of new problems because a change in the pattern of regulation of one industry changes the environment in which the other operates.

If there were a single intersection, or even a single type of intersection, between the banking and securities industries, our question today would be simpler. However, there are at least two distinct types of intersections between the two industries and several different intersections within each type.

The first type of intersection is what I would call a "competitive intersection" at which banks and securities firms offer the same or similar services to the same clientele. While banks and securities firms have traditionally offered somewhat different packages of service, the process of product extension is rapidly bringing them into competition along a broad front.

Securities firms engage in three basic kinds of activity—investment advice (to both individuals and institutions), execution of transactions in both exchange and over-the-counter markets, and market making both in outstanding securities and through the underwriting of new issues. Banks have also traditionally offered investment advice both to individuals and certain types of institutions; they have recently sought to expand the institutional side of this activity, particularly to include the rendering of advice to mutual funds. Banks have not thus far sought to go independently into the business of executing securities transactions; however, some have recently established plans under which they collect orders from a large number of customers and transmit them to securities firms for execution as a single transaction. In the market-making area, banks are prohibited from trading in equity securities for their own account or from underwriting corporate bonds. They compete actively with securities firms, however, in the underwriting of general obligation municipal bonds and are seeking to expand this activity into the underwriting of municipal revenue bonds.

With respect to traditional banking activities, securities firms have long competed with banks for the business of making loans to investors in securities; currently some securities firms are considering turning their margin accounts into a kind of charge account on which customers could draw to finance nonsecurities purchases.

The basic question with respect to these competitive intersections is whether we should aim for the removal of all barriers and permit firms that have traditionally operated as "banks" or "broker-dealers" to compete freely with one another for a wide range of financial services. There is a surface appeal to this kind of deregulation; it theoretically enhances competition by allowing the influx of a substantial number of new firms into an existing market. But we have to look more carefully into the future of the competition involved. If one group of firms is much larger or engages in other activities that give it competitive advantages or is regulated in an entirely different manner, we may simply create a situation in which one group runs the other out of the business.

It is also necessary to look separately at each individual competitive intersection to see whether the type of firm that is to be allowed into the field can offer the public a useful service not presently being provided. For example, banks, with their neighborhood offices staffed by modestly paid tellers, might be able to offer a simple and inexpensive way for people who have no contact with mutual funds or securities firms to invest in a diversified portfolio of equity or debt securities. On the other hand, there might be less benefit in utilizing banks as vehicles for direct investment in individual securities because bank tellers have no expertise in advising customers as to the risks and special characteristics of that kind of investment. Ironically, the interpretations by the courts of the Glass-Steagall Act have resulted in a situation in which banks are permitted to offer their customers a means of investing in individual stocks but are forbidden to offer them a means of investing in a diversified portfolio.[1] While this distinction rests on a defensible reading of the language of the Act, it also indicates the need for congressional reexamination of the underlying policy.

The question whether banks should be permitted to underwrite municipal revenue bonds raises similar questions. How much benefit would municipalities receive from the increased competition for their issues? Would this benefit outweigh the possible dangers to the financial soundness of the banks or to the viability of securities firms? Economic data may be of some help in answering these questions, but ultimately basic value judgments will have to be made.

The second type of intersection is what I would call a "cooperative intersection," in which banks and securities firms serve complementary functions rather than competing directly with one another. In the area of extension of credit to securities purchasers, for example, banks and securities firms, while they may compete, may also cooperate, with the banks lending money to the securities firms, which the securities firms in turn lend to their customers to finance margin purchases. The area of margin purchases is also an interesting example of cooperative regulation, with the rules being written by a banking agency, the Federal Reserve Board, and enforced by a securities agency, the SEC.

A second and more controversial cooperative intersection between banks and securities firms involves the clearing and settlement of transactions, the aspect of securities trading that precipitated the infamous "paperwork crisis" of 1967-68 and almost caused the collapse of the securities industry. Securities

firms and exchanges, through their clearinghouses, are responsible for determining at the end of each day's trading, who must deliver what securities to
whom to settle the transactions taking place during the day. Banks have also
been heavily involved in this process in two ways. First, they are transfer agents
for most stock issues, responsible for cancelling old certificates and issuing new
ones to reflect changes in record ownership. Second, they act as custodians for a
large proportion of the securities traded in the markets, including stock hold by
the banks themselves in a fiduciary capacity or held as custodians for other types
of institutions such as mutual funds.

This is one area where there is general agreement that a more rational and
efficient system is needed to reduce the cost of effecting securities transactions,
as well as reducing the incidence of mistakes, thefts, and other mishaps. Yet the
efforts to develop a better system, which is technically feasible, have been
delayed and hampered by squabbling and maneuvering for competitive advantage between banks and brokers, between New York and out-of-town banks, and
between NYSE members and other securities firms. The jealousy between banks
and brokers led to the ridiculous provisions in the 1975 Securities Acts
Amendments under which jurisdiction over transfer agents and clearing agencies
is allocated either to the SEC or one of the three federal banking agencies,
depending on the status of the entity involved.[2]

A second complicating factor, in addition to the number and variety of
intersections involved, is the difference in the types of regulation to which the
banking and securities industries have traditionally been subject. These differences are found both in the theory and stated purpose of the regulations applied
and in the nature of the agencies set up to administer them.

The stated purpose of much of our banking regulation has been to assure
the solvency and stability of each bank, in view of the importance of banks to
the communities in which they operate. To these ends, we have restricted entry
into the field, restricted branching by existing banks, regulated the rates that
banks can pay on deposits, and conducted investigations in a secretive manner to
avoid the possibility of customer panic. These techniques have not always been
terribly effective, as the recent collapse of several large banks has indicated, but
they have offered a consistent rationale for the prevailing pattern of regulation.

The theory of federal and state securities regulation, on the other hand, has
been generally to assure adequate disclosure about securities and to prevent or
minimize various types of fraudulent practices, with no attempt to limit entry
into the field or to assure the profitability or solvency of any particular firm.
This is not really a complete picture, however, since the federal scheme of
regulation was superimposed on an existing system of "self-regulation," which at
least as practiced by the NYSE, involved very strict restrictions on the types of
firms that could enter the field, the types of activities in which each firm could
engage, and the rates to be charged to customers. While recent years have seen
the elimination of some of these restrictions, this has been accompanied by an

increase in the regulation of financial aspects of the operation of securities firms by the government. The passage of the Securities Investor Protection Act by Congress in 1970 was a major step in conforming the regulation of securities firms to that of banks, and the promulgation by the SEC of net capital rules and rules for segregation of customers' securities,[3] applicable to all firms, are also steps toward the types of regulation traditionally imposed on banks.

With respect to the types of agencies involved in the regulatory process, both the banking and securities industries have a mixture of government regulation and "self-regulation," but the mixture is quite different in the two cases.

The securities industry has historically been characterized by a high degree of self-regulation. Some of the principal self-regulatory organizations in the industry, such as the New York and Philadelphia stock exchanges, have been in existence for almost 200 years. The jurisdiction of the securities industry self-regulators is not in terms of individual firms but in terms of markets, so that a single firm that effects transactions in a number of different markets is subject to regulation by several different industry organizations. While this arrangement has the potential for considerable overlapping and duplication of regulatory effort, in practice, there is an informal "pecking order," under which firms that are members of the NYSE are regulated in their internal affairs by that exchange, firms that are only members of regional exchanges are usually regulated by the principal regional exchange to which they belong, and the NASD to which almost all securities firms belong regulates the internal affairs only of those firms that are not members of any exchange.

In the Securities Exchange Act of 1934, Congress did not eliminate or restrict this system of self-regulation but superimposed on it an additional layer of federal regulation. The SEC was given direct power to regulate certain aspects of the operation of securities firms, plus oversight authority over the exchanges and the NASD with respect to the areas of activity traditionally subject to self-regulation. Partly because of this two-level setup and partly because the SEC's regulatory power is directed primarily toward disclosure and prevention of fraudulent practices rather than toward regulation of rates or entry into the business, the SEC has attained a unique reputation for independence from the industry it is charged with regulating.

An additional aspect of the regulatory mix in the securities business is that most large securities firms do business on a national basis so that most of the significant regulation of the industry takes place at the federal level. While most states require registration of broker-dealers and have government agencies charged with regulating their activities, this regulation affects mainly the smaller firms that do business only in a single local area.

The situation in the banking industry is entirely different. Banks, even the largest ones, are generally limited to doing business in a single state, or even in a limited part of a state. (This situation is changing; in their commercial lending operations and in their credit card operations, many of the larger banks are beginning to do business on a national basis, which is inevitably going to require changes in the regulatory pattern.) Banks are subject to significant regulation at both the state and federal levels; for example, the policy with respect to branching by either state or national banks is set by the state banking agencies, while the rate of interest that can be paid on time deposits by either state or national banks is set at the federal level.

In contrast to the two levels of regulation of securities firms, each bank is regulated at the federal level by a single agency that combines features of government regulation with self-regulation. The Comptroller of the Currency and the members of the Federal Reserve Board and the Federal Deposit Insurance Corporation are presidential appointees, but the funds to run their agencies come from assessments on member banks rather than from congressional appropriations. Partly because of this structural feature and partly because of the regulatory focus on assuring the solvency and stability of banks, rather than dealing with improper practices, the banking agencies tend to be identified strongly with the interests of the banks that they regulate. This identification of interest is encouraged by the fact that the federal banking agencies in effect compete with one another for business since a bank, by deciding whether to seek a national or state charter and whether or not to join the Federal Reserve System, can decide by which of the three regulatory agencies it wishes to be regulated. In fact, changes in the rules or policies of one or more of these agencies can result in pronounced shifts of banks from one jurisdiction to another.[4]

With this background in mind, we can now turn to what we mean, or should mean, when we talk about deregulation of the intersection between the banking and securities industries. Obviously we cannot answer that question unless we also know what types of regulation and deregulation will exist within each of the industries. But assuming those questions can be answered, I think the deregulation of the intersection poses three basic questions.

First, at the competitive intersections, to what extent should banks and securities firms be permitted to compete with one another in the same line of business? The standard "free market" or "deregulatory" answer is that all restrictions should be removed. My answer would be the opposite; I believe that direct competition between banks and securities firms should be restricted to a greater extent than it is now or totally eliminated.[5] I think that the basic approach of the Glass-Steagall Act is a sound one and should be extended. I think that banks should be excluded not only from the management of mutual funds but from the management of all types of pooled investment funds, including pension funds. In fact, I would strongly support the proposals for separation of trust departments from commercial banks, at least in banks above a certain size.[6] In the area of underwriting, rather than letting banks into the business of underwriting municipal revenue bonds, I would consider excluding them from the underwriting of all municipal bonds (again possibly with an exception for local activities by smaller banks). This would not necessarily result in any lessening of competition for municipal issues since the banks would be able to spin off the departments that engage in underwriting activities into separate entities, just as they did with their corporate underwriting departments after the passage of the Glass-Steagall Act.

You may naturally inquire why I would take this superficially anticompetitive approach to regulation of these competitive intersections. Basically, I believe that the idea of genuine competition over an extended period between banks and securities firms is illusory. Because of the competitive advantages that can be obtained by combining securities activities with commercial banking, I suspect that in the long run the firms without commercial banking connections would either be absorbed or driven out of the business altogether. This would result in an increased concentration of economic power and a dramatic increase in conflict-of-interest situations without any significant countervailing benefits to consumers.[7]

It is very difficult to impose and enforce limits on the size of individual entities or the degree of concentration within a particular line of activity. Indeed, it is usually difficult to find any satisfactory theoretical justification for doing so. On the other hand, a restriction against combinations of activities is relatively easy to impose and enforce and provides the most effective protection against the types of reciprocal arrangements, tie-ins, and coercive pressures that flourish in noncompetitive pockets within broad product or service markets.

There has been a tendency in these proceedings to equate all types of restrictions on entry—to assume that a restriction on the number of firms that may enter a given line of activity or a requirement of a minimum capitalization or minimum level of competence is the same as a restriction on firms engaged in one line of business from also engaging in another line of business. Each type of restriction must be evaluated on its own merits, relating its distinctive benefits to its distinctive costs.

I do not believe a restriction on combinations of activities is inconsistent with a general program of deregulation. In fact, it can complement a deregulatory program by eliminating the practices that involve the greatest expenditure of regulatory time and expense and the greatest difficulty in separating proper from improper activities.

There has also been an assumption throughout this conference that the question is one of "competition" versus "regulation"—that the natural tendency of firms in an unregulated environment is to compete and that regulation is a set of restrictions on their ability to do so, imposed by an outside force called "government."

I view the situation rather differently. While I do not share the current "revisionist" idea that most regulation was instigated by business firms for their own protection, I do believe that regulation, once in place, is heavily utilized by business firms to preserve or enhance their competitive position. In fact, to paraphrase Clausewitz' statement about war and politics, regulation is simply the continuation of competition by other means.

It has been my observation that the principal aim of the managers of most business firms is to insulate themselves, so far as possible, from the competitive forces that could lead to the firm's demise. There are three basic techniques for achieving this objective—regulation, expansion, and diversification. If they are denied the protection of regulation, firms will move in one of the other directions—either expanding to occupy so large a share of the market that their position is unassailable or (more frequently) diversifying, through mergers or acquisitions, into enough different fields that adverse developments in any one of them will not significantly affect the viability of the enterprise as a whole. We have seen both of these developments taking place in the securities industry over the past three years in the aftermath of the elimination of fixed commission rates.

I think that the really important question to be addressed—in the banking and securities industries as well as in other fields—is the relative impacts and merits of these alternative techniques by which firms attempt to shield themselves from the winds of competition. This is a question to which economists might profitably turn their attention if they could abandon their fixation with "fixed rates" and "barriers to entry." The economic and social effects of corporate giantism and conglomeration may be considerably more serious and more difficult to deal with than the relatively fragile system of regulation, which is difficult to enforce and is always subject to review through the political process.

I do not mean to suggest in any way that regulation is always more desirable than expansion or diversification. Expansion may in some cases promote efficiency, and diversification may give a firm greater flexibility in responding to challenges to one of the activities in which it is engaged. All I am suggesting is that the consequences of various forms of regulation be balanced carefully against the consequences of the developments that are likely to occur if the regulations are removed.

Second, at the cooperative intersections, particularly the one involving clearing and settlement of securities transactions, what type of regulation or deregulation would be most effective in bringing about the cooperation between banks and securities firms required to achieve a rational and efficient system? One problem is that, whatever merits regulation may have as a means of preventing people from doing bad things, it is woefully ineffective as a tool for getting people to improve their performance in permitted activities. In this area, the carrot is definitely better than the stick, but the problem is how to build the necessary incentives into the system to encourage banks and securities firms to devise the most flexible and efficient mechanisms.

To my mind, the most constructive idea that has surfaced in this area is the concept of the "transfer agent depository," under which the record of owner-ship of shares or other securities of any particular issuer would be maintained by the transfer agent (usually a bank) for that issue. This would allow the maximum amount of competition for the provision of clearing and settlement services, with the only necessary monopoly element being the switching mechanism by which the transactions by thousands of brokers, banks, and other entities were separated and routed to the transfer agents for the particular securities involved.

Unfortunately, the dominant elements in both the banking and securities industries, with a view to protection of their own competitive advantages, have favored a monolithic clearing and depository organization, which poses much greater risks of breakdown and offers far fewer opportunities for innovation than a more flexible and competitive system. The existence of such a monolithic central system unfortunately increases the need for government regulation to assure that all firms in both the banking and securities industries have fair opportunities for access to the central system on competitive terms. Unfortu-nately, as a result of vigorous opposition by the banks to any extension of SEC jurisdiction over them, Congress, in the 1975 amendments, opted for a split regulatory system under which a clearing agency or transfer agent is regulated by either the SEC or one of the three federal banking agencies, depending on the form in which it is organized.[8] This approach of giving each entity the choice of which agency will regulate it is even less excusable in an area where cooperation and coordination is required than in an area where differences in regulation simply lead to competitive advantages or disadvantages.

This brings us to the third, and probably most important, question—who will do the regulating that is determined to be necessary? The present situation might be analogized to a traffic intersection with four policemen, one to regulate large trucks, one to regulate small trucks, one to regulate buses, and one to regulate cars, each in accordance with a different set of rules.

Should there be a single agency to regulate all intersections between banking and the securities markets? I do not see any more reason why there should be a monopoly of all aspects of regulation in financial services than why there should be a monopoly on providing the entire range of services themselves by a single class of firms. But if there are to be several agencies involved in the regulatory process, the division between them should be functional rather than by the constituency involved. In other words, there should not be one regulator for the securities firms and one regulator for each type of banks, but one regulator for each activity or group of related activities that logically lend themselves to a similar type of regulation. For example, the SEC, with its greater expertise in disclosure, insider trading, market manipulation, and clearing and settlement, should have jurisdiction over those activities, regardless of who was engaging in them. On the other hand, banking agencies, with greater expertise in custodial responsibilities and safeguarding of funds and securities, could be given general responsibility for those areas.

It is not always recognized that regulatory agencies compete with one another, in a manner not totally dissimilar to the way in which firms compete. One type of competition is for markets as, for example, when the SEC contests with the Labor Department for jurisdiction over pension plans, or with the Commodity Futures Trading Commission for jurisdiction over futures contracts. This type of competition is often expensive and unproductive for either the regulated firms or consumers, whose interests are better served when Congress draws a clear jurisdictional line.

Another kind of regulatory competition is the competition for customers, which takes place in industries where the firms are given a choice as to which agency will regulate them. This is the present situation in the banking industry. Some think it is a good idea since it limits the ability of any single regulatory agency to impose unreasonable restrictions on its clientele.[9] It may certainly have that effect, but it may also go further and prevent the regulatory agencies from imposing even the most salutary restrictions, unless they can persuade all the competing agencies to adopt similar policies. This problem is exemplified by state corporation laws, which have become largely enabling acts because no state can impose any significant restrictions on the management of its corporations without losing business to states that do not impose any such restrictions.

It is not necessarily a bad idea to have a safety valve to enable regulated firms to bypass an agency that follows unduly restrictive policies. In the securities industry, for example, the regional exchanges have served the function of enabling firms to avoid unreasonable restrictions imposed by the NYSE. However, this type of approach presupposes that we do not really believe in the type of regulation the agency is empowered to impose. If we have prohibitions against practices that are considered deleterious to consumers or to the markets, they should be administered by independent agencies whose rules cannot be avoided by fleeing to the jurisdiction of another agency.

As to the appropriate mixture between government regulation and self-regulation, I believe that industry self-regulatory organizations can only deal effectively with fringe practices of which a substantial majority of the firms in the industry disapprove. With respect to practices in which a significant proportion of the firms in the industry engage, only a truly independent government agency can exercise an effective supervisory role.

If the regulation of these intersections is restructured along the lines I have suggested, we may anticipate, or at least hope for, a simpler and more rational system of regulation with resulting benefits to banks, securities firms, and the public.

Notes

1. Compare *Investment Company Institute* v. *Camp*, 401 U.S. 617 (1971) (banks are forbidden to operate a commingled fund for managing agency

accounts), with *New York Stock Exchange* v. *Smith,* 404 F.Supp. 1091 (D.D.C. 1975), dismissed on other grounds, 562 F.2d 736 (D.C. Cir. 1977) (banks may operate an "automatic investment service" providing for periodic investment in stock of one of the 25 largest publicly held companies).

2. Securities Exchange Act of 1934, §3(a)(34)(B), 15 U.S.C. § 78c(a) (34) (B).

3. Securities Exchange Act Rules 15c3-1, 15c3-3, 17 C.F.R. §§240.15c3-1, 240.15c3-3.

4. See Scott, "The Dual Banking System: A Model of Competition in Regulation," 30 *Stanford Law Review* 1 (1977):23-36.

5. I recognize, as other speakers have pointed out, that other countries permit banks to engage in all aspects of the securities business and that American banks and securities firms are able to combine banking and securities activities in those countries. I also recognize that there are special problems when a firm is permitted to engage in a particular kind of business in one jurisdiction, which it is forbidden to conduct in another jurisdiction. However, I do not believe that this is an argument for abolishing U.S. regulations unless there is strong evidence that the system in the other countries produces greater benefits to the society, and that those benefits could be expected to carry over to the U.S. environment.

6. See Hunsicker, "Conflicts of Interest, Economic Distortions, and the Separation of Trust and Commercial Banking Functions," *Southern California Law Review* 50 (1977):611.

7. See Mehle, "Bank Underwriting of Municipal Revenue Bonds: Preserving Free and Fair Competition," *Syracuse Law Review* 26 (1975):1117.

8. Securities Exchange Act of 1934, §3(a)(34)(B), 15 U.S.C. §78c(a)(34)(B).

9. See Scott, "The Dual Banking System," pp. 32-36.

Comment

Robert C. Pozen

Introduction

In reading the four papers prepared for this session, I perceived that there were two main sets of issues raised by the entry of banks into the securities business. One set of issues appeared to be internal: whether the entry of banks into the securities business would increase conflicts of interest and jeopardize the solvency of banks to the detriment of their customers. The other set of issues appeared to be external: whether the entry of banks into the securities business would result in destructive and unfair competition with regard to broker-dealers.

In order to focus the discussion on these two sets of issues, I will briefly analyze a recent legislative proposal, H.R. 7485,[1] that would permit national banks to underwrite revenue bonds issued by municipalities. As you probably know, national banks are now permitted to underwrite only general obligation bonds backed by the general credit of a municipality and not revenue bonds that are backed by the income flow from particular municipal projects. Since the SEC has publicly stated that it does not have an opinion with respect to H.R. 7485,[2] I feel relatively free to analyze this legislative proposal in light of the internal and external issues delineated above.

Internal Issues

H.R. 7485 attempts to meet the concerns that the underwriting of revenue bonds by banks will increase conflicts of interest and jeopardize bank solvency. While this attempt is not wholly successful, it does appear to demonstrate that such internal issues could be resolved by properly drawn legislative restrictions on bank underwriting of revenue bonds.

H.R. 7485 would permit national banks to underwrite revenue bonds subject to certain conditions. First, the bill would prohibit a national bank, acting as underwriter or dealer, of revenue bonds, from *selling* such bonds to its trust accounts unless lawfully directed by court order. This condition is apparently aimed at reducing conflicts of interest, which might arise if a bank could bolster its underwriting activities by selling revenue bonds to accounts over which the bank exercises investment discretion. But note that this condition does not prohibit a bank from *buying* revenue bonds for these accounts from other members of the underwriting syndicate.

The Securities and Exchange Commission, as a matter of policy, disclaims responsibility for any private publication or speech by any of its members or employees. Accordingly, the views expressed herein are those of the author and do not necessarily reflect the views of the Commission.

Second, the bill would prohibit a national bank, acting as underwriter or dealer of revenue bonds, from purchasing such bonds for its fiduciary accounts from another member of the underwriting syndicate until the syndicate has closed. This second condition is apparently aimed against methods of circumventing the first condition through reciprocal practices. For example, if bank *A* and bank *B* were members of the same underwriting syndicate for a revenue bond, absent this second condition, bank *A* could sell revenue bonds to bank *B* for its trust accounts, and bank *B* could sell the same revenue bonds to bank *A* for its trust accounts. Although the second condition eliminates the potential for such reciprocal practices *while* the syndicate is open, it does not deal with the possibility of reciprocal purchases that are consummated *after* the close of the syndicate.

Third, the bill would limit total bank holdings of revenue bonds of any one obligor or maker, as a result of underwriting, dealing, or purchasing for its own account, to 10% of the bank's actually paid-in capital and surplus. This condition is apparently aimed at protecting the solvency of the bank, which might invest heavily in the revenue bonds of certain issuers. While diversification of investments usually reduces the exposure to risk, this condition could be more finely tuned with regard to the objective of risk reduction. For example, it does not take into account the diversification level of the bank's total portfolio or the bank's holdings of revenue bonds as a percentage of the outstanding revenue bonds of any one issuer.

Fourth, the bill would require a bank to disclose in writing its capacity as underwriter or dealer of revenue bonds when the bank sells such bonds to its depositors or to its borrowers or to its correspondent banks. This condition is apparently aimed at increasing the level of self-policing against the abuse of conflict-of-interest situations by a bank. While such a disclosure requirement would probably have a salutary effect, there is probably no need for new legislation on this subject since the Municipal Securities Rulemaking Board (the MSRB) is already authorized to impose such disclosure requirements subject to SEC approval. For example, Rule 15c1-6[3] currently requires any bank, acting as an underwriter or dealer in municipal securities, to disclose any financial interest in any distribution of such securities to any customer from whom it receives a fee or the promise of a fee, before effecting or inducing a transaction in such securities for a customer's account.

External Issues

In contrast to the internal issues raised by bank underwriting of revenue bonds, the external issues raised by such underwriting may not be resolvable through properly drawn legislation. To begin with, there is a factual dispute about the impact of bank underwriting on the cost of issuing revenue bonds to municipalities. Mr. Stevens, an officer of a large bank, argues in his paper that the entry of banks into the field would lead to more competition for underwritings and therefore lower costs to municipal issuers. On the other hand, Mr. Rowen from Merrill Lynch asserts in his paper that the brokerage community doubts that large savings to municipal issuers will result from bank underwriting of revenue bonds. In my view, the proposed legislation would probably increase competition, but mainly between *large* banks and *large* brokers for *large* issues of revenue bonds. At present only about one sixth of competitively bid general obligation bonds of under $1 million received more than one bid,[4] despite the fact that banks as well as broker-dealers are permitted to underwrite such general obligation bonds. And there is little reason to predict under the proposed legislation that large banks would rush to bid on small issues of revenue bonds or that small banks would attempt to compete against large brokerage firms for large issues of revenue bonds.

As to the competition between large banks and large broker-dealers for the underwriting of large issues of revenue bonds, the question is whether the competitors would be subject to "equal regulation." On this question, Edwards suggests that banks and broker-dealers can be placed under similar rules if that is the desired policy choice. By contrast, Ratner is quite cynical about the possibility of achieving fair competition between banks and broker-dealers. In my view, it is quite feasible to place banks and broker-dealers under similar rules with respect to the underwriting of revenue bonds, but such similar rules do not guarantee fair competition between these two types of financial institutions.

Since 1975 the underwriting of municipal securities has been subject to the rules of the MSRB, which must first submit these rules for SEC approval. The MSRB is a self-regulatory organization with statutory jurisdiction over all broker-dealers and all parts of banks that deal in municipal securities. As a result, the same MSRB rules for the underwriting of revenue bonds would apply to both banks and broker-dealers.

However, the MSRB is empowered only to issue rules; it is not empowered to enforce them. With respect to brokers, MSRB rules are enforced by the SEC; with respect to banks, MSRB rules are enforced by the appropriate bank-regulatory agency—the Comptroller of the Currency, the Federal Reserve Board, or the Federal Deposit Insurance Corporation. Given the differential capacities for and approaches to enforcement among these governmental agencies, I believe that it would be unlikely for banks and brokers, in practice, to be subject to equal regulation with respect to the underwriting of revenue bonds.

Moreover, even if all MSRB rules were enforced by the same government agency, I believe there probably would not be fair competition between banks and broker-dealers for the underwriting of revenue bonds because of the different economic functions performed by these two financial institutions. For the equal regulation of economic unequals is inherently unequal.

One of the most important differences between banks and broker-dealers is that banks may engage in commercial banking activities (that is, accepting deposits, giving loans, and providing checking services) while broker-dealers are generally prohibited by banking laws from engaging in such activities (except for margin accounts). On the other hand, broker-dealers may sell securities to the investing public on a retail basis while the brokerage activities of banks are limited by the Glass-Steagall Act to placing orders for the accounts of customers.[5] Given these differences in spheres of economic activities, both banks and broker-dealers enjoy an established, and somewhat exclusive, client base to whom they could sell revenue bonds. The brokers argue that the banks have an unfair advantage in selling revenue bonds because banks can exert great pressure on their commercial customers. To the brokers, this unfair advantage would not be eliminated by requiring banks to disclose any conflicts of interest before selling revenue bonds to their commercial customers. The bankers, of course, argue that the brokers have an unfair advantage in selling revenue bonds to their brokerage customers. The bankers emphasize that brokerage firms may develop offices throughout the nation without the geographic restrictions generally imposed on branch banking.

In addition, there are economic differences in the relative size of banks and broker-dealers. As Rowen points out in his paper, the large banks are considerably larger than the large brokerage firms, even after the wave of mergers in the brokerage industry. To the brokers, the full entry of banks into the underwriting business raises the spectre of destructive competition in which the large banks drive all the brokers out of the underwriting business. In response, the bankers would argue that they are subject to the antitrust laws to the extent they engage in predatory practices, as opposed to doing a better job at underwriting than brokerage firms. In any event, the bankers emphasize, barriers to entry are low in the underwriting business so that abnormally high profits would quickly attract new firms into the business.

Conclusions

In short, the internal issues concerning bank underwriting of revenue bonds could be resolved by properly drawn legislative restrictions. By contrast, the external issues related to the underwriting of revenue bonds raise more general concerns about the economic functions of banks and broker-dealers. These concerns are extremely complex and cannot be easily resolved through legislative restrictions. Thus before passing legislation permitting banks to underwrite revenue bonds, Congress should develop better empirical data on the economic functions of banks and brokers and would have to make some fundamental policy decisions about the relative roles of these two financial institutions.

Notes

1. 95th Cong., 1st sess., 1977.

2. Letter from Harold M. Williams, Chairman of the Securities and Exchange Commission, to Bernard Martin, Chief, Economic Science and General Government Branch, Office of Management and Budget, 23 May, 1978.

3. 17 CFR 240.15cl-6.

4. This figure is derived from an informal survey of the computerized municipal securities data base, managed jointly by the Public Securities Association and the State University of New York at Albany, for a period during the second half of 1977.

5. 12 U.S.C. §24 (Seventh Power).

Comment

Howard H. Newman

The four papers we heard this afternoon do an admirable job of describing both the present intersection of the banking and securities industries and the regulatory landscape that governs that intersection. Rowen's paper is particularly useful in this respect, although I was surprised that his list of products and services with banker-broker competition omitted Merrill Lynch's Cash Management Account (CMA)—an omission quickly corrected by Citibank's Stevens. Rowen, however, was very even-handed in omitting the more controversial areas of intersection. Thus there is no mention of Citicorp's broker-dealer subsidiary, Citicorp Person-to-Person Investments, Inc., which is engaged in the direct sale of notes to individuals in the Southwest. Finally, there was no mention of Market Inventory Funds, a product that some observers see as a move by banks into the securities exchange business. Other areas Rowen omitted include the entire back-office side of the securities business—the clearing, transferring, and registering of securities and the depository functions. Fortunately, Ratner's paper fills in that gap in our taxonomy.

There is one major area of broker dealer—bank competition that has not been mentioned today, namely, competition in the credit markets. Yet the competition here has been intense. As we all know, short-term credit was traditionally provided by banks through their loan facilities. To service their clients' short-term credit needs, brokers countered by pioneering and promoting the commercial paper market. Banks in turn have introduced below prime-rate borrowing facilities to recapture a portion of this demand for short-term funds. A similar competitive phenomenon is observable in the medium- and long-term segments of the market. Banks, by gradually lengthening term loan maturities to the 8-, 10-, and 12-year range have moved into the heart of the so-called investment bankers' preserve by providing long-term funds. In response to this proliferation of revolving credits coupled with term facilities, investment banks have been active in making public and private offerings of fixed-rate debt with shorter maturities. In some instances, there have been offerings consisting of a series of notes with one, 3- and 5-year maturities, thereby duplicating many of the cash-flow characteristics of medium-term credits, except that interest rates are fixed, not floating.

This competition in the credit markets is a little different from those intersections discussed here today in that one could argue that Glass-Steagall was directly responsible for its development. If all financial institutions could offer all services, no long-term competitive advantages would be available from the development of new credit instruments that largely duplicate the characteristics of existing ones. Thus without Glass-Steagall, it is difficult to imagine what form

341

of economic pressures would have caused lending institutions to develop commercial paper, which, as we all know, is often a considerably less expensive (and therefore less profitable) form of credit than a bank loan. Similarly, what economic rationale would have caused the development of long-term bank credits? It is noteworthy that those products have been developed in those capital markets with a broker-banker separation and exported to those countries with fewer restrictions on the activities of deposit-taking institutions.[1]

Less satisfactory is the treatment given to certain economic issues underlying the debate over the removal of Glass-Steagall. In the broadest economic sense, the question is whether such removal would result in an increase, or decrease, in competition, and therefore, an improvement in, or an impairment of, allocative efficiency. As is well known, barriers to entry are a necessary condition for noncompetitive performance in an industry. Whether the Glass-Steagall Act represents such a barrier, however, is an empirical, not theoretical, question. Other than Glass-Steagall, what is the condition of entry into the respective industries? Does the existence of the Glass-Steagall barrier alter the condition of entry? These questions were briefly touched in Edward's paper, and we will not get into the argument over whether entry into banking is or is not blocked by state and other regulatory structures. Rather we will focus on whether removing the Glass-Steagall wall would *necessarily* increase competition and allocative efficiency. In this endeavor, we are taking the opposite tack to Edwards.

In order for increased competition to bring its theoretical benefits, certain conditions must be satisfied. One of these necessary conditions is that the private costs and social costs facing the potential and actual competitors do not diverge and that, accordingly, competition between groups is both fair and equal. If not, then the first order conditions for allocative efficiency may not be satisfied (except possibly privately), and we have what economists call a "market failure." In such cases, the competitive model is of little use.

An example of a divergence of social and private costs would be a subsidy. If a firm receives some form of government aid that reduces its costs of business, say, proportionately to the use of one of many inputs, the firm will expand to a point greater than it could without the subsidy. From the standpoint of the firm, it may be maximizing: From the standpoint of the economy, it may be overproducing.

The implications of any such subsidy, or other divergence of social and private costs, vary on the circumstances. If all competitors in all industries have them, it may be that they do not alter the outcome of competitive encounters. If only one group is so advantaged, however, the potential for that group to apply its "subsidy" to another area must be examined in order to understand the competitive and allocative consequences of any such transfer. If the subsidy were created to encourage the expansion of one industry, its use in another industry also has broad public policy implications.

From a purely economic standpoint, the first question is thus: Do banks, or securities firms for that matter, possess competitive advantages that would make them effectively unassailable in the other area? If so, the second question is, why. If there is an advantage, is it a natural one such as inherent skill, or is it a socially contrived one, created perhaps, for some bona-fide public purpose? In the first case, economics seems to offer little comfort to the disadvantaged group. The winners may choose to collect their "rent" as they see fit, and if the advantaged industry is highly competitive, there seems to be little threat to allocative efficiency. However, if their advantage is not "natural," then neither economics nor public policy countenances a transfer of the competitive advantage from one industry to another. This point is particularly telling when that advantage takes the form of a legislated divergence between private and social cost.

A large part of the Glass-Steagall debate is thus one of facts. Today's discussion, however, was not focused in that direction. For example, Stevens responded to his own charge that "banks have unrestrained financial muscle and overwhelming competitive advantages" by noting that "banks are not interested in the equity and debt underwriting business." When this competitive advantage is identified as the ability to lend money, he quotes a sample of one to indicate that banks, like securities firms, have competitors. Finally, he used 1975—a year when money market conditions caused banks to withdraw from the municipal business—to demonstrate their lack of competitive advantage. 1977, when banks had a market share of the G.O. business of approximately 50%, would be a fairer test.

What evidence exists on this point? Those opposed to bank entry into other businesses—whether securities, manufacturing, or other—often talk about the particular status banks have by virtue of their deposit-taking powers and their ability to grant credit. Scale economies and other factors associated with the concentration of funds are also a common topic of discussion. Securities firms also point out that banks, unlike all other taxpayers, are allowed for income tax purposes to deduct interest paid on funds borrowed to purchase tax-exempt securities. For the ten largest banks, I have estimated this advantage for 1977 alone to be over $100 million—or approximately one half of the total profits earned that year by all NYSE member firms doing a public business.[2]

More important than these factors, however, is that banks and their affiliates have access to funds with a risk-adjusted cost below the free-market rate. Indeed, our entire bank-regulatory apparatus is designed to bring about this effect. Restrictions on entry, restrictions on interest rates paid on time and demand deposits, federal deposit insurance, the discount window—the principal goal of these regulatory features is to reduce the riskiness of being in the banking business. The papers presented here today confirm that point. In an economic sense, their net result is to transfer the risk of the banking business to the depositor and, more importantly, to the taxpayer.

Of course, reducing the cost of capital to banks may have a valid social purpose. And I believe it does, for by reducing this important cost, the cost of intermediation is also reduced; these savings in turn should be passed on to entrepreneurs and other banking customers. In this way, capital formation is promoted by a socially directed reduction in the cost of private capital. Used in this fashion, there can be little objection to the benefit. One must ask, however, whether banks should be allowed to use these savings to enhance their competitive position—or that of their affiliates—in nonbanking areas. Our banking laws, which restrict banks to banking, answer this question unambiguously. Why then should bank entry into the securities industry be any different than entry into other industries?

You may wonder what evidence exists to support this point about the risk-return trade-off in banking. Formal studies are still scarce since the idea is a relatively new one, but a recent study by Michael Jessee (1976) demonstrated that bank holding companies tend to operate their nonbank affiliates with higher degrees of operational and financial risk than their independent competitors. Similarly, banks have a distressing habit of advancing funds at below market rates to their affiliates. Behavior that indicates a desire to assume additional risk or earn below normal returns is consistent with the hypothesis that the risk-return trade-off in banking is out of line. Clearly, much more work needs to be done to answer this question before an elimination of Glass-Steagall can be seriously considered.

I would like to conclude with a brief discussion of the evidence cited by Stevens regarding potential savings to issuers associated with bank entry into the municipal revenue bond business. Briefly, the argument is that bank entry would result in buyers' paying higher prices for municipal securities than they currently do. Behind this seemingly counterintuitive result is the "search" theory of competition propounded by Stigler (1961) and applied to the municipal bond area by Kessel (1971). In this theory, competition among underwriters is assumed to take place by a more extensive search for customers. Increasing the number of potential underwriters intensifies the search process; more search uncovers new buyers, which in turn means a larger market. Larger markets mean higher prices to issuers, and the result follows at once.

From the viewpoint of an investment banker, this explanation has the world upside down. True, bank-eligible securities are offered with lower yields; and true, this phenomenon no doubt is the result of a larger market for those securities. But is it reasonable to believe that the larger underwriting group causes the larger market instead of the naturally larger market supporting the increased underwriting competition? That is, are not credit, "legality,"[3] and investment policy the determinates of market size rather than the nature of the underwriting process? Recent evidence by Hopwell and Kaufman (1977) that bank eligibility does not result in an increase in the number of underwriting groups would support my alternative hypothesis. Again more studies are in order before Stevens's point can be conceded.

Notes

1. For a theoretical discussion of the economic effect of geographical restrictions on competition (which restrictions are analytically similar to the product restrictions set forth by Glass-Steagall), see Preston (1965). Interestingly, Preston concludes that such restrictions may lead to a more extensive coverage of the market than would unrestricted competition.

2. Brokerage firms must estimate the percentage of their interest expense incurred to carry tax-exempt securities. That percentage of interest expense is then disallowed as a deduction for Federal income taxes. The ratio of average municipal inventories to average total assets is commonly used to estimate the disallowed interest portion, with specifically financed assets excluded from the calculation. Thus my calculation for banks is:

$$1/2 \left(\frac{\text{average municipal assets}}{\text{average total assets}} \right) \cdot \left(\text{interest on domestic time deposits} \right)$$

where $1/2$ is an approximation to the marginal tax rate. This calculation excludes interest on federal and other purchased funds, foreign liabilities, and long-term debt on the assumption that banks could identify taxable assets financed by such sources of funds; no offsetting reduction in average total assets was made for this assumption, however, so the resulting estimate is too low. In addition, to the extent to such "dollar chasing" is not possible, our estimate is too low.

3. "Legality" statutes govern the investment behavior of most institutional investors. In most cases, the statutes restrict or prohibit the purchase of certain securities, either absolutely or to an amount less than a specified percentage of an institution's total assets. In general, investments in general obligations are less restricted than investments in revenue bonds.

References

Hopwell, Michael H., and Kaufman, George G. "Commercial Bank Bidding on Municipal Revenue Bonds: New Evidence." *The Journal of Finance* 32, no. 5 (December 1977):1647-1656.

Jessee, Michael A. "An Analysis of Risk-taking Behavior in Bank-holding Companies." Unpublished doctoral dissertation, University of Pennsylvania, 1976.

Kessel, Reuben. "A Study of the Effects of Competition in the Tax-exempt Bond Market." *J.P.E.* 79, no. 3 (July/August 1971):706-738.

Preston, Lee E. "Restrictive Distribution Arrangements: Economic Analysis and Public Policy Standards." *Law and Contemporary Problems* 30, no. 3 (Summer 1965):506-529.

Stigler, George J. "The Economics of Information." *J.P.E.* 69, no. 4 (June 1961:213-225.

Comment

Franz P. Opper

Although this particular discussion has been entitled "The Intersection of Banking and Securities," as is clear from the remarks we have heard, the traffic pattern—to borrow Ratner's metaphor—is more a one-way street than an intersection. With the single exception of Merrill Lynch's cash management account (which endeavor does not seem to have the endorsement of the rest of the securities industry), what we are viewing is the inexorable movement of banks into the business that traditionally had belonged exclusively to the securities industry. This is not meant to suggest that this trend is necessarily bad. There are, however, certain probable consequences of this activity that cannot be ignored and that have not really been addressed by the speakers.

First, the speakers have talked about the conflicts that may or may not arise as a result of the interaction of the banking and the securities industry. Most of this discussion is in the context of the concern expressed by the Supreme Court in *I.C.I.* vs. *Camp*, that underwriting clients gain at the expense of trust beneficiaries. Stevens may be right that this potential "dumping" of securities probably would not happen in the real world. The regulators and the bankers are probably far too aware of their responsibilities and, indeed, their liabilities, in this regard. Perhaps we can presume that the Chinese Wall does work for these purposes. The conflict that has *not* been discussed, however, is the one that exists because of the bank's role as both investment banker and potential lender to the same issuer. Besides distributing the issuer's securities, the investment banker functions as the issuer's financial adviser. The bank advises the issuer as to capital needs and structures the offering. It is a sensitive and delicate role and requires the advice be given in a disinterested manner. A bank assuming that advisory role may also be an investor (lender) in the issuer. The question that just begs to be asked is how, under those circumstances, can the bank provide disinterested advice? Stated another way, how can the bank, as underwriter, act solely in the best interest of the issuer if it has a separate and sometimes conflicting obligation to its depositors and shareholders? I do not know the answer, and indeed, I do not know if there can be a satisfactory one. Chinese Walls simply do not lend themselves to this situation. Moreover, no other kinds of institutions share this kind of conflict.

Many of us expected some discussion of this problem in the recent private placement study by the three federal banking agencies. Unfortunately, there was none. It may be that the agencies did not understand the business, it may be that they just chose to ignore the problem, or it may be they felt that the problem was not significant. But whatever the reason, the absence of any discussion is very disappointing.

Another problem that merits additional analysis is the impact of the investment banking business on the overall riskiness of the bank. Edwards suggests that it is impossible to generalize whether investment banking activities will increase or decrease the bank's overall riskiness. Stevens states that it is a nonissue.

Those positions may too lightly dismiss the similarities between the risks associated with commercial and investment banking. One that immediately comes to mind is a correlation of cash-flow risks. Factors influencing adverse cash flow to banks are likely to be the same as those that cause difficulties in the prompt resale of an underwriter's issue. These factors include unexpected interest rate increases and the reduction of the volume of funds flowing through the financial markets. As an example, when these events occurred in 1966, 1969, and 1974, insurance companies suffered cash-flow problems similar to those of the banks and reduced their acquisition of corporate debt.

It is clear that before any determination can be made, a study should be conducted comparing the recent cycles in bank earnings to those for investment banking firms. If such a study shows corresponding cycles, the conclusion would have to be that the merger of the commercial and investment banking functions would exacerbate rather than complement banking risks. In that case, we would have to ask whether our financial markets would be so improved by bank entry into investment banking that the additional risk to banks and the banking system would be worth bearing.

Finally, an area that requires further study is the competitive effect of investment banking activities of banks on the securities industry. Because of their portfolio of commercial loans, banks enjoy a unique advantage. This provides them with a close on-going relationship with potential issuers, particularly those that only infrequently use the securities markets.

Normally one of the greatest challenges for any investment banker is determining who a potential issuer is and then persuading the potential issuer to use that investment banker's services. Banks, on the other hand, are not necessarily faced with that same challenge. They have ready access to financial inside information on a stable of potential issuers, and they have the kind of continuing relationship with such issuers that surely makes it easier to obtain the business.

In addition, there is much more capital in the banking industry than in securities firms. It is difficult, therefore, to escape the conclusion that banks do have a competitive edge over securities firms. This is troublesome because that advantage is not necessarily gained because they would perform any better than the securities firms.

The conflicts, the possible increase in risks, and the apparent anticompetitive effects are all issues deeply intertwined with bank involvement in the investment banking business. There may be substantial public benefits to such bank activities that outweigh these possible adverse effects. But before we move from here to there, we need careful analyses to determine first if those perceived adverse effects do exist, and second if our securities markets and banking system would be so improved by bank entry that any such costs are worth either bearing or insuring against.

Comment

Almarin Phillips

With some important exceptions noted below, the papers presented in this session are remarkable in two respects. First, they reflect a blissful ignorance—or, better, a benign neglect—of the technological and market changes that have occurred, are occurring, and will occur among historically defined classes of financial institutions. Second, they reflect an unrealistic view that regulation, private or public, can succeed in reinstituting or at least preventing the further erosion of the "walls" segmenting commercial and investment banking.

The presentations remind me of two stories, which like many stories are somewhat flavored by the discussion at hand but which, nonetheless, contain important elements of truth.

The first story is about an old Virginia farmer who was plagued by frequent visits from a college-trained county agricultural agent. The agent was urging contour plowing and crop rotation—practices in which the farmer had never engaged. After repeated visits, the farmer kicked the agent off his farm with warnings of the dire consequences to transpire should he return. Afterward, complaining to a sympathetic neighbor, the farmer said, "That gol-danged whippersnapper is trying to tell me how to farm. Why, gol blast it, I've wore out three farms already, and I don't need him to tell me how to do it!"

The old farm is now a residential community, with green lawns and a lovely view of the Blue Ridge Mountains. Markets and technologies change—and they change radically when those accustomed to the old regime refuse to adapt to the new.

In a later year, 1971, my colleague, Don Jacobs, as codirector of the Hunt Commission, was wandering in California. He was interested in learning more about credit unions. He discovered one that was issuing share drafts to members on a line-of-credit basis. Don was a bit incredulous. He said: "Hey, you're paying interest on checking accounts."

"No, we're not," was the reply.

"These books of perforated drafts look like checks. They say, 'Pay to the order of' on them," Jacobs said.

"But they aren't checks," was the reply.

"Do your members use them like checks?"

"Yes, but they are not checks!"

"Do they get interest on their account balance until the check clears?"

"Yes, but understand, they aren't checks!"

"Do the checks—I mean drafts—clear through the system like bank checks?"

"Yes, but they aren't checks!"

Resolute, Jacobs continued, "Well, if they look like checks, are used like checks, and clear like checks, why aren't they checks?"

Without hesitation, the credit union official gave the perfect reply: "Because we aren't allowed by law to have checking accounts."

The legality, narrowly construed, of credit unions and other thrift institutions engaging in third party payments services continues to be argued today. Yet whether technically legal or not, those who wish to offer such services, including investment banking firms and bank trust departments, are effectively in that field. The "walls" erected by the Banking Act of 1933 are rapidly crumbling. They are crumbling not only in the third party payments area but quite generally.

All the papers seem to agree that investment banks are, in fact, engaging in commercial bank loan and deposit functions through mutual funds, money market funds, cash management accounts, and so on. All agree that the commercial banks are in fact engaging in investment banking in their agency, advisory, custodial, and fiduciary functions, "solely upon the order, and for the account of, customers."

Franklin Edwards sees this, and he recognizes the procompetitive influences that could emerge from removing restrictions on interindustry competition. Edwards treats the "safety and soundness" and "conflict of interest" problems in a novel and imaginative way. He favors a formal destruction of the "walls" of 1933, including a realistic approach to the interpretation of 10(b)-5 information transfers. My only criticism is that he fails to see the inevitability of the "intersection" being discussed. And, unhappily, he does not stress the fact that without the relaxation of present regulations, the intersection will have second-best, evasive qualities—qualities that encourage crises-bred change rather than orderly change.

My comments on the other papers are best prefaced by remarks by Dee W. Hock, president of VISA/U.S.A., Inc. Hock sees the new technology that heralds the inevitable intersection. Says Hock:

> [A]n accelerating evolution in the exchange of value will unlock a value reservoir to which [buyers and sellers] have never had access. . . . [I]nvestment houses, insurance companies, mortgage companies and other repositories of value will provide card access to the value reservoirs they hold. . . . When cards [and other devices] reach their full potential, they will identify a [payor] from anywhere in the world in full possession of his assets, whether credit, deposit, investment, or equity—a customer ready to exchange them for whatever you sell.[1]

David Ratner thinks that new walls can be created to maintain separate markets in this new technological environment. Walls can of course be erected— as the Maginot Line was—only to invite flights over or invasions around it. Ratner appears to think that some firms may possess such efficiency advantages that the older market structures will be threatened. Well, the older structures not only will be but are now threatened. New, more efficient organizations replace old ones. What is the social value of preserving the status quo when other mechanisms are demonstrably superior? Or, argumentatively, why worry about the new forms since, if they are not superior, they will not succeed in their attempts to enter?

Harvey Rowen recognizes this, but in a backward way. He is concerned about banks' entering the markets of investment bankers but peculiarly unconcerned about the reverse tendencies. After all, he says, no investment bank would be large relative to Citicorp or Bank of America—but what if the latter came into the securities markets? Suppose banks underwrite revenue bonds. Would society suffer? Suppose bank trust departments, without subterfuge arrangements with securities dealers, could offer commingled agency accounts? Would society suffer? If the public is, indeed, being well served by the "sufficient competition among those now providing the services," why would anyone, bank or otherwise, seek entry? Rowen, in conclusion, bemoans the proliferation of regulation at the same time that he urges new modes of regulation to keep banks out of the securities industry.

James Stevens's paper is paradoxical. On the one hand, he minimizes the interests of banks in amending Glass-Steagall, while representing the bank involved in *I.C.I.* v. *Camp,* in the Special Investment Advisory Service announcement of 1967 (an arrangement in cooperation with Merrill Lynch, coincidentally) and in numerous other ventures—many to the public benefit—to circumvent regulations. On the other hand, Stevens sees quite correctly that the deposit financial institutions are indeed in competition not only with the securities industry but among themselves as well as with many nondeposit institutions. The question is why deny it when the matter of banks—even Citibank—wanting to get into others' markets is raised?

Comments, with stories or without, should not be as long as the papers being discussed. In short, I regret the failure of this session to come squarely to grips with the EFT technology and its effects on the efficacy and efficiency of present regulations. Glass-Steagall, Regulation Q, the prohibition of interest on demand deposits, the regulation of asset portfolios, restrictions geographically and by service on asset transfers just cannot be effective in the new technological environment. Even if effective, they would be inefficient.

But make no mistake. Those who fret about the viability of the structures of their own industries are correct. There will be changes in structures—through entry, failures, and mergers—whatever the course of regulation and legislation. Modest re-regulation could make the changes less difficult to achieve in orderly fashion.

Note

1. Reported in "Visa Head Says Public Will Never Go Cashless," *Computerworld,* 28 November, 1977, p. 9. Copyright 1977 by CW Communications/Inc., Newton, Mass. 002160.

List of Conference Participants

Edward I. Altman, professor of finance, New York University

Ernest Bloch, Charles William Gerstenberg Professor of Finance, New York University

Franklin R. Edwards, professor of business, Columbia University

Lawrence G. Goldberg, associate professor of finance and economics, New York University

Robert C. Hall, executive vice president, operations, New York Stock Exchange

Gilbert A. Heebner, executive vice president, Philadelphia National Bank

Patric H. Hendershott, professor of economics and finance, Purdue University

Donald M. Kaplan, president and managing associate, Kaplan, Smith & Associates, Inc.

Barbara Goody Katz, assistant professor of economics, New York University

Michael Keenan, associate professor of finance, New York University

Roger Klein, executive director, Public Securities Association

P. Michael Laub, director, Economic and Finance Research Division, American Bankers Association

Robert Lindsay, professor of finance and economics, New York University

Simon Lorne, visiting associate professor of law and acting director of the Center for the Study of Financial Institutions, University of Pennsylvania

H. Michael Mann, professor of economics, Boston College

Morris Mendelson, professor of finance, University of Pennsylvania

C.F. Muckenfuss, III, deputy comptroller, Office of the Comptroller of the Currency

Howard H. Newman, vice president, Morgan Stanley & Co., Inc.

Edward I. O'Brien, president, Securities Industry Association

Franz P. Opper, counsel for the Consumer Protection and Finance Subcommittee, House of Representatives

Almarin Phillips, professor of economics, law, and public policy, University of Pennsylvania

Susan M. Phillips, associate professor of finance, University of Iowa

Lee A. Pickard, Esq., attorney, New York and Washington, D.C.

Robert C. Pozen, assistant general counsel, Office of General Counsel, Securities and Exchange Commission

David L. Ratner, professor of law, Cornell University

Michael A. Redisch, economist, Program Analysis Division, General Accounting Office

Dan Roberts, graduate student, University of Iowa

Joshua Ronen, professor of accounting, New York University

Harvey A. Rowen, assistant to the president, Merrill Lynch, Pierce, Fenner & Smith, Inc.

Arnold W. Sametz, professor of finance; director, Salomon Brothers Center for the Study of Financial Institutions, New York University

Roy Schotland, professor of law, Georgetown University

Neal M. Soss, deputy superintendent of banks, New York State Banking Department

James W. Stevens, senior vice president, Merchant Banking Group, Citibank

Robert Swinarton, vice chairman of the board, Dean Witter Reynolds, Inc.

Donald E. Weeden, chief executive officer, Weeden Holding Corporation

Lawrence J. White, associate professor of economics, New York University

Benjamin Wolkowitz, section chief, Division of Research and Statistics, Board of Governors, Federal Reserve System

Richard Zecher, dean, College of Business Administration, University of Iowa

About the Editors

Lawrence G. Goldberg is associate professor of finance and economics at the Graduate School of Business Administration, New York University. He received the B.A. from the University of Rochester (1966) and the M.A. (1969) and Ph.D. (1972) from the University of Chicago. His major fields of interest are regulation of financial institutions, health economics, and industrial organization. He is coauthor (with Warren Greenberg) of *The Health Maintenance Organization and Its Effects on Competition* (Federal Trade Commission, 1977) and author of numerous articles in economics journals such as *The Review of Economics and Statistics, The Journal of Law and Economics,* and *The Journal of Finance.*

Lawrence J. White is associate professor of economics at the Graduate School of Business Administration, New York University (on leave, 1978-79, with the U.S. Council of Economic Advisers). He received the B.A. from Harvard University (1964), the M.Sc. from the London School of Economics (1965), and the Ph.D. from Harvard University (1969). His major fields of research include industrial organization, regulation, and antitrust policy. He is the author of *The Automobile Industry Since 1945* (Harvard University Press, 1971), and *Industrial Concentration and Economic Power in Pakistan* (Princeton University Press, 1974) and articles in leading economics journals, including the *American Economic Review,* the *Quarterly Journal of Economics,* and the *Bell Journal of Economics.*